WILLIAM DUDLEY PELLEY

Religion and Politics
Michael Barkun, *Series Editor*

William Dudley Pelley

"Far and wide across the nation, in the opening months of 1933, went the high tocsin to America's Christian patriots to form the Legion of the *Silvershirts!*"

—from *The Door to Revelation*

WILLIAM DUDLEY PELLEY

A LIFE IN RIGHT-WING
EXTREMISM AND THE OCCULT

Scott Beekman

SYRACUSE UNIVERSITY PRESS

Frontispiece: William Dudley Pelley. From his autobiography,
The Door to Revelation (Pelley Publishers, 1939).

The paper used in this publication meets the minimum requirements of
American National Standard for Information Sciences—Permanence of
Paper for Printed Library Materials, ANSI Z39.48–1984.∞™

Library of Congress Cataloging-in-Publication Data
Beekman, Scott.
William Dudley Pelley : a life in right-wing extremism and the occult / Scott.—1st ed.
p. cm.—(Religion and politics)
Includes bibliographical references and index.
ISBN 0–8156–0819–5 (hardcover : alk. paper)
1. Pelley, William Dudley, 1890– . 2. Authors, American—20th century—Biography. 3.
Political activists—United States—Biography. 4. Antisemitism—United States—
History—20th century. 5. Politics and literature—United States—History—20th
century. 6. Cults—United States—History—20th century. 7. Silver Shirts of America
(Organization) I. Title. II. Series.
PS3531.E32Z56 2005
818'.5209—dc22
[B]
2005015040

Manufactured in the United States of America

*Dedicated to the memory
of Lucile May Beekman*

Scott Beekman is visiting assistant professor of history at Ohio University. He lives in Athens, Ohio, with his wife, historian Kimberly K. Little, and son, Miller.

Contents

Acknowledgments

A STUDY OF THIS NATURE is only possible through the generous assistance of librarians and archivists—and I have benefited from the expertise of many. I owe special debts of thanks to Kim Kumber of the North Carolina State Archives, Ann Wright of the Asheville (N.C.) Pack Memorial Library, Nancy Massey of the Noblesville (Ind.) Southeastern Library, Tim Blevins of the Pikes Peak Library District, and all the friendly folks at the Indiana University Government Records Archive. The interlibrary loan staff at Ohio University's Alden Library tracked down obscure materials for me too many times to mention.

I also garnered assistance from individuals with a personal interests in William Dudley Pelley. Independent Pelley scholar Vance Pollock provided invaluable information pertaining to Pelley's publications and life. Toward the end of this project I made contact with members of Pelley's family, who offered personal insights about the man. I am especially indebted to Pelley's daughter, Adelaide Pearson, and her husband, Melford. While I suspect Mr. Pearson will disagree with many of my views on his father-in-law, I sincerely hope he will at least find that I have portrayed Pelley's beliefs accurately and fairly.

This study had its origins in a discussion that arose during Charles C. Alexander's colloquium on the 1930s at Ohio University. From the outset, Dr. Alexander has guided this project with insight, patience, and constructive criticism. This work has been greatly improved by the suggestions offered by Katherine Jellison, Norman Goda, Richard Vedder, Michael Barkun, and John Werly. Mary Selden Evans and Glenn

Wright of Syracuse University Press have been both sympathetic and a calming influence on this oft-nervous writer.

Ohio University has been my home for many years now, and my time here has been very pleasurable thanks to the assistance of numerous Athenians. History Department secretaries Sherry Gillogly and Kathy Cooper led me through the labyrinth of forms, guidelines, and minor headaches endemic to the academic world. My fellow graduate students have created a network of support and friendship in Athens. I owe special debts of gratitude to the League of Athens Poker Players (LAPP), the Memphis Mafia, the Pike County Players, and all the long-gone attendees of Farrell-Fest.

Finally, I wish to thank my family. My parents have provided support of all kinds during my work on this manuscript. My wife, Kimberly K. Little, tirelessly aided my research (particularly during a rather trying year spent with the ladies of Tutor Time) and patiently listened to my frequently rambling discourses about Bill Pelley; she deserves a coauthor credit on this book. And, as always, this work is for Miller.

Introduction

IN A 1994 *American Historical Review* symposium, Leo Ribuffo posed the question, "Why is there so much conservatism in the United States, and why do so few historians know anything about it?" Ribuffo not only assailed historians who failed to discern the presence of a conservative movement in American history but also issued a clarion call for future research on the political and ideological right. Since Ribuffo made his challenge, a small coterie of historians has begun exploring not only conservatism but also right-wing extremism. Thanks to the pioneering work of Glen Jeansonne, Michael Barkun, and Jeffrey Kaplan, the farther shores of politics are being mapped. This study attempts to add to the burgeoning body of literature on right-wing extremism by detailing the career of William Dudley Pelley.[1]

During the 1930s the American extreme right achieved a level of popular success it has never again reached. Distraught by the Depression's massive economic dislocation and increasingly cynical over the inability of the existing two-party system to address the nation's ills, a significant portion of the American people sought answers to their woes in the utopian visions of radical politics. While American historians have focused their attentions on the Popular Front aspects of the "Red decade," the extreme right also attracted large numbers of Americans who believed some form of authoritarianism could answer the country's problems. A meaningful percentage of these right-leaning Americans looked to William Dudley Pelley for guidance.

Pelley's career as an agitator during the Depression era represents one of the more successful efforts in American history to create a paramilitary, anti-Semitic political organization. His Silver Legion of America, at its peak, boasted several thousand members, and Pelley garnered attention in the national media as one of America's leading "star-spangled fascists." Pelley, then, was a significant player in the extreme right of the period. By outlining his career, I hope to document his beliefs and to place Pelley within the context of this vibrant, extremist world. This study, the first full-length biography of Pelley, is intended to add to the prior works of Ribuffo, Jeansonne, and Francis MacDonnell and to help further scholarly understanding of 1930s extremism.

As these authors have noted, the extreme right attracted support throughout the decade, which propelled a backlash, the so-called "brown scare," as the United States geared up to enter World War II. Pelley, as one of the leaders of the radical right, helped create the loosely knit network of extremist organizations that peaked during the mid-1930s, and he became a martyr for the cause as a result of his 1942 sedition conviction. His story is an excellent case study of the rise and fall of the Depression-era right.

Pelley also proved to be a literate and prolific writer in a world of badly typed screeds and cheaply produced, emotionally driven extremist newsletters. The Silver Shirt chief spent the first half of his life as a journalist, fiction writer, and screenwriter during Hollywood's wildcat era of the early 1920s. His experience in the literary world gave Pelley a unique perspective on the published products of right-wing writers. Pelley took great care in producing books and magazines that were professionally designed and edited. As an obsessively prolific author, Pelley also issued an enormous quantity of materials to promote his views. Lawrence Dennis may have been the theoretician of American fascism, but Pelley was its Elbert Hubbard.

Pelley was also far more than a simple, authoritarian anti-Semite. He buttressed his attacks on "Jewish-Communism" and the New Deal with a Christian millennialism developed from his own spiritualist-Theosophical eschatology. Pelley's religious system, known as Liberation doctrine, marked him as a distinctive figure on the extreme right. At a time when figures such as Gerald L. K. Smith and Gerald Winrod assaulted the same enemies with ammunition derived from the Bible, Pelley armed himself with ideas obtained from clairaudient "Ascended Masters." He mixed spiritualism, Theosophy, Christianity, and pyramidism into a potent concoction that gave him supporters in both anti-Semitic and metaphysical circles.

Pelley's unique belief system led many contemporary critics to brand him as an opportunist, psychotic, or confidence man and later scholars have, unfortunately, often followed their lead. Frequently self-serving, these characterizations ignore the disquieting fact that during the 1930s many thoughtful and educated Americans attempted to alleviate their anxieties with anti-Semitic bigotry. Pelley's opponents always described him as well-spoken and intelligent and found it hard to believe that such a man would develop an organization based on hatred.

These critics ignore both the long history of bigotry in the United States, among all social classes, and the concerns over modernization, industrialization, and urbanization that fed the fears of traditional individuals such as Pelley. A parochial New Englander at heart, Pelley felt truly uncomfortable in modern, urban America, yet his drive to make a name for himself as a respected writer forced him into close quarters with that alien world. Unable to make sense of the society in which he operated and, perhaps even more important, convinced that his small-town America was systematically being destroyed, Pelley found it easier to explain the changes as part of a vast conspiracy than to confront the fact that America was not developing in accordance with his views.

Pelley's unhappy experiences as a screenwriter in Hollywood presented him with the opportunity to put a face on the conspiracy and to blame Jews for all that was wrong with this country. He never wavered in his hatred of the Jews, even after it became economically unprofitable and politically suicidal, and it is clear he adopted a career based upon bigotry because it offered a means of countering dreaded modern "isms," not financial remuneration. As Pelley himself noted, his income as a screenwriter in "Jewish" Hollywood far exceeded what he earned as head of the Silver Shirts. Contemporary critics quite rightly attacked the validity of his anti-Jew pronouncements and beliefs, but the suggestion that Pelley adopted these views to make a quick buck is patently false.

Those critics who attacked Pelley as a psychotic invariably based their criticisms on his religious system. His beliefs were atypical and, on the surface, difficult to connect with his otherwise conservative views, but the easy characterization that Liberation doctrine must be the ravings of a madman appears to be a gross over-simplification. Pelley led a national organization, operated a thriving press, ran for president, gave cross-country speaking tours, and published voluminous writings—a record difficult to reconcile with the notion that he was thoroughly mentally unbalanced.

Pelley was an orthodox Christian, although not a very diligent one, until 1928. In that year, significantly while he was still working in Hollywood, Pelley underwent a conversion experience, undoubtedly brought about through exhaustion related to his workaholic personality, that permanently changed his metaphysical beliefs and began the process that led to the development of Liberation. While it is impossible, from the distant vantage point of the twenty-first century, to make an exact determination of what happened to Pelley that year, it is clear he emerged from the experience a different man.

His opponents usually cited this event as the point at which Pelley went "insane" and buttressed their assertion by documenting the unorthodox nature of his Liberation system. Pelley's beliefs were controversial, even among the Silver Shirt faithful, but are consistent with his personality. Despite the ad hoc nature of Liberation, Pelley always maintained he was a Christian, in keeping with his generally traditional views, and that Liberation doctrine represented no more than the corrected teachings of Christ. Pelley removed what he believed to be the Jewish corruptions from Christianity by downgrading the importance of the "falsified" scriptures and replacing them with his own clairaudiently received messages. These messages, which Pelley transcribed on an almost daily basis, served as a religious bulwark for Pelley's political beliefs. Pelley, then, could claim that his anti-Semitic political program was not only in the country's best interest, but also had divine support.

The Silver Shirt chief was supremely confident that he had a significant role to play in world affairs. He frequently trumpeted his important "brevet," and the messages he received were often egotistical and self-aggrandizing. Pelley was a man obsessed with establishing himself. He harnessed a boundless energy to work, frequently long into the night, and cranked out writings at an astonishing rate. Pelley's conviction of his own importance, coupled with his exceptional work ethic, pushed him to establish the Silver Shirts and Liberation doctrine in an attempt to make himself a significant player in both political and religious affairs.

Pelley's sincerity and sanity are taken for granted in the present study. I have found no evidence to support the allegation that Pelley created the Silver Shirts as a money-making venture, adopted anti-Semitism as a perceived political expediency, or consciously fabricated clairaudient messages to bilk gullible spiritualists. Pelley's views, both political and religious, were unusual—and at times intentionally hurtful and narrow-minded—but he seems to have truly believed in both a Jewish conspiracy and a series of discorporate spheres of existence. Combined with his ego and overarching desire for public recognition, these beliefs propelled Pelley's public career in the Depression decade.

Released from prison in 1950 after serving eight years for his sedition conviction, Pelley began a virtual second career by developing his Liberation system into a full-blown religion, known as Soulcraft. Enjoined from engaging in political activities under the terms of his parole, Pelley dedicated himself to establishing Soulcraft as a viable cult, and he published more than two dozen volumes of Soulcraft materials, thereby ensuring that dedicated Soulcrafters would have a lifetime's worth of scriptures to study. Liberation and Soulcraft eventually served as models for a variety of similar Theosophically oriented organizations. There is a direct link from Pelley to Mighty I AM, Summit Lighthouse, the Church Universal and Triumphant, and countless other metaphysical groups. Pelley was also an important figure in the development of the Aquarian New Age movement in this country and deserves study for his role in twentieth-century American alternative religion alone.

Although Pelley's political work has received attention from scholars, his important religious activities are not thoroughly documented in any of the previous studies of his career. This monograph is the first work to detail Pelley's life fully and give equal attention to his literary, political, and religious works. Pelley's other endeavors help give context to his activities with the Silver Shirts, which are generally regarded as the most significant aspect of his public life, and an examination of his nonpolitical work is essential to a proper understanding of the man. The cluster of dissertations and chapters that focus on Pelley concentrate on the Silver Shirts and only discuss his religious beliefs as an ancillary topic—and none of these prior works discusses his post–Silver Shirt religious system.[2]

Pelley's two careers, extremist politics and metaphysical teachings, are the pillars of this study. His work in those two areas represents a significant chapter in the substantially uncultivated history of both fields. That Pelley managed to intertwine the seemingly disparate realms of authoritarian bigotry and esoteric religion marks him as an atypical figure with a unique legacy; that he spent a lifetime following his peculiar muse gives the researcher a marvelous opportunity to explore his beliefs fully. This work, then, is a venture into the eclectic world of William Dudley Pelley.

WILLIAM DUDLEY PELLEY

1

Early Years
1890–1915

ON JUNE 29, 1936, a large crowd, estimated by some at more than a
thousand, gathered in Seattle's Moose Hall. Restless after being subjected
to several verses of the "Battle Hymn of the Republic," the congregated
immediately came to attention as a diminutive figure sporting a Vandyke
strode to the podium. The curious and the converted alike listened atten-
tively as the speaker railed about Franklin Roosevelt's "Jew" Deal and its
corruption of America's Christian principles. The impassioned speaker
declared that only he and his loyal band of followers could save gentile
America from falling into the clutches of marching Communism. At the
end of his vitriol-laden speech, amid a storm of applause, the speaker
quickly marched off the stage to meet privately with his staunchest supporters; members of his entourage then diligently packed up banners and
display materials for the next stop on the Silver Cavalcade. The "star-
spangled fascist" William Dudley Pelley, Christian party presidential candidate and head of the anti-Semitic Silver Shirt Legion of America, had
come to town.[1]

William Dudley Pelley was born in the coastal city of Lynn, Massachusetts, on March 12, 1890. He was the only son born into a family of
staunch Methodism, a desire for wealth, and a tradition of economic failure. Pelley's perceived pastoral New England youth deeply affected him.
Looking back in his 1939 autobiography, *The Door to Revelation,* the Silver Shirt chief found a great deal to be proud of in his upbringing. By the
time his autobiography was published, Pelley was a national figure (or to

1

many, a national villain), and his memoir served the dual purpose of demonstrating both his proper ethnic background and the long, strange journey of his life. Pelley hoped the detailing of his unusual career would convince friend and foe alike of his qualifications to be a political leader.[2]

William Dudley Pelley devoutly defended the pure English blood on both sides of his family. He claimed in his autobiography that his racial pride came honestly, inherited from his father. As his son pointed out, William George Apsey Pelley "took a vast amount of pride in the assumption that the Tribe of Pelley could trace its genealogy back in an unbroken line to one Sir John Pelley, knighted sponsored by Good Queen Elizabeth."[3]

The knighting of Sir John began a period of prosperity for the Pelleys. Some of his (many) progeny established themselves as minor members of the peerage in the Southampton area (what Pelley referred to as the "ancestral acres"). William Dudley's paternal great-great-grandparents departed from England early in the eighteenth century for North America. Once ensconced in Newfoundland, the Pelley clan found economic success and rapidly multiplied until, as Pelley noted in his inimitable style, the name was "as common in Newfoundland as Finkelbaums in the Washington government."[4]

The Pelley line arrived in the United States, in the persons of William Dudley's paternal grandparents, Frederick William and Mahala, in 1875. Frederick William had spent most of his life in the fishing business but had a midlife epiphany. He had become aware of the desperate need for water-tight footwear on fishing ships. After some experimentation, Frederick William had latched upon the idea of selling leather boots thoroughly soaked in cottonseed oil. Flush with the success of his boots among Newfoundland and Labrador fishermen, Pelley decided to move his family to Lynn (a city built upon shoe manufacturing) in the mid-1870s. His goal was to make a fortune by breaking the Pelley boots into the American market. Frederick William's dream proved illusory before the increasing development of watertight boots made from vulcanized rubber. His business acumen, however, led to the development of a successful real estate and building concern, the benefits of which allowed Frederick William to utilize his retirement years to study English history and spend "weeks at a time in searching his Scriptures."[5]

William Dudley's father, William G. A., was the eldest son (one of eight children) of Frederick William and Mahala. William G. A. worked as a foreman at the Valpey & Anthony Shoe Factory in Lynn during the day and attended ministerial preparation classes at Boston Theological Seminary (now the Boston University School of Theology) at night. It was while working at Valpey & Anthony that he, who bequeathed his son "neither blood taint nor soul taint," met Grace Goodale.[6]

Although they had been residents of the Danvers, Massachusetts, region since the Puritan decades of the seventeenth century, the late-nineteenth-century Goodales did not possess the same status as the Pelleys. William Dudley addressed the disparity in their financial status in his autobiography, but he made no mention of any controversy (on either side of the family) surrounding the marriage of Grace and William G. A. In any event, two years after their wedding their first child, William Dudley, was born.

William G. A. demonstrated little of his father's business sense, at least early in life, and his lack of economic success led the family to make numerous moves during the first years of William Dudley's life. In 1892 William G. A. accepted the pastorate of a small Methodist church in East Templeton, Massachusetts. With a tiny congregation, financial remuneration was scant. When the depression of 1893 arrived, even the small amounts of currency and barter previously granted virtually ceased.

In response to this economic hardship William G. A. gave up the ministry. He moved his family to nearby Templeton Center and opened a dry-goods shop. Faring financially no better as a shopkeeper than he had as a minister (and faced with the increased economic hardship of supporting a daughter, Edna Grace, born in 1894), William G. A. moved his family back to East Templeton in 1895 and became a cobbler. While the family only spent a few years in East Templeton, the experience left a lasting impression on young William Dudley. It was while residing in this small town that Pelley learned to read and published his first work—two very significant events for a man who made his career as a writer and publisher.[7]

During this second period of residence in East Templeton, the Pelleys lived on a small farm colloquially referred to as the Fairbanks Place. As part of the terms of sale, the last of the Fairbanks family, known in the area as "Grandma" Fairbanks, reserved two rooms in the house for herself. It was this woman who taught William Dudley how to read by guiding him through a copy of *Aesop's Fables*. With this basic literacy Pelley was able to compose a contribution to the "Youth's Letter-Box" section of the local newspaper. This rather inauspicious beginning to a long and copious writing career detailed young Bill's prowess as a gardener.[8]

Pelley's introduction to politics occurred during this second East Templeton period. After being confronted by a gang of boys at school who demanded to know if he supported William McKinley or William Jennings Bryan, Pelley consulted his father regarding the family's political affiliation. William G. A. informed his son that William Dudley was a Republican "because I'm a Republican—and you happen to be my son." The younger Pelley would later note, "thus I discovered that politics had much in common with religion—or for that matter citizenship itself. . . . [Y]ou are born into all of them." [9]

East Templeton also played a role in Pelley's later fiction. He looked back very fondly on the village and utilized it as a model for the town of Foxboro Center, located "just over the mountain" from Paris, Vermont (the primary locale for his stories). Pelley noted the town was the "perfect idyl of New England existence." [10]

Before the family left East Templeton, again for economic reasons, Pelley underwent his first mystical experience. As detailed in his autobiography, he found himself contemplating the nature of human existence while sitting on a small knoll behind his parents' home. Pelley later claimed that "a corner of the veil of Eternal Mortality was flashingly lifted," and he gained his first insight into the reincarnation theory he promoted as an adult. Regardless of the validity of this incident, it is obvious that the thoroughly religious nature of the Pelley household left a mark on William Dudley and certainly helps explain the curious mixture of Christianity and mystical occultism he was to develop in the 1930s.[11]

The Pelleys' nomadic existence led them to West Gardner, Massachusetts, in 1896. William G. A. accepted a job as a reporter and advertising solicitor for the *Gardner Journal*. This occupational change would prove to be far more significant for William Dudley than for his father. Young Bill spent his evenings in the *Journal's* print shop watching the workers lay out the next edition. He set up lines of print for himself when no one else was around. The brief period in which his father was employed by the *Journal* led William Dudley to decide that his own fortunes lay in the newspaper business.[12]

William G. A. apparently experienced no similar epiphany concerning the world of journalism, and he quit the *Journal* shortly after the family arrived in West Gardner. He subsequently set up an auction room and furniture store, once again seeking to duplicate his father's business success. Despite initially having to stock the store with many of his family's own home furnishings, William G. A. parlayed this humble start-up into a profitable venture. His success permitted the family to move into a far more substantial house in the prosperous northwest part of town.[13]

It was in this home that Pelley stayed up late one evening to usher in the new century. For Pelley the change in centuries represented a signal event. His autobiography spoke approvingly of the sylvan nineteenth century of a "clean, wholesome, untarnished America" where "each year . . . four holidays [were] sacredly observed in the best Nordic tradition: Memorial Day, Independence Day, Thanksgiving, and Christmas." However, the twentieth century ushered in a far deadlier, dangerous, and un-Christian period. With typical vitriol Pelley posited that the new century created a situation in which "the spawn and scum of renegade immigration, with no character and less stamina, now flaunts it before young America that war is 'brutal' and 'inhuman,' that we must boycott militarism, that all men should be 'brothers,' . . . [and are] expanding their subtle villainies to overthrow, subvert, or emasculate the American tradition."[14]

Although Pelley built much of his career on railing against the takeover of the United States by these "alien locusts in human form," his parents apparently felt some parts of the country were still uncontaminated. To escape the "too many Polocks" flooding into the West Gardner region, the Pelleys moved to Springfield, Massachusetts, in June 1900. As John Werly has pointed out, "the Pelleys probably resented eastern European immigration into pure Anglo-Saxon country as much as other New Englanders, as alien prejudice provided a handy scapegoat for economic fluctuations." While Werly is undoubtedly correct that the Pelleys harbored common anti-immigrant sentiments, Pelley's assertion that the move to Springfield was an attempt to escape eastern Europeans is probably an overstatement. Springfield was more economically prosperous than West Gardner, but it was also a major destination for new immigrants, including a large number of Italians and Russian Jews.[15]

While living in Springfield William Dudley first became a publisher. With a loan from his father he purchased a used hand press and also salvaged items discarded by local presses, and then contracted with his father to print up business cards for William G. A. in return for the money to buy a dozen fonts of job type. He set up the completed press in the barn behind their home, a building that quickly became the focal point of his daily routine.[16]

Using his homemade press, Pelley began publishing his first newspaper at the precocious age of twelve. The *Junior Star* was intended to be distributed to his classmates during recess periods. Possessing several copies of Elbert Hubbard's *Philistine,* Pelley tried to emulate "the sage of East Aurora . . . [his] patron saint." Pelley would later write that he was "steeped in the sweet vitriol of the erstwhile Fra Elbertus." Much of Pelley's later newspaper and magazine work evinced a heavy and continued Hubbard influence.[17]

The New York polymath Elbert Hubbard enjoyed a meteoric rise (in part by demonstrating behavior that today would be classified as workaholic) as a writer and became a national celebrity from around 1895 until his death in 1915 (he went down with the *Lusitania*). The sheer variety and volume of Hubbard's career (his published writings run to approximately seven million words) have created challenges for later scholars and, consequently, his significance has been unfortunately obscured. As Freeman Champney (one of the more successful Hubbard biographers) noted, "to place and judge a man—now or in history—you have first to plot his position . . . then or now, Elbert Hubbard didn't stand still long enough for such a procedure to work." Still, Hubbard's public stature rested on two distinct and discernible pillars—his writings and his craft community.[18]

Along with Gustave Stickley and Frank Lloyd Wright, Elbert Hubbard helped popularize the arts and crafts movement in America. The movement initially arose in nineteenth-century England as a response to the social injustice, disease, and crime associated with industrialization and the overwrought, machine-made interior decorations of the Victorian era. Looking back to a "golden age," English social critics attacked current social conditions and sought to rally English society around the idea of a return to the values of the Middle Ages (hand-crafted goods, a guild-based worker fraternity, and a commitment to work).[19]

Hubbard helped propel the arts and crafts movement in this country with his 1895 establishment of the Roycroft Press in East Aurora, New York. The success of his printing venture helped lead to the creation of the fourteen-building complex known as the Roycroft campus, a virtually self-sufficient community. The Roycrofters produced a wide variety of products known for their quality, but they never developed a unified artistic vision similar to Stickley's furniture designs or the architecture of Wright. Hence, one scholar has noted that the principal legacy of Roycroft was "the creation of the community and the transformation of the village of East Aurora into a center, however brief its existence, of real intellectual ferment."[20]

Although Pelley admired Hubbard's commitment to rural life, community, and hard work, it was the Roycroft founder's writings that most influenced the young New Englander. Hubbard's initial recognition came from his magazine *The Philistine: A Periodical of Protest*, first issued in June 1895. The monthly presented Hubbard's own idiosyncratic worldview. Barbed jibes, attacks on cultureless "culture," quotations and epigrams, heavy-handed humor, withering attacks on organized religion, and unauthorized editing of literary classics filled the pages of Hubbard's very personal "little magazine." Hubbard would tolerate no ignorance or hypocrisy, and his magazine should be recognized as a precursor to H. L. Mencken's *American Mercury* and the college lampoons of the 1920s. To Pelley the magazine was a revelation. He would co-opt the form and attitude of *The Philistine* in his own early magazines. Hubbard's difficulty in dealing with writers, editors, and coworkers who did not share his vision would also be repeated by Pelley during his own publishing heyday in the 1930s.[21]

Along with his magazine, Hubbard kept up an exceedingly high pub-

lication rate (an example Pelley would follow). *The Philistine* was augmented by monthly installments of Hubbard's *Little Journeys.* The *Little
Journeys* series involved Hubbard visiting the homes of great writers,
artists, and public figures, then writing a pamphlet detailing the subject's
career along with Hubbard's views of their work (and houses). Hubbard
would eventually write 170 of these short works. Pelley would pick up
the idea in the 1930s with his similar *Little Visits* series.[22]

In the wake of a furor surrounding an article concerning young Bill's
teacher, William G. A. attempted to warn his son off publishing potentially inflammatory articles in the Hubbard-inspired *Junior Star.* William
Dudley, however, did not learn the lesson until a neighborhood bully,
Philip Taft, broke his nose in response to a story addressing the large size
of Taft's mouth. Because of the beating, Pelley gave up the *Junior Star.* Pelley later claimed the experience taught him that "in militant journalism
. . . whatever you print is just about as safe from reprisal as your opponent's secret dread of you."[23]

William Dudley would once again become a publisher at Springfield
Technical High School. In his sophomore year, along with becoming
president of the school's debating society Pelley began issuing *The Black
Crow.* In his own words it was a "pretentious and successful monthly
magazine."[24]

In 1907, Pelley's *Black Crow* fell victim to yet another family trans-
planting when they moved to Fulton, New York. Initially it was only
William G. A. who went, but he quickly decided to move the entire family there. William G. A.'s move resulted from his becoming a partner in
the Fulton Toilet Paper Company. This concern would finally be the financial success he had sought for more than a decade.

William Dudley was far less enthusiastic about the move than his father. He was forced to give up *The Black Crow* and a comfortable high
school environment. Further, his father determined that it was in William
Dudley's best interest to go to work for the toilet paper company. After
little more than a year of high school, the younger Pelley would enter the
working world. William Dudley Pelley's formal education ended in
Springfield; from that point on he would be completely self-taught.[25]

While the Fulton Toilet Paper Company (whose Pathfinder Toilet

Rolls "added years to your life") proved an economic success for William G. A., it was his ambitious son who benefited most from the concern. William Dudley rose quickly within the ranks of the company, and he eventually became treasurer and general superintendent of the firm. Pelley achieved a great deal at Fulton and was justifiably proud of his accomplishments. His time with the company hardened his senses of both business and independence. Pelley later posited that working at the Fulton Company provided him with the qualifications to present "a wholly new concept of social economics" (detailed in his book *No More Hunger*). Without his being "sold to the galleys" at the toilet paper company, Pelley claimed, his credibility would have been as nonexistent as a "Brain-Trust Professor out of the Jewish NRA."[26]

Pelley never again entered a school (as a student) after Springfield Tech, but he began a lifelong course in self-education while working at the Fulton plant. Determined to obtain a proper education in his spare time, William Dudley eschewed most social companionship (especially after a disastrous love affair with young Canadian woman named Mabel). He developed a voracious appetite for works of history, biography, and economics. Attempting to cram as much knowledge as he could into a short period, Pelley would read until he fell asleep at night (a practice he continued until the end of his life). During the years in New York, Pelley "drugged . . . [himself] with reading."[27]

Along with developing his own educational techniques, Pelley again became a magazine publisher while living in Fulton. *The Philosopher* represents the first Pelley publication of any real significance. Pelley began issuing the "religio-sociological" monthly from Fulton in June 1909. As Leo Ribuffo has noted, *The Philosopher* was "at bottom . . . a declaration of adulthood."[28]

Although Pelley tried to established himself as an independent and mature individual in *The Philosopher,* he also claimed to have special insights into America's youth. He proudly proclaimed himself the youngest publisher in the United States. Not surprisingly, Pelley's magazine focused much of its attention on America's children and young adults.

Pelley decried current child-rearing practices, which he felt led to violence and self-loathing. He noted that babies were born innocent but quickly fell afoul of parents, who believed them to be unruly. In response, parents inflicted corporal punishment on children and threatened them with damnation because of the "allegorical crime" detailed in the book of Genesis. This "forced obedience" and "physical authority" was "the by-product of the devil." Such an environment, according to Pelley, naturally led to warfare and crime.[29]

Pelley's views on childhood reflected many of the Progressive concerns of the period. The social reformers of the first two decades of the twentieth century also decried the treatment of children in this country, and they shared Pelley's view that the future of the United States depended on proper treatment of future generations. Progressive reformers helped establish settlement houses for abused women and children, created juvenile courts, organized the Boy Scouts of America, promoted child labor laws, and helped create the U.S. Children's Bureau. Pelley's hero Elbert Hubbard, during the same period, advocated lenient child-rearing practices (a campaign William Dudley clearly supported). However, few reformers would have agreed with Pelley's program of not permitting children under ten years of age to see books so that they could focus all energies on "physical culture."[30]

Pelley also mirrored elements of the Progressive movement in advocating clean living. In *The Philosopher* he claimed not to smoke tobacco, drink alcohol, frequent the "lewdery" of the theater, or eat unwholesome food. He argued that proper human progress (and economic rewards) required "self-control and purity of heart." Earthly punishment (he had disputed the existence of Hell in his teenage magazine), in the form of sickness and mental disability, awaited those who violated the "laws of health, chastity, and reason."[31]

Pelley's views on the proper way of life reflect the influence of New Thought. New Thought encompassed a variety of views and religious perspectives, as adherents refused to promote any specific dogma or institutional structure. As a result, their views are difficult to summarize. Still, the basic tenets of the movement included healthy living and thinking, an optimistic perspective on humanity, a firm belief that evil and sin are illusory and surmountable, the unity of God and man, and free will. Pelley found much with which to concur in New Thought beliefs (and dubbed his version "the Religion of Laughter").[32]

The *Philosopher* editor condemned most churches (excepting the Salvation Army) not only for erroneous dogma, but also for ignoring both the plight of the poor and the destructiveness of warfare. Pelley criticized many ministers for choosing unthinking, comfortable careers in mainstream denominations rather than continuing their studies or lobbying for activist social legislation. The *Philosopher* editor's views on churches and ministers echoed popular themes from the Social Gospel movement.[33]

Pelley's *Philosopher* began appearing shortly after Walter Rauschenbusch, the Social Gospel's most famous proponent, issued the classic statement of the movement's thought, *Christianity and the Social Crisis.* No hard evidence exists that Pelley read Rauschenbusch's work, but, given Pelley's interests, reading habits, and the book's success, he most certainly was familiar with both it and the movement Rauschenbusch promoted. The Social Gospelers advocated the improvement of society through good works, defended the rights of labor, promoted the restraint of competition through brotherly love, and called for an end to the abuses of laissez-faire economic policies.[34]

The society Pelley hoped to build upon this Social Gospel foundation mirrored Edward Bellamy's utopian conceptions. This intention is not surprising, inasmuch as Pelley readily admitted his support for Bellamy and his ideas. Bellamy's fame rested almost solely on his 1888 novel *Looking Backward*. In that novel Bellamy described a mythical future for the United States in which, thanks to a society based upon organic Christian brotherhood, socialistic perfection had occurred by the year 2000. The Christian ordering Bellamy envisioned—he called it the "religion of solidarity"— took its inspiration "in about equal measure from Christian liberalism, Transcendentalism, and Auguste Comte's Religion of Humanity."[35]

Pelley believed his program could create a Bellamy-like society within fifty years. He claimed that an army of intelligent, liberal theologians (the "Federation of Religious Leaders") would marshal the forces of society to abolish poverty and create safe, clean environments for work and play. In this newly constituted Christian community all individuals would be taken care of by all-encompassing social welfare programs. Pelley's program, however, fell short in providing the details for creating this utopian society. Instead, he frequently fell back on the slogan "instead of lifting men from the gutter, abolish the gutter."[36]

Given his Social Gospel-like calls for the protection of workers, Pelley's promotion of socialism in *The Philosopher* is not surprising. He proposed, in a manner similar to Bellamy's, that rather than be dismantled, giant corporations be operated for the common good of the people so that all citizens would receive a "fair share" of the national wealth. His defense of the sanctity of labor and of societal "producers" (farmers, mechanics, and craftsmen) reflected the mechanic ideology that dominated his childhood home of Lynn, Massachusetts. Methodism was the predominant denomination among the shoe factory workers of the city, and Pelley undoubtedly was exposed to the mechanic ideology on a frequent basis.[37]

Pelley's program combined technical expertise with grassroots democracy. Weekly national plebiscites and universal suffrage would be the order of the day. In stark contrast to his later pronouncements, the Pelley of 1909 believed people of all races and religions should benefit from the reorganized society, but the "foreign uneducated heathen element" would not be allowed to vote. Further, Pelley declared that the blood of ten nationalities would mingle in the United States to create an eleventh "mightier than them all."[38]

Pelley never did set out the specifics of his social program in *The Philosopher,* which folded after nine issues in 1909. Almost certainly a dearth of subscribers spelled its ruin, although Pelley never publicly admitted it. As an adult Pelley would come to regret many of his pronouncements in *The Philosopher.* He noted that "my twaddle and blither were piling up to give me such heartburn in later years when I came to see that I merely took out on God what I should have taken out on an inhibited environment."[39]

Despite Pelley's later disavowal of the magazine, his writings in *The Philosopher* represent the earliest examples of themes and ideas he carried into his later public careers. Already at age nineteen Pelley recognized the need for theocratic social planning and for overhauling of the current system, with a strong leader (he noted, "our second Christ will be a dictator") running the country. Embryonic examples of Pelley's later religious system can also be discerned in his discussions of Christ's imminent return, karmic retribution, and an evolutionary system for souls in which "men are gods in the chrysalis." These ideas lay dormant as Pelley spent the next twenty years engaged in material pursuits, but all bubbled to the surface as undergirdings of his philosophy in the 1930s.[40]

William G. A. Pelley lost financial control of the Fulton Toilet Paper Company in 1911; William Dudley did not last much longer at the firm. Thanks to the economic success they had previously enjoyed, the break was not a hardship on either of them. Desirous of continuing his writing career, Pelley returned to Massachusetts and accepted a position as a feature news writer for the *Springfield Homestead.*

Shortly after beginning work at the *Homestead,* Pelley met Marion (he usually called her Mary Ann) Harriet Stone in the paper's office. A native of Massachusetts, Marion worked as a proofreader on the paper (she had begun her career with Houghton, Mifflin, and Company). In his autobiography Pelley was quick to point out that Mary Ann's mother came from a line of people who signed the Mayflower Compact. After a brief courtship they were married on December 16, 1911. Pelley believed his betrothal was a signal event in his development. In *Door to Revelation* he noted that after asking Mary Ann for her hand in marriage "she said she might . . . thus my majority."[41]

By his wedding day, Pelley had left the *Springfield Homestead* to become western Massachusetts night editor for the *Boston Globe.* Pelley had to work on the paper every night, but he appreciated that his afternoons remained free from work duties. Although the income derived from his work on the *Globe* proved to be adequate, Pelley chafed at being under the dictates of an employer. As he noted, "it was anathema to my temperament." During this period Pelley also became a father for the first time. Marion gave birth to a daughter, Harriet, in Springfield in 1912.[42]

In order to start his own newspaper, Pelley moved his family just north of Springfield to Chicopee, a small city located at the confluence of the Connecticut and Chicopee Rivers in the Pioneer Valley. Pelley later portrayed the interlude in Chicopee as an example of his own moral high ground. This claim is an interesting perspective on his period there, because Pelley moved his family to Chicopee as part of a rather cynical arrangement with Mayor Frank A. Rivers. Although his desire to become his own boss is understandable, Pelley's willingness to become a politician's personal propagandist in order to achieve independence makes his positive spin on the escapade debatable.[43]

Rivers was running for reelection on a reformist platform. As part of his program, the mayor called for reducing the number of Chicopee saloons from seventy-five to forty-two. Fearing the loss of lucrative advertising from liquor concerns, the local newspapers all came out against him. Faced with this opposition, Rivers agreed to fund the establishment of a new newspaper, edited by Pelley, with the understanding that the new *Chicopee Journal* would be completely supportive of his reelection campaign.[44]

As Pelley readily admitted, he agreed to support the candidate solely to obtain control of his own newspaper. Although Pelley advocated temperance, the mayor's platform was of little consequence to the *Journal*'s editor. He noted that limiting the number of saloons would do little to curb excesses in the city. Pelley posited that "a city of Polocks could get just as drunk in five saloons as fifty: it simply meant that five would get ten times the business." For Pelley, it was only the newspaper that mattered.[45]

Pelley, however, quickly lost interest in operating a newspaper in Chicopee. Disgusted by local political machinations and "the Better Classes . . . [expecting] too much reprint of Sunday sermons in the *Journal* and the papers . . . becoming too flossy to sell," Pelley sold the paper and moved to Wilmington, Vermont. Still, he believed the events there had helped him prepare for future struggles. Pelley noted that the Chicopee experiences were "a pocket-handkerchief edition of what I was to go through nationally when I fought a vaster lechery."[46]

The night before the Pelleys left for Vermont, William Dudley's father came to visit them. William G. A. Pelley borrowed money from them, spent the evening discussing the Watch Tower Society, then departed (allegedly for New York). Pelley never saw his father again. The elder Pelley sent a few letters back from Pennsylvania, was spotted on a street in Wichita, Kansas, and then "his trail wended into the Mist."[47]

In Vermont, Pelley took a job as a printer on the *Deerfield Valley Times.* The *Times,* an eight-page boilerplate weekly, was owned and edited by a crusty old newspaperman named George Dixon. Pelley accepted the position for low wages in the hope that he would eventually purchase the newspaper, and because the location placed them closer to Marion's wid-owed mother.[48]

Pelley's residence in Wilmington, however, proved short-lived and painful. He immediately clashed with Dixon and then quickly fell out with the group that subsequently purchased the *Times.* In the winter of 1913 the Pelleys' daughter, Harriet, died of cerebral meningitis. The tragedy also left Pelley in a precarious financial situation; Harriet's med-ical expenses left Pelley in heavy financial debt for the first time in his life. Then, in July 1914, the new *Times* owner decided to remove Pelley from the *Times* and replace him with a new editor.[49]

To escape the dire circumstances of Wilmington, Pelley moved his family to Bennington, Vermont, and he took up duties as a foreman on the *Bennington Evening Banner* on the signal date August 4, 1914. Unlike the *Deerfield Valley Times,* the *Evening Banner* was an economically profitable venture, and Pelley laid the credit for the paper's success at the feet of its vet-eran editor "Clate" Kinsley, a man whose entire life revolved around the *Banner's* office. While Pelley still desired to edit his own paper, he found this period working for Kinsley in Bennington to be extremely beneficial to his career—a "thorough education in the small-town newspaper business."[50]

Bennington, a small city located in the extreme southwestern corner of Vermont, was not all that dissimilar to Wilmington. This Vermont city of ten thousand residents embodied near perfection to Pelley. He noted approvingly that it was a "sedate yet sprightly community . . . [with] no swollen wealth and on the other hand no squalor." This "brick sidewalk, maple tree bowered sort of town" left a lasting impression on Pelley. His successful career as a fiction writer was built almost entirely upon stories set in Bennington (dubbed Paris, Vermont, in Pelley's tales).[51]

Financial concerns initiated Pelley's forays into the world of fiction. His job at the *Evening Banner* paid only $16 per week. While this was suf-ficient to keep his family fed (even with the addition of a daughter, Ade-laide, born in September 1914), Pelley faced insurmountable debts from Harriet's extensive medical treatments. After reading about a contest for unpublished writers in John Slidell's *American Magazine,* Pelley decided to undertake the writing of short stories as a way to pay off these substantial medical debts.

The potential for income from selling his stories pushed the hard-working Pelley into a very rigorous daily schedule. He spent his days working in the *Evening Banner*'s print shop, rushed home to eat dinner, then spent the evenings working on his stories. To strengthen his style, Pelley studiously examined volumes of O. Henry's short stories.

Pelley's efforts finally paid off with a sale in December 1914. He received $50 from Street & Smith's *Popular Magazine* for his story "Spirit of the West." Pelley quickly sold additional stories to Arthur Hoffman's *Adventure Magazine* and George Horace Lorimer's *Saturday Evening Post*. The sale of "Li'l Son of a Gun" to the *Post* brought Pelley a great deal of local acclaim and a much-needed windfall of $300.[52]

The spate of sold stories allowed Pelley to pay down his debts, move into a large home in Bennington, and quit his job at the *Evening Banner*. He accepted a part-time position as treasurer of the Bennington County Fish and Game Association. The job with Fish and Game required William Dudley to travel throughout the county. He accepted the position primarily because this travel would give him an opportunity to collect anecdotes and material from individuals throughout the area.

Pelley was forced to search out new material because he was finding it increasingly difficult to develop new ideas. His early stories were primarily adventure tales, including many westerns. As Pelley had never been farther west than New York, he came to believe these tales were quickly growing stale. He later noted that his stories of Montana cow-punchers were "asinine." Pelley recognized that if was going to establish himself as a reputable writer something in his work had to change.[53]

2

Paris and Asia
1916–1919

DESPITE LEAVING THE *Bennington Evening Banner,* Bill Pelley still spent a great deal of time at the newspaper offices. It was during a late-night talk in the offices with Clate Kinsley that the direction of Pelley's fiction would undergo a permanent shift. After listening to Pelley discuss the problems he faced in developing original plots, Kinsley suggested that he focus his energies on writing local color stories based on Bennington incidents. Kinsley was able to persuade Pelley that he should write about the area he knew best, Vermont, and that a great deal of exciting material could be derived from stories depicting small-town life.[1]

Not only did Kinsley give Pelley the idea of focusing on local color stories, but he also gave him an example of small-town stories to study. *The Banner's* editor gave Pelley a copy of William Allen White's 1906 best seller *In Our Town,* and instructed him to read and study the volume closely. Pelley was captivated by what he read. He soon realized not only that he could write similar stories set in Vermont, but that these tales held real significance. Pelley noted that the characters in White's stories lived "their unwept, unhonored, and unsung lives as nobly as they could, representative Americans who displayed their poignant heroisms the clock around with never a thought that they were composing the true saga of our century."[2]

Inspired by Edgar W. Howe's *Story of a Country Town,* William Allen White built a very successful career as a writer of small-town fictions during the first quarter of the twentieth century. White located his stories in his native Kansas, basing many of them in Emporia. *In Our Town,* the best of his eight books, consisted of eighteen simple morality tales, all previously published in magazines, that blended comedy and pathos rife with sentimental optimism. White sought to depict the "generous, charitable, and merciful" residents of Kansas rising above their failings. In White's fictional world, crime and vice were present, but all difficulties could be overcome through the unity of neighbors. Heavily influenced by the Social Gospel, White "invited his readers not to join him in small-town America but to use the small town to cast reform upon their own communities and the greater community—to mold an American culture incorporating the best of *Gemeinschaft* within an emergent *Gesellschaft* order."[3]

White not only inspired Pelley to focus on the incidents of his own small town, but White's usage of the newspaper office as the narrative center in many of his stories also affected Pelley. White owned and edited the *Emporia Gazette,* and his experiences working there shaped much of his fiction. He saw the newspaper's office as the clearinghouse for the life stories of any town. As a result, many of his stories revolved around "life as seen through the window of a small-town newspaper office." Pelley, having similar life experiences, eventually based many of his stories around the newspaper office in his fictional Paris, Vermont, and used a young newspaper foreman as his narrator.[4]

As Leo Ribuffo has pointed out, Paris, Vermont, was a "Yoknapatawpha County for sentimentalists." Most of Pelley's Paris stories involved the offices of the *Paris Daily Telegraph,* where hard-bitten editor Sam Hod placed current events in the context of his years of human observation, frequent visitor "Uncle" Joe Fodder (owner of the stables and "town philosopher") provided insights and wisdom, and the young *Telegraph* foreman, Bill, often served as the "crusty" narrator. Young love blossomed frequently in the starlit New England night, and even the most cynical residents came to understand the simple pleasures of life. In Paris friendship and camaraderie were how a man was judged, not economic status. Pelley's Paris, Vermont, stories clearly reflected what critic Henry Seidel Canby referred to as the "vivacious dullness which was the note of the period."[5]

Hardship and tragedy, however, were prevalent in Pelley's fictional world. Class conflict, while muted, did occur. In one story a bitter (and deadly) strike erupted at the local knitting mill, possibly modeled after the violent shoe factory strikes of Lynn, Massachusetts. Families also faced the challenges of spousal abuse, crime, failed romances, financial difficulties, and the death of children. However, the overwhelming majority of such travails served only as obstacles to be overcome by the successful pursuit of love and happiness, or by the altruistic self-denial of Pelley's invariably heroic heroines. For example, the knitting strike caused a personal tragedy for the central character but served only to teach him a lesson about keeping the right sort of people in charge of the local church. Further, the villains in these tales were frequently strangers who had arrived in Paris under mysterious circumstances (or locals who had obtained vast wealth and lost their traditional New England values), not the peaceful lifelong residents of the community.[6]

Pelley's work, like that of William Allan White, maintained the traditional lofty position of the small town in American literature. Small-town writers such as these two men argued that within provincial life one could find refuge from the vicissitudes of modern industrial life. In these communities conformity, thrift, industry, and compassion brought comfort, joy, and the realization of American ideals. As Pelley put it, "American life all over the nation isn't reflected by the cities; it is reflected by the people of the communities of ten thousand inhabitants and under." Pelley, then, clearly reflected the love among the tradition-minded of his generation for what Robert Wiebe termed the "island community." Wiebe posited that the essential aspect of these communities was the ability to "isolate the individual" and judge him on his own merits, but with urbanization and the intrusion of the previously distant outside world it became difficult both to isolate the individual and to determine what an individual did and what was done to him. To Pelley, Paris, Vermont, was a refuge from the increasingly impersonal, urbanized modern life that continued to encroach upon his notions of idyllic New England life.[7]

Whereas White attempted to use such communities as a metaphor, as a means to create a "progressive alternative within the modern order," Pelley's Paris, Vermont, was a town trapped in the past. The residents of

Paris were clearly uneasy about the rapid changes brought about by the twentieth century. Pelley himself frequently appeared troubled by the modernization around him. As a result, many of the Paris stories took place during the final decades of the nineteenth century, a period when modernization had not fully affected the lives of a rural Vermont town.[8]

Pelley's narrative focus would change only gradually over time. His dogged maintenance of genteel themes undoubtedly hurt his short-story career during the 1920s, as literary critics turned on the village myth with a vengeance. The changes in literary tastes, in part, help explain his shift toward writing scripts and, infrequently, novels as a means of supporting himself during that decade. While he continued to write short stories, his production of them tapered off as his publication rate declined.[9]

In 1917, however, William Dudley's shift toward writing local color stories paid immediate dividends. In August of that year the *American Magazine* published Pelley's story "Their Mother" (subsequently expanded into his 1919 novel *The Greater Glory*). This was to be the beginning of a long and productive relationship between Pelley and the magazine. *American* editor John Slidell greatly admired Pelley's work, and he saw to it that his stories appeared in the magazine frequently. Pelley's name appeared in the *American's* table of contents almost every month throughout 1917 and 1918. The publicity garnered from his frequent appearances in the *American* helped Pelley sell stories to several other magazines, including *Pictorial Review, Adventure, Popular Magazine,* and *Red Book*. He quickly became one of the country's best-known short story writers (he later claimed to have published over two hundred stories during his career) and won the prestigious O. Henry Award in 1920.[10]

Pelley's successful career as a fiction writer eventually provided the financial security he needed to purchase his own newspaper. His love for publishing never diminished, and while he found great pleasure in his writing career, he desperately wanted to own his own newspaper. Always possessing a strong work ethic, Pelley believed he could operate a paper during the day and leave his evenings free to compose his tales of small-town life.

Pelley's plan to purchase his own newspaper came to fruition early in 1918. Clate Kinsley not only suggested the shift in Pelley's fiction focus but also gave him the tip that led William Dudley to obtain the *St. Johns-bury (Vermont) Caledonian*. During one of their evening conversations in the *Banner's* office, Kinsley mentioned to Pelley that the long-established newspaper had recently gone bankrupt and suggested that Pelley should utilize his bank account and newspaper talents to resuscitate the moribund *Caledonian*. Pelley thought it an excellent idea because it would "give him a diversion to his magazine work and because a man who has once been in the newspaper business has difficulty in ever entirely weaning himself from the interesting phases of that work." [11]

Located on the banks of the Passumpsic River, St. Johnsbury had been home to the *Weekly Caledonian* since 1837. In 1909 the newspaper was purchased by Walter J. Bigelow, previously the night editor of the *Burlington (Vermont) Free Press*. Bigelow turned the paper into a daily in 1916. He failed miserably, primarily because he "was unfortunate in making his paper a morning instead of an evening daily." Pelley reasoned that an evening newspaper would succeed in St. Johnsbury because New Englanders would have more time to read in the hours after work than in the mornings. He purchased the paper on February 26, 1918, and promptly converted the *Daily Caledonian* into the *Evening Caledonian*. [12]

In an effort to remold the paper in his own image, Pelley made other changes to the *Caledonian* as well. He concentrated more on local news, including separate social news columns for all the surrounding communities. Pelley also utilized the skills he had honed writing small-town stories by adding "a series of pert paragraphs . . . concerning the homely incidents that had transpired beneath . . . [his] observation during each intervening day." To add variety (and fill space during slow news days), Pelley added advice and recipe paragraphs, famous quotations and homilies, and odd little stories from around the country (for example, a short report on a man dying of a heart attack while his barber son was shaving him). [13]

To defuse any rumors concerning the new editor's past experiences as a somewhat less-than-independent newspaper publisher, Pelley issued editorials declaring his freedom from outside influence. He posited that the newspaper was an institution of the community, one that served as a mirror for the town in which it was published. For the reflection to be true, the paper "must have no politics and no religion." Pelley soothed the fears of those concerned that he would be a partisan editor by noting that he owned the *Caledonian* "personally, with no clique, faction, or individual behind him, either financial, political, or any other way."[14]

Although he was no longer the teenage socialist he had promoted himself as being in the *Philosopher,* Pelley's work on the *Caledonian* betrayed vestiges of the Social Gospel and Progressive thought that had influenced him as a young man. Pelley's interest in motion pictures and the theater led him invariably to report all performances at the Colonial, Globe, and Please-U theaters (the last two were movie houses). He frequently wrote brief recommendations for those stories that were "based on honest sentiment" and happily noted the "decline of the problem and sex plays, and those which depend on unhealthy moral themes." While Pelley continued to report on sensational crime stories, the *Caledonian* editor gently reminded his readers that "poverty is the principal cause of crime." He cited approvingly the work of social scientists who argued that hard work and high wages could eliminate crime entirely.[15]

Although Pelley was able to maintain some of his older beliefs during his tenure at the *Caledonian,* he did fall victim to the ethnically directed propaganda so prevalent during World War I. He routinely referred to the Germans as "Huns," claimed that the influenza epidemic was unleashed on the United States by cowardly German secret agents dropped off by submarines, that Germany was the "plague spot of Europe," and that the "Teutons are . . . imitators [rather] than originators."[16]

Pelley later claimed he did not learn of the truly diabolical nature of Jews (and their black minions) until his trip to Japan and Siberia at the end of 1918, and his articles from early 1918 seem to prove his assertion. Unlike the vitriolic attacks Pelley would level at Jews one decade later, his *Caledonian* articles demonstrated no hatred of the group. Among the frequent short articles concerning drafted soldiers were a few detailing the festive farewell parties thrown by the Young Men's Hebrew Association of Burlington for Jewish draftees. A reprint of an editorial by George Harvey in the *North American Review War Weekly* praising the Jews, Slavs, and other unfree peoples who "from their bondage struck with fettered hands brave blows for freedom and humanity" also appeared in the *Caledonian.*[17]

Pelley's views on Blacks were not quite as progressive, but they were probably no more racist than the typical small-town resident with limited exposure to minorities of the time. He noted approvingly the War Camp Community Society's program to create clubhouses for black draftees who had been forced to relocate to distant training camps. However, Pelley mentioned the segregation of the armed forces without comment, reprinted a story with a black character who spoke in a stereotypical dialect, and, while he normally used the then-acceptable terms "colored" and "negro," he once used the term "nigger" in an article.[18]

Although his perspectives on Jews and Germans would later undergo significant alteration, his opinion of Communism had hardened by 1918. Pelley would later argue that Communism was synonymous with Judaism, but during the war, echoing a popular belief, he blamed the Germans for the Bolshevik Revolution. In the *Caledonian* he argued that the Kaiser's government trained and financed the Russian Communists to create disruptions within the Czarist military. Pelley also stated that the Germans' ultimate aim was to utilize the Bolsheviks (and their "anarchist" allies) as the vanguard of an international revolution that would cripple the war efforts of Germany's enemies. Having been beguiled by the German master plan, the only hope for the Russian people was that they "begin to show signs of waking up the morning after the night before."[19]

Pelley's views apparently found acceptance in St. Johnsbury, because the revamped *Caledonian* became a money-making venture for the first time since it became a daily paper in 1916. Pelley later self-servingly argued that a man who resuscitates a bankrupt newspaper could succeed at any task "that requires executive management—and I am not excepting the United States of America as a nation" and promoted political tickets made up entirely of "practical newspapermen."[20]

Although his success as a New England newspaperman never earned him the presidency, his work on the *Caledonian* (and his fame as a short-story writer) did garner Pelley the opportunity to travel halfway around the world as a representative of the Methodist Centenary. Pelley's 1918 trip to Asia would prove to be a turning point in his life. It not only brought him face-to-face with the dreaded Bolsheviks but was also his first exposure to the anti-Semitism that would, within a decade, come to dominate his public life.

When the offer to travel came to William Dudley Pelley, he had never been farther from New England than the state of New York. Although he kept abreast of events around the globe (and avidly read works on world history), Pelley evinced no interest in international travel as a young man. While he would later crisscross the United States numerous times, Pelley was thoroughly parochial during his New England newspaper years. In 1918 it was a very specific set of circumstances that led Pelley to leave his home and venture across the Pacific Ocean.

In late summer 1918, Bishop Fred B. Fisher of the Methodist Episcopal Church visited Pelley in the offices of the *Caledonian*. Acting as a representative of the Methodist Centenary movement, Fisher offered to fund a trip around the world for Pelley and his wife. Dr. S. Earl Taylor of the Centenary needed a writer to travel abroad both to survey conditions in existing foreign missions and to investigate possible sites for future Methodist missions. He wanted the person hired to travel to Japan, Korea, and India, then return to the United States by way of Palestine and Egypt. Taylor decided upon Pelley after reading several of his stories in the *American Magazine*.[21]

Pelley, although excited by the proposition, faced obligations in Vermont that could have forestalled his acceptance of the offer. A satisfactory arrangement was quickly established, however. He found two men to run the *Caledonian* in his absence, convinced his mother-in-law to care for Adelaide during her parents' trip, and entered into a lucrative financial deal with the Centenary. The organization agreed to pay Pelley's expenses and provide an additional five thousand dollars in return for writing a series of articles on foreign missions to be published exclusively in Methodist publications.[22]

In August 1918 the Pelleys left Vermont and traveled by rail to Los Angeles. They then departed from San Francisco and, after eighteen days at sea aboard the *Tenyu Maru,* reached Japan. Pelley developed a strangely ambiguous opinion of the country during his time there, which he never fully discarded. His 1918 stay left him with a primarily negative view of Japan, but he found some aspects of the culture commendable (particularly later, after Japan became allied with Hitler's government).

All of Pelley's views of Japan were underscored by his opinion that the Japanese people were, at best, "half-adults." He noted that the residents of this "rice-paper nation" were "children and naught else." Pelley posited that Japan only made sense when one learned an essential truth about the country: "Nippon was a nation that had been left to propagate or starve on scoria rock." What the Japanese needed most was "a [Herbert] Hoover."[23]

Pelley argued that, unable to overcome their inherent poverty, the Japanese became warlike and aggressive. Only through military strength could they become a significant player in world politics. The Japanese military, however, presented little threat to the Western powers. Japanese forces appeared strong, but, in reality, fell far short. They exhibited only the "impertinence of small people who realize they are small."[24]

Still, Pelley perceived some inherent strengths of the Japanese people. Not surprisingly, given the audience he was writing for, he believed Christianity held the key to future Japanese success. He noted that those Japanese who had adopted Christianity frequently exhibited good judgment, diplomatic and business prowess, and a healthy countenance. Christian Japanese had cast off the "blank, expressionless, soulless masks of fatalism" and moved into the modern world of international finance and politics. When melded with the "natural" efficiency and respect for order of the Japanese, these Christians could propel Japan into a position of global prominence.[25]

Pelley also saw the Japanese as a stabilizing influence in the region. He commended their incursions into Korea because the people of that country were "not capable of self-government." Japan had "cleaned up the age-old filth," given Korea "good water systems, sewerage, [and] a few model cities," as well as efficiency and, he hoped, Christian values.[26]

Pelley never developed a wholly positive attitude toward Japan, but he eventually came to admire significant elements of Japanese culture. Despite his criticisms, Pelley claimed to be always a friend of the Japanese people. In 1939 (with the Axis war machine in high gear), he noted that if he had anything to do with the government of the United States, he would never permit a war to break out between the two countries.[27]

Pelley's itinerary called for him to depart for Korea and northern China after finishing his work in Japan. However, the decision to move

American and Japanese troops into Siberia in the wake of the chaos created by the November Bolshevik Revolution prevented his undertaking
that segment of his trip. The Japanese authorities requisitioned all passen-
ger ships plying the northern Pacific Ocean in order to facilitate the
transportation of infantry to Russia, leaving Pelley without a means to
continue his journey.

Stranded in Japan, Pelley undertook a cross-country tour, traveling to
as many missions as possible to obtain material for his articles. While in
Karuizawa he was approached by George S. Phelps, International YMCA
Secretary for the Far East. Phelps offered Pelley the chance to see the war
firsthand by going to Siberia under the auspices of the YMCA. The organization would help underwrite his journey and arrange for transportation in return for Pelley's writing reports on YMCA activities in the
region and scouting out possible locations for canteens the organization
hoped to establish for American servicemen stationed in Russia.[28]

Pelley sailed for Russia aboard the *Penza* from the Japanese port city
of Tsuruga. He later claimed that it was while spending a few days in Tsuruga waiting for the ship that he was first exposed to the "world-wide
Jewish question." According to Pelley, it was an unnamed American surgeon heading for Siberia, previously attached to Polish forces, who explained the causes of the war to the young New England newspaperman.
The surgeon told Pelley that Jews had orchestrated the assassination of
Austrian archduke Franz Ferdinand in order to bring about a bloody and
profitable war. Jewish plans during the war involved overthrowing the
Russian czar and creating a Jewish homeland in Russia. From this Russian base of operations, Jews would launch their plan for world domination. Pelley's confidant informed him that the Russian Revolution was
part of this program (and entirely funded by the Jewish-American banker
Jacob Schiff), and that V. I. Lenin was also a Jew.[29]

Pelley debarked in Vladivostok (which reminded him of the docks of
Hoboken, New Jersey) to receive specific instructions from the staff at the
headquarters of the YMCA's Red Triangle in that Siberian city. He later
claimed he was immediately besieged with anti-Semitic pronouncements
in Vladivostok. Pelley noted that these sentiments prevailed among the
American and Czech troops in Russia as well as with his traveling companion from Japan, George Gleason.[30]

Pelley's commission with the Red Triangle involved traveling throughout Siberia in a canteen car attached to Allied troop trains. He was instructed to take pictures of conditions in the region and to write reports for the YMCA on the most efficient means of turning the youth of Russia away from "satanic Leninism." Pelley claimed he was a combination "Red Triangle secretary, war correspondent, espionage agent, secret photographer, canteen proprietor, and consular courier . . . striving to plant sanity, decency, and political stability in a land being slowly mutilated and mangled by Communism."[31]

Pelley's excursion kept him primarily behind the Allied lines, but the frequently shifting position of the front often left him dangerously close to combat. His first and most significant experience in a combat zone occurred in the city of Blagovyeshchenck. Pelley's car was attached to a Japanese troop train sent in as reinforcement during the fight for the city. Arriving after most of the fighting ended, Pelley witnessed the entire city go up in flames. He was deeply moved by this "terrible and unforgettable sight . . . as magnificent as it was tragic."[32]

In November 1918 the most picaresque episode of Pelley's Siberian adventure began while he was staying in Irkustsk to watch the ceremonies that gave Admiral Aleksander Kolchak formal control of all the White Russian forces. At the American consulate he was persuaded to accompany two representatives of the International Harvester Company, three-quarters of a million dollars in company funds, and Washington-bound diplomatic documents from American ambassador David R. Francis to Harbin, in Manchuria. Harvester officials sought to rush the money out of the country before it fell into Bolshevik hands. Pelley's credentials, local authorities believed, would prevent the funds from seizure along the road to Harbin. Pelley chaperoned a money-loaded canteen for twenty-six days. Already fearful of being robbed, Pelley found the journey even more harrowing because of the vicious weather of the Siberian winter. When the cold and hungry trio reached Harbin, they learned the war had ended during their treacherous trip.[33]

While he possessed nothing but scorn for either the red Bolsheviks or the white Cossacks ("predatory hetmen"), Pelley's accounts demonstrated a genuine sympathy for the Russian peasants. He decried the treatment of these people caught in the middle of a war they neither understood nor wished to participate in. Much as he did the rural folk of the American southwest, Pelley found the Russian peasants to be hardworking, friendly, and quietly noble. To Pelley they were the "prototypes" of the generous New Englanders he grew up with, and their wholesale dislocation was a pitiable consequence of the Revolution.[34]

Pelley blamed only the Jewish Communists for the tragic destruction of the peasantry. He argued that the boxcar loads of refugees he traveled with were victims of a revolution perpetrated by "two hundred and seventy-six Jews from New York's East Side." Pelley later claimed that witnessing the actions of the "scavenger Jews" in Siberia led him to understand the Jewish plot to take over the world, the Russian Revolution being merely the first step in this program. He used his experiences in Siberia as first-hand "evidence" of the fate awaiting Americans if the Communists took over this country. Pelley believed that Russian atrocities could "happen in Kansas, Indiana, New Jersey . . . if this Communist peril becomes guerrilla warfare."[35]

With the war over, Pelley traveled back to Vladivostok by train, and booked passage on the *Penza*. Twenty pounds lighter and prematurely gray, Pelley returned to Tsuruga and Marion, who had remained in Japan to teach English at a Methodist missionary school in Tokyo during her husband's Siberian adventure. Owing to wartime conditions, neither Pelley had obtained any mail from the United States while in Japan; now, with the war over, they received a flood of letters from home. Among the old letters given to them was one detailing the death of Marion's brother Ernest from influenza. Although Ernest had died almost two moths prior to their belated notification, the Pelleys decided to cut their trip short and return home to help care for their family, particularly Marion's aged mother.[36]

The Pelleys returned to America aboard the *Siberia Maru*. Rocked by family tragedy, the three-week journey was a bleak affair. Marion found the delay in returning home interminable and sank into a depression. Her husband tried to bury himself in his work. Pelley studiously shaped his voluminous Siberian notes into articles, but he quickly tired of the project. During the first week of their journey Pelley discovered a copy of the *American Magazine* containing the story he called his "epochal prizewinner, 'Their Mother.' " Facing a long, tedious trip, Pelley decided to expand the story into a full-length novel, *The Greater Glory*.[37]

Pelley had based "Their Mother," the first of his Paris, Vermont, stories, upon an event in his own life. Pelley's paternal grandmother had died when he was a young child, and the scene at her deathbed—surrounded by her five "clean, fine" full-grown sons, who owed their "manhood, their virility, their careers to her"—had deeply affected him. Pelley believed his grandmother represented true motherhood. Determined to celebrate his grandmother's memory (and symbolism), he had composed "Their Mother" in a fevered rush.[38]

Narrated by a young newspaperman named Bill, *The Greater Glory* related the story of Mary Wood, the abused stepdaughter of "Silent" Wheeler, a drunken thug. Forced out of the family home by Wheeler's violent tendencies, Mary accepts a job at the *Paris Telegraph,* a situation that causes great harm to her reputation. Courted by both John Purse, a struggling newspaperman, and Herb "Slug" Truman, sporting heir to a local fortune, Mary is faced with "the problem old as Eden itself . . . [to] choose poverty with love or riches with dissatisfaction." Mary selects John to be her husband and lives happily until he dies suddenly from pneumonia. Mary returns to work at the *Telegraph* and forfeits her own happiness to raise five honest sons on her meager income.[39]

The centerpiece of the novel is a heavy-handed subplot about a twenty-dollar gold piece. As teenagers, the group Mary associates with buried the coin in an old cabin. They agree to meet thirty years later, dig the gold piece up, and award it to the one who has been most successful in life. Despite the fame and fortune obtained by several of the surviving members of the group, they unanimously agree to give the coin to Mary for her success as a mother.

Shortly after she receives the gold piece, Mary travels to New York to hear her newspaper reporter son Tom give a religiously oriented speech. Basking in the success of her son, Mary "came into the blessing of her heritage through an emotion that is known by no other save the mother-heart, it was her great and all-consuming . . . moment of power and glory—the greater glory—the greatest glory." Having achieved the "greater glory," Mary can die in peace.[40]

The novel served primarily to promote Pelley's view that self-sacrifice and motherhood were the highest achievements of women. Mary's youthful companions all find economic success but die broken-hearted and pathetic because they sought financial riches instead of love and family. Pelley stated that Mary truly succeeded in life because "woman's work" in the home was "just as important and noble as anything a man could do outside the home."[41]

As demonstrated in *The Greater Glory,* Pelley never reconciled his ambiguous feelings toward women. In the novel, Mary represents both the modern, liberated woman who doggedly struggles to build her own career and the maternal homebody. As Leo Ribuffo has noted, Pelley's writings, throughout his life, displayed his difficulty in determining which of these two roles women should undertake.[42]

On one hand, Pelley promoted the rights and equality of women. He endorsed women's suffrage, and defended feminist leader Carrie Chapman Catt. Pelley even published an article entitled "Why I Am Glad I Married a Suffragist." In the article Pelley defended the actions of his wife, Marion, in establishing her own sphere. He complimented his wife for her knowledge of politics, business, and baseball. To Pelley, a proper wife must possess intellectual capabilities and a sense of civic responsibility.[43]

Pelley also argued that proper female companionship was essential for productive men. He declared that it was impossible for a man to achieve true success without a female companion. Only with a respected and intelligent female "help-mate" by his side could a man find the strength to face the vicissitudes of life.[44]

Still, Pelley's desire to possess a woman free from "fads and isms" seemed to override his advocacy of female (or marital) equality. His writings are rife with defenses of "homebodies" and self-sacrificing mothers. For example, the longest speech in *The Greater Glory* is a soliloquy by a character decrying the development of labor-saving devices within the home because they led women to look beyond "the homes and motherhood." Pelley often posited that women only wanted to be "dominated by the right man." He defended Marion's suffragist tendencies as long as she still took care of the children, cooked his dinner, kept house, and remembered that he was "boss." For Pelley, a woman could focus her energies outside the home as long as she remembered that home came first, and that the proper attributes of a woman were "patience, reticence, gentleness, altruism, kindness, graciousness, long-suffering, sobriety of conduct and concept, and a general reaction to life in terms of conserving acquiescence."[45]

Pelley would desperately need the proceeds from *The Greater Glory* because the *St. Johnsbury Caledonian* slid into financial difficulty while he was in Asia. He had left the newspaper in the care of Walter J. Bigelow and Arthur Stone, who, during Pelley's absence, had tried to extract as much profit from the paper as possible by reducing both the number of pages and the quality of material published. Their actions resulted in a sharp downturn in subscription revenue and advertising. Pelley arrived in Massachusetts to find his paper $20,000 in debt and himself skittering toward bankruptcy.[46]

Pelley threw himself into saving the *Caledonian*. Always a hard worker, Pelley undertook a rigorous schedule of activities. He struggled to maintain the *Caledonian,* published *The Greater Glory,* wrote numerous essays and short stories, and gave public speeches on current conditions in Russia and Japan. To keep his creditors at bay, Pelley retained a crafty Bennington lawyer named Robert Healy, who would go on to a very successful career as a jurist.[47]

Pelley's work on the *Caledonian* after returning in December 1919 showed little alteration from his pre-Siberia trip articles. He continued to offer down-home homilies, breezy features, and stories (including a serialization of *The Greater Glory*) as the backbone of the paper, although an increased focus on international affairs did creep in. Pelley advocated a lenient peace and promoted increased awareness of foreign markets as a means to bolster the American economy.[48]

Not surprisingly, given his experiences in Siberia, Pelley also devoted frequent columns to the threat of Communism. He decried the chaotic activities of the Bolsheviks and regaled his readers with firsthand accounts of horrors from the Russian Revolution, which he continued to claim was German-sponsored. The *Caledonian* editor believed his personal experiences made him especially qualified to comment on international affairs.[49]

Pelley feared the growth of domestic radicalism with equal alarm. He
decried the activities of the Industrial Workers of the World (IWW) and
the nascent American Communist movement, warning his readers of
their nefarious plans. To deal with these domestic perils, Pelley advocated
swift and forceful governmental action. He noted approvingly the actions
of Attorney General A. Mitchell Palmer and Lee Overman, chairman of
the U.S. Senate Subcommittee on Bolshevik Propaganda. Pelley's support
for antiradical measures reflected a consensus of American opinion at the
time.[50]

Eventually the strain of his vigorous schedule caught up with Pelley.
His financial difficulties were also compounded by marital discord. Pelley
realized that he and Marion had different interests and worldviews. As he
noted, they did not "see life alike . . . [and] probably never shall." Determined to alleviate all of his difficulties at once, Pelley heeded the advice of
Red Book editor Karl Harriman and, in June 1919, sold the *Caledonian,*
wired some of the money to Marion in Vermont, and bought a train
ticket to San Francisco. Pelley soon returned to his family, primarily because he learned that Marion was again pregnant, but his interlude in
California left a permanent impression on him. While staying in San
Francisco, Pelley was briefly introduced to the spiritualism and clairvoyance that, along with anti-Semitism, helped form the foundation of his
public career during the 1930s.[51]

3

Hollywood

1920—1927

WILLIAM DUDLEY PELLEY'S DESIRE to escape the confines of home led him to California. His prior pleasant experience in that state played a part in the Vermonter's decision to migrate there, but other factors also affected his choice of location. Pelley hoped to alter the focus of his writing career in California, and he wanted to meet a young woman who had entered into a regular correspondence with him. Conveniently, the woman and *Sunset,* the magazine in which he hoped to publish a series of articles, were both located in San Francisco, which became Pelley's home for the summer of 1920.

During 1919 Pelley had published five articles in *Sunset Magazine* based upon his Asian adventures. He hoped to persuade George Fields, the magazine's editor, to publish a second round of articles in 1920. Pelley believed Japan represented one of the "burning issues on the Pacific Coast," and that his experiences in that country made him especially qualified to address the subject. He proposed a series of articles that would set "forth the situation with the Japanese in a way that might contribute to constructive statesmanship." Given Pelley's generally negative view of Japan, it is difficult to imagine anything "constructive" developing from these articles. Fields apparently found the writings questionable as well, and published only one piece by Pelley, "Behind the Dreadful Mask." [1]

However, Pelley's contact with his female correspondent proved more fruitful. The woman Pelley referred to in his writings only as "Lillian" worked for a San Francisco newspaper. In her spare time she flew airplanes and studied spiritualism, particularly the clairvoyance on which Pelley began focusing his own energies later in the decade. "Lillian" initially contacted Pelley because she wanted to write a series of articles on the "more romantic side of aviation." Finding it difficult to get publishers interested in her work, she believed collaborating with an established author might create more attention for the articles. Excited about aviation himself, Pelley agreed to meet with her as soon as he arrived in San Francisco.[2]

Pelley later claimed that he engaged in a strictly platonic relationship with "Lillian," and that he "entered into no intimacies with this girl, in the accepted sense." While there is no evidence to the contrary, Pelley's writings about her make it clear that he felt a strong attraction to the aviatrix. Pelley described her as an "exceedingly clever woman" with a "characterful face, a strangely penetrating eye, a disconcerting poise . . . [and] a trace of the exotic."[3]

Pelley appeared to have no interest in returning to New England, but events quickly developed that led him to return home. In August he received a letter from Marion stating that she was pregnant and due to give birth in September. Pelley did not want to leave his recuperative interlude in California but finally determined that his familial concerns must be his first priority. His return to the East Coast effectively ended Pelley's relationship with "Lillian." They "parted in some enmity because of the nature of the circumstances."[4]

The birth of son William Ernest in September 1920 did nothing to ease Pelley's marital difficulties. Pelley had little interest in continuing his relationship with Marion, but he felt compelled to take care of his expanded family. Faced by increased expenses (and problems getting his Asian articles published), Pelley once again turned to fiction writing to survive.

Although Pelley intended to focus on writing short stories immediately after his son's birth, his exposure to a soon-to-be-released novel led him to begin working on a longer work. Wanting Pelley to write an editorial on whether it accurately portrayed the tenor of rural life, the editor of Street & Smith's *People's Magazine* gave him an advance copy of Sinclair Lewis's *Main Street*. Pelley found the novel a "distorted, reprehensible libel on the American small town." Determined to rectify Lewis's attack on the American village, Pelley decided to write his own "pen-picture" for young men and women "to help them grope their ways out of the fog of adolescence and out upon the clean high table-lands of unobstructed life-traveling." [5]

Although Pelley believed *Main Street* aimed solely to undermine the sanctity of the American small town, perceptive critics have noted that Lewis did not intend the novel to be simply a screed against rural dwellers. Rather, ambivalence, attacks on social folly, and the shift from village to city as a metaphor for the closing of the frontier lie at the book's heart. It is understandable, however, that from the perspective of a man like Pelley, the novel represented an attack on all that was sacred. Although communities of only twenty-five hundred residents qualified as urban, news of the nation's shift to urban population predominance in the 1920 federal census already had defenders of a dwindling insular lifestyle concerned. Pelley's knowledge of current literary trends also fed into an increasing paranoia over the death knell of life in Paris, Vermont. Culturally and economically, Pelley faced an increasingly incomprehensible society as the 1920s unfolded. [6]

The Fog, published in the summer of 1922, was the most autobiographical of Pelley's six novels. Although the author claimed he wrote the book as an antidote to Sinclair Lewis's portrayal of small-town America, Pelley's characters are as despicable as those living in *Main Street*'s Gopher Prairie. Further, Pelley's depiction of marriage is just as critical as Lewis's (both authors were undoubtedly influenced by their own marital woes). [7]

The plot revolves around the "freckled Forges" of Vermont, products of the "disgustingly prolific lower classes." Family head John wants to be a minister, but his marriage to an older woman (and premature creation of a family) leads him to become an unhappy cobbler—a situation reminiscent of Pelley's father's life. The story's autobiographical protagonist, Nat Forge, is a repressed young man in love with Madge Theddon, adopted daughter of a wealthy widow. In a clearly autobiographical plot twist, Nat wishes to become a writer, but family difficulties force him to quit school and begin working in the Gridley Tannery. [8]

Through sheer dint of hard work and a creative spirit, Nat is able to balance family economic responsibilities and his dream of becoming a successful writer, but his lowly social position forestalls any relationship (or, in Pelley-speak, "the Amethyst Moment") with Madge. The young writer then finds solace in a hasty marriage to slatternly factory girl Milly Richards. While he is trudging through Siberia (for truly unclear reasons) during the Bolshevik Revolution, Milly dies in a sabotage attack on a New Jersey munitions plant. Nat is then involved in a train wreck, captured by the Communists, and (somehow) makes a miraculous escape in a blinding blizzard. He awakens in a field hospital and is cared for by a Red Cross nurse, none other than Madge. The two quickly fall in love and decide to wed.[9]

Although a stronger work than *The Greater Glory, The Fog* still suffers from a trite (and unbelievable) plot. Further, significant plot twists are never explained. Pelley's determination that Nat and Madge must not meet until the book's end—the story's "surprise" twist that he believed guaranteed big sales—leaves gaping holes in the plot and Pelley scrambling to make sense in the closing chapters of the preceding two hundred pages. Seemingly to assist the reader through this tangled mess, Pelley abruptly stops the narrative on two occasions to spend three or four pages recapping the entire plot.

Despite the book's obvious flaws, *The Fog* turned out to be a financial success for Pelley.[10] The novel's profitability (it eventually went through seventeen printings) spurred Pelley to attempt to rejuvenate his languishing short-story career. During the summer of 1922 he quickly completed a new serial entitled "White Faith." Pelley sent the story to *Red Book* editor Karl Harriman. Although Harriman liked the story, he was afraid that the plot, premised upon the appearance of the Holy Grail in America, would offend his more conservative readers. Hoping to help Pelley, Harriman, upon his own initiative, sent the story to New York film producer Larry Giffin.

Pelley did not learn that Giffin wanted to buy the story until October. An avid swimmer, he had contracted typhoid in July 1922 after an ill-advised plunge into the polluted waters of the Passumpsic River. Delirious for nine weeks, Pelley lost a considerable amount of weight and his sense of smell (which never returned). He was unable to get out of bed until October.

The slimming down of his physique was the final development in

Pelley's physical appearance for the rest of his public career. He stood a slight five foot six and weighed only 135 pounds, with piercing blue eyes offset by his shock of prematurely gray hair. Pelley's personal affectations included pince-nez, a Vandyke, and a perpetual cloud of smoke (thanks to his constant use of cigarettes, cigars, and a pipe). And along with losing his sense of smell, Pelley was partially deaf.

Shortly after regaining his health Pelley learned that Larry Giffin had offered to buy the film rights to "White Faith" for $7,500. Financially strapped by his inability to write during his illness, Pelley ecstatically agreed. Giffin wanted the story for wealthy New Yorker Jules Brulatour, who was in the midst of a lengthy (and ultimately unsuccessful) attempt at making a film star of his wife, Hope Hampton, by financing the production of her movies.[11]

The Brulatour project inaugurated Pelley's active involvement in the production of motion pictures, but this was not the first time that his work had ended up on the silver screen. A film lover himself (he generally went to the movies twice a week), Pelley previously had sold the rights to three of his stories to film studios (who converted them into films: *A Case at Law, One-Thing-at-a-Time O'Day,* and *What Women Love*). Seeing motion pictures as a way to supplement his income as a writer, Pelley had readily agreed to sell these earlier stories in the full knowledge that studios would alter them with no possible recourse from the original writer.

These early film script sales derived from Pelley's success as a short-story writer. East Coast filmmakers often worked through magazine editors to purchase the rights to stories. Seeing these sales as a way to make extra money from stories that, having been published in national magazines, could not be resold, writers such as Pelley readily agreed to the sales but evinced little concern in the fate of the actual film project.

Pelley's first three films were neither particularly significant nor over-whelmingly successful. Released in November 1917, *A Case at Law* was a trite western that starred Dick Rosson in one of his patented anti-alcohol "message" films. The June 1919 release *One-Thing-at-a-Time O'Day,* based on a Pelley *Saturday Evening Post* story of the same name, featured future "Lone Wolf" detective series star Bert Lytell as a well-meaning buffoon who falls in love with a circus bareback rider, only to have to sway her affections away from the circus's nefarious strongman. *What Women Love* provided Pelley with the most acclaim of the three films. Released in August 1920, the film starred the notorious Annette "Diving Venus" Kellerman as a bathing suit-wearing libertine wooed by a chaste young man who saves her from the clutches of an aggressive professional boxer. Thanks to Kellerman's drawing power and exciting aquatic sequences (including an underwater fight and a seventy-five-foot dive into the Pacific by the film's heroine), *What Women Love* proved to be a mild critical and commercial success.[12]

Unlike these earlier films, however, the "White Faith" project allowed Pelley to delve into the motion picture business as an active participant. Contracted to rewrite the serial into a workable script, Pelley quickly realized the money-making potential of turning his writing attentions toward film. With his short-story career foundering, Pelley also understood that his sentimental style fit better with the prevailing mood in film than with the magazine fiction market. With *The Light in the Dark* (the script's new title) Pelley's "seven-year submergence in movies had begun."[13]

Pelley's shift toward motion picture work was aided immeasurably by the one lasting friendship that developed from working on *The Light in the Dark*. Although Jules Brulatour intended the film to showcase his wife, he also understood the need to flesh out the cast with more familiar names. Therefore, he contracted Lon Chaney, "the man of a thousand faces," to costar. Chaney, who began making films in 1912, became a featured performer after his appearance in *The Miracle Man* (1919). Working together on the film, Pelley and the "soft-spoken, jovial-mannered" Chaney became fast friends. When they were not filming, their two families spend evenings and weekends together in New York (with Chaney often cooking dinner for them). Their friendship ebbed at the end of the decade as Pelley became increasingly anti-Hollywood in his outlook.[14]

Directed by Clarence Brown, *The Light in the Dark* is the tale of coat-check girl Bessie, who is injured by the automobile of a society matron. The wealthy widow takes Bessie into her home to recover, and while there the girl falls in love with the matron's brother, J. Warburton Ashe (Elmo Lincoln, film's first Tarzan). Realizing that Ashe is only toying with her, Bessie returns to her boardinghouse, where she is nursed by small-time hoodlum Tony Pantelli (Lon Chaney). Meanwhile, Ashe goes on a hunting trip to England and brings back a chalice reputed to be the Holy Grail. Learning of the cup's recuperative powers, Tony steals it in an attempt to cure Bessie. Tony is arrested, but Ashe (having realized the error of his ways and now reunited with Bessie) refused to press charges. The police later discover that the cup's mysterious glow and powers (in Pelley's original story it truly was the Holy Grail, marking it as the beginning of what Andrew Mathis noted as Pelley's lifelong affinity for "Arthurian imagery . . . [and] medievalism in general") resulted from radium hidden within it by an unscrupulous merchant. When it was released as a multitinted print, critics found the "color" film beautiful to look at but dull and slow-moving. Pelley later claimed that the film's problems resulted from Brulatour's editing of the feature to emphasize Hampton's part. In a contemporary interview, however, he had nothing but praise for the feature.[15]

The filming of *The Light in the Dark* wrapped up on Christmas morning 1921 (Brulatour's reediting caused the film's release to be delayed nine months). After celebrating the holiday with the Pelleys, Lon and Hazel Chaney departed for California, taking a Pelley script, *The Shock* (based on Pelley's *Munsey's Magazine* story "The Pit of the Golden Dragon"), with them. Eventually filmed by Universal in 1923, *The Shock* helped spur Pelley's move to Los Angeles.

Having gained entree into the world of motion pictures, Pelley sold two more scripts to East Coast filmmakers in the summer of 1922. The first of these two films was released by New York's Aywon Studios in November 1922. *Back Fire* starred Jack Hoxie as "Lightning" Carson, a Texas ranger working undercover in a small town. This Alvin Neitz-directed programmer was one of the weakest (and most obscure) films of Pelley's career. *As a Man Lives* premiered in December 1922. Although clearly the superior of Pelley's two fall features that year, the film was a forgettable adventure film, and *Variety*'s film reviewer commended J. Searle Dawley's direction but found the plot "oft-time meager."[16]

While Pelley's film career began ascending in 1922, his troubled eleven-year marriage to Marion finally ended (they did not legally di-

vorce, however, for another fourteen years). Neither one wished to return to Vermont; Marion took up residence in Brooklyn (with the two
children); Pelley rented an apartment in Greenwich Village. Pelley later
claimed that the marriage had simply gone "sterile," but it seems clear that
he was suffering from a personal crisis and simply did not want to be tied
down to life's drudgeries with Marion, who, he posited, was too conservative in her outlook to understand a creative individual such as himself.
As Pelley noted in his inimitable style, he was compelled to move on because of his status as "a soldier-of-fortune with ivories in his pack,
zephyrs in his mess-kit, [and] a song in his heart for the highroad that
meant victories." [17]

To keep his affairs in order Pelley hired a personal secretary in New
York. Although his personal secretary arrived in Pelley's life at about the
same time as the termination of his relationship with Marion, her involvement in the decision finally to end the marriage is unclear. Pelley,
however, was obviously very attached to her. Even twenty years later Pelley recalled fondly his time with the "soft-spoken, dove-eyed" young
Iowan he referred to simply as "Beryl," with a "delightful . . . mark of
Satan" dimple in her chin. Pelley always maintained that his "help-mates"
were purely platonic friends, but Marion may have believed these relationships to be somewhat less innocent. Detailing the ending of his first
marriage, he defensively noted "in the eleven years that I had been husband to Marion, I knew I had not cheated, that was all that mattered, that
I knew it to myself." [18]

With most of his routine duties being handled, Pelley gave in to the
sort of wanderlust that befell his long-lost father. Pelley began going on
extended solo automobile trips throughout the United States. By the end
of the 1920s he had motored across America by himself seven times. Although Pelley claimed he used these trips to gain story ideas (he declared
that "America was my studio"), little of value really emerged from the ex-
cursions. Pelley's scripts continued to sell, but he lost many employment
opportunities because of frequent absences from both coasts. [19]

It seems more likely that Pelley, finally unburdened of his family,
sought only a release from the heavy schedule he had maintained since his
teens. After receiving news from Chaney of Universal Studio's interest in

buying the script for *The Shock,* Pelley decided to maintain his Greenwich Village apartment and obtain a residence in California, where most film production was now located. In 1923 Bill Pelley began the most financially successful period of his life—submerged in the "necromancy of movie making" in Hollywood. It was also while working for the Hollywood film studios that Pelley began developing the twin undergirdings of his later public career—anti-Semitism and spiritualism.[20]

While Hollywood gained a deserved reputation for decadence during the 1920s, much of the studios' output retained a conservative, Victorian veneer. Pelley's writing style, which did not appreciably change until late in the decade, fit perfectly with studio notions of "proper" script content, and he prospered immediately in Hollywood. His film scripts, taken in toto, reveal Pelley's attempt to stem the tide of social change he felt pressing against him. Pelley's film plots revel in the defeat of predatory wealth, criminality, and "alien" lifestyles, while celebrating the values of home, hard work, family, and true love. The great irony of Pelley's work during the 1920s is that he had to dwell among the libertine residents of southern California to produce defenses of traditional values.

Pelley's daily interaction with the "glamorous, cockeyed, crazy gang, booze-lit, and money-drunk children in Arabian nights palaces of papiermâché," however, proved significant for the scriptwriter. Increasingly distressed over the actions of screen stars and Jewish studio moguls, and their influence on American society, Pelley began to develop the racist attitudes that shaped the rest of his life. Already deeply troubled by the changes being wrought in America, in Hollywood Pelley found a ready scapegoat on which to pin the blame for "isms." It was his only extended contact with Jews, but it left a permanent impression on him. As he later noted, "for six years I toiled in their galleys and got nothing but money." In 1923, however, Pelley saw Hollywood as a means to make easy money and also to put a continent between himself and his New York-based family.[21]

Pelley found immediate success in Hollywood, selling the script he sent with Chaney for $2,000. The Universal Studios film *The Shock* featured Chaney, one of the studio's fast-rising stars. In the film Chaney plays Wilse Dilling, a crippled crook who falls in love with Gertrude

(Virginia Valli). Her father is embezzling funds from the bank where he works in order to pay off the blackmailing leader of a criminal gang (with which Wilse is affiliated). Wilse blows up the safe that holds the evidence of the embezzlement, but Gertrude is severely injured in the explosion. He then pays for the operation that cures her, and the two escape the clutches of the gang by fleeing to San Francisco. The criminals, however, follow them, only to be wiped out during the earthquake of 1906.

The film received poor reviews upon its release, and, as Chaney scholar Michael Blake has noted, "only Chaney's performance and the mildly interesting special effects that simulate the 1906 earthquake distinguish this film from the studio's other melodramatic productions." Despite negative reviews, *The Shock* proved to be highly successful at the box office, helping both Chaney's and Pelley's careers.[22]

The success of *The Shock* (and his relationship with Chaney) gave Pelley's burgeoning Hollywood career a great deal of momentum. Having proven himself in California, Pelley found his scripts attracting the attention of major studios. In 1923 Pelley sold two scripts to Metro Studios, both of which are good examples of Pelley's improving status in the film community. The film version of *The Fog* eliminates some of the novel's subplots but remains reasonably faithful to Pelley's 1921 book. In the film version Nathan Forge undergoes a series of trying hardships (which occur at a dizzying rate in a seven-reel feature), eventually finding himself working for the International Red Cross in Siberia. While in Russia he is reunited with Madelaine, a girl he loved from afar back home. Nathan discovers Madelaine has read a poem he wrote about her in the local newspaper years ago and has longed to meet the author. Thrown together by the vicissitudes of war, the two find love in each other's arms. Pelley's second film of the year, *Her Fatal Millions,* was a lightweight romantic comedy involving a series of misadventures, but it did star top-flight talent such as Violet Dana and Huntley Gordon.[23]

Pelley maintained his Greenwich Village apartment after making California his primary residence. He frequently returned to New York to visit friends, relax, and renew contacts with the Manhattan publishing world (frequently selling stories for extra cash to pulp magazines such as *Argosy All-Story Weekly* and *Short Stories*). On one of these visits he sank a portion of his film profits into the establishment of the Pelley Press on West 8th Street. The most significant product of the venture was the publication of Pelley's own promotional, "plot" magazine. In these illustrated hardback volumes he provided synopses of his available screenplays, mailing copies to the studios. Although most of the screenplays advertised went unsold, the effort did keep his name fresh in the minds of studio heads and probably contributed to the success he found in 1924.[24]

Pelley revealed himself to be as prolific with scripts as he was with short stories, and 1924 proved to be a very successful year for him, with three releases to his credit. None of these films proved particularly significant, but all of them featured top stars or directors. With other creative and business ventures soon occupying a considerable portion of his time, the year represented the pinnacle of his screen writing career.

Pelley scripted two westerns (the most popular film genre of the decade) released in 1924. Fox's *Ladies to Board* starred Tom Mix (the studio's top male performer). In this film, which was not one of Mix's more important works, the cowboy star saves an elderly woman from a car accident. She subsequently repays him by bequeathing to him her estate (consisting primarily of a home for aged widows), where he woos a nurse. A truly lightweight comedy, the film's moderate success derived solely from Mix's bankable name. Pelley's script was decried by one critic as "indifferent" and "overly sentimental." His second western, Universal's *Sawdust Trail,* starred Hoot Gibson as an eastern college boy who joins a Wild West show and falls in love with the show's leading lady, bronco-busting, man-hating "Calamity" Jane Webster (Josie Sedgwick). After Gibson assists Jane to escape from show business, the film ends with him winning her heart.[25]

Pelley's third release of the year, and probably the most prestigious of all his films, the crime drama *Torment,* was independently produced and directed by Maurice Tourneur. A former assistant to the sculptor Auguste Rodin, Tourneur earned recognition as "one of the great stylists of the early American cinema." *Torment* revolves around the crown jewels of the Russian royal family. During the Bolshevik Revolution (which, not surprisingly, Pelley casts in a highly unfavorable light) Count Boris escapes from Russia with the jewels, planning to use them to aid starving countrymen. Three international thieves travel to Yokohama to steal the jewels from Boris. But one of the criminals, Hansen (Owen Moore), falls in love with a young woman he meets there, and he decides to go straight. All parties involved are caught in an earthquake in Yokohama, with Boris being murdered during the chaos. After being rescued, Hansen and the young woman, now in possession of the valuable loot, pledge to get married and use the jewels to assist hungry Russians.[26]

In 1925, finding life in California pleasant and profitable, Pelley decided to dispose of his New York holdings. He gave up his Greenwich Village apartment and sold off the possessions of the Pelley Press. Realizing that pitching his stories to producers in person had proved more successful than sending them a magazine, Pelley also gave up the idea of issuing a "plot" magazine. Pelley used the proceeds of these sales to rent a house in Newburgh, New York, along the Hudson River, for the summer of 1925.

Written during his sojourn in Newburgh, *Drag* continued the developing autobiographical nature of Pelley's novels. The story revolved around young newspaperman David Haskell, and Pelley clearly poured much of himself into the character. In the novel Pelley glorified the work of industrious writers, the proper subservience of women, and the heroism of nurses, while heaping scorn on intrusive in-laws and the loveless trap of marriage. Although as overly sentimental and genteel as his earlier novels, *Drag* clearly benefited from the author's gaining a bit of worldliness in California.

The hero, David, grows up in the *Paris Daily Telegraph* office, where his father works. He is desperately afraid of women (clearly a healthy fear in the mind of author Pelley). The first third of the novel serves merely to establish the three female characters who will affect Haskell's life. First, echoing Pelley's own discomfort with sexuality, Haskell undergoes a harrowing confrontation with the "sordidly pretty" Lill Whalen, who possesses an "oversexed body." Second, the protagonist becomes friends with *Evening Telegraph* proofreader Allie Parker, a young woman looking for a husband and saddled with a gold-digging family (obviously modeled on Marion and "Mrs. Holbrook"). Finally, Haskell briefly crosses paths with altruistic nurse Carrie Flynt, who takes care of the invalid wife of local luminary "Big" Jim Thorne. Flynt represents the occupation, nursing, Pelley finds the most honorable, and her appearance bears a striking resemblance to Beryl.[27]

Falling under the sway of his romantic feelings, Haskell begins a disastrous relationship with Allie, which leads to a quick betrothal. Not surprisingly, the thrill of marriage quickly degenerates into drudgery, and Pelley frequently interjects bits of dialogue noting the detrimental effect of marrying too young. Not only does Allie's attitude toward her husband quickly sour, but her parents and siblings also move in with the newlyweds. The bulk of the novel consists of David's varied attempts to succeed in the world, which are all thwarted by the "drag" of his leeching extended family. Echoing Pelley's perception of his own career, Haskell is a failure at his own newspaper (because of other people) and in marriage (again because of other people), and is forced to eke out a living writing for someone else, while supporting an estranged family who offer him no assistance.

Drag benefited from the New York- and California-related expansion of Pelley's parochial views but offered little that was new or original. Reflecting Pelley's embitterment over the dissolution of his own marriage, the novel is one of the darkest works of his career. Even the pat happy ending is ambiguous; David closes the novel by nonchalantly noting that Allie has custody of their children and is teaching them to hate him for being a failure as a father. The book's negative tone, and rehashing of *The Fog*'s plot, did nothing to help sales, and *Drag* found neither the critical nor the commercial success of that earlier novel.

After completing the novel, Pelley, at the behest of a friend, New York film producer Larry Giffin, traveled to Washington, D.C., to discuss a new film project. While the proposed film on the criminal justice system proved abortive, Pelley once again found himself in contact with worried anti-Semites. Pelley later maintained that a group of Washington newspapermen and Justice Department officials (never disclosed by name), with whom he met as part of the film project, spent most of the trip detailing the machinations of Jewish Communism around the world, including a claim that the Teapot Dome scandal served merely as a smokescreen to keep public attention away from plans to set up an unofficial government to control the economy.[28]

Pelley's Washington contacts undoubtedly contributed to his growing concern over racial and ethnic issues during the decade. His frequent
contact with Jewish studio heads also helped propel Pelley toward anti-
Semitism. He found the moguls, many of whom were first-generation
Jewish immigrants, ignorant and uncultured. Reiterating a frequent
screenwriter complaint, Pelley decried the manner in which the unlet-
tered studio bosses tinkered with his scripts. Angered over his treatment
by the studios, Pelley even contemplated organizing a union for film
writers, a plan that came to naught.[29]

Pelley was not alone in fearing the effect of decadent Hollywood on
American society. The film enclave suffered numerous scandals during
the early 1920s, and the publicity surrounding the trial of Roscoe "Fatty"
Arbuckle and the mysterious deaths of director William Desmond Taylor
and producer Thomas Ince led many Americans to perceive Hollywood
as a seething modern Babylon. Further, the fact that Jewish studio chiefs
controlled film production caused much latent anti-Semitism to boil over
into public outcry over the behavior and influence of the "Oriental custodians of adolescent entertainment." For example, Henry Ford's notorious "The International Jew" series of articles in the *Dearborn Independent*
frequently condemned "Jewish Hollywood" as part of Ford's campaign to
expose Jewish machinations.[30]

Although Pelley increasingly came to question the motives and
morals of his Hollywood employers, he made no move to extricate himself from the "fleshpots of Hollywood." He decision to continue focusing
on film work partly reflected the difficulties Pelley faced in selling his
short stories to mass circulation magazines as the 1920s progressed.
Pelley's style of genteel fiction was increasingly marginalized as established magazines sought out stories by authors considered to be young
radicals. As the *Ladies' Home Journal, Saturday Evening Post,* and other previously staid publications began snapping up stories by writers such as F.
Scott Fitzgerald and Theodore Dreiser, the market for homespun Paris,
Vermont, tales evaporated, leaving Pelley with few alternatives but to
continue working in Hollywood while selling occasional stories where
he could.[31]

Pelley shifted his operations back to California in 1926 and resumed his studio work, shortly to be augmented by a series of business ventures. His return to California also led to a significant development in Pelley's personal life. Spending so much time on the East Coast, Pelley maintained only a furnished room in Matie Shaw's Pasadena boardinghouse. On his 1926 return to California, Pelley discovered that an attractive young woman named Helen Wilhelmina Hansmann ("Mina" to Pelley) also now resided at Shaw's. Pelley was smitten with Helen the first time he saw her "clad in the most beautiful of all feminine apparel, the free-falling cape of the Red Cross nurse." Much to Pelley's pleasure he discovered that Helen had also spent time in Russia during World War I and had even stayed with Pelley's Siberian traveling companion George Smith and his wife in Omsk for an extended period. The two quickly began a romantic relationship (Pelley noted that she was "a chalice to drink from that offered an elixir that my lips had never tasted"), which would eventually lead to marriage.[32]

Pelley also developed a number of close personal contacts with individuals involved in filmmaking. Along with Lon Chaney, Pelley cultivated friendships with future Hopalong Cassidy star William Boyd and actor Neil Hamilton (best remembered for his role as police commissioner Gordon on the 1960s television program *Batman*). Pelley's post-1924 shift away from script writing was facilitated by his budding friendships with two nonactors involved in the film business, Grant Dolge and Eddie Eckels.

Film agent Grant Dolge became Pelley's Hollywood representative in 1924. Highly successful during the 1920s, Dolge had film clients who included topflight stars Henry Walthall, Chester Conklin, Mack Swain, Huntley Gordon, Blanche Sweet, and Charles Emmet Mack. As the decade progressed, Dolge, like Pelley, became increasingly disgusted with doing business in Hollywood. Something of an anti-Semite himself, Dolge helped reinforce Pelley's increasingly racist attitudes.[33]

Pelley's other close friend, Eddie Eckels, possessor of a "philosophy of rampant materialism," worked in the publicity department at Metro-Goldwyn-Mayer (and had previously edited the *Exhibitors Trade Review*). The two men formed the Pelley and Eckels Advertising Agency, based at the Guaranty Building in Hollywood, to handle a variety of business ventures. According to Pelley, their joint operations earned a great deal of money during the middle of the decade before personal difficulties led to the dissolution of their partnership.[34]

The first of their projects involved managing publicity and promotions for the clients of their mutual friend Dolge. To promote Dolge's actors they established *Hi-Hat Magazine*. Subtitled the "roundtable of the film community," *Hi-Hat* was little more than a thinly veiled promotional packet, and it quickly began faltering. Eckels eventually bought out Pelley's interest in the magazine, rechristened it the *West Coaster*, and tried to broaden the magazine's contents, but he still stopped publishing it in early 1930.[35]

The agency's other ventures, often well outside the field of advertising, proved considerably more profitable. Pelley and Eckels snapped up a large tract of real estate on Sunset Mountain and converted it into the Filmanor subdivision. With the proceeds from disposing of their properties, Pelley and Eckels bought a chain of ice cream parlors.[36]

Fresh off these successes, Pelley and Eckels enlisted their friend Dolge in an attempt to cash in on the post-Lindbergh solo flight craze. The three men hired pilot Dick Grace to attempt to be the first person to fly by himself from Hawaii to California. A protégé of wing-walking pioneer Owen Locklear, Grace established himself as one of the preeminent motion-picture stunt pilots during the 1920s, including holding the position of stunt coordinator in the classic *Wings* (1927). Pelley and his associates funded the trip hoping to benefit from the publicity engendered and to manage Grace's postflight career.

The flight, however, proved ill-fated from the beginning. Grace's plane did not perform properly in the tropical climate, the plane malfunctioned on takeoff, and weather conditions aborted several other attempts. Replacement parts had to be shipped from the mainland, leading to costly delays. Having been in Hawaii since late June, Grace finally got his plane airborne on July 4, only to have the tail break off, forcing a crash landing. Although Grace (and the dog that flew with him) were unhurt in the accident, his backers decided to cut their losses and end the venture after this failure. Although Grant Dolge continued to finance Grace's aerial exploits (including competing in one of the Pacific air races sponsored by the Dole Fruit Company), Pelley found the project tiresome and quietly ended his participation in the enterprise.[37]

With business ventures appropriating so much of his time, Pelley's studio work dwindled precipitously. For example, he only sold two scripts in 1927. *Ladybird,* released by the small studio Chadwick Pictures, was a low-budget crime feature distinguished only by the fact that the heroine utilized martial arts to defeat a gang of criminals. *The Sunset Derby,* based upon Pelley's 1926 story of the same name, was released by First National Pictures, but the lightweight horse-racing yarn was not one of the studio's successful products that year.[38]

By 1927 Pelley's hectic schedule finally began to catch up with him. Finding little satisfaction in the constant round of speculative ventures (and believing his creativity stifled by his focus on financial gain), Pelley ended his professional relationships with Dolge and Eckels. In late summer 1927, financially solvent, Pelley determined to scale back his workload and "withdraw into quiet."[39]

Pelley decided that he needed a home of his own to provide seclusion and quiet to renew his strength. To that end he selected an out-of-the-way bungalow on Altadena's Mount Circle Drive. Under California law one's spouse is entitled to half equity in any real estate, and Pelley, who had never bothered to divorce Marion, did not want his estranged wife to have a claim to his new home. To eliminate this potential problem, Pelley gave Helen Hansmann the money to buy the bungalow and put it in her own name. The house on Mount Circle Drive proved especially significant in Pelley's later career. As Pelley said, "this bungalow had been built—left there waiting—to contribute its bit to the nation's spiritual history."[40]

Although he ostensibly purchased the house as a place of extended relaxation and contemplation, the hard-working (and money-hungry) Pelley found it impossible to retreat entirely from worldly affairs. In early 1928 he established the Pelley Corporation as a real estate venture. In a partial attempt to limit his involvement in the daily affairs of the corporation, Pelley hired local businessman Al Burke to manage the company. One of the corporation's ventures involved the creation of a fast-food chain, the Briefmeal Company, based upon the principles of the Harvey

Houses that Pelley had admired so much during his cross-country train rides.[41]

Pelley also continued to focus attention on his literary career while staying in Altadena. Although an attempted Broadway translation of his novel *Drag* fell through owing to financial difficulties, Pelley managed to publish several stories in late 1927 and early 1928. He continued to sell his work to the *American Magazine* occasionally, but Pelley found the editors of *Collier's* more receptive to his stories. *Collier's* also published a serial of Pelley's in the late spring of 1928 that eventually was released in novel form as *The Blue Lamp* in 1931.

The story revolves around mysterious blue lights and an amnesiac woman associated with a mansion built just outside Paris, Vermont, and clearly reflects a broadening of Pelley's horizons. The plot includes appearances by eccentric scientists, a Hungarian prince, a hunchback, and a wise attorney named Hubbard. Like many of Pelley's plots, *The Blue Lamp* also features an intrepid young newspaperman—in this case the "trimly tailored, magnetic, [and] aggressive" Jimmy Battles—who proves to be fearless and intelligent. In classic Pelley style, Battles not only saves the day, but ends the novel falling in love and living happily ever after with the amnesiac young lady.[42]

Despite the rather cheesy ending, *The Blue Lamp* is the best of Pelley's novels. While strangers are still to be feared and distrusted, at least the residents of Paris are engaged in livelier activities. And with the exception of the framing pieces, the entire novel transpires in one forty-eight-hour period, which keeps the plot and pacing tight and prevents the sort of meandering that afflicts many of his longer works.

The "Blue Lamp" serial began running in *Collier's* in May 1928. In that same month Pelley underwent the mystical experience that permanently changed his life. His public career was about to take a wholly unexpected twist, one that left Pelley much less financially secure but far happier.

4

Seven Minutes in Eternity
1928–1929

WILLIAM DUDLEY PELLEY's increasing focus on race and ethnicity during the 1920s placed him in large company. Although North American anti-Semitism dated back to the rule of Peter Stuyvesant in New Amsterdam, American Jews, when compared to Europe, faced little organized hostility in this country until the turn of the twentieth century. The presence of large numbers of eastern European Jews among the "new" immigrants of the late nineteenth century helped propel a wave of anti-Jewish sentiment unprecedented in American history.

Prior to the late nineteenth century the small communities of Sephardic and Ashkenazic Jews in the United States experienced muted discrimination and infrequent attacks, usually instigated by renewed claims of their status as "Christ killers," but the influx of almost four million clannish, poor, eastern European Jews at the end of the century deeply troubled American nativists. In their attempts to limit the flow of "inferiors" into the United States, immigration restrictionists began developing theories that Jews belonged to a diseased racial stock that, paradoxically, possessed the business acumen to control America's financial system.[1]

Nativist sentiment that recent immigrants represented degraded, unassimilatible races received supportive evidence from the developing field of eugenics. The eminently respectable eugenicists argued that swarms of enfeebled and morally crippled "lower" racial stock immigrants threatened to overwhelm the superior Anglo-Saxons, requiring restrictive immigration, repatriation, and sterilization to prevent, in Madison Grant's famous phrase, the "passing of the great race." Strange to old-stock Americans in appearance and customs, the new Jewish immigrants became prime examples of racial distinctions to nativists and eugenicists alike. These anti-Semitic ideas found popular dispersal in new English translations of Houston Stewart Chamberlin's *Foundations of the Nineteenth Century* (English version available in America in 1910), Count Joseph Arthur de Gobineau's *The Inequality of Human Races* (1915), and Werner Sombart's *The Jews and Modern Capitalism* (1913). An explosive development in anti-Jewish sentiments and incidents, culminating in the 1913 lynching of Leo Frank in Georgia, spurred American Jews to establish protective organizations such as the American Jewish Committee (1906) and the Anti-Defamation League of B'nai B'rith (1913).[2]

Anti-Semitic sentiment boiled over in the 1920s. Spurred by alleged links between Jews and the Bolshevik Revolution, American Jews came to be viewed as a moral, economic, and political menace. These ideas spread thanks to works such as Henry Ford's infamous "International Jew" series in the *Dearborn Independent* and Theodore Lothrop Stoddard's bestsellers *Revolt Against Civilization* and *The Rising Tide of Color*. At the beginning of the decade, Boris Brasol's English translation of the *Protocols of the Learned Elders of Zion* also appeared in the United States.[3]

Allegedly the minutes from a Zionist conference in Basil, Switzerland, the *Protocols* detail Judaic attempts to control the international political and economic system (using their Freemason stooges as proxies). Russian mystic Sergei Nilus first published the *Protocols,* concocted by the Russian secret police, in 1905. Although disclosed as a forgery shortly after being translated into English (much of the work was directly plagiarized from an 1864 novel by Maurice Joly), the *Protocols* received a warm welcome during the 1920s, including a full reprint in Ford's newspaper.[4]

In the midst of expanding anti-Semitism and a general conservative retreat from the reforms of the Progressive era, Pelley's shift toward the political right is not surprising. As early as the mid-1920s he was already questioning the role of Jewish movie studio moguls in affecting American morality. Increasingly distressed over the treatment of his work by the studio bosses, Pelley found solace in the view that Jews were both conspiring against old-stock Americans like himself and inherently inferior people. His shift toward business ventures and his distancing from film production can be viewed as a symptom of his mounting concern over affiliation with "Jewish" Hollywood.[5]

Seeking escape from the film industry and his hectic business schedule, Pelley retreated to his Altadena bungalow. Increasingly isolated from friends and colleagues—Mina Hansmann appears to have been his only consistent visitor—Pelley utilized his time to reflect on his life and career. These meditations also led Pelley, like Houston Stewart Chamberlain before him, to focus his attention on the question of defining "what is race."[6]

While studying the question of race at the bungalow on the night of May 28, 1928, Pelley underwent a mystical experience that led him to focus his energies and writings on metaphysics. Before the night of his "seven minutes in eternity," Pelley had little exposure to spiritualism and the occult (although his experience was greater than he admitted), but he threw himself into examining the topic after his visit to the "other side." Although much of Pelley's later career calls into question the sincerity of many of his religious pronouncements, it is clear he underwent a life-changing conversion event in Altadena.[7]

On the night of his conversion experience, Pelley went to bed early and read ethnological tracts until dozing, only to be awakened early in the morning by an inner voice shrieking "I'm dying." He felt a physical sensation like a "combination of heart attack and apoplexy." This physical distress subsided as Pelley plunged "down a mystic depth of cool blue space not unlike the bottomless sinking sensation that attends the taking of ether for anesthetics."[8]

"Whirling madly" into the blue mist, Pelley closed his eyes and hoped for the quick end of the experience. Feeling hands holding him up, he opened his eyes and found himself lying naked on a marble slab in an environment reminiscent of a Maxfield Parrish painting, with two men in white uniforms attending to him. The two vaguely familiar helpers told Pelley not to be afraid and not to try to see everything in the first "seven minutes." They instructed him to bathe in a nearby reflecting pool, which caused Pelley to lose his self-consciousness over being naked.[9]

One man left and the remaining white-clad individual, "William," explained to Pelley that he had gone "over" while stationed at a military camp in 1917. William told Pelley that everyone has lived hundreds of times before, because earth is a classroom where souls learn and move up the spiritual hierarchy. This hierarchy accounts for human races, which are simply "great classifications of humanity epitomizing gradations of spiritual development, starting with the black man and proceeding up-ward in cycles to the white." Having completed his first spiritual lesson, the blue mist reappeared to return Pelley to the bungalow.[10]

Although Pelley awakened to conscious awareness of his earthly exis-tence, he remained in contact with the spirit world, as William continued to speak to him clairaudiently. He instructed Pelley to relax and return to the "Higher Reality." This time the marble portico was full of people, and Pelley realized that he knew all of them and that they were all saintly in-dividuals, with "no misfits, no tense countenances, no sour leers, no pre-occupied brusqueness, nor physical disfigurements." After a brief chat with these folks Pelley, again enveloped by the blue mist, returned to his bedroom, but now possessing "strange powers of perception" to assist him in completing a specific errand on the material plane.[11]

Shaken by the experience, Pelley determined to regain his sense of the material world by visiting his office the next morning. He related that his employees found him to appear like a different person who stood straighter and healthier and less wrinkled. The experience also eliminated his troubling insomnia and anxiety.[12]

Pelley's description of the results of his "seven minutes in eternity" clearly reflect the effects of a conversion experience as outlined by William James. Pelley's conversion follows the Jamesian pattern of an ex-hausted "sick soul" (Pelley posited that "something hard and brittle had broken in my spirit") escaping through a "self-surrender" conversion pro-pelled by faith that has previously hovered at the edges of consciousness. Having pushed beyond "egotistical worry," the converted individual feels rejuvenated (Pelley noted he "had somehow been reborn") and possesses a new, and frequently permanent, sense of determination and strength.[13]

In Pelley's case the rejuvenation was permanent. The "seven min-utes" began what can be viewed as the second half of Pelley's career. After this conversion he abandoned script writing and only pushed his short stories as a means to raise capital quickly. Giving up his old pursuits, Pelley zealously threw himself into spiritual affairs and politics.

Pelley decided that the "fleshpots" of Hollywood could not help him understand his metaphysical experience, so he traveled to New York to meet with friends there. While crossing New Mexico by train, he underwent a second experience. As he was reading Ralph Waldo Emerson's essay "The Over-Soul," a brilliant shaft of white light poured down on Pelley. A disembodied presence explained to Pelley that Jesus Christ was an "actual Personage," and that existing churches and ministers were not only wrong about Christ's teachings but were leading millions of people astray. The presence instructed Pelley to continue to receive clairaudient messages by utilizing the "hidden powers" within him and to spread the correct understanding of Christ.[14]

In New York, Pelley met with his friend Mary Derieux, fiction editor for the *American Magazine*. Deeply immersed in spiritualism herself, Derieux excitedly joined Pelley in exploring his new powers. During the summer of 1928 they spent two weeks engaged in automatic writing.[15]

The beings from the other side instructed them that the Music of the Spheres (a concept swiped from Pythagorus) is the very center of the mystery of universal creation. Within this universe there is no force but love; hatred and evil are merely the absence of love. These beings also explained to Pelley and Derieux that they dwelled on the "harmonious plane" (which is the next level above the earth) and communicated with certain earth-dwelling souls to promote love and harmony.[16]

A large portion of these messages focused specifically on the role of Pelley in spiritual history. The voices allegedly explained to Pelley that he would apprentice in tribulation, then achieve financial independence so he might be ready for freedom and service to higher beings. He had been chosen because art is the "handmaiden of God," and artists like himself are the true chosen priesthood.[17]

As chair of the publications committee of the American Society for Psychical Research (ASPR), Derieux provided Pelley with entrée into New York spiritualist circles. These contacts garnered Pelley exposure to current theories and writings on psychical research and undoubtedly helped him develop his own ideas. Further, Pelley's account of visiting another plane made an immediate splash in the psychical community, as it placed him squarely within the debate over the most divisive spiritualist issue of the period—reincarnation.[18]

Established in 1884 by, among others, physicist William Barrett and psychologist William James, the ASPR staggered through a tumultuous early career. Unlike the older English Society for Psychical Research, the ASPR faced chronic underfunding and a lack of full-time psychical researchers. Owing to financial difficulties, the ASPR was absorbed by the English society in 1889, only to reappear as an independent organization in 1909, thanks primarily to the dynamic leadership of Columbia professor James Hervey Hyslop.[19]

Although Hyslop died in 1920, the Society reached the pinnacle of its public success in the ensuing decade, propelled by vigorous researchers such as Walter F. Prince and Lamarckian psychologist William Mc-Dougall. A spate of best-selling books, including Sir Oliver Lodge's *Raymond* and Baird T. Spaulding's five-volume *Life and Teachings of the Masters of the Far East;* successful speaking tours by Lodge, Sir Arthur Conan Doyle, and the playwright Maurice Maeterlinck; and the publicity surrounding annual international congresses helped push psychical research into the headlines. In the early 1920s even Thomas Edison became involved, spending parts of his final years working on a spiritual communication machine.[20]

The seriousness with which psychical research was taken is illustrated most clearly by the establishment of the first university-affiliated psychical laboratory, at Duke University in 1928. Headed by J. B. Rhine, who originally moved to Duke to work with McDougall, the lab investigated scores of mediums and psychics. Rhine initially studied the question of life after death but, realizing the pitfalls of this line of inquiry, quickly restricted his focus to "corporeal parapsychical" material (mental or subjective phenomena, excluding spiritualism). Rhine, who worked at Duke until 1965, published a series of best-selling books and coined the terms "parapsychology" and "extra-sensory perception."[21]

Despite growing public awareness of the Society, psychical researchers faced increasing schisms within the movement. Issues such as reincarnation and ectoplasmic evidence divided the ASPR into warring factions. When disputes arose over the validity of trance medium (and ectoplasmic material spewer) "Margery," local branches of the Society left to organize themselves into independent organizations.[22]

Although never a member of the ASPR, Pelley found a great deal of interest in the debates swirling within the Society during the late 1920s. Needing to get his business affairs in order, however, he returned to California in summer 1928. Pelley and Mina began automatic-writing sessions almost as soon as he returned to the Pacific coast. During these sessions Pelley became increasingly convinced of his own spiritual importance. Pelley related that one of his California spirit contacts noted that, in numerous previous incarnations, he had been one of those "people who kicked up more of a rumpus on the human stage than humanity especially liked at the time, and always in some proselytizing capacity that wrought alterations in the mode of humanity's living." This developing sense of self-importance, coupled with the urging of Mary Derieux, led Pelley to publish the account of his conversion experience.[23]

Returning to New York, Pelley rented a room at the Commodore Hotel and, through a process he later called "super radio," wrote the narrative of his "seven minutes in eternity" in less than two hours. Derieux presented the article to her boss, *American Magazine* editor Merle Crowell, who agreed to run the story and to pay Pelley $1,500 for it. Appearing in the March 1929 issue of *American,* Pelley's tale of travel to other planes of reality generated a mass of mail both to the editor and to the writer. The *American* boasted a subscription list of over 2,200,000 people at the time, and Pelley's tale became one of the most widely read accounts of paranormal activity in American history.[24]

Stunned by the response to his article—the *American*'s offices received thousands of letters concerning the "seven minutes"—Pelley decided to move to New York in summer 1929. He rented part of a 53d Street brownstone for himself and paid for a room in the Allerton Hotel for Women on Lexington Avenue for Mina. Pelley spent much of 1929 responding to his voluminous correspondence and participating in Manhattan séances and spiritualist meetings.[25]

During one of these meetings, Pelley made the acquaintance of trance medium George Wehner. Something of a "psychic to the stars," Wehner carved out a very successful career for himself during the 1920s. Pelley attended séances in which Wehner served as amanuensis for such diverse celebrities as Joseph Conrad, film scenarist June Mathis, various prominent American Indians, and Robert Louis Stevenson.[26]

Pelley eventually began contacting many of these same people during his own sessions. He claimed that Robert Louis Stevenson provided him with an unused chapter and asserted that Joseph Conrad clairaudiently dictated an entire novel to him. Pelley published this work of fiction in summer 1929 as *Golden Rubbish,* allegedly to answer many of the questions readers raised in response to his *American Magazine* article.[27]

Golden Rubbish revolves around the spiritual awakening of Louise Garland. Designed to present Pelley's developing beliefs in a form amenable to his spiritualist friends and fans of his earlier fiction, the novel meanders for four hundred pages. Pelley attempted to graft a quest for spiritual understanding onto the undergirding of one of his traditional Paris, Vermont, tales and failed miserably on all levels. Neither portion of the work stands on its own, and the two subplots suffer from a jarring discontinuity. Although most of Pelley's fiction has aged badly, *Golden Rubbish* is the only one of his novels that is simply unreadable.

Louise Garland's transformation from a callous Manhattan restaurant owner to a spiritually enlightened humanitarian develops from her relationship with George Robling. Louise seeks out Robling after discovering that her recently deceased father's fortune was money bilked from him. Determined to make amends, Garland, who has "got too many brains t' be a woman," travels from Paris, Vermont (where her father died), to Robling's palatial estate in California (he is a skyscraper architect). The cross-country journey gives Pelley, through the characters, a chance to decry western urbanization and tell a few Jewish jokes.[28]

Upon finally meeting George Robling, Louise and friend Basil Buss discover that he now possesses a deep mystical power. George, when not building skyscrapers, undergoes visions and works as a spiritual counselor. He finds Louise desperately needs his guidance. She "had not attained to a 'transformation' in those days, and her hair was dispirited—a brand of straw yellow." Not surprisingly, Louise is immediately smitten with George.[29]

Attempting to help Louise, George, who has "coffers of wisdom in maturity's treasure-house," expounds his spiritual philosophy to her. Most of his lengthy speeches concern the power of light. George explains that it is the "basis of Matter," "a movement of the Eternal Benefaction," and "the power of the Godhead, vitalizing creation where ever there be need." He finally concludes by noting that "thinking, by and large, is a receiving of billions upon billions of sublimated light granules from the sun of Universal Intelligence, impacting upon brain cells, demanding a housing, seeking conversion into the proper vibratory velocity for practical employment." Seeking the wisdom of George's teaching, Louise opens her heart and begins a soul-searching self-examination.[30]

Before Louise can truly find herself, however, Christ appears, utilizing the body of George as a vessel. He booms empty platitudes, then quickly disappears. When George awakens he has aged almost thirty years and remembers nothing that has happened in the decade since the war. Louise and Basil discover that George, before he aged, made them trustees over his fortune. They are to use the money for an excavation project in Palestine to uncover Christ's true teachings—which have been perverted over time. While the duo will be attacked by the religiously conservative, they need not fear because, in one of the earliest examples of Pelley's millennialism, Christ will reappear to protect them. Having found spiritual peace, financial security, and a sense of mission, Basil and Louise decide they are truly in love and should travel together "into the World's Sunrise on Wings."[31]

Wooden, purple, and pretentious beyond belief, *Golden Rubbish* is simply god-awful. During the last 150 pages the plot completely disintegrates, and the book becomes a turgid religious tract of banalities posing as profundities. During one of George's interminable blatherings Louise notes, "it seemed like too much descanting for one day"—a fitting summation of the book itself. *Golden Rubbish* marked the end for Pelley as a popular novelist. His next—and last—novel did not appear until twenty years later, and then only as a self-published work.

Pelley's sudden fame also led to the resuscitation of his faltering short-story career. Not surprisingly, most of his 1929 stories appeared in the *American Magazine*. These tales, still centered primarily around events in Paris, Vermont, continued the pattern of sentimental fluff Pelley had cranked out during the decade but added bits derived from his newfound spiritual awakenings. The "Dark Happiness" serial, for example, includes discussions of reincarnation, "original cosmic energy," persecution of religious dissidents, and a character with "supra-normal" spiritual gifts, before reaching its pat happy ending.[32]

Pelley's 1929 fiction is among the weakest of his career. A combination of recycled plots, an increasingly faltering eye for local color, and changing literary tastes already hampered his success during the decade; the addition of religious themes made his work even more difficult to read. The sudden and surprising attention given Pelley after the publication of the "seven minutes" rejuvenated his fiction-writing career, but this brief flash of public illumination proved short-lived. The sheer mediocrity of Pelley's fiction during this period made a full-fledged comeback unlikely and, as the excitement over his mystical experience faded, his writing career again receded into the background, although Pelley later maintained that he gave up a highly successful literary career to study metaphysics.[33]

Although Pelley spent most of 1929 in New York, Hollywood proved to be interested in his newfound fame as well. Pelley had not sold a screenplay in the two years preceding the *American Magazine* article, but in the aftermath of the "seven minutes," three films written by him were produced. Although Pelley clearly felt uneasy about his continued relationship with the Hollywood moguls, he agreed to involvement in these final productions because he needed the money. Also contributing to his decision was that none of the projects required a great deal of work on his part; one film was a remake and the others were novel and story adaptations.

Pelley's 1929 features are significant only in that all utilized newly developed motion picture sound systems. Based upon Pelley's story "The Stolen Lady," *Come Across* detailed a criminal swindle thwarted by love. *Drag,* directed by future two-time Academy Award winner Frank Lloyd, was released in July 1929. Based on Pelley's 1925 novel of the same name, the film faithfully followed the book's plot. As in the novel, the story revolves around the fate of a young New Englander stifled by a poor marriage choice who eventually finds love. The December 1929 Universal release *Courtin' Wildcats* became Pelley's final motion picture. In a remake of 1924's *Sawdust Trail,* Hoot Gibson reprised his role as an Eastern college boy who joins a wild west show. *Courtin' Wildcats'* only significant departure from the 1924 version was the use of Movietone sound. Intended as no more than a programmer, the film played at the first-run Loew's New York house for only one day (Dec. 17, 1929), and even then only as part of a double feature.[34]

Pelley faced a critical situation by the end of 1929. Although his name was more widely recognized than ever before, he was at a career dead end. Unwilling to continue what he perceived as a morally harmful association with Jewish moguls, he no longer felt welcome in Hollywood, nor did he see anything but spiritual bankruptcy in his various business ventures. Although he wanted to continue his career as a fiction writer, this option was not viable. *Golden Rubbish* garnered disappointing sales and earned Pelley a tongue-lashing from his editor at Putnam's. An editorial shake-up at the *American Magazine* cost Crowell and Derieux their jobs, and Pelley became an unwelcome writer of sentimental fluff and religious "hokum," effectively ending his relationship with the magazine. In the wake of the "seven minutes" hoopla, Pelley steadfastly maintained that he wanted neither to establish his own religious organization nor to "convert anyone to anything," but, faced with dwindling opportunities, that is exactly what he endeavored to do in 1930.[35]

5

Liberation
1930—1932

AS WILLIAM JAMES NOTED, "divided selves" often find peace outside established religious forms. Thus William Dudley Pelley's adoption of an anti-Semitic worldview, like his immersion in spiritualism, may be seen as a reflection of his need to find an explanation for a world of which he neither felt a part nor completely understood. Working under the thumb of Jewish studio moguls he perceived as immoral and unappreciative, Pelley found a convenient scapegoat for the disquieting aspects of American society. While his anti-Semitism remained relatively muted at the dawn of the 1930s, it is clear that Pelley already felt threatened by Jews and their suspected machinations. Pelley's conversion experience pushed spiritualism to the forefront of his energies (and career), but his developing anti-Semitic views always remained in the close background. He spent the first few years of the new decade establishing his credentials in metaphysical circles, but spiritual studies never assuaged Pelley's concerns over the "Jewish problem." [1]

Pelley's decision to focus his attention on developing a reputation in spiritualist circles arose from both limited opportunities and his increasing acceptance within the world of metaphysical studies. He developed invaluable contacts within the New York City spiritualist community, thanks to the "seven minutes" article and his friendship with the well-connected Mary Derieux. Pelley also garnered a positive review in the *Journal of the American Society for Psychical Research,* which gained him attention among metaphysical researchers across the United States and England.[2]

By early 1930 Pelley was already earning money utilizing his new-found psychical powers. He began making his clairaudient messages available to the public and presenting lectures to groups of spiritualists. His claims about the messages he channeled became increasingly fantastic as Pelley sought to establish the validity of his alleged powers. Pelley posited that his clairaudient messages occasionally came to him in Sanskrit and that the automatic writings flowed from him backwards (requiring a mirror to translate them). After reading Emanuel Swedenborg approvingly, Pelley co-opted the Swedish mystic's alleged ability to glean knowledge of an item's past owners by holding the object in his hand. Pelley claimed he "could handle a handkerchief or bit of clothing and know accurately all there was to be known about that person, including some of the most intimate affairs of their lives."[3]

In spring 1930, Pelley decided to begin publishing his own magazine. Pelley's *New Liberator,* under the imprint of the Gallahad Press, appeared in May, with a subscription rate of $3 per year. Pelley wrote all the articles, and his spiritualist friend Margaret Christie, a "big-bodied, athletic, go-getting spinster," edited the magazine. Pelley's mission statement for the *New Liberator* stressed the promotion of Christ's teachings (in Pelley's version) and an exposition of the "vast machinery, operating with infinitesimal precision and accounting for every event on our present plane of consciousness." Pelley clearly felt this was a significant undertaking, but he noted with false modesty that he accepted "this brevet in no spirit of grandiose evangelism or fanatical proselytism, but as one who would take his universal brethren up into New Mountains of Transfiguration, bidding them behold with their own eyes that Religion and Science, or Spirituality and Materialism, are but mosaic facets of the same Eternal Jewel."[4]

Despite Pelley's contention that the magazine contained material of spiritual import, the first issue of *New Liberator* proved to be a tentative step. Clearly still developing his approach to the larger spiritualist community, Pelley's articles stretched across a broad spectrum of topics, from his own background to reincarnation and Russian atheism. Not surprisingly, the magazine generated only moderate interest.[5]

The inaugural issue of *New Liberator* promised the next number's release on May 25; the second issue, however, proved slow to appear. Pelley learned very quickly that his popularity within New York spiritualist circles did not automatically translate into financial windfalls. The *New Liberator* sold poorly, Pelley's savings dwindled to almost nothing (Mina also found employment difficult to obtain during this period), and the printer with which he had contracted to publish the magazine went out of business. Because of this dire situation, the next *New Liberator* did not appear until October 1930.[6]

The issuance of the October *New Liberator* inaugurated a short period of stability, and Pelley published the magazine on a monthly basis for the rest of the year. Pelley reorganized the editorial staff during this period, and brought Olive E. Robbins on board as business manager. Robbins, in a move that greatly aided the magazine's continued existence, managed to increase advertising revenue. The advertisements, however, proved to be something of a double-edged sword. In no position to refuse advertising dollars from any source, Pelley accepted money from a variety of shady metaphysical organizations, including the Ancient Mystical Order Rosae Cruces (AMORC) and Psychiana. Although the advertising revenue was desperately needed (and Pelley agreed with significant aspects of the teachings of these groups), affiliation with such organizations did nothing to promote the acceptance (or perceived validity) of Pelley's religious doctrine.[7]

Established by New York advertising man H. Spencer Lewis, also known as Wishar Spenle Cerve, the AMORC represents one of several Rosicrucian groups active in the United States. All of these groups claim that their teachings are based upon writings ascribed to the mythical seventeenth-century mystic Christian Rosenkreuz. Lewis, however, went on to posit that his organization's teachings actually dated from the reign of Thutmose III, circa 1500 B.C. In a sort of spiritual alchemy, the AMORC blends Christianity with Kabbalism and Hermetic theories, with the ultimate goal of transcending material form. Lewis skillfully mixed in Theosophical elements to separate his version of Rosicrucianism from his competitors (completing a circle begun with Theosophy founder Helena P. Blavatsky, who earlier swiped elements from European

Rosicrucianism for her movement). During the 1930s Lewis oriented much of his teachings toward the spiritualist mecca of Mount Shasta. His 1931 volume *Lemuria: The Lost Continent of the Pacific* placed the Atlantis myth in the Pacific Ocean, with Mount Shasta as the continent's highest peak and current home of cavern-dwelling Lemurian survivors. Owing to its image as a mail-order religion, AMORC has never been respected within the esoteric religious community.[8]

Frank B. Robinson established Psychiana in 1929 after undergoing a conversion process while living in Hollywood. In an experience very similar to Pelley's "seven minutes," Robinson claimed that God lifted the veil between mortals and the spiritual plane for him, warned that the spirit of holiness was not present in any current Christian church, and instructed the middle-aged pharmacist to develop his own body of teachings. Robinson's work mixed New Thought with Theosophy (he described himself as an "Adept"), and posited that God worked through an evolutionary process in which salvation is achieved through a developing relationship with the individual, bringing peace, happiness, and health through His cosmic powers. Robinson's heavy New Thought influence derived from intensive study of Robert Collier's work, particularly *The Secret of the Ages*. Like the AMORC, Psychiana was essentially a mail-order religion. Robinson utilized modern marketing techniques to spread knowledge of his organization (often placing ads in popular magazines with headlines such as "I spoke to God!") and estimated that more than one million people had received information on his group by the end of the 1940s.[9]

The tireless work of Olive Robbins, however, did not save the magazine from another crisis. Early the next year trusted employee Margaret Christie embezzled most of the *New Liberator*'s profits, leaving Pelley unable to continue publication of the magazine. Given the chaotic condition of his business records, Pelley realized that prosecution of Christie was impossible (no one involved with the venture knew where money came from or went). Determined to push forward, Pelley in February 1931 incorporated the Gallahad Press, shortly to be changed to Galahad Press. He divided one hundred shares of common stock among employees Mary Joyce Benner and Olive Robbins and himself, keeping a majority thirty-four, and sold $13,000 worth of preferred stock to fifteen people, at $10 per share, to finance the magazine. With this new cash in hand, Pelley published the first 1931 issue of the *New Liberator* in March and issued monthly installments through the summer of that year.[10]

Also that spring, Pelley renewed his friendship with Sumner Vinton. The two men had first met in Japan during the World War, and Vinton had also developed an interest in metaphysics in the ensuing decade. Already employed by the spiritualist Golden Rule Foundation, Vinton agreed to work for Pelley on a new venture. To help spread his message, Pelley organized the League for the Liberation, with Vinton handling most of the paperwork.[11]

The League for the Liberation served as an umbrella for local organizations known as Leagues of Liberators. Pelley envisioned the Liberators as a "great Christ-Force, international perhaps some day in scope, that should throw a stern gauntlet to the Satanic influences now seeking the debauchment of our present civilization." The Liberators met in weekly discussion groups, usually held on Sunday nights, to study materials mailed to them by Vinton. These materials, *Programs of Service,* were separate sheets enclosed with copies of the *New Liberator.*[12] Known at League headquarters as the "Pink Scripts" because of their color, these documents outlined a specific program for each weekly service. The Sunday night meetings began with an introduction to that week's topic, followed by an invocation. After the recitation of a clairaudiently received message (the "New Sermons on the Mount"), the local chaplain read the week's lecture, then led the group in a discussion of the "Script." The weekly meeting ended with a benediction. Pelley posited that the fifty-two scripts "projected an entirely new religious philosophy, a philosophy of Christian mysticism raised to ideality but minus the hatreds, vengeances, and preposterous absurdities of the Jewish God of Jealousy."[13]

Pelley developed a grand plan for the League. He proposed a national structure that divided the United States into thirteen departments, each under a department governor. Each of these departments, in turn, was to be divided into thirteen divisions, with a directorial board to oversee operations of local chapters (which were presided over by chaplains and clerks). Although this ambitious plan proved impossible to implement, by early 1932 the League boasted approximately four hundred local chapters, most—thanks to Pelley's ties to California and its thriving spiritualist community—based on the West Coast.[14]

In the midst of this organizational expansion, Pelley moved to Washington, D.C., in October and established a residence at the Hamilton Hotel. Pelley's decision to move derived largely from his need to accumulate funds for further growth of his movement. The nation's capital held one of the League's largest and most profitable chapters, headed by former International New Thought Alliance (INTA) president James Edgerton, and Pelley believed his presence there might convince members to invest more funds in the Galahad Press. Pelley's single-minded determination to raise capital quickly led him even to put his Altadena bungalow up for sale, advertising it in the *New Liberator* as "a property that may be worth much money in years to come because of Mr. Pelley's experience which occurred beneath its roof." [15]

Pelley's efforts paid off, and his magazine became a weekly publication in fall 1931. He successfully lobbied Liberators to purchase more stock in the Galahad Press and launched a successful lecture tour that took him across the eastern half of the United States. The new weekly version of the magazine also proved more profitable after Pelley raised the subscription rate to $6 per year, even though subscribers only received twelve more pages per month.[16]

Not content with merely providing weekly study materials for Liberators, Pelley decided to take a more active role in his developing movement. Here his connections within spiritualist circles paid a high dividend as Lillian E. Terry, a wealthy mystic and founder of Montreat College, offered to give Pelley a tract of land for a spiritual retreat. Terry gave Pelley title to three hundred acres at the base of Black Mountain in Asheville, North Carolina.[17]

In February 1932 Pelley incorporated the Foundation for Christian Economics, dividing one hundred shares of common stock among Mina, Galahad Press employee Robert Summerville, and himself. The Foundation's assets consisted only of one hundred shares of common stock from the Galahad Press and a $6,000 chattel mortgage. The creation of the Foundation and the mortgage developed solely from Pelley's abysmal financial condition. Several lawsuits were filed against the press for non-payment (as of Feb. 7, 1932, it had assets of $100), and League officials feared the publicity resulting from them would ruin both the movement and Pelley's reputation. Chattel mortgages hold precedence over other claims, and assigning the press's to the new foundation gave Pelley the ability to keep his printing concerns in business (which was essential to his organization) and his creditors at bay.[18]

Pelley decided that, rather than organize a traditional spiritualist re-treat, the Foundation should focus on developing a college, noting that "it became necessary to educate, enlighten, and train people in the meta-physical principles I was attempting to expound." To raise funds for the creation of a school and generate interest in the venture, Pelley sold stock in the Foundation and launched another speaking tour. He hoped to ex-tract large sums of money through personal appeals to a select few of his wealthiest followers; this plan failed miserably.[19]

The shift in Pelley's operations to North Carolina led to a significant shake-up in his organization. Not wishing to move to Asheville, Robbins and Benner left Pelley's employ. Vinton also left, but under less pleasant circumstances. Although unable to keep up with the League's growth, Vinton tried to micromanage the organization. As a result he fell behind in shipping materials; lost receipts, money, and followers; and greatly hin-dered both the development of the movement and Pelley's bottom line. These employees were replaced in importance by "Mont" Hardwicke and Donald Kellogg. The impractical nature of maintaining printers in New York led Pelley to search out a local press to issue his work. He quickly entered into a long relationship with Asheville's Biltmore Press, whose owners, Robert and Gladys Williams, already subscribed to the *New Liberator*.[20]

Pelley's Galahad College, utilizing buildings leased from the local YMCA, opened on July 5, 1932. He outlined the purposes of the college: "to overcome a general breakdown in religious conviction; to inspire psy-chical research; to help combat the menacing crime wave; and to instill the principles of Christ in the American industrial sphere." These grand plans were not mirrored either by the rented buildings or by the college's staff, which numbered three. With James Edgerton appointed dean, Pelley and

Henry Hardwicke handled most of the teaching duties. Hardwicke, father of Pelley associate "Mont" Hardwicke, was a well-known American spiritualist deeply involved in the "Margery" ectoplasm debate.[21]

Despite Galahad's obvious difficulties, one hundred students paid $150 each for the summer term. The bulk of the nine-week curriculum consisted of Pelley's 105 lectures, which took the students "through a metaphysical evolution of the world, from the projection of the planet down through every phase of secular and sacred history to the present." Most of the students agreed with Pelley's message; seventy-three graduated.[22]

In fall 1932, however, it became obvious to Pelley that Galahad College's initial success could not be sustained. Most of his devoted followers attended the first summer session; very few, however, enrolled afterward. Realizing that it was "impracticable to run a minor college of that nature," Pelley decided to convert Galahad into a correspondence school. This change proved to be a wise and profitable maneuver. Pelley charged $60 for regular mail-order courses and found many willing students. In one four-month period in 1932, five hundred people signed up for a course in basic metaphysics.[23]

To those students who signed up for the Galahad College Extension Fellowship Pelley promised "the knowledge which may get to the real principles governing life, and the present conditions abroad in the world." Correspondence students were also entitled to fifty-two lectures (the Galahad Scripts) originally delivered by Pelley to Galahad College's summer 1932 session, fifty-two weekly lectures (the Blue Scripts), and twelve issues of *Liberation* magazine. Each student was also assigned a "personal correspondence counsel" who replied to the quizzes students completed after reading the week's lecture.[24]

Despite the success of his mail-order mysticism, Pelley continued to face financial difficulties. These problems arose primarily from the related issues of Pelley's shoddy bookkeeping methods and his inability to choose efficient assistants. While Pelley possessed great oratorical skills and the ability to create grand organizational visions, he never developed an eye for details. This blind spot partly arose from Pelley's own ego. Perceiving himself as a great visionary, Pelley felt mundane paperwork and correspondence beneath him. His tendency to hire inefficient sycophants only exacerbated these problems. The Foundation for Christian Economics' finances became so unsound that, in late 1932, business manager George Anderson urged Pelley to resuscitate his moribund short-story career. This plan had limited success.[25]

Pelley's writings and lectures from this period represent a formidable, albeit flawed, theology. He read widely in metaphysics, and his Liberation Doctrine possesses a clear spiritualist undergirding. Upon this foundation Pelley added layers of Theosophy, Rosicrucianism, pyramidism, Jainism, and harmonialism, all topped with a peculiar Christocentric millenarianism. Claiming all his writings were dictated to him clairaudiently by "Masters," Pelley declared that his religious system reconciled creationism with evolution, free will with predestination, and Christ with eastern teachings.[26]

Pelley posited three significant forces in the universe. First and foremost was the Universal Spirit, "from which all things proceed and which is of all things the substance." Second was the Spirit of the Group, responsible for animating all the lower forms of creation. Finally, there was man, consisting of mind, body, and soul. The "Divine Mind" created every soul twenty-eight million years ago. Pelley noted that "there is now in each human soul a separate and distinct development of the Universal Spirit which has a body for expression and which is yet able to be aware of its kinship with Divine Essence, [so that] there must be an instrument for this awareness, and this instrument is Mind."[27]

Pelley's system included the Christian God, but only as one god among many. While he (and to Pelley God was always "he") may meet in council with other gods, God was a very old spirit living on a distant planet who was responsible for our solar system. While souls were not directly accountable to him, the Great Avatar (Jesus) visited God for instruction. Pelley noted that there was "no God in the sense in which the mortal theologian uses the term . . . [because] to name and personify Infinite Spirit would be to limit It."[28]

Pelley's theology was also Christocentric. He noted that Christ was spirit made "manifest for the moment." His status as "Pure Spirit" was significant, as "Spirit is the one Law and Force and Harmony that is Love." Pelley staunchly maintained that he was a Christian (and that Jesus dictated messages directly to him), but that his beliefs must be separated from the "man-made dogma" termed religion that men "ignorant of these great psychical fundamentals" had developed since Christ's death. Like the sixteenth-century cleric Thomas Müntzer before him, Pelley had little use for the "Bible thieves" who, for their own ends, buried the truth that Christ was "the greatest psychic who ever trod the earth" and who corrupted his teachings. Although the New Testament had been corrupted for materialistic ends, Pelley considered it far superior to the Old Testament. He noted that the Old Testament "is the record of the lives and works of the Negative Introvert Element in the human race, the effeminate manifestation of human nature in the social state, the New Testament is the record of the lives and works of the Positive Extrovert Element, the masculine exposition of aggressive and constructive spiritual accomplishment." Pelley believed it was his responsibility to instruct humanity in an accurate understanding of this "Positive Extrovert Element." Once the truth was disclosed, the true orthodoxy of Pelley's version of Christianity would be revealed.[29]

According to Pelley, in the beginning there was only Holy Spirit (or Consciousness). The solar system was made "for purposes of Love by Vibration." This Love was an attempt by Holy Spirit to comprehend its own limitless existence. Matter, then, was a corruption of Pure Spirit intended only as a learning tool. Ultimately all matter (including those fragments of Spirit known as souls) would revert to pure Spirit.[30] There were numerous universes, each with its own gods and conscious life forms. These systems all followed a similar evolutionary pattern, however. Initially, life on each planet was vegetable (assisted by Over-Spirit, or the region's god). Then lower animals developed with the assistance of Group Spirit. Planets eventually evolved human forms and, ultimately, purely spiritual beings.[31]

Pelley believed human life on Earth had developed in a particularly unusual manner. One group of souls in another planetary system, Sirius, migrated to Earth thirty to fifty million years ago. These "star guests" incarnated in certain animal forms. Initially they incarnated in a creature form with the body of a lion and the head of an eagle (the Sphinx is a tribute to this form). In lion form procreation was by thought. The "guests," however, switched to an ape-like body, causing the difference between human and primate "species." This shift to ape form led matter to become primates' "fetish and shibboleth," and they lost control over "thought-generation." They then "gradually became the races of man as society now recognizes them." Believing his system reconciled creationism with evolution, Pelley posited that the Genesis "daughters of men" were apes, and the "Sons of God" were "star guests." Hence, man was "half-monkey and half-angel," and the missing link had not been discovered because it was spiritual, not biological.[32]

Pelley argued that this type of creation also explained religion on Earth. The mysteries and apparent falsehoods of Christian scripture made sense once one understood that extraterrestrial material was both involved and forgotten. He noted that man built his incomplete faith in gods out of his longing for the "spiritual home from which so many long eons before he had started out on this cosmic journey." Pelley also posited that following an erroneous, established form of Christianity—Roman Catholicism, for example—indicated a very young soul.[33]

This evolutionary system also explained the different types of people on Earth. According to Pelley there were three castes of mortal life on this planet. At the bottom of the spectrum were the beast-progeny of the ape-mothers. Above them were the reincarnated spirits from the original Sirian migration. And, finally, there were the Goodly Company, the 144,000 souls who followed the Great Avatar here to promote his teachings and put humanity on the path of righteousness.[34]

At the heart of Pelley's theories on humanity was the concept of reincarnation (as he noted, "Death is Liberation"). He declared that each soul was reincarnated on Earth approximately every five hundred years. Between these incarnations was a period of "rest and refreshment upon the so-called Planes of Thought." On these astral planes a soul's last earthly incarnation was reviewed within the context of its entire "soul history." As each "Spirit Particle" achieved adulthood (on Earth) it was exposed to temptations; its response to tests determined the soul's next earthly incarnation. The return to "Earth-Life" was done at the "recommendation of those who no longer are obliged to go back."[35]

The underlying assumption was that souls would continue to

progress by following righteousness and "Light" in earthly incarnations until they achieved satisfactory spiritual development. While a soul's karma was cataloged during every earthly existence, souls had free will in deciding whether or not they would live proper lives. However, all souls were aware of the inevitable consequences of following the forces of darkness on Earth, thereby adding elements of predestination to the system.

Every incarnation, then, was to be a learning experience, one guided by the Goodly Company. Some souls, however, did not progress and continually gravitated toward darkness. For some this was a product of a continued attachment to their animal ancestry (the "Mark of the Beast"). Although he never fully explained why this occurred, Pelley posited that some souls stopped evolving and slowly reappeared as grosser, uglier, and stupider persons who became "mass antagonists of those who have not defaulted but are developing and mounting steadily." The demons of scripture were examples of these "crazy souls." Other souls who gravitated toward darkness simply became part of the cosmos and suffered identity extinction.[36]

Eventually souls, having learned all they could from earthly existence, transcended material bodies and lived solely on the astral planes, with a select few progressing to the point of godhead. Never particularly thorough or consistent in his teachings, Pelley was especially unclear concerning this process. He wrote voluminously on the reality of reincarnation and detailed life on the higher planes "Beyond the Veil," but Pelley never fully explained how or when this leap to spirit form occurred. His depictions of these higher planes did not outline which planes different types of people (in terms of spiritual development) reached upon death and how progress was made from one astral sphere to the next. Also, the number of reincarnations it took to get to particular planes, and why souls would willingly stop reincarnating to begin spirit life on a lower plane rather than reincarnate on Earth again to learn more and go to a higher sphere, remained vague.[37]

Regardless of how a soul eventually reached the higher planes, Pelley echoed common spiritualist teachings in his writings on higher levels of existence. Pelley's spheres, although he never specified where they were located, seemed to have a basic geographical component related to their proximity to Earth. On the First Sphere dwelled the "earth-Bound" spirits. Comparable to the Roman Catholic notion of Purgatory or Swedenborg's "The Hells," this plane bore no vegetation and existed in "almost total darkness." Vile people lived here, many of whom, because of their closeness to the earth, communicated with living friends or relatives and usually gave them bad information about life after death, as the disincarnated did not know what they were talking about. For example, Pelley argued that information received through ouija boards typically came from this low plane and was, therefore, unreliable.[38]

The Second Sphere was slightly better. Those dwelling here were the ignorant and weak of prior earthly incarnations. This sphere possessed more light that the First and better opportunities for progress to higher spheres. Still, psychically received information from this plane was suspect.

Souls that landed on the Third Sphere encountered a world similar to a purified version of Earth. The great mass of ordinary people, neither bad nor good, started from this plane. Pelley determined, after studying Sir Oliver Lodge's books, that the English spiritualist's son Raymond communicated from the Third Sphere. Progress upward from this plane was relatively easy, as most of the souls here contained inherent goodness. In order to ease the shock of leaving material existence behind, the Third Sphere (called by Pelley and most spiritualists "Summerland") was very "earth-like" and life on it resembled life there. On this plane everyone appeared to be about thirty years old and lived in a world of sunshine and happiness. There was no marriage in "Summerland," but souls paired off in purely spiritual "harmonious unions."[39]

The best mortals began on even higher levels. Pelley believed he visited the Seventh Sphere during his "seven minutes" experience. Masters, who occasionally traveled down to lower spheres and to Earth to assist other souls, dwelled on the Ninth and Tenth Spheres and possessed "a serene and lovely countenance, superb beauty and dignity, and a brilliance dazzling to the eyes."[40]

Pelley's promotion of advanced souls communicating (and visiting) with mortals demonstrates a familiarity with the doctrines of Theosophy. Although Pelley steadfastly refused to admit that his teachings came from any source other than clairaudient messages, he did admit his familiarity with Theosophical writings. While decrying their relegated status of Christ, Pelley noted that "the Theosophists are nearest to the true facts about the forces operating behind life of any of the so-called theological creeds or sects."[41]

Established by Russian émigré Helena P. Blavatsky (HPB) and Henry S. Olcott in 1875, Theosophy became the most successful occult system in American history. Blavatsky's bombastic writings attracted thousands of followers in America, India, and Europe. Like Pelley she claimed that her writings came to her through messages received from Ascended Masters. Blavatsky's system was a syncretic blending of Hinduism, Buddhism, Christianity, spiritualism, Egyptian Hermeticism, Kabbalism, and occultism. Theosophy is generally Buddhist and Hindu in doctrine and Christian in morality. Her cosmology outlined the development of seven root-races of humanity, each with seven subroots. These human forms (d)evolved from a purely spiritual form to a material one, with the ultimate, emanationist end of returning to immaterialism. Like Pelley, Theosophists promoted evolution, karma, reincarnation, and after-death states.[42]

Pelley's debt to Theosophy cannot be underestimated, yet he frequently decried Blavatsky's contention that Jesus represented simply one of many equally important Ascended Masters. Although at least two Theosophical splinter groups developed a Christocentric cosmology not unlike Pelley's system, Pelley never mentioned either Rudolf Steiner's Anthroposophical Society or the Arcane School of Alice Bailey in his writings. Given Pelley's voluminous appetite for metaphysical books (and the esoteric circles he moved in), it seems highly unlikely that he did not possess at least a rudimentary knowledge of these groups, particularly Bailey's group, which (like the Theosophists) was active in Los Angeles during the 1920s. Pelley's silence regarding these groups may have been an attempt to separate his movement from two theologies so similar to his own beliefs (and potentially capable of siphoning off Liberation followers).[43]

Pelley, like many other esoteric writers of the period, also borrowed the notion of ancient, advanced civilizations from the Theosophists (and buttressed these beliefs with "evidence" from the works of Isaac Newton

Vail). He posited that global cataclysms resulted in the destruction of highly developed societies in Atlantis and Lemuria. According to Theosophical teachings, Lemuria housed the third root-race (the first race to possess physical bodies, reproduce sexually, and bear responsibility for good and evil), while the fourth root-race, the last remnant of whom perished a few thousand years ago, called Atlantis home. The Atlantians are especially significant to Theosophists because they were the alleged composers of the "Stanzas of Dyzan," the book of knowledge upon which all world religions were based.[44]

For Pelley tangible proof of the existence of these ancient civilizations could be found by studying the time line preserved in the Great Pyramid of Giza. Pyramidists believe the passageway from the pyramid's entrance to the king's chamber is a prophetic account of the history of humanity. They discern the course of human history by dividing this time line into "pyramid" inches. The "pyramid" inch, slightly larger than the English inch, is one five-hundred-millionth of the earth's axis. Using this measurement, the pyramidists determined that the time line runs from 2624 B.C. to A.D. 2001. For most of its course the time line is one inch per year, but, at the year 1909, it becomes one inch per month, thereby giving even more specific prophetic messages. Although pyramidism reaches back into the nineteenth century, Pelley developed his ideas on the matter from David Davidson, pyramidism's leading twentieth-century proponent. Pelley's views on the Great Pyramid were taken almost verbatim from Davidson's writings.[45]

Pelley's support for Davidson's theories derived in part from the pyramidist's claim that May 29, 1928, represented a significant date in human history. This, of course, was the night of Pelley's "seven minutes in eternity." Following this lead, Pelley promoted the idea that this date began the "Time of Tribulation," which would end on September 16, 1936. Pelley placed great significance upon these dates, as well as several other "pyramid dates," such as January 31, 1933 (the day Hitler took power), August 20, 1953 (the potential end of the Piscean Age), and September 17, 2001. Pelley believed the 2001 date denoted the Second Coming of Christ or, as Davidson declared, "the final cleansing of the whole world for the full extension of the Kingdom of Heaven to all the earth."[46]

Throughout his career, Pelley steadfastly maintained his belief in the imminent return of Christ. His writings frequently alluded to the approaching Armageddon and the need for the godly to prepare. Bolstering his pyramidist theories with astrological "evidence," Pelley posited that the rapidly closing Piscean Age and the impending dawn of the Age of Aquarius heralded the Second Coming.

As John Werly has noted, a deep current of millenarianism ran through Pelley's career. Despite fleeting (and not surprising) inconsistencies in his writings, Pelley clearly demonstrated a pre-millennialist strain of millenarianism. Pre-millennialists hold that Christ's return will precede the creation of the millennium, or Kingdom of God, and he will personally rule the earth for a thousand years. Pre-millennialists, then, stress both immediate personal purification and vigorous proselytizing to prepare for Christ's imminent return. Typically less emotionally charged in their rhetoric, post-millennialists believe Christ's Second Coming will occur only after godly men establish a thousand years of paradise on Earth to welcome his return. Given his increasing concern over the condition of human society, it is not surprising that Pelley, troubled by changing social mores and economic dislocation, adopted the pessimistic, pre-millenarian version of millennialism, which holds that conditions on Earth will become increasingly nightmarish before Christ's return.[47]

Pelley's apocalyptic faith helped propel his attacks on existing churches. His constant claims that early church fathers corrupted the true teachings of Christ underpinned his assaults on faulty belief systems and ecclesiastical structures. Fearing the imminent return of Christ, Pelley felt compelled to exhort Christians to turn their backs on these ungodly churches and follow the righteous path, as determined, of course, by the Liberation chief.[48]

Pelley believed the worsening conditions around him demonstrated the ever-present existence of the Antichrist. Like most millenarians, Pelley inhabited a world of absolutes, in which compromise was equated with damnation. Pelley's writings during the Liberation period frequently referred to a world in which the forces of Christ squared off with the minions of the Antichrist over the soul of humanity. Although Pelley later equated Jews, Communists, Franklin D. Roosevelt, and Bernard

Baruch with the Antichrist, his Liberation writings got no more specific than pitting the "Sons of Light" against "Dark Souls."[49]

Pelley's pyramidist beliefs undergirded his millenarian views. He believed that, in accordance with Davidson's reading of the Great Pyramid, the "Time of Tribulation" would end in 1936 (although the current economic depression would not abate until the mid-1960s) and be followed by a period, ending in 1953, in which Christ's faithful servants would receive protection from the forces of evil. To Pelley the end of the pyramid's time line, in 2001, held only one possible meaning: the dawn of the Age of Aquarius inaugurated by Christ's Second Coming. After Christ's victory, the forces of good could look forward to continued spiritual development and eventual immaterialism and godhood, while the "hosts of darkness" would descend into "Everlasting Namelessness."[50]

Pelley's dogged faith in the pyramid prophecy, however, raised something of a dilemma. With human history mapped out and the victory of the "Sons of Light" assured, vigorous attacks and calls for change seemed unnecessary. Liberation students needed only to continue their studies and wait for 2001; active faith or engagement with the enemy made no sense if success was predestined. As with most of his inconsistencies, Pelley chose to ignore this difficulty rather than drastically revamp his eschatology.

Throughout his public career Pelley always maintained a religious system to augment his political and economic teachings. He adopted different names for his theology and made minor alterations, but the basic beliefs remained unchanged. The Liberation doctrine served Pelley very well during the 1930s; it gave him a spiritual explanation for the evidence of tribulation he perceived around him. In 1932 Pelley began to explore the economic condition of America in the light of his religious beliefs. A truly profound development arose from Pelley's increased concern over secular affairs, and the shadowy "Dark Souls" gradually gained Jewish faces.

6

Silver Shirts
1933

ALTHOUGH WILLIAM DUDLEY PELLEY focused the bulk of his energies on spiritual matters at the dawn of the 1930s, he also exhibited concern over economics and politics. Believing the sinister "Dark Souls" running amok in American society may have played a role in his own problems, Pelley began exploring financial affairs in *New Liberator Weekly* in late 1931. Although these early explorations quickly subsided in the face of expanding Liberation Doctrine and the development of the Asheville enterprises, his ever-decreasing revenue led Pelley to turn again, in 1933, to secular affairs. This 1933 shift proved to be the decisive turn in Pelley's life. His adoption of an openly anti-Semitic political program effectively ended any chance of reigniting his fiction career and alienated many friends and followers. Pelley clearly understood that such a move to the racist right meant, as William H. Schmaltz has noted, "there would be no turning back once such a venture began; traditional employment would be difficult to find if not impossible." Already pushed to the wall financially, Pelley felt that he had nothing left to lose. And with Liberation Doctrine providing explanations for the terrible events unfolding around him, Pelley undoubtedly believed that he must publicize the truth as part of his responsibilities as a religious leader.[1]

Pelley's political writings from early in the decade exhibit his long-standing concerns over Communism but do not explicitly refer to Jews. Still, these articles present the basic tenets of his anti-Semitic worldview in embryonic form. Pelley warned *New Liberator Weekly* readers that the

"Dark Souls" were marshaling Communist forces, under the guise of "peaceful hunger and non-employment" demonstrators, to march on American cities, thereby bringing the government to a standstill. These Communist elements worked in concert with "vast international financial groups" to control the economic and political life of the United States.[2]

This strange combination of Communism and international finance remained a lynchpin of Pelley's political thought throughout the 1930s. He maintained that the Communist hordes were but the visible vanguard of the "money barons" who possessed the "Mark of the Beast." Beyond the inherent inconsistencies of linking two groups in obvious conflict, Pelley's reliance on pyramid prophecy also raised the conveniently ignored problem of predestination. If, as he noted, the rising tide of events "fit perfectly into the Cosmic Plan," active opposition seemed pointless.[3]

Although Pelley did not specifically tie Jews to Communism and manipulative finance at this point (as he would later), he clearly implied the connection. Pelley noted that "the brains and brawn that have made America great [are] the Celts, the Scots, the clean-blooded Germans, the Anglo-Saxons." These backbone elements "who were born here, who come from Aryan, nordic blood, who uniformly worship the One Father and affinity idea of His Son, Jesus the Christ . . . [no longer] own their nation." While Pelley never mentioned the Jews by name, in answer to the rhetorical question "what can be done by the individual to save civilization," he advised his followers to start by reading Nesta Webster's anti-Semitic diatribe *World Revolution* and Albert Wiggam's eugenics classic *The Fruit of the Family Tree*.[4]

In 1933 Pelley's increasing distress over his own plight finally boiled over into open anti-Semitism. Angered over his inability to establish financial security, Pelley sought out a convenient scapegoat. Given his earlier warnings over Jewish machinations, Pelley's adoption of anti-Semitism could serve as a handy explanation for his own problems. His oracle also contributed to this stance. Pelley asserted that he received a clairaudient message that he should create a paramilitary organization immediately after an unknown house painter became chancellor of Germany. Heeding this rather dubious inspiration, Pelley established the

Silver Legion of America on January 31, 1933, observing that "the rise of Adolph [*sic*] Hitler to the German Chancellorship, with an immediate exodus of Hebrews from Germany, supplied the key that unlocked a staggering sequence in my own progression."[5]

Despite his claims of oracular advice, Pelley's decision to support Hitler most likely derived from a late 1932 meeting with Paul Lillienfield-Toal of the North German Lloyd shipping line. Lillienfield-Toal presciently predicted Hitler's rise to power and so advised Pelley. Pelley maintained a long relationship with the German, who eventually became the Silver Shirt chief's "foreign adjunct."

The creation of the Silver Legion benefited immensely from the prior establishment of Pelley's operations in North Carolina. He simply converted his spiritualist organization into a paramilitary political group with religious underpinnings. Pelley dissolved the League for the Liberation; Galahad College became the Liberation Fellowship; and *New Liberator Weekly* became *Liberation,* the official organ of the Silver Legion. Pelley's new publication was subsequently dubbed "the most pro-Nazi and racist publication in the United States."[6]

To generate the Legion's initial membership, Pelley bombarded his mailing list with announcements concerning the new group. He attempted to convince his followers that the Legion represented merely a more active, militant version of the League for the Liberation. Pelley maintained that the Legion would preserve the religious teachings of the League, but the addition of open anti-Semitism to the prior group's esoteric Christianity alienated many supporters. Fortunately for Pelley, the remnants of the League provided enough support to continue Legion operations until new followers began joining.[7]

As with the earlier League for the Liberation, Pelley outlined a grandiose plan for the Silver Legion. The Legion was to be headed by the national commander (Pelley), a treasurer, and a secretary. Pelley was to be assisted by the General Staff, consisting of the chief, the chamberlain, the quartermaster, the sheriff, and the censor. Elected for ten-year terms, the General Staff possessed the authority to appoint Divisional Executive and Local Executive Staffs. The Legion maintained its headquarters in Asheville and divided administrative duties, handled by the Divisional

Executive Staff (DES), into nine divisions. Each DES was presided over by a Divisional Commanding Officer, assisted by a treasurer and clerk. Although answerable to officials at the national headquarters, each division maintained Departments of Local Posts, Silver Rangers, Industrial Relations, Junior Activities, and Foreign Affiliates. The Silver Rangers, consisting of paramilitary bands of one hundred "actionists," would, in particular, cause Pelley future difficulties.[8]

Anticipating that the Legion would serve as the foundation of a new theocratic state, Pelley also created departments to handle specific issues, including Public Enlightenment, Patriotic Probity, Crime Erasement, and Public Morals and Mercy. The Department of Public Morals and Mercy was seen by Pelley as especially important as it would be in charge of placing all "vagabonds" in concentration centers, censoring the press, and arresting persons responsible for motion pictures that depicted violence.[9]

Membership in the Legion was open to all, save Jews and Blacks, over the age of eighteen who could afford the $10 annual dues and $6 for a uniform. Prospective members submitted a photograph and personal information, including racial heritage, military experience, financial records, and the exact hour and minute of birth, and signed a document agreeing to abide by the organization's principles. These "Christian American Patriots" pledged to "respect and sustain the sanctity of the Christian Ideal, to nurture the moral tradition in Civic, Domestic and Spiritual life and the culture of the wholesome, natural and inspirational in Art, Literature, Music and Drama; to adulate and revere an aristocracy of Intellect, Talent and Characterful Purpose in the Body Politic; to sponsor and acclaim aggressive ideals and pride of Craftsmanship rather than the golden serpent of profit, that the lowliest individual may aspire to a life of fullest flower; to exalt Patriotism and Pride of Race, and in the interest of progress and evolution, to recognize the integrity of every nation and seek to perceive his place in the Fellowship of Peoples."[10]

Because of their distinctive uniforms, Legion members became known to friend and foe alike as the Silver Shirts. Their outfits consisted of leggings, blue corduroy pants, a tie with the individual's personal membership number stamped on it, and a silver shirt with a scarlet "L" stitched to the breast. The "L" signified love, loyalty, and liberation. The letter was also found on the Legion's otherwise solid white flag. For the Legion's weapon Pelley chose the "Scourge of Cords, with which Christ drove forth the money-changers from the Temple" as it was "a doughty weapon that will withstand rough usage." The adoption of a uniform and name specified by color of attire was a conscious decision on Pelley's part to connect his organization to the Nazi and fascist "shirt" movements in Europe—a connection his critics quickly seized upon.[11]

New recruits attended nine weekly indoctrination meetings. Local Councils of Safety directed the proceedings at these meetings. The recruits received instruction on the threat of Jewish Communism and their responsibilities as Christian patriots. The bulk of these nine meetings was discussions of the "four primers" with which all Silver Shirts must be familiar: the anti-Semitic standards *The Hidden Empire* and *The Protocols of the Learned Elders of Zion* and two Pelley works. The Pelley writings, *The President Knows* and *No More Hunger,* outlined the theocratic (or "Christ Democracy") state the Silver Shirt chief hoped to create in the United States.[12]

No More Hunger detailed Pelley's program for establishing the Christian Commonwealth. With moderate alteration, Pelley maintained this governmental plan, like his religious system, throughout his public career. The Commonwealth, then, should be considered one of the twin pillars of Pelley's thought (Liberation/Soulcraft doctrine is the other). He never let the book go out of print during his lifetime and claimed it had sold over eighty thousand copies by the early 1950s.[13]

Pelley claimed that the Commonwealth was "a social system that is neither Capitalism, Socialism, Fascism, or Communism." In fact, the Commonwealth blended elements of all these ideas into a composite not unlike the ideas expressed by his adolescent hero Edward Bellamy and the iconoclastic Populist-Social Gospeler Richard T. Ely. The system meshed a theocratic, corporate state; centralized production control of government-owned industry; civil service-style employment protection with private ownership of personal property; and an all-encompassing social welfare program.

To assuage fears that he planned to overthrow the government (concerns easily deduced from his more vitriolic writings), Pelley staunchly maintained that the Commonwealth was consistent with the Constitution. Pelley claimed that the sheer rationality of the Commonwealth made its benefits obvious to all Christian Americans. Once all gained knowledge of the plan, it could be put into effect immediately and without "physical violence." According to Pelley, the plan was economic, not political. Therefore, all current political structures and offices would continue to exist. Only those involved in the "present Moscow-inspired federal bureaucracy" need fear losing their jobs.[14]

To insure maximum state efficiency, somewhat contradictorily, a vast Department of Commerce would be created. This agency would manage all importing, exporting, and domestic economic activities. As all means of production belonged to the Commonwealth, Commerce officials would oversee all manufacturing, labor assignments, and business transactions. To guarantee an adequate supply of goods, annual surveys and inventories were mandated.[15]

As part of their citizenship rights, all Americans would be stockholders in the corporate state. Each "native-born citizen of proper racial qualifications" received one share of common stock. This entitled the citizen to the franchise and a guaranteed annual income. Pelley claimed that citizens could also look forward to deriving dividends from stock ownership, but, as the Commonwealth system eliminated capitalist "profiteering," it was unclear how this would occur. By undertaking particularly beneficial endeavors for the state, individuals could also obtain merit stocks, redeemable for goods and services beyond the regular annual income.[16]

To acquire proper homes (and avoid rapacious rent-gouging), citizens earned realty stock. Like Frederick Jackson Turner, Pelley decried the ill effects of the closing of the American frontier, and, like many social reformers, including Ely, he feared the corrupting influences of urban areas. Therefore, he promoted the razing of congested cities and the elimination of apartment complexes, and he advocated spreading the populace out to give citizens adequate natural space. To ensure these social advances, realty stock guaranteed citizens the resources to purchase their own homes. The state owned all real estate but willingly sold land to citizens at reasonable prices, utilizing the freely granted realty stocks and a paycheck direct-withdrawal system.[17]

The Commonwealth plan outlined a rigid financial system for every American. Under the plan all citizens would receive checking accounts at the Commonwealth Bank (as part of their status as "stock holders in the sovereign corporation"). With the adoption of this system, paper money would disappear. To prevent hoarding and its concomitant creation of predatory wealth, all bank balances were to be canceled at the end of each year. For the same reasons, all inheritance, with the exception of family homes, was prohibited. Pelley hoped this system would eliminate "money crimes" (kidnapping, embezzlement, robbery), usury, advertising, private legal practices, and trade unions.[18]

Pelley's monetary system was derived from his close reading of Frederick Soddy's *Wealth, Virtual Wealth, and Debt*. Soddy, like Pelley, believed banking (defined as "the secret printing of money") was the root of all modern problems. He advocated issuance of "energy-certificates" (instead of Pelley's checks) to eliminate the "universal conspiracy" of private banking. While Soddy remained rather nonspecific as to the culprits behind the conspiracy, he was willing to entertain theories that Jews played a part. Pelley relied very heavily on Soddy's works for most of his career.[19]

The amount each citizen received in his or her bank account varied depending upon the nature of the citizen's work, but, like the Social Credit program promoted by Clifford H. Douglas, every citizen was entitled to an income. Each American would receive at least $1,000 per year (in Commonwealth parlance this was 1-Q status), which Pelley thought was sufficient for one to live comfortably. Even those who steadfastly refused to work were guaranteed this amount. Pelley hoped this income would encourage struggling young artists to follow their muses without having to scramble to feed themselves.[20]

This protection from starvation also reflected Pelley's religious beliefs, and again reflected Richard T. Ely's influence on his thought. Because all souls reincarnate in human existence to learn life-lessons and progress in spiritual development, they should be given freedom from basic needs to focus on matters of more cosmic significance. Also, protection from the "Hunger System" reflected the Christian value that all citizens had the "right and liberty . . . to live . . . devoid of barbaric duress from physical want."[21]

The system also placed limits on how much an individual could earn.

The Commonwealth plan prevented any personal income of more than $100,000 per year (10-Q). Those achieving this income level did so only because of their hard work and dedication to the state, with particularly high Q ratings going to those who generated national wealth from raw materials; favoritism and patronage would no longer factor into financial success. The particularly industrious might also obtain special merit and realty "stocks." Particularly meritorious citizens might achieve higher ratings, but these were purely ceremonial tributes from a grateful state.[22]

These material benefits, however, did not apply to all residents of the United States. Not surprisingly, women did not receive an equal status. Pelley believed that the guarantee of 1-Q status would prevent prostitution and the need for women to stay married to abusive husbands, but, despite his protestations that the Commonwealth promoted the "new status of Womanhood Ennobled," motherhood and maintenance of a proper home for their spouses remained the primary roles for women under the plan.[23]

Still, women fared better than others under the Commonwealth. Pelley feared the social effects of giving "the great slovenly mass of indolent and illiterate" Blacks the freedoms granted to others under the plan. He believed black men's overriding impulse was sexual relations with white women. Miscegenation led to "mongrelized" beings who actually slid downward in spiritual attainment. Therefore, like John C. Calhoun before him, Pelley advocated that all Blacks be made wards of the state and closely supervised, while providing a vast supply of domestic servants.[24]

The regulation of Blacks, however, paled in significance to the "one problem"—whether "Christian tenets could survive assault from the atheists of Judah." The creation of a free, Christian state hinged upon the elimination of the Jewish threat. Although the Commonwealth financial system guaranteed an end to Jewish monetary schemes, their mere presence portended other machinations. To eliminate this threat, all Jews would be required to live in one city per state, known as "Beth Havens." Commonwealth forces, directed by the Secretary of Jewry, would guarantee personal safety and full autonomy within these ghettos, but Jews who strayed from their confines risked execution.[25]

To reinforce the validity of the Commonwealth program, Pelley bolstered his assertions of its inherent efficiency with claims of cosmic significance. Pelley scaled back his esoteric teachings after establishing the Silver Shirts, but religious issues remained an aspect of the group's fundamental beliefs. He argued that the Silver Legion's Commonwealth plan was consistent with Christ's social teachings, the prophetic time line of the Great Pyramid, and clairaudient messages he received concerning the importance of the "Fifth Root race in the United States." Unlike descriptions of "Utopia thought out in any one man's brain," the Commonwealth "is GOING to happen" as part of God's plan for humanity. Pelley noted that the Commonwealth, "in the practical sense, . . .means the principles of Christ substituted for the civic precepts and practices of Lucifer." [26]

Although the mixture of spiritualism, economics, and Christianity promoted by the Silver Shirts represented a continuation of Pelley's teachings from the beginning of the decade, the Legion's public admiration of Adolf Hitler and open promotion of anti-Semitism came as a shock to many of his longtime followers. Pelley's prior enigmatic references to "Dark Souls" fit into his Manichaean cosmology without singling out any particular group as minions of Satan. With the creation of the Silver Shirts, however, Pelley permanently altered his public teachings to connect Jews with the "Dark Souls." This shift polarized Liberation students, and 40 percent of Pelley's pre-Legion followers deserted him. [27]

Convinced of the vast importance of his anti-Semitic pronouncements, Pelley refused to allow these defections to thwart his campaign. Even attempts by personal confidants such as business manager George S. Anderson failed to dissuade Pelley from launching the paramilitary Legion or his anti-Jewish attacks. Pelley, however, perceived the potential of an anti-Semitic program far better than his wavering Liberation students. The rabidly anti-Jewish Silver Shirts provided him with considerably more followers (and notoriety) than the League for the Liberation ever did. While some contemporary critics suggested Pelley adopted his anti-Semitic stance solely to derive income from his new supporters, there is no evidence to support the notion that he embraced his public anti-Jew stance for any reason other than a deep personal hatred.

In his work with the Silver Shirts, Pelley made Judaism the nation's most significant issue. His strident attacks on Jews mixed history, biology, and religion into a potent compound of hate that, as Geoffrey S. Smith has noted, "often verged on autism." Like his religious system, Pelley's anti-Semitic program was long on complexity and pseudoscholarship and short on coherence and consistency.[28]

Central to Pelley's campaign was the belief that Jews represented a distinct race. Echoing Lothrop Stoddard, Pelley argued that scientists had proven Jews were a "mongoloid-oriental" race. As Donnell Portzline has noted, the establishment of this blood theory allowed Pelley to ascribe to Jews whatever characteristics he desired. Their "other" status provided Pelley with a handy means of heaping accusations on American Jews without factual evidence or consideration of their rights. Repeating the racial views of Madison Grant, Pelley argued that Jews did not deserve the status of American citizenship.[29]

Pelley's "scientific" distrust of the Jews, however, served only as supportive evidence for the religious tenets of his anti-Semitic program. The "Dark Soul" Jews possessed the literal "Mark of the Beast" as a result of their descent from the original progeny of the "beast-mothers." Held over from Liberation Doctrine was Pelley's "star guests" cosmological blend of spiritualist Theosophy and millennial Christianity. Not surprisingly, Pelley's conflation created inconsistencies in his racial explanation of Jews. Seemingly oblivious of his own evolutionary scheme, Pelley occasionally explained the presence of Jews as part of God's cosmic scheme.[30]

Pelley never found a satisfactory explanation for the presence of Jews. When holding that they were part of God's cosmic plan, he explained that "it is an inexorable Law of Cosmos that these forces of destruction and debauchery are only permitted to exist in an educational capacity, and for the purpose of exhibiting to frail and underdeveloped mortals the fallacy of their worth." At times he favored an explanation more in line with Liberation Doctrine, but still displayed marked inconsistency. Along with the "beast-mother theory," Pelley occasionally posited that Jews were a "conglomerate" people developed from crossings of the yellow and black races.[31]

In keeping with his Liberation Doctrine views on evolution, Pelley found the belief in Jews as the "chosen people" untenable. He claimed it was simply a Jewish plot to establish their false superiority to Gentiles; the Jewish "tribal deity" deserved no attention from true Christians.

Conscious of their debased nature, Jews launched the "chosen people" publicity campaign in order to justify their very existence, which Gentiles must combat. Pelley argued that "Christianity and anti-Semitism are synonymous." [32]

In defense of his stance that the Jews had no special place in the past, Pelley argued that Jesus Christ was not a Jew. He posited that Christ was "not a Judaist, or any other kind of a Hebrew, but a Galilean" descended from immigrant Gauls. According to Pelley, Christ actually hated the Jews for violating God's precepts and "drove the Jews out of the Temple with a whip of ropes." Pelley noted that Christ "looked Gentile, thought Gentile, acted Gentile, came from a Gentile province, talked Gentile, died with Gentile courage for a principle, and withal was the world's outstanding anti-Semite of all time." [33]

In response to his teachings, the Jews executed Christ. Like anti-Semites for centuries, then, Pelley buttressed his hatred of Jews with claims of their status as "Christ-killers." Further, to erase Christ's stance as an "outstanding Jew-baiter," Jews rewrote the New Testament to obscure his beliefs. Pelley claimed that, after diligent study, he had found 175,000 instances where Jews inserted false material into the Bible. [34]

The murder of Christ and the cloaking of his teachings were but the opening salvos in a vast Jewish program for worldwide domination. Pelley believed, in classic "paranoid style," that the Sanhedrin, as in Christ's time, still led the global Jewish conspiracy. This conspiracy, then, reached deep into the past and represented a formidable opponent for the righteous Silver Shirts to combat. To demonstrate the strength (and evil) of Jewish machinations, Pelley rewrote history to suit his beliefs. He claimed that the hidden hand of Judaism had been present in almost all global difficulties for thousands of years. [35]

Small in number and dispersed without a homeland, Jews were forced to work behind the scenes to further their program of world conquest. Central to this campaign would be manipulation of national economies. Pelley argued that Jews controlled banking and finance as a means of exerting their influence on politics and policy. With their dominance of the world's monetary supply, they could disrupt the economy if governments balked at adopting policies acceptable to Jewish "international bankers." If sufficiently angered, the Jews created depressions, which propelled Gentile suffering and, because they were the primary creditors, added to Jewish power.

Because of their vulnerability to the whims of ignorant masses, republics and democracies were particularly subservient to the Jews. Elected officials needed to keep the voters happy to stay in power; only by working in collusion with the Jewish "power-brokers" could they hope to maintain peace and prosperity. In this country, for example, Jews were "trying to make the United States of America their personal Jewtopia." [36]

Given the lack of governmental regulation, Jews could also promote their views, and control politicians, through newspapers. Even those newspapers not owned by Jews followed their dictates or faced the consequences of losing Jewish advertising dollars; hence the major media outlets could not be trusted. Only an authoritarian regime not answerable to the populace, such as the Christian Commonwealth, possessed the strength to buck Jewish decrees and operate outside the Sanhedrin's authority with impunity. [37]

Ever resourceful, the Jews created the "freakish racial despotism" of Communism as their main weapon for global domination. Pelley steadfastly maintained that Communism, which was "as old as Judaism," represented the most destructive aspect of the conspiracy. The Silver Shirt chief argued that the Communistic nature of Jews was eternal and explained attempts to control them in pharaonic Egypt—attempts only thwarted by the craftiness of Moses, who was "the Stalin of his day." He posited that Karl Marx (real name "Karl Henrich Mordecai"), Friedrich Engels, V. I. Lenin, and Leon Trotsky (real name "Laiber Davidovitch Bronstein") were all Jewish, and that the financier Jacob Schiff had bankrolled the Bolshevik Revolution. [38]

All Communist parties possessed Jewish leadership or figurehead "Jew stooges." Pelley believed that the USSR, as the homeland of "Jewish Bolshevism," served as the base of operations for a final Communist attack on Gentiles. He predicted that Russian-sponsored Communism would "utilize the downtrodden workers of the world to emancipate world Jewry from any further domination by the Gentiles and put the Jews in control of all Gentile world governments." [39]

The Jews also found other underhanded means of gaining control over Gentiles. Like modern extremists fearful of "brainwashing" from fluoride in their drinking water, Pelley displayed alarm over proposed Wassermann inoculations to combat syphilis, believing that the shots contained poison that weakened Christians. Illegal drugs also demonstrated the "hidden hand" of Judaism in corrupting Gentiles. For example, Pelley claimed that the Chinese opium trade only began with the arrival of "Baghdad Jew" Sir Victor Sassoon in Asia.⁴⁰

Owing to its decentralized structure, the United States was already a tool of the Jews. Pelley found American history littered with devastating events engineered by the Jews. Perhaps Pelley's most notorious revision of American history involved his promulgation of the "Franklin prophecy." Pelley claimed he had seen "missing" pages from the diary of Constitutional framer Charles C. Pinckney relating to Benjamin Franklin's views of Jews. According to Pelley, Franklin believed that "the Jews constituted a menace to the country" and should be barred from the United States, as they would undermine the government within two hundred years. Although numerous scholars immediately attacked the work as a blatant forgery (Charles A. Beard, for one, noted the unlikelihood of Franklin using the words "vampire" or "chit chat"), the "prophecy" continues to circulate on the extreme right.⁴¹

Pelley also developed a remarkably convoluted explanation of the Civil War. According to Pelley, the war began when Lionel Rothschild, fearing the potential power of an intact United States, sent his emissaries to "exploit the question of slavery," with Judah P. Benjamin serving as his point man. Lincoln, who hated the international bankers, began issuing paper money to break their power and, therefore, had to be killed (by the Jewish John Wilkes Booth). England and France, following Rothschild dictates, sided with the south, while Emperor Maximilian arrived in Mexico in 1864 with two hundred million francs provided by the Rothschilds to carry out their program of Western hemispheric domination. Benjamin Disraeli then worked out a deal by which Napoleon III could have Texas and Louisiana, with the Confederacy's consent, if he sent French troops against the Union. This plan was foiled at the last moment when America's great friend, the Russian czar, sent his fleets to New York and San Francisco and put them at Lincoln's disposal.⁴²

Pelley's Rothschild-inspired account of the Civil War found its most

significant adherent in Ezra Pound (a fact of which Pelley was probably
unaware). Pound scholar Leon Surette has suggested that the modernist
poet's support for anti-Semitism and fascism can be traced to his reading
of Pelley's Civil War article. Pound accepted Pelley's revisionist history
whole cloth, became a *Liberation* subscriber, and shortly thereafter began
investigating material on the "Jewish question." While their mutual anti-
Semitism partly explained Pound's support of the Silver Shirts, Pelley and
the poet also exhibited very similar economic views. Like Pelley, Pound
was very fond of the work of Clifford H. Douglas and Frederick Soddy.
Pound actually corresponded with Silver Shirt leaders for a period but did
not deal directly with Pelley.[43]

The pace of the Jewish conspiracy in this country, however, had escalated with the "unconstitutional" creation of the Federal Reserve Board
and the subsequent Bolshevik Revolution. The revolution was a signal to
Jews to step up their program of conquest. In this country President
Woodrow Wilson's Jewish advisors (Colonel Edward House loomed
large among them) hoodwinked the country into both involvement in
the World War and the creation of the League of Nations. Pelley argued
that the League served as the first step in the creation of "a world state for
the more proper and efficient jurisdiction of Jewry over the Gentile
Christendom." Level-headed American Christians headed off the danger
in time and kept the United States out of the League, but this served only
to inflame Jewish animosity toward America.[44]

Realizing the strength of American Gentiles, the Jews stepped up
their attacks on the United States. Pelley argued that Jews controlled Herbert Hoover and started the Great Depression (he urged "say it in your
dreams, the Jews are to blame") to rivet the final chains of tyranny upon
Christians. Although the conspiracy's chief minions in this country were
Bernard ("the uncrowned prince") Baruch and Felix Frankfurter, they
could not openly admit their control because of the "fiction" of American
democracy. Rather, the conspiracy operated through the authority of the
man Pelley and like-minded American extremists came to see as the arch-
enemy—Franklin D. Roosevelt, the first "Jewish" president.[45]

Hitler's rise to power in Germany and Roosevelt's New Deal in this
country, then, served as catalysts for the growth of American right-wing

extremism. Hitler proved to be a shining example of how to combat Jewish Communism, and Roosevelt's "socialist" New Deal and official recognition of the Soviet Union whipped many on the radical right into a froth. Pelley may have been one of the first to profit from the combination of militant anti-Semitism and Red-baiting, but he quickly found the country filled with other potential "American fuehrers" competing to attract followers.

7

Extremists
1934

WILLIAM DUDLEY PELLEY's creation of the Silver Shirts early in 1933 made him one of the first Americans to create an organization celebrating the work of Adolf Hitler. But Pelley was hardly alone in his adulation of the German chancellor. A number of American political leaders emerged waving the banner of economic fascism and Nazi anti-Semitism. With his peculiar mixture of spiritualism and extremism, Pelley carved out his own niche on the political right, but his dreams of creating a vast national movement were stunted by the proliferation of other right-wing organizations competing for a limited number of adherents (and dollars) during the Depression decade.

There is no consensus on a label for people promoting right-wing extremism during the 1930s. Their general agreement on issues of corporatism, Communism, militarism, and hatred for the "socialist" elements of the New Deal put most American rightists firmly in the fascist camp. The avowed anti-Semitism many promoted also placed them in line with Nazi Germany. However, their promotion of nationalism (and concomitant disgust with "Jewish" internationalism) made some American extremists uneasy about linking to European right-wingers as part of a global movement. Also, the Christian orientation of leaders such as Pelley and Gerald Winrod placed them in sharp contrast with the anti-Christian Third Reich.

This complicated situation has led scholars to adopt a number of descriptive terms for American extremists of the period. Donald S. Strong, for example, dubbed them members of "national radical revolutionary" anti-Semitic movements. While Strong's terminology is more informative than David H. Bennett's "quasi-fascists," Geoffrey Smith's "counter-subversives," or Leo Ribuffo's "Old Christian Right," the sheer unwieldiness of Strong's phrase makes it impractical for regular use.[1]

In the present study I will use the term "protofascist" to describe these groups. While the definition of this term is still hotly debated, it will be used here to describe the American extremists of the 1930s who espoused the beliefs listed above. I chose the term "fascist" rather than "Nazi" because of the Holocaust connotations associated with the Third Reich. Although virtually all the individuals discussed here were anti-Semites, none (including Pelley) advocated outright extermination of American Jews (the minuscule National Liberty Party was almost alone in promoting genocide). The current term "neo-Nazi" is probably accurate in this context, but its usage would be anachronistic. Hence, the Italian term, with its more muted form of anti-Semitism, has been adopted.

The few scholars who have undertaken extended studies of Pelley continue to disagree on a proper terminology for his beliefs. Donnell Portzline found the Silver Shirts to be little more than a carbon copy of European fascism and liberally applied that label to the group. John Werly, however, argued that Pelley's economic and religious systems were inimical to both Mussolini and Hitler and, therefore, he should be dubbed a "millenarian rightist." Pelley himself was happy to use both "fascist" and "Nazi." For a period the masthead of *Weekly Liberation* read: "Washington was a Fascist because he led an insurrection against tyranny, and Lincoln was a Nazi because his issue of greenbacks smashed the control of Jewish financiers."[2]

Regardless of the appellation given to them, Pelley and like-minded rightists benefited significantly from the economic dislocation of the 1930s. The inability of the federal government to answer the challenges of the Great Depression left many Americans frustrated and open to previously marginalized political ideologies. Seeming to offer solutions to the grinding impoverishment of the Depression (the substitution of strong-willed autocratic rule for impotent democracy) and convenient causes/scapegoats (Jews, liberals, Communists), American right-wingers formulated emotional appeals calculated to attract the disgruntled and dispossessed. Pelley and his ilk created a host of organizations that played upon the fears of Americans with surprising success. As Raymond Gram Swing noted in his pioneering study of American right-wingers, a collision of factors during the 1930s (governmental failure in the face of economic collapse and concomitant erosion of public confidence, the impression of rising support for Communism, and the declining status of America's middle class) propelled extremism. These era-specific factors melded with the strong nativist impulse of the previous decade and older remnants of Populist rhetoric decrying the power of "Wall Street" bankers and international financiers to create a contingent of domestic fascists.[3]

The massive economic upheaval of the 1930s made the rise of American fascism possible. With savings wiped out, at least 26 percent unemployment in 1933, and the gross national product plummeting by one-third in just five years, the Depression created a reservoir of anxiety and ill-will that demagogues of all stripes played upon. With President Herbert Hoover seemingly unable (or unwilling) to address the nation's difficulties, radical alternatives to democracy and capitalism offered extraordinary solutions to extraordinary difficulties. The groundswell of support for extremists at both ends of the political spectrum demonstrated both the dire economic conditions and the degree to which many Americans felt traditional political systems powerless to address their problems.[4]

American right-wingers attracted not only those searching for alternatives to constitutional democracy, but also those looking for means of combating the potential rise of Communism. Conservative Americans looked aghast at the wave of "hunger riots" during 1930–31 and the "Bonus Army" encamped in and around the national capital during the spring and summer of 1932. Reports of Communist support for these incidents heightened fears of a left-wing threat and rekindled memories of the unrest resulting in the postwar Red Scare. Rumors of Communist direct action might frighten, but they could be disputed. Extremists on the right, however, pointed to electoral gains as factual indicators of the "Red menace." By 1930 socialist candidates began achieving significant success in municipal and state elections and ended a decade-long decline in their popular support. In the 1932 presidential election, the Socialist and Communist presidential candidates together garnered almost one million votes. That was a small fraction of the number cast for Hoover and Franklin D. Roosevelt, but the significant gains over left-wing candidates' 1928 results provided fodder for right-wingers looking for evidence of a Communist insurgency. The government's official recognition of the Soviet regime in 1933 and "socialist" New Deal policies only buoyed support for these claims.[5]

Benito Mussolini's successes in Italy and Adolf Hitler's startling ascension to power in Germany served as models for American extremists with delusions of grandeur. Their images as uniformed autocrats reorganizing their nations with martial spirit fed the ambitions of men such as Pelley, who saw themselves as potential leaders of a reformed United States. Also, the European dictators' hatred of Communism (and Hitler's explicit anti-Semitism) made them heroes to much of the American right.

The development of American fascism was aided by the establishment of domestic organizations supported by Italy and Germany. In 1925 both the Fascist League of North America and the National Association of Teutonia were established in the United States. While the Italian-backed organization struggled to build a base of support in the 1920s and staggered toward inconsequentiality during the 1930s, the Teutonia Society served as the launching pad for a series of increasingly successful Nazi-oriented groups on this side of the Atlantic.

In 1932 those belonging to the Teutonia Society automatically became charter members of the American branch of the German Nazi Party, headed by Heinz Spanknoebel. Owing to concerns over the potential protests arising from the creation of an official political party in the United States, the group was reorganized in summer 1933 and renamed the Association of the Friends of the New Germany. A subsequent shake-up gave the group its most famous name, the Amerikadeutscher Volksbund (German-American Bund). The Bund served as a conduit between Nazi Germany and American right-wingers throughout the decade. Most domestic fascists, including Pelley, had connections to the Bund, and almost all gave the group at least grudging support.[6]

Although Hitler's rise to the chancellorship in 1933 spurred a number of individuals to organize, several of the leading domestic extremists of the 1930s had already established religious, economic, or political groups during the preceding decade. In 1925 Elmer Garner began publishing his anti-Semitic newspaper, the *Malvern Review,* and Gerald Winrod founded his Defenders of the Christian Faith. Two years later "espionage expert" Harry A. Jung of Chicago established the American Vigilant Intelligence Federation, an ostensibly private security outfit that specialized in attacking "Jewish-Bolshevik" trade unions. By the dawn of the 1930s the nation was littered with right-wing groups such as the American Patriots, the Paul Reveres, and the Crusaders for Economic Liberty (the White Shirts)—organizations that used Hitler as a spark to ignite their own anti-democratic, anti-Semitic campaigns in this country.[7]

Pelley, then, represented merely one of several like-minded leaders who established Hitler-inspired groups at roughly the same time. The spring of 1933 saw the creation not just of the Silver Shirts but also the White, Blue, and Khaki Shirts and the refocusing of older groups such as the Anglo-Saxon Federation, the Industrial Defense Association of Edward Hunter, and Winrod's Christian Defenders. By the end of that year more than one hundred domestic fascist groups were vying for attention.[8]

Pelley developed connections to a number of these extremist groups. He cultivated relationships with, among others, C. Leon de Aryan of *The Broom* magazine, American White Guard leader and convicted forger Henry D. Allen, the "Wichita Fuehrer" Gerald Winrod, Reverend Gerald L. K. Smith, Colonel Edward Emerson, Harry Jung, James True (the inventor of the patented "kike killer" billy club), Royal Scott Gulden of the Order of '76, and various Bund leaders. Always jealous of his own status, Pelley frequently quarreled with other right-wing leaders. Usually these friendships ended either when Pelley tried to "absorb" their organizations into his own or when his esoteric religious beliefs became too much for his compatriots to stomach. Pelley's relations with domestic extremists suffered a devastating blow when he refused to back the Union Party in 1936 and ran for president on his own Christian Party ticket.[9]

A representative example of Pelley's difficulties in dealing with other right wing leaders was his relationship with Gerald L. K. Smith. A highly active "nationalist" fundamentalist minister of the era, Smith had connections to Huey "Kingfish" Long, Father Francis Coughlin, and William Lemke. Pelley actually contracted Smith to organize a deep south outpost of the Silver Shirts in 1933; the two, however, rapidly turned on each other over finances and Pelley's spiritualist system. Smith then left Pelley's organization and began ingratiating himself to Long.[10]

The rise of protofascist groups led to a wave of articles in American newspapers and magazines. The overwhelming majority of such reports were highly critical of the startling development of domestic protofascism. Liberal media outlets gave the groups the most attention and usually ascribed their growth to one of three overlapping explanations: mentally disturbed leadership, confidence rackets, or German-backed "Nazitern" fronts.[11]

Even a cursory glance at Pelley's writing demonstrates that he held rather unusual beliefs. Hostile reporters readily latched onto his Liberation Doctrine as an example of Pelley's mental instability. Most early articles about Pelley also mentioned his "seven minutes in eternity" experience as further proof that the Silver Shirts were led by a madman. As Donald Strong calmly noted, "Silver Shirt leaders appear to be rather unstable persons," while Arthur Graham singled Pelley out as being "mentally broken."[12]

Pelley's spiritualist beliefs also led investigators to assume that the Silver Shirts served only as a money-making scheme. Believing that Pelley's religious teachings were merely a way to exploit the gullible, several reporters concluded that Pelley created the Silver Shirts as a way to bilk a different segment of the populace. Dubbing Pelley "a mysterious demagogue who promises to ennoble," writers linked him with such obvious frauds as Art J. Smith of the Khaki Shirts. Even Congress concluded that the Silver Shirts, like many of the new extremist groups, was a "petty racket."[13]

Despite Pelley's vocal championing of Hitler in early 1933, the Silver Shirts had no sustained contact with Nazi Germany until the middle of the decade, and even then he did not receive direct financial support. Still, reporters took Pelley's pronouncements as evidence of official connections between Pelley and Hitler. Pelley did nothing to correct these reports, believing they only increased his stature in extremist circles here and abroad. While Pelley's reputation among rightists may have improved by celebrating and imitating Hitler, it also gained the attention of the authorities. Concerned over these purported linkages between domestic fascists and Nazi Germany, various state and federal governmental agencies began investigating American extremists in 1934. This proved to be the beginning of a costly battle that would land many domestic Nazi sympathizers, including Pelley, in prison.[14]

Observers at the time also found it difficult to determine how many American extremists were active. Conflicting figures developed from the proliferation of extremist organizations and fascist leaders purposefully inflating membership numbers to appear stronger. Many of these new groups were of the "one member and a postal box" variety, and weeding them out from those with legitimate memberships proved difficult. As a result, reporters surveying this hazy landscape arrived at wildly disparate figures. Some investigators put the total number of domestic protofascist groups at no more than one hundred, while others cited more than eight hundred.[15]

Determining who joined these groups also proved problematic. Many commentators at the time believed that the extremist groups attracted followers just as disturbed as the leadership. Unwilling to concede that educated Americans might turn to anti-Semitism and authoritarianism, reporters, with little or no evidence, posited that protofascist followers were drawn from among the urban lower class and criminal elements. More recent scholarship places most members in the middle socioeconomic class, with a smaller proportion drawn from the lower class and an even smaller percentage from professional trades.[16]

The most comprehensive study of national Silver Shirt membership was undertaken by John Werly. Although Pelley dreamed of "a million Silver Shirts by 1939," total membership figures never approached that lofty number. The best estimates are that the group had approximately eight hundred members by mid-1933, with membership peaking at fifteen thousand in 1934–35 and then falling to five thousand by 1938. Additionally, the Silver Shirts had an estimated seventy-five thousand nonaffiliated sympathizers. At its zenith, then, the Silver Shirt Legion was among the largest of the militant domestic extremist groups and only slightly smaller than the Bund (which reached a membership of twenty-five thousand). While Pelley's membership paled in comparison to the number of followers attracted by Coughlin and Winrod, his "actionist" cadre, with their violent rhetoric, provided a far more visible threat than the "passive" supporters of those two theologians. As one commentator noted, the Silver Shirt Legion was the "most vocal, most wild-eyed, and in some ways most dangerous" of all extremist groups.[17]

Although the evidence is fragmentary, it appears that the Silver Shirts primarily attracted members of northern European background from across the socioeconomic spectrum. Studying surnames on membership rolls, Werly determined that the overwhelming percentage of Silver Shirts came from northern European backgrounds (with British and German names predominating). Nationally the group had almost equal numbers drawn from the lower and middle classes. Approximately 15 percent of members came to the Legion from professional backgrounds (most of these were physicians). Eighteen percent were women, who were allowed to attend regular Legion meetings but were designated as "Nurses" rather than Silver Shirt "Spartans."[18]

Although Pelley claimed Silver Shirt branches in all forty-eight states, this statement is no more accurate than his membership figures. By late spring 1933 local groups were organized in eight states. By the next year there were branches in twelve states. Eventually more or less active units organized in twenty-two states. However, membership was not evenly distributed among the states. The Silver Shirts were found predominantly in the Midwest (primarily Ohio, Minnesota, Michigan, Illinois, and Pennsylvania) and in the far West (Washington and California).[19]

The midwestern groups appear to have been strongest in urban, industrialized areas. For example, most members in Ohio and Pennsylvania resided in steel-producing cities. While membership rolls are nonexistent for most local midwestern branches, newspaper accounts of mass meetings attracting one hundred to three hundred people are common. In his study of Pennsylvania right-wingers, Philip Jenkins estimated two thousand active members in a variety of extremist groups in the Philadelphia area alone, with twenty thousand less-involved supporters.[20]

The Silver Shirt Legion in the Pacific Northwest has been studied in more detail. Karen Hoppes found sixteen hundred members spread throughout twenty-six local branches in Washington state. While some of the local units had only ten active members, those in larger, urban areas attracted more than four hundred active members. Hoppes found the membership in the Evergreen state, like that nationally, divided almost equally between the middle class and manual laborers. The Washington unit was among the largest in any single state and highly organized (with its base at the Silver Lodge in Redmond).[21]

Pelley was very proud of the Washington branch and visited the area frequently. However, he did the state organization no favor by feuding with some local leaders and shifting others to alternative positions. Pelley fell out with state leader Frank W. Clark over finances, leading Clark to establish his own National Liberty Party and to take a number of Silver Shirts with him. He replaced Clark with the indefatigable Roy T. Zachary, but, in a move that vitiated the Washington branch, he soon assigned Zachary to head the Christian Party. Zachary proved to be an excellent organizer, and Washington was the only state with Pelley on the ballot in the 1936 presidential election. However, the state unit suffered because of Zachary's inattention and was further weakened by Pelley's decision to relocate Zachary to the national headquarters in Asheville as Silver Shirt "field marshal." One of Pelley's most loyal followers, Zachary readily agreed to the move, even though it entailed significant financial difficulties for him. Zachary's successor, Orville W. Roundtree, was just as dedicated to Pelley and was equally efficient, but he desperately needed the assistance Zachary could have provided.[22]

Of all the large state organizations, California created the most problems for Pelley. The first Silver Shirt branch opened in Los Angeles in 1933 and met with surprising initial success, with statewide membership reaching a peak of three thousand in 1934. Pelley was so pleased with the progress in southern California that in February 1934 he moved the *Silver Ranger,* his newest magazine, from Oklahoma City (which had become the organization's "second headquarters") to Los Angeles. That city eventually housed six different local branches. This concentration of units in one city, the most in the country, allowed Pelley to organize the branches with specializations. For example, there was a Los Angeles branch for those most interested in Pelley's religious system (the astrology-minded Nazi William Kullgren was associated with this group) and another unit, headed by "Captain" Eugene Case, for the violent "actionists." [23]

The Case unit, however, proved impossible to control. In 1934 Case and a few of his closest followers incorporated their own Silver Legion of America, California, Inc. While Case made this move to avoid sending money generated by the California branch back to Pelley, he claimed it was an attempt to thwart a Jewish takeover of Pelley's organization. Case quickly reconstituted the *Silver Ranger* as his own publication and sank deeply into debt. Pelley eventually bought out Case and his associates by assuming their debts and restarted the *Silver Ranger* with James Craig (who had already lost the job once for misappropriating organization funds) as editor. Case retaliated by establishing his own organization, the American White Guards.[24]

Pelley and Craig fell out again in 1935, leading to another attempted coup. Craig and Silver Shirt comptroller Frederick Beutel (whom Pelley hired after the Case incident to keep the California organization in line) used Pelley's mailing list in an attempt to attract his members to their own Constitutional Legion of America. These organizational squabbles sapped much of the strength from the Los Angeles branches, and the Silver Shirts never regained the force they had in 1934. During 1937 the Legion revived somewhat, thanks to a close relationship with the strong Bund movement in the city.[25]

While the Los Angeles branches created internal strife for Pelley and his organization, the San Diego branch foisted a surfeit of complications on the Silver Shirt chief. The San Diego group leader, Willard Kemp, had little use for Pelley's esoteric writings and focused his membership on preparing for armed struggle with Communist invaders. Not content to wait for the Communists to strike first, the San Diego chief proposed a series of violent schemes to his followers. In anticipation of bloodshed, Kemp armed his two hundred followers with rifles allegedly bought illegally from unscrupulous attendants at the North Island Naval Base armory and drilled them at a heavily fortified ranch near El Cajon. To insure that his men were ready for action, Kemp hired two U.S. Marine

Corps drill instructors (Virgil Hayes and Edward T. Grey) to train his men in military tactics and offered to buy any stolen weapons the two could procure.[26]

Kemp's indiscretions proved costly. Hayes and Grey reported Kemp's offer to their superiors, who instructed the two to infiltrate the Silver Shirts and report their findings to Naval Intelligence. The two marines and a number of Silver Shirts eventually testified about the San Diego unit's actions before an executive session of the Special House Congressional Subcommittee on Un-American Activities (the McCormick-Dickstein Committee) in August 1934. Already investigating Nazi propaganda in the United States, committee members were appalled by the schemes of the San Diego Silver Shirts, which included assassination of Jewish public officials and an armed march on San Diego during a May Day celebration. It proved to be the beginning of close governmental scrutiny of Pelley and his organization. Investigators quickly discovered irregularities in Pelley's financial activities. As 1934 dawned, Pelley began twenty years of legal entanglements.[27]

8

Tribulation
1934–1936

THE GROWTH OF THE SILVER SHIRTS and similar domestic fascist groups during 1934 created a wave of public and governmental interest. Most reporters attacked the politics of these groups, but Pelley could counter such exposés by claiming that Jews controlled the media. The publicity given to the Shirts by these articles, as Pelley astutely realized, helped propel the group into the public's consciousness. Governmental investigations and potential legal actions posed a far more serious threat. Pelley could lob claims of a Jewish conspiracy at the federal government, but he possessed no ability to deflect the real dangers posed by hostile government investigators. His counterattacks against the authorities resulted only in further scrutiny of his finances and organization, and Pelley's prophecies of tribulation certainly came true in 1934.[1]

The ill-advised activities of Pelley's California "actionist boys" spurred the first wave of government investigation. The Los Angeles Police Anti-Radical Squad maintained an ongoing investigation of the Silver Shirt branches in that city. Troubled by Willard Kemp's fiery rhetoric, local police also monitored Silver Shirt meetings in San Diego. Kemp's attempt to buy stolen weapons from U.S. Marines Virgil Hayes and Edward T. Grey proved especially costly. The two marines infiltrated the group and reported their findings to Naval Intelligence. These reports eventually reached Washington and came to the attention of several congressmen.[2]

Deeply troubled by the perceived threat of right-wing organizations (particularly the Silver Shirts), Congressman Samuel Dickstein (D-N.Y.)

proposed the creation of an investigative committee to determine the true nature of the danger. The House of Representatives accepted Dickstein's suggestion and in March 1934 placed John McCormack (D-Mass.) in charge of the newly constituted Special Committee of the House Un-American Activities Committee (generally known as the McCormack-Dickstein Committee). Congress believed that American extremists were agents of European fascists and established the committee "for the purpose of conducting an investigation first, of the extent, character, and objects of Nazi propaganda in the United States, second, of the diffusion within the United States of subversive propaganda that is instigated from foreign countries." The committee held hearings in Washington and New York before zeroing in on the Silver Shirts.[3]

Committee member Charles Kramer (D-Calif.) traveled to Asheville in April 1934 and subpoenaed most of the Legion's records. Kramer also heard testimony from former Pelley business manager George Anderson, "foreign adjunct" Paul von Lilienfeld-Toal, and James Craig. Not surprisingly, Pelley, whom Kramer believed to be so untrustworthy that he was never called to testify, blamed the Jews for launching an attack to destroy his organization under the guise of a governmental body and accused Kramer of coming to Asheville only to prove that "fornication had been rife at Silvershirt headquarters."[4]

Kramer also held closed executive sessions in Los Angeles, beginning in August 1934. The committee heard the testimony of marines Hayes and Grey during these sessions. Hayes detailed his encounters with Kemp and the San Diego Legion leader's attempts to purchase weapons from him. Grey's testimony was even more damaging. He claimed that the Silver Shirts plotted to attack Communist meetings, to execute San Diego's Jewish undersheriff, and eventually to overthrow the government. These sessions received national attention and widespread news coverage, and they fueled a wave of angry denunciations and rhetoric in the halls of Congress. Kramer eventually introduced a series of bills calling for more severe penalties and restrictions against extremists who established organizations "advocating overthrow of any government in the United States by force." Kramer's proposals, like those of his colleague Senator Richard B. Russell (D-Ga.), resulted in only limited changes to the law (primarily

restricting propaganda activities among servicemen), but the McCormack-Dickstein Committee, built upon the groundwork of 1930s Fish
Committee, began a long period of congressional investigation of domestic radicals, including close scrutiny of William Dudley Pelley.[5]

For Pelley, however, the actions of congressional committees in far-
off Washington and Los Angeles proved insignificant compared to troubles brewing in North Carolina. Kramer's May 1934 visit to Asheville also
spurred local authorities to investigate Pelley's organization. Less than
three weeks after the McCormack-Dickstein Committee's representatives arrived at Silver Shirt headquarters, the state of North Carolina indicted Pelley for fraud.[6]

Pelley's difficulties with local authorities arose from his shady financial activities. Although the Legion proved more profitable than the
League for the Liberation, Pelley continued to face monetary difficulties
thanks to poor record keeping and his inability to hire responsible associates. If anything, his anti-Semitic followers were even less efficient than
the coterie of starry-eyed mystics he had previously recruited, and creditors were already after Pelley and the Legion by late 1933.

Pelley's financial shenanigans caught up with him in early 1934. In
March the Washington printing firm of Stott and Company sued Galahad
Press for an overdue bill; no representatives from Pelley's company even
bothered to show up in court. In an attempt to protect the Silver Shirt organization, Pelley incorporated the Silver Legion in Delaware at the beginning of 1934, instructed office worker Harry Seiber to burn all
Galahad Press files, and filed for bankruptcy for the press in April. Pelley's
destruction of Galahad Press records was primarily a move of self-
protection. Federal judge E. Yates Webb, who took control of the press
after it went into receivership, impounded everything Kramer had left at
Pelley's headquarters. While he could find no evidence of wrongdoing
from the scanty surviving records, a later federal investigator determined
that Pelley's diversion of press funds into his own bank account had has-
tened the downfall of Galahad. The federal court for the Western District
of North Carolina declared the press bankrupt in May.[7]

During the investigation of Galahad Press, court officials read Pelley's
publications. Buried in a back issue of *New Liberation* was an advertise-

ment offering the Galahad Press for sale that claimed the corporation was financially solvent. The magazine was printed in North Carolina, but Pelley had failed to register the press with local authorities. A perfect example of Pelley's shoddy business practices, this oversight meant that Pelley had violated North Carolina's "blue sky" securities law.

On May 23, 1934, Pelley and associates Robert "Captain Bob" Summerville (editor of *New Liberation*) and Donald Kellogg (Galahad Press secretary) were indicted on sixteen counts of securities violations. Local authorities arrested Summerville and Kellogg the same day; Pelley surrendered after his return from a trip to California (to deal with the power struggles in local Silver Shirt branches) on June 15. All three were released on $2,500 bond. The court seized all records pertaining to the Silver Shirts, Galahad Press, and the Foundation for Christian Economics and ordered Pelley to halt publication of *Liberation*. Confined to North Carolina and unable to contact his followers directly, Pelley issued a circular in June claiming he was an innocent victim of Jewish machinations.[8]

His indictments proved only the beginning of a tumultuous summer for Pelley. Judge Yates sold off Galahad Press's assets, which raised only a fraction of the money owed to creditors and stockholders. Pelley claimed that the Press's insolvency (and later failure to raise enough to pay off the company's $35,000 debt) resulted from the public's ignorance concerning the quality of materials Galahad produced and the valuable information contained in its publications.[9]

Pelley's personal life also altered that summer. He decided to divorce Marion, from whom he had been separated since the early 1920s, and marry (fifteen days after his divorce) his longtime companion, Helen "Mina" Hansmann. His decision finally to straighten out his personal life may have been an attempt to present a more respectable appearance to jurors and followers alike. Also, under North Carolina law a wife may not testify against her spouse in a criminal case; the Pelleys' hasty marriage, then, may have been an attempt to prevent Hansmann from being subpoenaed.[10]

While Pelley's personal life appeared more reputable, local authorities picked over his records for signs of irregularities. Pelley's claim that he was guilty of only a "technical breach" was reasonably accurate, but it was a breach nonetheless. Even the local authorities had trouble making sense of the press's chaotic records. The overlapping employees, publications, and memberships of the Foundation for Christian Economics, Silver Shirts, and Galahad Press, coupled with the destruction of most press files, made it impossible to determine what had actually transpired at Pelley's headquarters (and Pelley probably did not know either). Before the trial even began, prosecutor Zeb Nettles was forced to drop thirteen of the sixteen indictments against the defendants for lack of evidence.[11]

When the trial finally began on January 7, 1935, Pelley, Summerville, and Kellogg stood accused of advertising the sale of stock not registered with the state, selling stock not registered with North Carolina, and advertising stock for sale for an insolvent company. The proceedings lasted only thirteen days, and, as Pelley correctly noted, the jury of local farmers was clearly befuddled by him and by the prosecution's case. Nettles, however, received invaluable assistance from the testimony of disgruntled former Pelley business manager George Anderson, who had left Pelley's employ shortly after the shift toward anti-Semitism. Anderson's testimony shed some light on the confusing business practices of his former boss but did far more service to the prosecution by painting a lurid picture of Pelley's character.[12]

The jury acquitted Kellogg on all counts and, after five hours of deliberations, found Summerville and Pelley guilty on the two lesser charges. They were rightly acquitted of selling unregistered stock in North Carolina. Judge Wilson Warlick sentenced both to one to two years hard labor (suspended for five years on provision of good behavior and their abstinence from publishing materials relating to the sale of stock) and heavy fines, which neither could pay. Pelley paid off his by issuing a circular (which actually netted more than the $1,000 needed). Although angered by what he perceived as the ignorance of the jury, Pelley took comfort in clairaudient messages he received from Christ that he would be protected from future Jewish persecutions and in the fact that the court lifted the ban on his publishing career.[13]

Pelley's divine protection, however, did not prevent followers from deserting him on this plane of existence. His legal troubles led Pelley's energies away from the Legion, and the torpid organization suffered as a result. The chief's inability to leave North Carolina left local Silver Shirt leaders to fend for themselves, leading to serious internal squabbles such as those previously mentioned in southern California. Further, Pelley's conviction led many of his followers to believe that the Silver Shirts possessed a crooked (or at least horribly inefficient) leader and a doomed future. A number of Pelley's already dissatisfied followers, such as Henry Allen and James Craig, took this as a sign to abandon the Silver Shirt ship. Silver Shirt membership never again reached the 1934 level.[14]

While many of Pelley's anti-Semitic supporters followed Craig and Allen into other fascist organizations after his trial, most of his esoterically minded followers deserted him as well. The League for the Liberation provided the initial membership reservoir of the Silver Shirts, but Pelley's increasingly strident anti-Semitism alienated many League members. The notoriety of the Silver Shirts, Pelley's increasing focus on political and economic matters at the expense of his religious teachings, and a general disillusionment following the "blue sky" trial pushed the remnants of the League out of Pelley's orbit. Most of these dissatisfied spiritualists joined the rapidly expanding Mighty I AM group.[15]

Established by former Chicago fortune-teller Guy Ballard and his wife, Edna, the Mighty I AM (the "inner reality of the divine") achieved startling success during the 1930s. The Ballards' cult melded Christian Science, Unity, Rosicrucianism, and Pelley's teachings (which they borrowed freely) with Theosophy. While I AM represented the most popular diffusion of Theosophy ever attained in this country, one scholar has quite accurately posited that the Ballards "reduced the resulting mishmash to the mental level of the comic-books." The cult began in 1930 when Guy Ballard allegedly met the legendary magician Comte de Saint Germain on Mount Shasta. Ballard swiped most of Helena Blavatsky's religious system, placing Saint Germain and Jesus Christ at the top of a pantheon of Ascended Masters. While Guy Ballard developed ideas from Theosophy (and a few meetings with Psychiana's Frank B. Robinson), Edna Ballard began holding esoteric classes based on material she lifted from Pelley's League for the Liberation writings. The group peaked in the mid-1930s. At the height of its success their meetings attracted more than six thousand devoted followers. Guy Ballard's death in 1939 and a series of fraud trials against Edna, beginning the next year, spelled the end of their prominence. The I AM Foundation continues to this day, but only with a shadow of its former grandeur.[16]

Although the Ballards claimed that their teachings came directly from Saint Germain, they did reveal a debt to Pelley. Their writings included references to "Christian Democracy," citations of *No More Hunger,* and a decidedly Pelley-like, anti-New Deal, conservative political perspective. Part of the Ballards' appeal was the nationalist overtones of I AM doctrine. They argued that the Masters lived in the United States (primarily in the far West), that humanity began in America, and that this country would be the vessel of spiritual light. The Ballards essentially filled the void (with admittedly much greater success) left by Pelley when he formed the Silver Shirts. Their doctrines were almost interchangeable, and the Ballards promoted a pro-American, conservative agenda very similar to Pelley's pre-anti-Semitic position. It was not surprising, then, that Pelley's spiritualist followers deserted him for the I AM organization.[17]

As a tribute to Pelley, Guy Ballard, in his second book of I AM doctrine, even named a lesser Master "Pelleur." The Ballards' acknowledgment of influence, however, did not prevent them from raiding Pelley's membership for I AM converts. The Ballards attracted both rank-and-file League for the Liberation veterans and close Pelley associates. For example, Harry Seiber, the man who burned the Galahad Press's records in anticipation of the bankruptcy proceedings, left his post as Silver Shirt treasurer in the wake of Pelley's trial to become the associate director of the Saint Germain Activities.[18]

Pelley's legal difficulties and the resultant loss of followers accelerated his discomfort with the Roosevelt administration. Like Father Francis Coughlin and subsequently the American Communists, Pelley initially supported Franklin Delano Roosevelt and the New Deal. The Silver Shirt chief, however, began to turn away from the New Deal because of a developing belief that Roosevelt's program did not present the necessary central planning to alleviate the nation's economic woes. Roosevelt's piecemeal programs may have been politically expedient, but to individuals such as Pelley who sought fundamentally to alter the political and economic systems of the country, the New Deal appeared a futile attempt.[19]

Pelley's personal problems reinforced his theories of a governmental conspiracy to silence true patriots and to end free speech. Pelley argued that Roosevelt served as a tool of international "Jewish Bolshevism." Seeking to put a positive spin on his own problems with the authorities, Pelley posited that the attacks on him demonstrated that the government feared the Silver Shirts and hoped to eliminate them through the machinations of a corrupted legal system. Pelley also occasionally claimed that clairaudient authorities informed him that the assaults launched against him, and the apparent setbacks resulting from them, were merely obstacles placed in his way to strengthen his resolve.[20]

According to Pelley, Roosevelt was descended from Dutch Jews with the last name "Rosenfeld." The Silver Shirt chief used this as evidence that the president worked undercover for the international Jews. Pelley believed that most of the people involved in the New Deal were Jewish Communists. The number involved varied, but Pelley usually cited the figure of twenty-five hundred Communists serving in New Deal agencies. He scrutinized employee lists for individuals with Jewish-sounding names and, when this failed, occasionally claimed that New Dealers' names were aliases (for example, Secretary of Labor Francis Perkins's real name was "Matilda Wutski").[21]

Pelley posited that Roosevelt sought to create a dictatorship in the United States; the New Deal represented the heart of this Jew-backed plot. New Deal programs—the National Industrial Recovery Act loomed large in Pelley's theory—gave handouts to desperate Americans to make them both compliant and under government control. Those who rebelled against this program of dominance faced persecution by the courts and, if this quasi-legal method failed, darker ends at the hands of the Federal Bureau of Investigation.[22]

Although Roosevelt was the "first Communist president," the influential financier Bernard Baruch was "the real leader of international Jewry in the western hemisphere." Pelley declared that the Communist conspiracy would eventually order Baruch to replace Roosevelt ("another Kerensky") with an openly Jewish dictatorship. Based upon his reading of pyramid prophecy, Pelley believed that Jewish control would end quickly, thanks to the Christian guardianship of the Silver Shirts, and that the "pyramid" date September 16, 1936, would bring a resolution to Christian Silver Shirt–Jewish New Deal conflict.[23]

Heeding the call of prophecy, Pelley created the Christian Party of America (CPA) on August 16, 1935 (also a "pyramid" date). Pelley planned to establish the CPA as the third national party and to propel his followers into positions of political authority, from which they could protect the interests of the "forgotten man." Spearheading this campaign was his own candidacy for president in 1936. He converted *Pelley's Weekly* into the "official organ of the Christian Party" and filled the periodical's pages with attacks on Roosevelt. Pelley claimed to represent the only Christian alternative to the Jewish puppets promoted by the two established parties, and utilized "Christ or Chaos?" and, echoing the nineteenth-century Covenanters, "For Christ and Constitution" as his campaign slogans. To help spread his message, Pelley published a new, even more stridently anti-Semitic political treatise, *Nations-in-Law,* based upon his earlier *No More Hunger.* He also issued a hastily mimeographed autobiography, *The Door to Revelation.*[24]

Pelley's grandiose plan came to little. Unable to generate enough support to complete petition requirements in most states, he appeared on the ballot only in the Silver Shirt stronghold of Washington state. Refusing to acknowledge defeat, Pelley launched a national speaking tour. The candidate slowly wound his way west, speaking to small groups of Silver Shirts before arriving in Washington, where he spent the better parts of 1935 and 1936. Pelley later estimated that he traveled almost thirteen thousand miles during his "Silver Cavalcade" campaign.[25]

While in Washington in February 1936, Pelley organized the Christian Party convention (and added "From Washington to Washington" to his list of campaign slogans). This meeting at Redmond rubber-stamped his platform and nomination for president and selected fifteen candidates for state and federal offices. Among the most significant candidates were the fiery San Diego Silver Shirt leader Willard Kemp (Pelley's running mate), insurance salesman Orville W. Roundtree, and dentist Dwight D. Clarke. To facilitate party growth, Pelley organized nine-person Councils of Safety. Each member was instructed to organize nine new followers into another council in a political Ponzi scheme.[26]

Party organization in Washington was aided immensely by the groundwork laid by the defunct Liberty Party. The aged Populist veteran William H. "Coin" Harvey established the party in 1932 with himself as its presidential candidate. The Christian Party attracted numerous former Liberty Party members, including Clarke, Seattle restauranteur Roy Zachary (who proved to be one of Pelley's most devoted followers), and "bonus march" organizer Frank W. Clark (who fell out with Pelley and established the even more violently anti-Semitic National Liberty Party). In 1932 Harvey had garnered 30,308 votes in Washington; Pelley believed that the addition of Harvey followers to the Christian Party guaranteed him at least that many votes in the 1936 election.[27]

Pelley stepped up his campaign in summer 1936. He gave speeches almost every other day to crowds of up to one thousand. Buried in his public excoriations of Roosevelt, Jews, bankers, and Communists were references to his esoteric beliefs. Pelley tried to rally his wavering followers disappointed by his inability to get on the ballot in forty-seven states by frequently noting the spate of impending "pyramid" dates (particularly Silver Shirt entrance into the "king's chamber" on September 16, 1936). He noted that these dates portended monumental events that would foist the Christian Party into national prominence and end Communist conspiracies.[28]

Pelley's electoral difficulties were compounded by his inability to reach common cause with other extremist leaders. Although the Silver Shirt chief boasted of his political connections (and occasionally wrote positive articles about other domestic fascists), he found it impossible to attract the active support of like-minded organizational leaders. These difficulties derived partly from the decentralized nature of the extreme right wing, which teemed with tiny independent-minded groups, but Pelley's own eccentric beliefs also hampered the effort. Many extremist leaders corresponded with Pelley but balked at giving public support to the candidacy of a convicted felon who promoted a spiritualist doctrine they neither agreed with nor completely understood.[29]

During the election Pelley did involve himself in one attempt to help organize American fascists and, he hoped, obtain their unified support for his candidacy. In late summer 1936 the Reverend Ralph Zollner, head of the America Forward Movement, organized the National Conference of Christian Ministers and Layman and invited more than two hundred clergymen to attend the gathering in Pelley's hometown of Asheville to discuss ways of combating atheistic Communism. Zollner denied any anti-Jewish bias, but he allowed a number of anti-Semitic "laymen," including James True and Harry Jung, to participate in the meeting. When these anti-Jewish delegates proposed that the conference approve anti-Semitic statements, the more liberal attendees cried foul and successfully pushed through a vote inviting two rabbis to speak before the assembly. The anti-Semites, including Gerald Winrod, left to organize their own conference. However, even this rump meeting of forty-five, with Louis T. McFadden as chairman, began to fall out, and a proposed second meeting in October never occurred, thereby ending any chance Pelley had of obtaining a blanket endorsement from a united anti-Semitic front.[30]

Pelley's campaign was also undercut by the creation of the Union Party, headed by Father Coughlin, Gerald L. K. Smith, and the advocate for the elderly, Dr. Francis Townsend. These three "little foxes" (in James McGregor Burns's term) combined their varied inflationary economic panaceas into one semicoherent platform and nominated the bland North Dakota congressman William Lemke for president. Lemke attacked Wall Street and Communists but steadfastly refused to engage in Jew-baiting during the campaign (Smith felt no such compunction). The Union Party attracted the conservative protest vote that Pelley so desperately needed to give his own bid legitimacy. Unable to devise an effective counter to Lemke's success within his own potential voter base, Pelley simply ignored the Union Party during the campaign.[31]

The election proved disastrous for the Christian Party. The prophesied September 16 groundswell of support never materialized, and Pelley's total proved to be minuscule—1,598 votes, just one-twentieth of the Liberty Party's 1932 tally. William Lemke received sixteen thousand more votes in the state of Washington than Pelley got (and garnered the bulk of the national protest votes). Even worse, the Christian Party candidate finished behind both the Socialist and Communist presidential nominees in the state.[32]

The debacle of the election left Pelley in a quandary. Having built much of his movement on the pyramid timetable, he now faced the dilemma of all failed prophets. Initially Pelley lashed out at American voters and blamed them for letting him (and the country) down. Later he promoted the idea that the forces of Communist evil in America were so strong that they even overwhelmed the pyramid time-line. However, in an attempt to save face, Pelley posited that he might have misinterpreted the prophetic event as resolving the "Jewish problem" on September 16, when in fact that date represented only the beginning of the end for Communist Jews. To support this theory, he cited a victory by General Francisco Franco over Spanish Communists on that date as the possible "signal" for work to begin in earnest. In early 1937, looking to deflect attention away from the election and his prophetic inconsistencies, Pelley devoted himself anew to "Christ's men in silver raiment" and began a dangerous campaign of ignoring the "good behavior" provisions of his criminal sentence.[33]

9

Silver Shirts Redux
1937–1939

THE COMBINATION OF LEGAL DIFFICULTIES, defection of supporters, and the failure of September 16 to propel him into the White House
forced William Dudley Pelley to choose between retrenching and giving
up his public career. In the late 1930s, with nothing left to fall back upon
(his adverse publicity as a "Nazi" effectively ended his already faltering
writing career), Pelley decided to renew his publishing enterprises and
rebuild the Silver Shirts. Pelley believed that he could attract more followers by separating his political and esoteric writings as much as possible, thereby offering material for both non-anti-Semitic spiritualists and
orthodox Christian political extremists. As with most of the Silver Shirt
chief's campaigns, this attempt to broaden his support met with mixed
results.

Pelley hoped to avoid further legal difficulties by creating a tangled
web of corporations and company names that investigators would find
impossible to follow. In September 1937 he incorporated the Skyland
Press, the name on his movement's bank account. Followers joined the
Silver Legion of America, but the mail they received bore the label Little
Visits. Those who requested material be sent to them by express mail,
however, found their packages shipped by the Foundation Fellowship. Finally, Pelley issued his monographs under the Pelley Publishers imprint.
This complicated structure did not stop federal and North Carolina
agents from investigating Pelley's organization, and it kept his Asheville
headquarters in chaos.[1]

Central to the renewal program was the recommencement of Pelley's periodicals. For spiritualists he issued a monthly "magazine of practical esoterics," called *Reality*. Pelley hoped this purely metaphysical journal would interest readers disaffected by his political pronouncements. His notoriety as an extremist politician, however, kept most mainstream spiritualists away. One of Pelley's less successful ventures, *Reality* attracted only those already in Pelley's orbit and ceased publication in 1939. Undeterred, Pelley issued a spate of metaphysical volumes that fleshed out his Liberation doctrine but reached a limited audience.[2]

Pelley's long-standing interest in American history blossomed into a monthly magazine in 1937. Each issue of *Little Visits with Great Americans* contained a short biography of significant figures from the past. Based upon a series written by his adolescent idol Elbert Hubbard, the *Little Visits* served primarily to provide "historical" underpinnings to the work Pelley and his group did against Jews and left-wingers. To make the figures examined seem more personal, Pelley adopted Anglicized or modern nicknames for them. For example, Giovanni Verrazano, the "original discoverer of Atlantic City," became "Johnny" and Jacques Cartier was "Jack Carter." Betraying his New England heritage, Pelley partially rehabilitated the Puritans by noting they were "made the victims of an attempt to cross-breed the Jewish theological system with a strain of ultra-conscientious Nordics," while the Pilgrims represented "the Silver Shirts of the period who didn't like the chicaneries of the religious New Dealers." Initially issued twice monthly, the *Little Visits* series met with limited success and was discontinued in 1939.[3]

To keep the remaining Silver Shirts abreast of political affairs, Pelley began publishing *New Liberation*. Although he claimed the magazine would avoid metaphysics, Pelley still interjected the occasional prophetic message into the journal. *New Liberation* contained attacks on all the same targets previously found in *Liberation*'s crosshairs: Jews, organized labor, Franklin Delano Roosevelt, and the New Deal. Perhaps embittered by his electoral failure and perceived persecution, however, Pelley increased the violent rhetoric in his new magazine. He stepped up his vocal support for Hitler ("the outstanding statesman-leader of the world") but also began hinting that Roosevelt might be the victim of bloody revolution, one that might also end tragically for American Jews. To demonstrate his new focus to the "actionist" boys, Pelley frequently referred to his close relationship with the bloodthirsty anti-Semite James True.[4]

Pelley also devoted a great deal of space in *New Liberation* to attacks on his old employer—Hollywood. Pelley's crusade against the film industry had begun in 1934 (he was particularly disturbed by George Arliss's performance in *House of Rothschild*), but his trial, with its injunction against publishing, ended that campaign. He renewed his vitriolic onslaught against "Little Russia" shortly after the ban was lifted. Pelley argued that Hollywood was "one hundred percent Jewish-controlled" and played an active role in maintaining Roosevelt's power in this country. The Silver Shirt chief posited that Hollywood Jews not only kept Gentiles in political chains but also destroyed the virtue of Caucasian maidens. He detailed the horrors of the Jewish casting couch, where the "Oriental custodians of adolescent entertainment" maintained the "concupiscent slogan of screendom: don't hire till you see the whites of their thighs."[5]

Although Jews did continue to dominate top studio positions in the 1930s, Pelley's overall attack on Hollywood was unfounded. Throughout the decade the moguls attempted to downplay the Jewish presence in film; Jewish names were removed from credits and some studios would provide, upon request, medical documentation that male stars were not circumcised. These attempts to limit claims of Jewish control of Hollywood here and abroad meant, as one historian has noted, that "for most of the thirties the Jew as a recognizable character practically disappears from the screen."[6]

Fearful of losing European revenue, the studios refrained from making openly anti-Nazi films until the Third Reich banned all American motion pictures in 1939. Although the studios, particularly Warner Brothers, then began to issue films dealing with European politics, their efforts were still circumscribed by government intervention. Troubled by possible connections between Communists and the anti-Nazi sentiment of Hollywood productions, the United States Senate began investigations of the film community in September 1941. These hearings halted because of the attack on Pearl Harbor, after which the shift in American foreign policy (and Hollywood's essential role in wartime propaganda activities) made such investigations irrelevant.[7]

Whereas Pelley fastened his attention on criticizing motion pictures, American novelists actually proved more effective in undermining domestic extremists. Rex Stout's *The President Vanishes* and Nathaniel West's *A Cool Million* were early attempts by fiction writers to warn Americans of the danger of incipient fascism. West's National Revolutionary Party head "Shagpoke" Whipple is clearly modeled on Pelley. In the novel, New Englander Whipple forms the Leather Shirts to battle Jewish international bankers and Bolshevik labor unions. The most famous of all antifascist novels during the period was Sinclair Lewis's *It Can't Happen Here.* Lewis's work details the career of demagogic politician Berzelius "Buzz" Windrip, who, after being elected president, creates a dictatorship with the help of his "Minutemen" (and directly quotes Pelley along the way). Although most reviewers found the novel to be a political screed rather than a work of fiction, Lewis's book reached fifth place on the best-seller list for 1936. Lewis was apparently unaware of his own role in creating Pelley's public career; his earlier novel *Main Street* had directly inspired Pelley's Paris, Vermont, stories. Nor did Pelley acknowledge any debt—he lumped the author with Communist Party head Earl Browder and Roosevelt as the "killers of American culture." [8]

As part of his reorientation campaign Pelley began exploring the possibility of building bridges to groups previously outside the Silver Shirt orbit. During 1937–38 Pelley launched a program to attract Native Americans and Japanese to his movement. In classic Pelley style, this drive mixed political considerations with religious overtones.

The attempt to recruit Native American followers represented one of Pelley's most unusual campaigns. The Silver Shirt chief believed the Department of the Interior's Bureau of Indian Affairs (BIA) had fallen completely under Communist control, leading to the exploitation of Native Americans. By coming to the aid of these victims of Bolshevik New Dealers, Pelley hoped to earn their support for his larger political programs. Recognizing that support for Native Americans did not mesh with his prior racial and political statements, Pelley sought religious explanations for his policy shift. He declared that Silver Shirts should reach out to Native Americans because these oppressed people were actually survivors of Atlantis. This background meant they represented "pure-

bred Constitutionalists" and "natural-born psychics." Given their Atlant-
ian heritage, Native Americans possessed special insights into "the racial
conspiracy of the Jew and the secret Communistic structure of the New
Deal." [9]

Pelley's appeals to Native Americans met with little success. Despite
claims that once the Christian Commonwealth was established he would
place an "Indian representative" in the executive branch and convert
reservations into Jewish "Beth Havens," few Native Americans found
supporting the Silver Shirts an appealing proposition. Pelley certainly did
not help the campaign by writing Native American-directed articles in a
stereotyped Hollywood Indian version of English, presumably to demonstrate "Chief Pelley of the Silver Tribe's" empathy with their plight. [10]

The only connection Pelley made with Native Americans involved
the eccentric Elwood Towner. Falsely billing himself as "Chief Red
Cloud of the River Rouge Tribe," Towner spoke at Silver Shirt and German-American Bund meetings throughout the Pacific Northwest. "Red
Cloud" usually dressed in swastika-covered buckskins at these rallies and
loudly defended Hitler while excoriating Jews, Roosevelt, and BIA head
John Collier. Although Pelley thought Towner might provide a useful
conduit to other Native Americans angry at the federal government, the
relationship came to little; Pelley could not provide the financial support
Towner demanded in return for his assistance in reaching the tribes. [11]

If Pelley hoped to attract followers by reaching out to Native Americans, his campaign to support the Japanese represented an attempt to improve his financial condition. After Japan joined the Anti-Comintern
Pact in 1936, Pelley began to perceive that nation as a significant member
of the global anticommunist crusade—a dramatic shift from his opinion
of Japanese military strength during his war visit. Believing the Japanese
now to be in agreement with his political stance, Pelley hoped that their
government would provide money for his publishing ventures. [12]

In December 1937 Pelley began making overtures to Japanese residing in the United States. He requested a list of "key Japs" in the Pacific
Northwest from Washington Silver Shirt leader Orville Roundtree in
order to begin making contact. Fearful of being branded an enemy agent,
Pelley did not want the Japanese to make an open contribution to the Sil-

ver Shirts; rather, he wanted them to place large orders for his magazines. Pelley hoped the Japanese government would sign up for "several thousand subscriptions," then distribute the periodicals in Japan.[13]

To show his support for the Japanese cause, Pelley began publishing pro-Japanese articles in his magazines. He claimed that the Japanese were battling Communism (personified in Pelley's bizarre reading of Asian affairs by Chiang Kai-Shek) in China and needed the support of all true patriots. Pelley argued that the Jews created anti-Japanese sentiment in this country out of fear of losing control over China and the "Jewish trade in Chinese dope." If Japan lost the war, Communism would control Asia and begin preparing for an invasion of America by flooding the United States with narcotics.[14]

For several reasons Pelley's campaign among the Japanese was unproductive. First, allying with a convicted felon and his band of extremists promised little positive reward for the cautious Japanese government. Second, the Japanese had made a concerted propaganda effort among American Blacks, an effort that would have been wasted by creating a united front with the rabidly "anti-Negro" Silver Shirts. Finally, Pelley's own racial animosity toward the "lower" "yellow races" (and the latent anti-Japanese sentiment of many West Coast Silver Shirts) sabotaged the relationship. While trying to extract money from the Japanese, Pelley refused to let them join the Silver Shirts. He placated members concerned about the developing relationship with the Japanese by noting that they were "entirely right about keeping the Silver Shirts Aryan."[15]

Pelley's efforts with German-Americans and Nazi Germany proved more fruitful than attempts to connect with Native Americans and the Japanese. Pelley's political and racial concepts hewed much closer to the Nazi line than to that of imperial Japan. Although his unorthodox religious beliefs gave concern to Bundists, Pelley's commitment to Hitler and anti-Semitism gave the Silver Shirt leader cachet among Nazi supporters in the United States. As a result the Bund (and, to a lesser extent, the Third Reich) began to cultivate a closer relationship with Pelley at the tail end of the decade.[16]

Rocked by defections, exposés, and government investigations, the Bund, beginning at its 1938 convention, adopted a "Free America" approach as a means of self-preservation (which included changing the name of its newspaper to *Deutscher Weckruf und Beobachter and the Free American*). Nazi Germany ended all official ties with the organization that year, and the Bund inaugurated a campaign to reach out to other domestic supporters of Hitler, including Pelley. Beginning in the summer of 1938 the Bund began purchasing large quantities of Silver Shirt literature—thirty to fifty copies of every pamphlet Pelley issued and twenty-five to thirty copies of each issue of *New Liberation*.[17]

Pelley's relationship with Nazi Germany also intensified at the end of the decade. The Germans approached Pelley with some trepidation, not wanting a potential ally to be branded an enemy agent. Pelley's religious thinking also contributed to this arm's-length relationship. Although the Nazis invited Pelley to the Third Reich's Erfurt Anti-Comintern Congress in 1938, the Silver Shirt leader's espousal of Christianity and spiritualism gave the Nazis pause. Pelley exchanged large amounts of material with German propaganda outlets, including the German World Service and, in particular, Oscar Pfaus of the *Fichte Bund,* but these Third Reich agencies specifically requested only his anti-Semitic works (and never directly sent him cash payments). This relationship (and Pelley's vocal championing of Hitler) aside, claims that the Silver Shirt leader was an agent of Nazi Germany, as the federal government announced in 1944, were clearly erroneous.[18]

To help rebuild the Silver Shirts, Pelley brought Washington state leader Roy Zachary back to Asheville with him. The move created serious personal problems for Zachary (who left a wife and a restaurant, which quickly faltered, in Seattle), but the newly appointed "field marshal" became one of Pelley's most dedicated followers. Zachary risked his own safety (he suffered injuries in several car accidents and at anti-Legion riots) traveling throughout the country to recruit new members. His efforts proved successful; Silver Shirt membership, after a severe mid-decade decline, reached five thousand in 1939.[19]

The rejuvenated Silver Shirts brought much-needed monies into Pelley's coffers. Congressional investigators concluded that Pelley earned $91,000 from the sale of literature between 1935 and 1939; he also received numerous large contributions (of up to $2,000) from a variety of

supporters, including George B. Fisher of the Crowell Publishing Company and "Doctor" John R. Brinkley. To keep orders up to date, Pelley
purchased the Biltmore-Osteen Bank Building for $20,000 and employed thirty staffers.[20]

Zachary's recruitment campaign, however, met with sporadic animosity. Anti-Nazi demonstrators routinely picketed Silver Shirt meetings. Occasionally these confrontations spilled over into violence. Rallies
were broken up in Washington, Pennsylvania, Ohio, and Illinois. In November 1938 alone three Chicago meetings ended in riots, including a
melee that left Zachary hospitalized with severe head injuries (and fined
fifteen dollars for disorderly conduct).[21]

These clashes with anti-Nazi forces represent one aspect of a larger
movement to discredit (and silence) domestic fascist elements—the
so-called Brown Scare. The development of the Brown Scare was tied directly to the actions of Nazi Germany. The Sudeten crisis and pogroms of
1938 made many Americans, for the first time, cognizant of the totalitarian nature of Hitler's regime. American Jewish organizations, civil libertarians, pacifists, and German-Americans all began to express heightened
alarm about European developments. The support for, and self-professed
ties to, Nazi Germany expressed by American extremist leaders such as
Pelley made them ready targets for disquieted Americans.[22]

The rising tide of anti-Hitler sentiment coupled with fear of Silver
Shirt-like groups provided the impetus for individuals ranging from liberal to Communist to form organizations countering their propaganda.
The most significant of these organizations was the Friends of Democracy. Headed by Reverend Leon M. Birkhead, the Friends sponsored lectures, radio programs, and numerous publications and flyers. The group
received wide support, was the largest of a host of similar organizations,
and counted John Dewey, Thomas Mann, and Rex Stout among its most
illustrious members. Despite (or perhaps as revenge for) memories of
their own recent persecution during the postwar Red Scare, American
Communists joined the fray and funded several anti-Nazi organizations.[23]

The mass media also helped fuel anxieties over a Nazi fifth column in
America. Liberal magazines such as the *Nation* and *New Republic* regularly
excoriated domestic extremists, while middle America received a steady

diet of antifascist exposés in *Life, Time,* and the *Saturday Evening Post.* Popular commentators, most significantly newscaster Walter Winchell and columnist Drew Pearson, frequently utilized their positions as platforms to detail the unchecked machinations of nefarious protofascists looking to destroy democracy.[24]

Domestic fascists also faced difficulties from government bodies. Concerned over the growth of extremist groups at home and abroad, elected officials and policing agencies began to increase their scrutiny of possible troublemakers. Both the executive and legislative branches of the federal government took interest in right-wing figures such as Pelley. Federal government investigations proved disastrous for the Silver Shirt chief, but, even though he was cognizant of the dangers, Pelley continued to press forward in his campaign against the "Jewish" New Deal. He undoubtedly felt emboldened by his ability to avoid going to prison after he was found guilty in his "blue sky" trial, but this confidence, and the recklessness it inspired, only fueled his own downfall.[25]

Given his strident assaults on Roosevelt and the New Deal, it is not surprising that the president eventually explored means of silencing Pelley's cranky attacks. In October 1938 Roosevelt asked FBI director J. Edgar Hoover to look into prosecuting Pelley for libel. That attempt came to nothing, but in spring 1939 FBI field operatives began interviewing *Liberation* subscribers across the country and drew fire from Pelley for their efforts. For Roosevelt the final straw was Pelley's pamphlet *Cripple's Money.* In this short diatribe the Silver Shirt leader asserted that the money raised for the Warm Springs Foundation for Crippled Children during the annual President's Birthday Balls actually went into Roosevelt's pocket as "the nation's birthday gift." Pelley claimed that this "contemptible racket and hoax" by the "lowest form of human worm" served only to line the pockets of Jewish benefactors. This time Roosevelt approached Attorney General Frank Murphy about possible litigation; Murphy offered to file libel charges against Pelley but warned the president he would undoubtedly be subpoenaed by the defense. Fearful of providing a forum for the Silver Shirts, the president did not pursue the matter.[26]

Along with the president, Congress began to explore means of dealing with alleged Nazi sympathizers in the late 1930s. In 1938 they passed the Foreign Agents Registration Act (FARA), which forced those receiving financial support from Nazitern states (and the Soviet Union) to file disclosure forms with the State Department. Although the act placed no restrictions on the type of propaganda "foreign principals" could disseminate, they were required to disclose publicly that they acted on behalf of a foreign state. The act was altered in 1939, with stiffer penalties for failure to comply and the inclusion of U.S. citizens and organizations financed from abroad under the enlarged definition of "foreign principals" being the chief adjustments. By 1940 more than four hundred people had registered under FARA's provisions.[27]

Although most Americans never heard of FARA, Congress also established an investigative body in 1938 that brought the threat of foreign-inspired revolutionaries to the attention of people across the nation. In May of that year the House of Representatives created a new Special Committee on Un-American Activities (HUAC). Under the chairmanship of Martin Dies (D-Tex.), HUAC investigated extremists across the political spectrum (although Nazis and New Deal "subversives" seemed favorite targets). Although Dies steadfastly maintained that the body sought to root out all types of "un-American" behavior, those believed to be allied with Nazi Germany received an inordinate amount of Committee attention. Not surprisingly, the committee began investigating the Silver Shirts soon after its establishment.[28]

Individual states began passing antisubversive statutes at the same time. Most of these legislative actions were directed at the Bund. That group's ostentatious displays of militarism, the creation of several training camps, and a massive February 1939 rally in Madison Square Garden created a flurry of concern over possible Bund-led insurrections. States in which that organization flourished, particularly New York and New Jersey, passed laws aimed at curbing the Bund's ability to drill, recruit, and operate in secrecy. To deal with hate-mongering organizations, states toyed with the idea of passing group-libel legislation. New Jersey's hate speech law was probably the most famous of these measures. For example, in 1940 nine Bundists were convicted there (the conviction was later overturned by the Supreme Court) under the law because of their anti-

Semitic pronouncements. Most states, however, proved uninterested in passing legislation against fascist sympathizers (and those states that did pass group-libel laws used them against Jehovah's Witnesses more frequently than right-wing extremists) and preferred to wait for the federal government to take action.[29]

Although group-libel legislation proved an ineffective means of dealing with domestic anti-Semites, existing laws dealing with personal libel and slander provided a means for American extremists to counter their critics. Hundreds of suits alleging defamation of character were filed by anti-Semites and hard-line "nationalists" during the 1930s and 1940s. Typically the litigation was directed at newspaper reporters (Walter Winchell and Drew Pearson were favorite targets) and authors. Because of his position as chairman of HUAC, Martin Dies was probably the most sued man in America during this period. While he also had to defend himself from suits launched by left wingers, extremists on the right sponsored most of the actions against him. Most of these lawsuits never even made it to court, but the constant attempts to disrupt HUAC activities with frivolous litigation caused a great deal of consternation on Dies's part.[30]

Pelley brought his own lawsuit against Dies in September 1939. Claiming that, without any evidence, HUAC had branded him a Nazi spy, a racketeer, and a public enemy, the Silver Shirt chief sued Dies for $3,150,000 in damages. Pelley's case created a good deal of publicity (which was probably all he had hoped for to begin with), but nothing came of it. He withdrew the suit even before going to court.[31]

The Silver Shirt chief's first significant contact with the Dies Committee involved a shadowy character named Frazier Gardner. In 1939 Gardner applied for a job working for HUAC and during his interview claimed never to have been affiliated with any of the groups investigated by the Committee. Subsequently, information came to light that Gardner was connected with Pelley. The exact nature of their relationship was never determined (Pelley's later explanations varied), but investigators discovered that Gardner was employed by Pelley's Skyland Press and communicated with the Silver Shirt leader frequently. Although Gardner claimed that Pelley did not instruct him to apply for a position with the

Committee (and no direct evidence to that effect ever surfaced), Dies believed that the Silver Shirt leader hoped to place Gardner within HUAC to sabotage their activities. This certainly seems a logical explanation for the escapade, but Pelley's plan came to naught (and Gardner went to prison on perjury charges).[32]

Pelley's difficulties with the authorities did nothing to halt his attacks on the government. In fact, sensing the late 1930s drift toward war, he escalated his criticisms of Roosevelt. Enamored of Hitler and, at best, dubious of the British, Pelley found the administration's overtures toward assisting Hitler's enemies another example of Jewish machinations at work in Washington. Apparently giving up on the idea of using the courts to expose conspirators, Pelley launched another wave of articles detailing the Jewish domination of the New Deal.[33]

Pelley claimed that Jews had orchestrated American involvement in World War I, and that they sought to involve this country in another European conflict. He argued that Jews in America and England desperately wanted war to break out against Hitler to increase the power of "Jewish internationalism" and to prevent the German dictator from strengthening the white race's position in a purified Europe. In Washington, "Jew stooge" Roosevelt hoped to settle a racial grudge against Hitler and to focus attention away from domestic crisis.[34]

For Pelley, then, U.S. involvement in a European conflict on the side of the British would amount to a Jewish attack against the last, best chance for Gentiles to regain control of their European "homeland." Believing that Jewish propaganda (and political clout) made entering a war allied with the Germans highly unlikely, Pelley advocated nonintervention. He claimed that American Gentiles had nothing to gain by entering into an alliance with the British, except defeat. Pelley argued that Hitler wanted only Germany for the Germans and meant no harm to the United States unless the Roosevelt administration provoked him by aiding "our traditional oppressors." Further, assistance to the British left America prostrate and open to a German invasion. Pelley argued that the overwhelming majority of Americans wanted no part in another European war, but, echoing Charles Lindbergh, the Roosevelt government was leading the country into it by only paying attention to "the British, Judaists, and Bolsheviks."[35]

Pelley was certainly not alone in assailing Roosevelt's interventionist posturings. Old-line Progressives and isolationist conservatives within the government decried participation in continental political affairs. People from a variety of political persuasions recoiled at involvement in another European conflict, citing the duplicitous actions of munitions makers and financiers, recently scrutinized by the Nye Committee, during the Great War. Many claimed that two oceans permanently separated the United States from European and Asian conflicts and promoted "continentalist" self-sufficiency, which made any involvement in non-Western Hemisphere affairs dangerous and unnecessary. The mood of most Americans was reflected in Congress by the passage of a spate of neutrality acts during the late 1930s.[36]

The twists of Soviet foreign policy also led to the creation of common noninterventionist ground between those on the radical right and American Communists. Since 1935 the Communist Party-USA (CPUSA) had built bridges with liberals through the auspices of various Popular Front organizations, only to have its painstaking efforts destroyed when the Nazi-Soviet Non-Aggression Pact was signed in August 1939. Overnight the party's policy went from staunch antifascism to alliance with Nazi Germany. Most non-Communist Popular Fronters found the pact disillusioning and the shift in policy untenable. The party faithful, however, accepted Moscow's directives and began publicly supporting a noninterventionist position that allied the party with right-wing extremists.[37]

For those of Pelley's ilk the pact was a surprise but, perhaps owing to their more cynical perspective on politics, created no crisis of faith. Pelley never wavered in his mistrust of the Soviet Union, and explained the pact as merely a Machiavellian expedience. Although he frequently cited noninterventionist "authorities" to back up his own stance, Pelley never acknowledged the CPUSA's work for the cause, nor did he lessen his unrelenting attacks on Communism.[38]

Despite the espousal of similar sentiments of nonintervention by members of Congress, Pelley's antiwar stance placed him on dangerous ground. After war broke out in September 1939, those advocating intervention gained the moral high ground. The dissection of Poland by Hitler and Stalin left Americans on both political extremes in the position of defending blatantly aggressive regimes. As public opinion shifted against the fascist states, people such as Pelley faced public chastisement as Nazi propagandists or agents of a foreign power. Such "un-American" behavior did not escape the attention of the Dies Committee or the FBI.[39]

Pelley's difficulties are not surprising, as even reputable noninterventionists faced adversity. Those who sought to stanch the tide of totalitarianism successfully undermined the noninterventionist stance by branding them subversives. The most prominent—and respectable—of the noninterventionist organizations was the America First Committee. Established in autumn 1940, America First eventually claimed eight hundred thousand members spread throughout 450 local chapters. While most people involved with the America First Committee honestly hoped to keep the United States neutral, the "lapses into bigotry" of members such as Charles Lindbergh and Senator Robert Rice Reynolds undermined much of the organization's credibility and were frequently played up by the group's bête noire—William Allen White's Committee to Defend America by Aiding the Allies. Noninterventionists confronted a difficult situation in which they had to defend a position that seemed to turn a blind eye to European injustice and put them in opposition to a popular president.[40]

For his part, Roosevelt helped undermine the noninterventionists by publicly attacking America First and ordering government surveillance of those opposed to his foreign policy. In an environment in which even the cloak of respectability offered no protection from the winds of governmental investigation, radicals such as Pelley faced imminent disaster. Pelley's dogged determination to hold his line in 1939 left him totally exposed to the forces propelling the Brown Scare—a situation his enemies exploited to their full advantage.

10

Sedition

1940–1949

THE BEGINNING OF WORLD WAR II in September 1939 created severe difficulties for Hitler supporters such as William Dudley Pelley. Although most Americans continued to favor neutrality in any European conflict, President Roosevelt made no bones about his support for Great Britain and France. Those espousing alignment with Germany faced an opponent in the executive office willing to utilize all the means at his disposal to eliminate dissent. In increasing numbers, alarmed Americans also came to believe that Nazi espionage efforts threatened American security. For people such as Pelley, unwilling to alter their political stance, the 1940s would prove to be a very difficult decade.[1]

While they sought to distance themselves from domestic fascists, the America First Committee fell victim to a highly successful publicity campaign that lumped them with the disreputable wing of extremists and Nazi apologists. Although Charles Lindbergh and other members professed a respect for Hitler, most members exhibited no tendencies that could be construed as subversive. Still, the attacks from interventionist organizations such as the Friends of Democracy helped discredit the organization and their cause. Anti-America First propaganda also helped lead Roosevelt to initiate FBI investigations and infiltrations of America First as early as November 1939.[2]

As Francis MacDonnell has noted, Roosevelt was unwilling "to recognize a distinction between legitimate opposition and treason." Given his willingness to unleash the FBI on the respectable end of the noninter-

ventionist movement, it is not surprising that Roosevelt also ordered surveillance and reports on the extremists promoting nonintervention. Pelley, James True, Joseph "Joe McNazi" McWilliams, and others faced
increasing attention from the FBI throughout 1940. Because the United
States was not officially at war, Roosevelt's machinations accomplished
little, as the extremists violated no laws.[3]

However, the president's fiery denunciations, increasing fears of Nazi
propaganda activity, and a shifting congressional perspective on aiding the
Allies led to new legislation to augment the Foreign Agents Registration
Act. While most bills died on the floor of Congress, the magnitude of the
perceived threat is illustrated by the fact that more than one hundred alien
and sedition bills were introduced in Congress in the two years before
Pearl Harbor. Those bills signed into law severely circumscribed the
rights of both aliens and native-born extremists. The 1939 Hatch Act
called for the automatic termination of federal employees with membership in subversive organizations. The next year Congress passed the
Voorhis Act, aimed at curbing the excesses of domestic hate-mongering
groups, and the Alien Registration Act (or Smith Act), which called for
the fingerprinting of millions of aliens residing in the United States.[4]

The upshot of these governmental efforts (and state statutes directed
at paramilitary organizations) was a host of trials that effectively silenced
many on the extreme right. The German-American Bund leadership was
among the first to fall afoul of the law. In November 1939, Bund leader
Fritz Kuhn and several of his top aides were convicted on a variety of
charges involving misuse and misappropriation of funds. Other Bund
leaders faced prosecution under New Jersey's group libel law. In December 1941, shortly after the declaration of war, the federal government shut
down the Bund.[5]

Those outside the Bund also faced legal difficulties. Joseph
McWilliams, leader of the paramilitary Christian Mobilizers, began a series of short stints in jail and mental hospitals in 1940, usually for disorderly conduct. Violating the terms of FARA also led to convictions for
aviatrix Laura Ingalls, most famous for dropping isolationist propaganda
from her plane on the White House; Transocean News Service operator
Manfred Zapp; and writer George Sylvester Viereck, owner of the rabidly
anti-Semitic Flanders Hall publishing house.[6]

Viereck was a paid German propagandist during both World Wars, but his conviction stemmed directly from the notoriety he gained during the so-called "franking scandal." Using German funds, Viereck purchased millions of copies of anti-interventionist speeches extracted from the *Congressional Record*. When the cost of mailing them became prohibitive, Viereck convinced several noninterventionist congressmen, New York's Hamilton Fish being the most conspicuous, to send the speeches out in congressionally franked envelopes. That people with foreign ties were sending out masses of propaganda at taxpayer expense led to a wave of protest both within and outside Congress. Although Fish aide George Hill went to prison for perjury during hearings dealing with the scandal, none of the twenty-four congressmen involved faced any legal actions. However, their activities further helped discredit nonintervention.[7]

Pelley and the Silver Shirts also faced difficulties as the weight of the government swung against pro-Axis noninterventionists. HUAC investigators Robert Barker and John Metcalfe, as part of their inquiry into extremist organizations, studied the Shirts and posited that Pelley was little more than a racketeer and possibly insane. Former Legion members testifying before the committee did little to help Pelley's cause; the disgruntled Henry Allen provided particularly damaging details. Pelley would have undoubtedly been subpoenaed to testify anyway, but Frazier Gardner's harebrained scheme to infiltrate HUAC led to an immediate call to Washington in August 1939.[8]

Still on parole for his 1934 conviction, Pelley was concerned about possible ramifications of his testimony before HUAC. In a truly poor decision he decided to ignore his subpoena and go on another of his frequent cross-country speaking tours. Throughout fall 1939 he eluded the congressional committee and even wrote *Liberation* articles detailing how he had outwitted them. However, the state of North Carolina took a far dimmer view of his antics. Judge Zebulon Nettles, the prosecutor in Pelley's first trial, ordered the Silver Shirt leader to appear in Buncombe County Court for parole violations. Nettles publicly explained his decision in a series of politically charged interviews, claiming that Pelley was an "un-American" exploiting the racial prejudices of gullible people. Obviously concerned about going to prison, the Silver Shirt chief avoided returning to North Carolina (but attacked the case in print), and

Nettles quickly ordered his arrest as a fugitive from justice. With Pelley still at large, state officials raided Silver Shirt headquarters in October; HUAC's Robert Barker arrived the same month to peruse the confiscated materials.[9]

Evading two subpoenas, Pelley spent the rest of 1939 traveling undercover and staying with friends. In February 1940 he suddenly surfaced unannounced at the HUAC hearings. Pelley's surprise appearance created some confusion within the committee, particularly inasmuch as Martin Dies was sick and not in attendance; little of value, then, came from his first two days of testimony. Pelley's third day before the committee, however, veered into the surreal. Committee investigator Barker grilled Pelley at length and openly branded him a racist, racketeer, and fifth columnist, but Pelley denied he was a criminal and maintained a conciliatory attitude toward the proceedings. The Silver Shirt leader disclaimed any desire to establish National Socialism in America, argued that his program dealt "humanely" with Jews, and offered his support for the fine work the committee did in rooting out subversives. Much to the consternation of acting chairman Joseph Starnes (D-Ala.), Pelley offered to disband the Silver Shirts if the committee would continue to track down and punish Communists and Red New Dealers. Pelley's testimony was clearly self-serving, although he had previously published articles supporting Dies's anti–New Deal stance. It gained him no allies on the committee.[10]

The most bizarre element of Pelley's appearance, however, revolved around a series of letters. David Mayne, an unhappy former HUAC employee with ties to Pelley, forged the letters, which purported to show that Pelley and Dies were secret allies. Mayne claimed that Pelley had sent him the letters, and he sold them to Dies's political enemies in a plot to discredit the HUAC chairman. During his testimony Pelley called attention to the forged letters and agreed to assist the committee by exposing them as fakes. In return for this service he asked that the committee do him the favor of keeping him on the stand until February 18, the date on which he was no longer subject to punishment in his home state. The committee declined to assist Pelley and dismissed him on February 10; he was arrested when he left the hearing. Unable to make bail, Pelley spent two nights in jail, then began a lengthy appeals process.[11]

In late 1940 Pelley decided that he needed a fresh start. To that end he announced that the Skyland Press was for sale and he was leaving North Carolina to move to Noblesville, Indiana. As part of this plan Pelley disbanded the Silver Shirts. In keeping with his HUAC testimony, Pelley claimed this move was prompted by the fine work of congressional investigators in assailing Communists within the government. However, declining membership and revenue, the time-consuming work involved in operating the organization, and the adverse publicity it now provoked combined to create a more likely explanation for Pelley's decision. Although there was no longer a formal national organization, a few of the local branches, particularly on the West Coast, continued to meet for the next year.[12]

In November 1940 Pelley incorporated the Fellowship Press in Indiana and began the process of moving his concerns to that state. Pelley no longer felt comfortable in North Carolina and believed that authorities there sought to silence him in any way possible. The move, then, may have been an attempt by Pelley to stay out of prison by leaving North Carolina voluntarily. He claimed he selected Indiana because it was a solidly Republican state that also exhibited northern tolerance. However, personal connections also led Pelley to choose the Hoosier state as his new home.[13] Pelley's secretary, Agnes Marian Henderson, with whom he was developing an increasingly personal relationship, hailed from Indiana and probably spurred his decision to relocate to the Indianapolis area. Henderson and longtime supporter George Henry, an Indianapolis lawyer, introduced Pelley to Carl Losey, who was appointed president of Fellowship Press. Losey, a former Indiana state trooper with a checkered past, had connections with the Ku Klux Klan and the "nationalist" Christian Crusaders.[14]

At the same time that Pelley's printing equipment came north, Losey attempted to purchase the *Noblesville Times.* Losey maintained that Pelley was not involved in the abortive *Times* deal but did admit that Charles Wren Swift, a former Klan newspaper editor, helped raise the purchasing funds. Also in December 1940, former Indiana Klan Grand Dragon David C. Stephenson became eligible for parole from his 1925 murder conviction. Stephenson's possible release, coupled with Pelley's move to

Indiana to work with his former associates, gave rise to rumors of a reju-venated Klan with the Silver Shirt chief helping to lead a "deep, dark plot." Pelley and Losey did nothing to squelch such talk. Pelley, despite being spotted frequently in Indianapolis, refused to acknowledge that he ever even visited Indiana, while Losey denied that Pelley was involved with the Fellowship Press or that he was connected to Stephenson.[15]

Pelley's move, however, met with some protest. Several Indiana newspapers, the American Legion, and Governor Clifford Townsend spoke out against Pelley upon learning of his move to the state. With memories of the 1920s KKK political machine fresh, columnists decried the potential revival of race-baiting, violence, and corruption they per-ceived Pelley might instigate. Adopting a direct-action approach, a group of unidentified men smashed the windows of the Fellowship Press shortly after it opened.[16]

Pelley finally returned to North Carolina at the end of October 1941. With the assistance of two followers, Pelley was able to post $10,000 bond and avoid jail. Presiding judge Don Phillips, clearly angered by Pelley's flight from the jurisdiction and the critical statements he made during the appeals process, found the Silver Shirt chief guilty of multiple parole vio-lations on January 21, 1942, and sentenced him to two to three years in prison. Pelley was in Indiana during most of the proceedings and was not even present when Phillips handed down his ruling. Pelley refused to re-turn to North Carolina (forfeiting his benefactors' bond in the process) and immediately began another round of appeals.[17]

During this period of legal difficulties, Pelley attempted to reorganize his publishing ventures. *Liberation* had ceased publication after the January 1941 issue. In its stead Pelley issued two magazines. In keeping with his late 1930s attempts to separate his political and religious followers, the journals presented different types of material. For his metaphysical fol-lowers Pelley published *Revelation*. This twelve-page weekly contained Pelley's channeled messages and prophetic narratives. Pelley suspended publication of the magazine in fall 1941. For most of that year he had also issued *Roll Call,* the "voice of the loyal opposition." Pelley devoted this weekly's pages to defending Hitler and to detailing American foreign pol-icy and Roosevelt's role in drawing the United States into the European war. After Pearl Harbor, Pelley stopped issuing *Roll Call*. Although the publisher claimed patriotism and the sudden anachronism of noninterventionism as his reasons, some measure of self-preservation undoubtedly played a role in this decision.[18]

The end of *Revelation,* however, did not mean that Pelley had cast his metaphysical followers aside. He quickly replaced it with *The Galilean* in late 1941. Initially *Galilean* closely resembled its forebear and focused exclusively on religious matters. Despite his political difficulties, Pelley still commanded an admittedly reduced following. *Galilean* had 1,500 subscribers and he typically printed 3,000–4,000 copies of each sixteen-page weekly issue (it was initially a monthly). However, many of these subscribers probably never read the magazine and only subscribed to help support a "martyred" fellow extremist.

The decision to halt publication of *Roll Call* left Pelley with no outlet for his political views. Despite the inherent danger, Pelley could not keep from publishing anti-Roosevelt and pro-Axis material; *Galilean,* then, became a *Liberation*-style religio-political magazine in late December 1941. With "Spiritual Significance of America's Armageddon" and "The Religious Truth Behind World Conflagration" on the magazine's masthead, Pelley continued to attack Jews and Communists but also blasted the Roosevelt administration for forcing the Axis to declare war on the United States. He claimed that we should be "legally" considered "accessory before the fact," and that the destruction of the American fleet at Pearl Harbor and loss of the Philippines were examples of "divine justice punishment for our crime."[19]

Not surprisingly, *Galilean* came to the attention of the government. In February 1942 Pelley was ordered to submit all new issues to postal inspectors for approval prior to distribution through the mails. Unwilling to have his magazine censored, Pelley decided to cease publishing *Galilean* in late March. He announced his intention to devote the Fellowship Press to the publication of books for the duration of the war, but continued legal entanglements curtailed his plans.[20]

On April 4, 1942, FBI agents arrested Pelley at longtime supporter George Fisher's home in Darien, Connecticut, and charged him with seditious activities under the 1917 Espionage Act. Agents also raided his

offices in Indiana and carted off most of his records. After being trans-
ported to Indianapolis, Pelley spent six nights in jail before his daughter,
Adelaide, raised his bail. The indictment charged Pelley and Fellowship
Press employees Lawrence Brown and Agnes Marian Henderson with
twelve counts of sedition. Most of the counts involved allegations of hin-
dering the war effort and causing insubordination within the military; the
counts involving the military hung tenuously on a single thread—that a
copy of *Galilean* was found in a soldier's duffle bag.[21]

Pelley spent the spring filing a series of defense motions, including
one claiming the indictment was invalid because no women served on the
grand jury. All the defendants eventually pleaded not guilty, and the trial
began in July. Undaunted by the failure of the motions filed on his behalf
by attorney Oscar F. Smith, Pelley publicly proclaimed his belief that he
would be fully exonerated and allowed to continue his "patriotic" work
without government interference.[22]

Pelley's optimism, however, proved unfounded. The prosecution
brought a well-prepared case to court, helped greatly by an assistant pros-
ecutor appointed by the attorney general, former Democratic National
Committee vice-chairman Oscar R. Ewing. The prosecution used an
Office of War Information study to demonstrate the pro-Axis nature of
Galilean articles, before assailing Pelley as a modern-day Benedict Arnold.
After a Federal Communications Commission official testified about the
most common Nazi propaganda themes, the prosecution called its star
witness—the eminent political scientist Harold Lasswell, then head of the
Division for Research on War Communications of the Library of Congress. Utilizing the "content analysis" technique he pioneered, Lasswell
claimed he found 1,195 statements in *Galilean* consistent with Nazi propaganda, with only forty-five contradicting the Berlin line. Based upon
this study, Lasswell concluded that Pelley was for all intents and purposes
an agent of Nazi Germany operating to the detriment of the American
war effort. Despite their free-flowing technical jargon and battery of
charts, the prosecution established no direct links between Pelley and
Nazi Germany (or United States military personnel), but the defense
team seemed oblivious to this lack and failed to bring it to the attention of
the jury.[23]

In sharp contrast to the clearly planned case of the prosecution, Pelley's defense team, now augmented by Floyd Christian of Noblesville, seemed both confused and incapable of countering the government's expert witnesses. In their opening statement, Pelley's attorneys attempted to present him as a simple religious patriot who operated a "little country paper of religious nature." Apparently they did not clear this stratagem with their client, because Pelley tried to convert the case into an exposé of the Jewish-Communist conspiracy at work in the American government. Although Pelley never called most of his long list of elected officials, U.S. Supreme Court justices, and journalists to the stand, the defense did add a bit of zest to the proceedings by calling several prominent defense witnesses. Among those called to testify were Federal Reserve Board chairman Marriner Eccles, former congressmen Rush Holt (D-W.Va.) and Jacob Thorkelson (D-N.Dak.), Charles Lindbergh, and the radical right's abortive "man on a white horse"—General George Van Horn Moseley.[24]

Although the defense created a flurry of excitement over its prospective witness list, only Pelley, Thorkelson (who may have helped Pelley to avoid the Dies Committee in 1939), and Lindbergh (who had never met or corresponded with any of the defendants) actually testified. Their two days of testimony did nothing to help Pelley's case. As Lindbergh, who was on the stand for a total of twelve minutes, later noted, "the defense seemed extremely incompetent; [they] asked questions which had no relationship to the trial." Pelley's testimony proved as embarrassing as Lindbergh's was useless. He spent his time on the stand positing his patriotism and hope for an Allied victory, while backtracking on his defense of Nazi Germany. While the verdict was probably never in doubt, Christian did not help by accidentally referring to the defendant as "Mr. Hitler."[25]

The jury of farmers and small businessmen took three hours to find the defendants guilty. Pelley was found guilty on eleven counts, with Brown and Henderson guilty of one count, and the Fellowship Press guilty as a vehicle of sedition. On August 13 Judge Robert Baltzell sentenced Pelley to fifteen years in prison, Brown to five years, and Henderson to two years suspended, and he fined the Fellowship Press $5,000. Two days later Pelley entered the federal penitentiary at Terre Haute, Indiana; he quickly began a futile appeals process.[26]

Although he publicly pledged that civil liberties would not suffer as they did during World War I, Roosevelt made a series of moves during the new war that violated the rights of American citizens. He ordered the FBI to begin interning "dangerous" enemy aliens shortly after the declaration of war in December 1941. Under Executive Order 9066 Roosevelt gave the United States Army the authority to relocate more than 100,000 American citizens to special camps simply because they were of Japanese, Italian, or German ancestry. Virtually all Japanese-Americans ended up in the camps, but the great majority of German and Italian-Americans remained at liberty. However, most of those still free faced dusk-to-dawn curfews on the Pacific coast and potential forced removal from their homes because they lived in "prohibited zones." Members of extremist political groups, conscientious objectors, and Black Muslims also faced increased FBI surveillance and coastal exclusion during the war. Many former Silver Shirts, including Roy Zachary, found themselves prohibited from visiting the Pacific coast because they were listed on the FBI's prewar Custodial Detention Index (CDI).[27]

While Pelley was fighting his sedition indictment in Indiana, he became a player in a massive legal struggle involving the leading protofascists in America. The Silver Shirt chief was one of twenty-eight people indicted in Washington, D.C., in July 1942. The indicted came from a variety of backgrounds and included Pelley associates Court Asher, H. Victor Broenstrupp, and James True. Pelley and three others were arraigned on August 18, with all four pleading not guilty. Tracking down and arraigning the other twenty-four defendants proved to be a difficult and time-consuming task. With the process dragging on interminably, the Justice Department decided there was nothing to lose by expanding the scope of the investigation and, in January 1943, added five more defendants and charges of "conspiring to impair the morale and loyalty of the armed forces" to the case. After much wrangling, the government issued a final set of indictments for *United States v. McWilliams* one year later, with thirty defendants listed.[28]

Special prosecutor William Power Maloney's decision to allege that the defendants represented a vast conspiracy stemmed from his desire to try all the accused together and in a place of his choosing, in this case

Washington, D.C. Conspiracy trials were typically easier to prosecute because circumstantial evidence was admissible, and juries could convict without evidence of meetings between individuals. Maloney's actions pleased Roosevelt, who had hounded the Justice Department for indictments against his most outspoken critics as early as December 1941, but Maloney ran afoul of civil libertarians (and old noninterventionists) in Congress concerned about a return to World War I-era excesses, and he was criticized in the media for his theatrical antics. As a result, Attorney General Francis Biddle replaced Maloney with O. John Rogge, the youngest person ever to receive a Harvard law degree, before the trial began.[29]

Prosecutor Rogge based his case on alleged connections between the defendants and the government of Nazi Germany. He accused the group of conspiring to overthrow the government of the United States and replace it with a National Socialist regime. Utilizing Lasswell's content analysis techniques, Rogge posited that the similarity of themes promoted by the thirty demonstrated both their subservience to Germany and their participation in a vast Nazi conspiracy. Although all did exhibit a fondness for the Hitler regime, hatred of Roosevelt, and some measure of anti-Semitism, the government's ill-conceived prosecution was severely hampered by the simple fact that no direct connections existed between the defendants. The indicted also got great play out of the fact that Rogge placed them at the center of a vast international conspiracy that threatened democracy, but only asked for $2,500 bail apiece.[30]

The trial did not actually begin until April 17, 1944, and eventually stretched over seven months. Although the defendants were required to stand together, each was allowed his or her own attorney, and all witnesses could be questioned by each of the thirty's legal counsels. The defense attorneys took every opportunity to file objections, cross-examined prosecution witnesses at length on irrelevancies, and totally exasperated Judge Edward Eichler. The defense objected to every prosecution witness, and Eichler offered to allow one objection to stand for all thirty defendants. Fearful that this might be used to demonstrate a "conspiracy," the accused declined his offer; as a result, the trial screeched to a halt every time a new witness was called. Courtroom decorum also deteriorated as the trial progressed; Eichler cited several defendants and attorneys for contempt in a futile attempt to maintain order.[31]

As the proceedings staggered forward, most observers realized that the government's case was very thin and, if looked at objectively, should have been halted. Rogge succeeded in presenting many of the defendants as unsavory, bigoted, and undemocratic, but he presented no evidence of a conspiracy. As defendant Lawrence Dennis noted, "there was and still is no law against anti-Semitism, anti-Communism, and isolationism." Several of the defense attorneys howled that it was a show trial—and they were correct—but it was more of a circus than a purge. When Judge Eichler died of a heart attack in November, with only thirty-nine of the prosecution's one hundred witnesses having appeared, a mistrial was declared. Rogge attempted to renew the case, but the U.S. District Court in Washington ruled that a revival of the government's moribund prosecution "would be a travesty on justice."[32]

After his Washington sojourn, Pelley spent the remainder of the decade in prison. Beginning in 1946 he undertook a long, unsuccessful attempt to obtain his release under a writ of habeas corpus. In 1948 Pelley became eligible for parole. That year and the next he was denied by the parole board, despite favorable letters from Baltzell and Ewing. The second refusal prompted Pelley's attorney T. Emmett McKenzie to lash out publicly at the "Communist conspiracy" keeping his client in prison.[33]

Pelley was not, however, inactive while in prison. During his incarceration he wrote a novel and a number of metaphysical works—none of which was published until after his release. He also organized a "Great Books" discussion group for prisoners and helped edit a pictorial history of the Terre Haute penitentiary that was displayed in offices of the Federal Bureau of Prisons. Pelley later claimed that his time in prison was eased because of his ability to make astral visits to friends, family, and the Fellowship Press facilities.[34]

Pelley's advocates took his case public in hopes of garnering a pardon for him. His name began to appear in conservative newspaper editorials as part of the emerging Cold War rhetoric. Columnist John O'Donnell labeled him a "political prisoner" and questioned the level of Communist infiltration in the Truman administration. Pelley's daughter, Adelaide, also launched a letter-writing campaign that sent "Free Pelley" materials to all congressmen, Justice Department officials, and the president. This campaign met with some success. Senator William Langer (R–N.Dak.) eventually called for, but was denied, the establishment of a congressional investigative body to examine whether Pelley was being held for political reasons.[35]

Adelaide's husband, Melford Pearson, served as Pelley's chief advocate. In 1947 he published *The Price of Truth,* which claimed that Pelley was a political victim of the Roosevelt administration. Pearson argued that his father-in-law's prosecution resulted from Pelley's "courageously assailing Communism" and his recognition of the "diabolical strategy of the international banking interests that not only had brought about the Revolution in Russia but were the manipulating force behind the New Deal regimentation of America." For this "unpardonable sin" the "twentieth century's outstanding patriot" became, in Pearson's curious analogy, the "American Dreyfus." Pearson also organized the "Justice for Pelley Committee" to continue the letter-writing campaign. Pearson's promotion of Pelley as an anti-Communist proved an astute move, and the political climate's shift in his favor finally garnered Pelley his freedom. In February 1950, with American Communists having replaced right-wing extremists as the country's leading boogeymen, the former Silver Shirt chief was abruptly granted his parole.[36]

11

Soulcraft
1950–1965

WILLIAM DUDLEY PELLEY's release from prison in 1950 was perceived by his supporters as a victory over the Communist conspiracy, but it left the former Silver Shirt chief in difficult straits. Although Melford and Adelaide Pearson had kept Pelley's publishing ventures afloat during his incarceration, the absence of new materials and the adverse publicity surrounding his conviction led to ever-decreasing sales. The terms of his parole also limited Pelley's opportunities to rebuild his career. He was enjoined from engaging in political affairs, making a resuscitation of the Silver Shirts impossible. Restricted to Hamilton (and, after 1952, Marion) County, Indiana, Pelley could not undertake the cross-country speaking tours that had proved successful in publicizing his name and raising money before his conviction. Such demanding undertakings would have been difficult anyway; Pelley's advancing age and increasing heart problems slowly sapped him of the boundless energy he had exhibited during the 1930s. At the dawn of a new decade, then, Pelley's fight for freedom represented only the opening salvo in a battle against legal restrictions and marginalization.

Upon his release from prison, Pelley's most pressing problem involved an effort by the state of North Carolina to revisit his 1935 fraud conviction. Claiming that Pelley had violated the provisions of his parole, North Carolina authorities wanted him to serve out his sentence. To that end, Pelley was arrested immediately upon leaving the Terre Haute penitentiary. Indiana governor Henry Schricker readily agreed to extradite

Pelley, but the parolee's attorneys successfully forestalled the transfer and obtained Pelley's release on a $1,000 bond. Pelley and his supporters countered the North Carolina charges by claiming that Communists, operating under cover of the Tar Heel state's government, sought to silence him permanently. In December 1950 Hamilton County circuit judge Thomas White ruled that Pelley did not have to serve the North Carolina sentence. Demonstrating a determination that only reinforced Pelley's belief that the Communist conspiracy was behind the proceedings, North Carolina launched a series of appeals that did not terminate until January 1952, when the Indiana Supreme Court refused to hear the case. Thus, seventeen years after his "blue sky" trial, Pelley's legal wranglings with the state of North Carolina finally came to an end.[1]

Encouraged by the success of his battle against extradition, Pelley launched a campaign to have his sedition conviction overturned. He filed his first petition in September 1953, then hired Chicago attorney Albert Dilling, husband of *Red Network* author Elizabeth Dilling, to handle the case for him. Dilling appealed the conviction without success in a series of motions, until the matter eventually ground to a halt in January 1955, when the U.S. Supreme Court refused to hear the case. Unable to overturn the conviction, Pelley continued to make monthly visits to his parole officers until his parole period finally ended in August 1957.[2]

Although legal affairs engaged Pelley for the first half of the decade, he devoted most of his energies to rebuilding his spiritualist movement. In April 1950, along with Melford and Adelaide Pearson, he established the Soulcraft Press, incorporated as a nonprofit organization in 1955 as the Soulcraft Fellowship. Operating out of the Fellowship Press's old plant, the new concern focused on publishing Pelley's metaphysical works. Because of his travel restrictions, Pelley spent most of his time writing. This devotion resulted in a mass of literature devoted to his new Soulcraft religious system. Pelley's absorption in Soulcraft matters eventually led him to build an apartment for himself on the floor above the printing press, which he eventually shared with his third wife, longtime "personal pivot" Agnes Marian Henderson.[3]

Pelley's first publication under the Soulcraft Press imprint was the novel *Road Into Sunrise*. Written during his incarceration, the work is a turgid and stilted attempt to present the basics of his religious system in novel form. *Road Into Sunrise* details the spiritual growth of Egyptologist Norval Grane. After writing a book about the pharaoh Ikhaton, Grane is summoned to New York by his publishers and contracted to write another book entitled "Road Into Sunrise," which will lay out the spiritual needs of a country currently bereft of proper religious and philosophical values. Grane falls in love with Sophie Bicker ("the happy combination of two of our finest racial stocks"), the publishing house receptionist, and takes her on his cross-country quest to find the information he needs to write the book. Out on the road Sophie goes into a hypnotic trance and discovers that she was Nefertiti in a previous incarnation. She subsequently leaves her present incarnation personality behind and "becomes" an ancient Egyptian. Back in New York she catches pneumonia and dies. Grane is so distraught that he develops amnesia. While he is sans memory, one of the press's owners, Melissa Codden Sheppard, marries him, nurses him back to health, and has his baby. Grane regains his senses two years later and begins developing a metaphysical system. He posits that reincarnation is real, that we progress to higher octaves through regeneration, and that the people we associate with in this life are individuals we have had relations with in previous incarnations. In the end Grane is able to convince a coterie of high-powered New York businessmen to fund the creation of a foundation that will focus on spiritual research to help humanity get on the "road to sunrise," an endeavor essential in an era in which "all the phenomena of a spiritual trend that's of the ethereal elements is congealing in religious significance."[4]

Similar to the earlier and equally dreadful *Golden Rubbish, Road Into Sunrise* sinks in a morass of metaphysical musing, wooden dialogue, and one-dimensional characters. The only levity is that Grane's dog is named "J. Edgar Hoover." The book also showed that Pelley continued to have difficulty seeing women as equals. For example, wealthy career woman Melissa admits to Grane at one point that she "would do anything in the world for the man who'd boss me and make me mind him."[5]

Road Into Sunrise demonstrated that the O. Henry award-winning fiction writing skills Pelley earlier evidenced had irreparably eroded. He published no other fiction during the remainder of his life other than occasional, anonymous stories in his own magazines, but he refused to admit this fact. Rather, Pelley declared that there was no point in his publishing fiction because his work was "blackballed all over the nation by the pro-Kremlin element."[6]

Although political activism was denied to Pelley under the terms of his parole, the former Silver Shirt chief could not bring himself to refrain completely from social and political commentary. Pelley continued to believe that the "Jewish conspiracy" spearheaded the program that led to his incarceration, but he toned down the anti-Semitic statements in his writings. However, Jews, Communists, and "New Dealism" remained Pelley's archenemies, even if he wrote about them in a newly circumspect fashion. As *Indianapolis Times* reporter Ted Knap put it, "in Pelley's current writings you get anti-Semitism in hints and spoonsful, not in barrels of venom as before." Pelley also added the United Nations to his list of Communist efforts to control the American people.[7]

Unable to create a political organization or to travel beyond central Indiana, Pelley was forced to rely on his writings to spread his political message. He came dangerously close to violating his parole by issuing new versions of *No More Hunger, Nations-in-Law,* and other Silver Shirt-era tracts. However, believing that it was his attacks on Jewish Communism that created his legal difficulties, Pelley sanitized the revised editions of these works. That the government did not arrest him after the publication of these deracinated versions only fueled Pelley's belief that Jews controlled the United States and actively squelched anti-Semitic agitators.

Pelley's revised editions continued to promote his Christian Commonwealth as the centerpiece of his political program but removed all explicit references to racial qualifications for citizenship and the ghettoizing of American Jews. The Commonwealth plan remained virtually unchanged from its original 1930s presentation. Pelley continued to promote the creation of the "Great Corporation of the United States" with all citizens as shareholders, total corporate control of production and land, the elimination of money in favor of individual, state-issued checking accounts, and income at pre-established levels according to one's "Q Status" as the answers to the country's ills.[8]

However, the removal of explicit attacks on Jews, Communists, and

Franklin D. Roosevelt left Pelley in the awkward position of promoting a revolutionary plan without any real explanation for why the current system needed to be replaced. Without targets for his bilious pen, even Pelley had trouble generating excitement over the Commonwealth plan. Pelley conceded that he was "not particularly worried over who shall set the compensations of any given profession . . . [or] classification of craftsmanship" and that the only alternative to the United Nations he could come up with was international trade based purely on the barter system. Not only did Pelley excise references to the "rapacious Jewish moneybund" from his political works, but he also edited out most of the optimistic predictions concerning the eminent establishment of the Christian Commonwealth. Instead, the chastened firebrand posited that "an ideal Utopian structure is no more possible of attainment than the complete termination of wickedness is possible by merely passing legislation."[9]

Despite his pessimistic attitude about current political affairs, Pelley continued to promote the adoption of the Christian Commonwealth as a bulwark against the United Nations' creeping global dictatorship. Pelley argued that the United Nations, modeled on the Soviet Union, was a "kosher-manipulated," Communist-led attempt to destroy individual freedom. Even worse, the "Stalinist" United Nations sought to level out all racial differences. Pelley argued that "true internationality" involved the maintenance of racial and national groups so that "each may fulfill its offices to the other." While Pelley's vision of international relations was currently impossible given "the strategies of nonsocial races to[ward] the peoples of Christendom," clairvoyant sources told him the United Nations would soon collapse because of events in the Middle East.[10]

Pelley believed, based upon messages he received clairaudiently, that international relations faced an imminent shake-up because of Middle Eastern conflict. He predicted that the Chinese demonstrated a racial strength, owing to their Lemurian ancestry, that made it impossible for the Russians to protect themselves from the inevitable "Oriental invasion." After taking control of the Soviet Union (which was weakened by its "racial mongrelization"), the Chinese would invade the Middle East, occupy Israel, and "finish off the Zionists . . . [who] have asked for it." This conflict, predicted to start in October 1956, will lead to the creation

of two armed camps, the Chinese-led Moslem Asiatic Treaty Organization (MATO) and the American-dominated Pan-Aryan Federation.
Eventually MATO would succumb because "the forthcoming Armageddon is the pitting of the Yellow egotist against the White entrepreneur in
the earth-scene, with the White winning out eventually because he is
possessed of greater virtues." When war did not break out as predicted,
Pelley simply pushed the starting date back to late 1959.[11]

Pelley derived his predictions of the coming Middle Eastern apoca-
lypse from his studies of race. Although this topic was a favorite of Pelley's
during the 1930s, he devoted even more time to exploring and writing
about race following his release from prison. He posited that there are
three "pure" races (white, black, and yellow), plus a fourth, "step-race"
(brown). Within each race are gradations of spiritual development. These
races are reflections of the "atmospheric components" of the different
planets from which these "Star Guests" migrated to Earth. As a result of
their divergent backgrounds, the different races have different aims. The
Whites (who are the most spiritually advanced) are trying to reproduce
the utopia of "Sixth Plane Ethereality" on this planet, while the Yellows
are trying to perfect society based solely upon earthly perceptions—they
do not comprehend the spiritual realms. Blacks are merely "a factor of
Cosmic Ignorance in its pure state" and, therefore, are uninterested in the
"cosmic climb." Semites are a "hybrid race" and are properly placed
"around the bottom region of the White Plane, shading off into the Yellow . . . not exactly Yellow, not exactly Brown in the true sense of these
skin colors."[12]

These racial (or cosmic) distinctions, then, would lead to global conflict. After MATO conquered Israel, the Arabs (the Whites' "Racial
brethren") would defeat them and conquer Asia. Realizing their spiritual
inferiority to Nordics, the Arabs would continue to control Asia but
would interact with the "pure" Whites in a subservient fashion. In 1960,
during this "Third World War," Christ would appear before an assemblage
of statesmen as a "stupendous display of Light Vibrations that should give
them the jitters for a year and a day." After that the most spiritually developed souls on the planet controlled the earth.[13]

Not always coherently, Pelley grafted this racial system and millennial prophecy onto his Soulcraft religious system. Soulcraft represented the culmination of the metaphysical studies Pelley had begun immediately after his "seven minutes" experience and occupied most of his post-incarceration time. The fundamentals of Pelley's religious system remained unchanged from his League for the Liberation doctrine (materials from which he frequently republished unchanged as "new" Soulcraft writings), but Pelley also significantly fleshed out his ideas. Pelley, or, as he typically referred to himself, "the Recorder," issued a staggering amount of material for Soulcraft students to digest. During the 1950s Pelley published more than two dozen books (including the mammoth twelve-volume *Soulcraft Scripts*), three magazines (*Valor, Bright Horizons,* and *Over Here*), a weekly "Script," a weekly "Nostradamus Letter," and almost fifty "Famous Voices" audio tapes detailing the Soulcraft system.

Soulcrafters were expected to familiarize themselves with all these works (especially the *Soulcraft Scripts* and *Golden Scripts*). To facilitate a proper understanding of Soulcraft doctrine, students were asked meet in the home of their local Soulcraft chaplain to discuss each week's "Script" and the ideas contained in the full-length works. Heedful of the experiences he faced as head of the Silver Shirts, Pelley kept the movement decentralized and did not charge a membership fee (he made his money selling the literature, which was available only through him), making exact calculations about Soulcraft impossible. Pelley did admit that almost all Soulcrafters were in the forty- to seventy-year-old age range, and that most had been associated with his Liberation doctrine during the Depression era. In late 1953 Pelley proposed holding Soulcraft conventions in every state on one weekend, but, despite his claim that there were 1,250,000 Soulcrafters in the United States alone, he only listed twelve states that would hold conventions under his abortive plan. It seems likely that Soulcraft never boasted more than a thousand members at any time; the number that purchased the entire costly Soulcraft library (subscription to the "Nostradamus Letters" alone was $60 per year) was certainly much smaller.[14]

The religious system that Soulcrafters studied mixed Theosophy, Christianity, Jainism, spiritualism, and Hindu elements. Soulcraft, like Liberation, promoted humanity's interstellar origins, reincarnation, multiple levels of consciousness, and karma. The system was convoluted, complicated, and contradictory; the Soulcraft books were bizarrely organized and obtuse. Donnell Portzline has characterized the Soulcraft belief system as "so pervaded with mystical references that they almost defy a mundane precis."[15]

Pelley posited that the fundamental force in the universe is Divine Thought (also referred to as Holy Spirit, Universal Spirit, Over-Spirit, and the Godhead), which is "self-functioning, and out of it in its nonphysical state comes all Matter and all Substance and all Protoplasm, being the author and creator of these in the atomic and material sense." All creation arises out of Divine Thought, which fractures into Spirit Particle to create souls. These souls are found on various planets across the universe and also in several nonmaterial planes of existence.[16]

The various planes of existence are at the heart of Soulcraft doctrine. Pelley taught that all souls go through earthly incarnations, usually one every five hundred years or so, to increase their spiritual awareness. During discorporate periods, the souls (or Spirit Particle) inhabit purely spiritual planes. There are six or seven of these planes "Beyond the Veil" (here Pelley waffled a bit) that correspond to a soul's level of spiritual development. Each soul, then, undertakes a Platonic development that eventually leads to assignment as the deity over a distant planet.[17]

Pelley posited that earthly existence was solely for the educational purpose of "developing the individual consciousness to complete [the] realization of itself and of its source." After souls reach the Fourth Plane (the "idealized earthplane" or "Summerland"), they realize their deficiencies and reincarnate in order to improve their spiritual development and obtain the requisite amount of knowledge to progress to the Fifth Plane (the "Plane of Radiance"). After a soul achieves Fifth Plane status, earthly reincarnation is strictly optional. A few highly developed souls, however, willingly choose to return to material existence to serve as mentors for humanity.[18]

These earthly mentors are, according to Pelley, the 144,000 members of the biblical "Goodly Company." They return to earth periodically, following the lead of Jesus Christ (the "Great Avatar"), from the Sixth Plane (the "octave of amalgamation with one's spiritual affinity") to direct human affairs along a proper spiritual path. Most humans need this spiritual assistance because they are unwitting victims of spiritual ignorance owing to the peculiar nature of human creation.

Pelley taught that humanity developed on this planet sometime between thirty and fifty million years ago as the result of "Star Guest" material forms arriving on earth and mating with primate life-forms. These "beast-progeny" became humans. While they are part of the constant oscillation between the Earth-Plane and the Thought-Planes, humans need assistance from the mentors because they are prone to irrational behavior thanks to the "dormant racial and sodomic heritage" within the physical body.[19]

Pelley argued that the different races reflected different planetary origins for the original "Star Guests." He claimed that the progenitors of the white race came from Sirius, but he never explained from which planetary systems the ancestors of other races arrived. Race proved to be a problematic topic in the Soulcraft system. Pelley staunchly maintained that Whites formed the top of the racial pyramid, but he found it difficult to explain why the souls of people of color had not evolved to the point where they also reincarnated as Whites. At times he claimed that those incarnated in yellow-skinned bodies forsook spiritual development to focus on wholly material pursuits, but Pelley frequently contradicted this position by noting that the yellow race was second only to the white in the racial hierarchy.[20]

Jews also proved difficult to explain. Pelley claimed they were a "hybrid" race of mixed Berber, Assyrian, and Ethiopian origins, a mixture that "for some reason has been permitted by the Higher Powers." These "primitive and eccentric people" caused mischief in the world but, for unknown reasons, did not spiritually progress.[21]

Although this belief system remained basically unchanged from the original Liberation doctrine, Pelley expanded upon it with the vast Soulcraft library. However, Pelley's detailed explanations of individual theological points often served only to obscure (and contradict) his earlier teachings. Pelley was a voracious reader of metaphysical materials, and he frequently cited other esoteric sources to buttress his own assertions. These outside sources only confused matters further, as they did not always completely correspond with Pelley's teachings on specific matters. In a futile attempt to help befuddled Soulcrafters, Pelley began issuing *Bright Horizons,* a monthly magazine, in October 1953. *Bright Horizons* consisted entirely of Pelley's answers to questions sent in by Soulcraft students perplexed by the morass of convoluted materials pouring from Pelley's Noblesville press.[22]

Whereas most of the Soulcraft doctrine was simply an expansion of Liberation teaching, Pelley did add several new elements to his system. Pelley not only began making increasingly outlandish claims concerning his extrasensory communications but also introduced discussions of unidentified flying objects (UFOs) into his metaphysical system. His decision to involve UFOs in Soulcraft partly derived from difficulties he faced in utilizing his traditional prophetic backing—pyramidism. The Great Pyramid time line reached a critical prophetic date of August 20, 1953. On that date the pyramid time line reached the south wall of the King's Chamber. Most pyramidists, seeing this as an indication of cataclysmic events for humanity, predicted a momentous event for that year. Pelley, for example, had earlier posited this date would be the dawning of the Age of Aquarius. Faced with the eternal problem of explaining a failed prophecy, Pelley latched upon the novel explanation that the arrival of the UFOs represented the fulfillment of pyramid predictions for 1953, and that the occupants of the spacecraft would provide humanity with new knowledge and help usher in the Aquarian age.[23]

Pelley attributed enormous power and intelligence to the "spacemen" but, characteristically, had trouble deciding exactly what they were doing on Earth. He claimed they were mentors for humanity, but that Earth residents might scare them away with our warlike tendencies (exemplified most distressingly, in Pelley's unique perspective, by the violence in motion picture westerns). Pelley also posited that the "saucer-men . . . constitute the advance guard of the Christ Cohorts, prefacing the Second Coming," yet these "semi-angelic people" were not permitted to "alter earth destiny." Pelley also speculated that the saucers may serve as vehicles to "lift the Christ people off earth to leave the planet to the purely materialistic souls." Despite his confusion over the role of space beings in human affairs, Pelley steadfastly maintained that "no other happening that has occurred in the world within historical time matches it in importance." [24]

Just as he did with metaphysical materials, Pelley read widely in the burgeoning field of ufology. Kenneth Arnold's 1947 sightings and the reported Roswell, New Mexico, crash during the same year sparked a wave of public excitement, government investigations, and hastily published saucer accounts; the UFO mania crested in the early 1950s with publications by Donald Keyhoe, Gerald Heard, and Frank Scully and the legendary Washington, D.C., sightings of 1952. Pelley demonstrated a familiarity with all the leading ufology works of the period and frequently cited them in his publications. Apparently desperate to prove the validity of his "Star Guests" theory, Pelley accepted all the UFO sighting accounts he encountered and refused to retract his support even after specific works (such as Scully's *Behind the Flying Saucers*) were demonstrated to be hoaxes. [25]

Pelley not only hailed the arrival of the UFOs in his publications; he became actively involved in the ufology movement. He claimed to have sighted a UFO in October 1953 and frequently reported sightings by Soulcraft employees. The most important of these employees was a young anthropologist named George Hunt Williamson, who began working for Pelley in 1953. Williamson was deeply interested in ufology and wrote a regular column on UFO sightings in *Valor* until 1954. Williamson then left Pelley's orbit and began a long and eccentric career investigating ufology, unexplained phenomena, and the occult. [26]

Williamson was already well-known by 1953 because of his connections with one of the most controversial figures in the UFO movement, George Adamski, who died in 1965. An opportunist of dubious morals, Adamski established himself as a minor metaphysical teacher in the 1930s, when he created the Royal Order of Tibet. "Professor" Adamski's teachings were swiped whole cloth from the I AM movement, and the Royal Order eked out a meager existence until the late 1940s. Inspired by the Arnold sightings, Adamski began lecturing on flying saucers (of which he claimed to have seen 184 by 1950) and writing science-fiction stories. [27]

During the early 1950s Williamson had traveled to California to meet Adamski and discuss UFOs. In November 1952 Williamson,

Adamski, and five others ushered in the "contactee era" by allegedly conversing with a Venusian near Desert Center, California. The spaceman encountered was described as "Aryan" looking, with long blond hair and blue eyes, a point that critics familiar with the backgrounds of Adamksi and Williamson quickly seized upon as evidence of both fraud and racism. Adamski spent the rest of the decade writing about his frequent encounters with aliens (including rides into outer space) and promoting the spiritual teachings the spacemen allegedly imparted to him. That the spacemen's religious system was identical to Adamski's prior Royal Order of Tibet teachings (and that his pictures of the spaceships bore a striking resemblance to out-of-focus ceiling light fixtures) is usually cited as irrefutable evidence of Adamski's chicanery.[28]

Despite the highly questionable aspects of Adamski and Williamson's stories, Pelley continued to trumpet his association with them and the validity of their alien encounters. In *Valor*, Pelley recounted their adventures and reprinted letters he received from Williamson, Adamski, and Adamski's secretary, Lucy McGinnis (who ghostwrote all of his books). When Adamski began publishing accounts of the spacemen's spiritual system, which, being I AM derived, bore close similarities to Soulcraft, Pelley approvingly noted the material as further extraterrestrial evidence of the validity of his own religious teachings.[29]

Pelley's promotion of extraterrestrials was not particularly unique during the 1950s, but other claims by the Soulcraft guru placed him far beyond generally accepted beliefs. Pelley claimed he was working on "Univision," a system of "ultra-violet light and piezo-quartz lenses" that would allow "discarnate soul-spirits" to be seen on television screens. He also began stressing his ability to engage in both astral projection and the voluntary materialization of his "etheric double." Pelley's fascination with invisible bodies peaked with his claim that "violet-light photographs have been taken of imbeciles, amnesia victims, and others of impaired mentality showing their living bodies equipped with two heads." The Soulcraft Recorder also asserted that he was the reincarnated soul of the apostle Simon Peter and published a full-length study of his interaction with Christ, *As Thou Lovest*, in 1955.[30]

As Thou Lovest was, to put it mildly, a revision of Christ's teachings. In

the book Pelley alleged that Christ had an invisible playmate from another planet, that he was (like all the Galileans) forced to become a Jew
(but did not practice the religion), and that he was placed on this planet
by a higher power to "destroy the scourge of Jews." The book is also written as an adventure novel ("it would fill my history with tedious repeti-
tions if I pause to recount all the healings and minor miracles") replete
with Pelley's trademark wooden dialog (Nicodemus to Christ: "Marco
the cheese-buyer beheld you with companions in the Street Called
Straight today").[31]

Along with his increasingly bizarre claims, Pelley became enamored
of Michel Nostradamus ("the patriarch"). A sixteenth-century French
seer and physician, Nostradamus gained notoriety during his lifetime and
lasting fame in some occult circles with his prophetic quatrains. Pelley
said that Nostradamus began speaking to him in 1952 (he later revised this
date to 1929). From that point on, Nostradamus became Pelley's primary
conduit for information from the nonmaterial planes. Nostradamus
spoke to Pelley on a regular basis; these conversations were collected in
the weekly "Nostradamus Letter" sold to Soulcrafters. The French seer
also dictated new quatrains to Pelley that were the source of his prophecies (including the Asian-inspired Third World War and 1960s Second
Coming) after the pyramid date in August 1953 failed to prove decisive.[32]

The most unusual part of Pelley's relationship with Nostradamus was
that the French seer put the Soulcraft Recorder in contact with the discarnate souls of historical figures. Beginning in summer 1958, Nostradamus introduced a steady stream of famous people at the séances held
regularly at the Soulcraft headquarters. Typically, several figures appeared
at every sitting. For example, in one March 1959 night the disembodied
voices of Horace Greeley, George Bancroft, James Fenimore Cooper,
William Henry Seward, and William Lloyd Garrison spoke.[33]

Pelley made these conversations available to Soulcrafters in a variety
of fashions. The weekly "Nostradamus Letters" frequently included tran-
scripts, but the information was primarily made available to students
through the "Great Voices" program. Beginning in the early 1950s Pelley
tape-recorded all the séances held in Noblesville (with Bertie Lily Candler frequently serving as the medium). Once the historical figures began

conversing with Pelley's group, he decided to make the tapes available to a larger audience; Pelley sold these "Great Voices" tapes to Soulcrafters for $10 each. The complete collection of tapes included conversations with almost fifty figures from American history. To provide the information obtained from the Nostradamus-led encounters with additional contextualization from Pelley, Soulcraft began issuing *Over Here* magazine.

Subtitled "the magazine of historical foreknowledge," *Over Here* presented a dizzying array of figures from American history who provided information concerning life on the higher planes of existence and their views on current events. Not surprisingly, the voices offered a view of discorporate existence that reflected Soulcraft teachings. For example, Paul Revere reinforced Pelley's claims that the Christian scripture has been corrupted by the spiritually bankrupt, and Theodore Roosevelt noted that the higher planes of existence were pleasurable but somewhat "tedious . . . except for watching Soulcraft develop." Alexander Hamilton agreed with Roosevelt and explained that, lacking anything better to do, the cofounders of the Republic meet after every session of the United States Congress to discuss current affairs.[34]

The "Great Voices" spent a great deal of their time observing current affairs and, again, their perspectives on international events bore a striking resemblance to Pelley's views. "Jewish" Communism figured heavily in their discussions. Mark Twain explained that the U.S. government was secretly funding Communists (apparently behind President Eisenhower's back, because according to William Seward, Eisenhower was doing a fine job running the country), and Henry Ward Beecher posited that Communists were behind desegregation and the Civil Rights movement. Samuel Adams was so angry that "overseas rascals permeated" the government that he planned to reincarnate as a political agitator. Typically, the "Great Voices" also commended Pelley for the work he had done on behalf of the American people. George Washington commented that when Pelley passed over, "we may meet on the celestial stairs and have a moment of handshaking."[35]

Beyond the increasingly bizarre notions he was promoting, Pelley's work also demonstrated that he was rapidly declining by the end of the decade. While his publications continued to be printed in a professional fashion, the issues were filled with typos and misspelled names, an obvious indication that the always exacting editor was slipping mentally. Physical ailments also slowed Pelley; he increasingly faced heart difficulties. Pelley decided to retire from active involvement with Soulcraft in 1961, and he turned over control of the press to Melford Pearson. Although Nostradamus had told him that he would live until 1989, Pelley died of heart failure on July 1, 1965. Pelley, however, refused to go quietly. Noblesville residents awoke on the morning of Pelley's burial to discover that unknown persons had burned an eight-foot cross on the front lawn of the funeral parlor where he lay.[36]

Epilogue

GIVEN HIS VARIED CAREER, it is not surprising that William Dudley Pelley left a diffuse legacy. Many of his books are still in print, and the Internet has made a great number of his more obscure pamphlets and magazine articles available to readers uninterested in tracking down these materials in dusty archives. This widespread availability, when coupled with the broad scope of his interests, has given Pelley a unique position as a spiritual godfather in widely disparate circles. His work is cited in a variety of underground movements—from politics to ufology and spiritualism.

Pelley's most devoted disciple has been his son-in-law, Melford Pearson. In the early 1960s Pearson (along with his wife and his brother Walter) established the Aquila Press in Noblesville to publish Pearson's own writings. Pearson's works are focused exclusively on promoting his father-in-law's political program. From 1963 to 1970 Pearson edited *The Eagle's Eye,* a magazine of political commentary. According to Pearson, Aquila Press and *Eagle's Eye* were established "for researching and documenting corporate monopolistic power and promoting the proposals in Mr. Pelley's book [*No More Hunger*]." Since then Pearson has written three books promoting Pelley's corporatist system (Pearson, however, changed the name from Christian Commonwealth to "National Cooperative Commonwealth"). Pearson's program is identical to Pelley's plan, except that income figures have been adjusted for inflation. Like Pelley's 1950s version of *No More Hunger,* Pearson avoids explicit references to Jews, but attacks "bankers," the elite who control the money supply, and the multinational corporations who control the two major political parties.[1]

Pelley's widow, Agnes Marian, operated the Fellowship Press until her death in 1970; then Pearson and Adelaide took full control of the organization. Without a steady stream of new publications to make available to Soulcrafters, and bereft of Pelley's leadership, the Soulcraft movement began a gradual decline from which it has never recovered. Slowed by age, the Pearsons decided to retire from active Soulcraft involvement in 2000. Soulcrafter Jack Kerlin now handles all orders for materials and publishes infrequent new editions of Pelley's books from a plant in Utah.

The Soulcraft movement today is rapidly dwindling. Jack Kerlin estimates that no more than six hundred persons remain on the Soulcraft Enterprises mailing list (the name Fellowship Press was abandoned in August 2001). Almost all of these remaining followers were involved in Soulcraft during Pelley's lifetime and, given their advancing age, even this paltry number will drop significantly within the next decade. Nor are any active study groups meeting on a regular basis. Kerlin is confidant that the Internet will facilitate a revival of Soulcraft, but even he acknowledges the difficulty posed in competing with the plethora of current New Age materials that correspond "in many respects to that of Pelley but written in modern idiom free of outdated references."[2]

Pelley's religious ideas have also continued to circulate through the efforts of his former disciples. Individuals such as George Hunt Williamson and Benn Lewis promoted Pelley's metaphysical system but did so without official connections (or sanctions) from Soulcraft. While both of these men have modified Pelley's teachings to a degree, their work was overwhelmingly reflective of Soulcraft-Liberation doctrine.

Benn Lewis became involved in the Soulcraft movement in the late 1950s. A Washington-based artist, Lewis painted the portraits of historical figures that graced the covers of Pelley's *Over Here* magazine. After Pelley's death, Lewis drifted away from Soulcraft and established his own small metaphysical organization, the Washington Cosmic Center, but Lewis's doctrine was almost identical to Pelley's. The primary difference in Lewis's teaching was a focus on faith-healing. Like Pelley, Lewis claimed to be in contact with discarnate souls on higher planes of consciousness. In fact, Lewis avowed that he received most of his messages from the deceased Pelley, a claim hotly contested by the Pearsons and Soulcraft. Like Pelley, Lewis asserted he was a reincarnated apostle, in his case John. Lewis is best remembered in metaphysical circles for his account of this prior life, published as *I, John*. In this book Lewis not only claimed to receive messages from Pelley and Nostradamus but also assailed Jews and Franklin D. Roosevelt (who noted that Lewis was "assigned to correct my errors").[3]

George Hunt Williamson took Pelley's ideas into areas far beyond Benn Lewis's orthodox Soulcraft system, but throughout his eclectic career Williamson maintained beliefs firmly grounded in the teachings of his former employer (despite his claims to have distanced himself from the Soulcraft Recorder). While Pelley utilized the flying saucers as supportive evidence for his religious system, Williamson focused his attentions on the spacemen, then worked a religious system into the "reality" of the saucers. His ufological studies involved receiving transmissions from Martians via short-wave radio. These messages instructed him that humanity developed as Pelley had depicted in "Star Guests"—by the mixing of apes and aliens. However, Earth has been visited by three types of extraterrestrials since then. According to Williamson, the "Harvesters" travel to Earth from Sirius and help defeat evil on this planet. Earthly evil is a product of the violent machinations of the "Intruders," from Orion. Humanity is assisted in its spiritual development by the "Migrants" (Williamson occasionally adopted Pelley's terminology and referred to this group as the "Goodly Company"). Like Pelley, Williamson stressed reincarnation and a golden "New Age" that will dawn after the apocalyptic battle that inaugurates the Aquarian Age.[4]

Williamson eventually became obsessed with uncovering artifacts from the lost continent of Lemuria and spent much of his time exploring Himalayan ruins. Although his later works focused on these endeavors, his 1950s works on "Star Guest" activities resonated with a number of writers. Williamson's Pelley-inspired notions encouraged metaphysically oriented ufologists such as George Van Tassel, Max Flindt, and Erich von Daniken and insured an audience for his creation theories well beyond the limited sphere of Soulcraft.[5]

Several scholars have noted that Pelley's teachings fit well with the totalitarian (if not openly racist) attitudes of much alleged extraterrestrial communications. Frequently the "star men," as in Williamson's books, outline a human prehistory that presents certain elements of humanity as members of an evil plot that must be eliminated. It is not a great leap to assign, as Pelley did, these dark characteristics to specific groups and advocate discrimination by citing extraterrestrial authorities. Further, pronouncements of outer space residents that they possess superior knowledge and technology, which they may bestow upon their chosen followers on Earth, help promote social hierarchy and authoritarianism. As has been previously noted, the "Aryan" appearance of the aliens described by numerous contactees has also been cited as evidence of the latent racism found in the UFO subculture. Pelley's ideas, then, dovetail nicely with beliefs frequently found on the dark underbelly of ufology.[6]

Pelley's religious ideas have also continued to circulate third-hand through the various offshoots of the I AM movement. I AM itself continues to operate out of its Chicago headquarters, but, like Soulcraft, the organization is a shadow of its former glory. I AM's bastardized Liberation-Theosophy doctrine, however, has continued to circulate widely. Among the best known of I AM's spiritual descendants have been Bridge to Freedom, Summit Lighthouse, Christ's Truth Church, and the Aetherius Society. The largest of the neo-I Am groups is Elizabeth Clare Prophet's Church Universal and Triumphant (CUT). Prophet co-opted the I AM doctrine to create a classic authoritarian mind-control cult with militant overtones. CUT practices a racially charged millennialism that betrays the group's origins in the doctrines of Pelley and Guy and Edna Ballard. Within the last decade the cult has come under increased government scrutiny as a result of former-member lawsuits and arrests for illegal firearms purchases. CUT's Montana headquarters is now an armed camp and widely believed to contain large weapons caches as the group prepares for Armageddon.[7]

Since his death in 1965, Pelley's political beliefs have also found proponents. A number of right-wing radicals cut their political teeth in the Silver Shirts and went on to join conservative groups such as the John Birch Society, the American Legion, and the Reverend Fred Schwartz's Christian Anti-Communism Crusade; others established their own organizations. Pelley is also recognized as a martyred hero among American neo-Nazis, who view the Silver Shirts as a progenitor of the modern paramilitary, anti-Semitic far right.[8]

In 1960 a group of unreconstructed Silver Shirters, including former Silver Legion Washington state chief Orville Roundtree, established the National Party of America (NPA) in Portland, Oregon. The group, in fact, promoted itself as the legitimate successor of the Silver Shirts. The NPA issued pronouncements against Communists, Jews, and liberals and picketed outside public schools they thought to be teaching "un-Americanism." Never boasting more than a few dozen members, the NPA drifted into oblivion in the mid-1960s.[9]

The most significant organization to be developed by a former Silver Shirt is the Posse Comitatus. Established in 1968 by ex-Legion member Henry L. "Mike" Beach, the Posse holds that there is no legitimate authority above the county level and refuses to answer to any law enforcement agency except the county sheriff. Because of their localist beliefs, Posse members refuse to pay taxes, make Social Security payments, or purchase driver's licences. Posse members often adopt survivalist tactics, and many are linked to the racist Christian Identity movement (which holds that Jews are descendants of Cain's demonically developed "seed line"). Since the mid-1970s, Posse members have been involved in several violent confrontations with law enforcement officers, most dramatically a 1983 gunfight that left Posse member Gordon Kahl and two federal marshals dead.[10]

Pelley is also often cited as a hero by modern neo-Nazi organizations. Typically, these groups celebrate Pelley's work with the Silver Shirts as a representation of militant anti-Semitism while downplaying, if not outright ignoring, his religious systems and 1950s backpedaling on the "Jewish question." The global neo-Nazi community has used the information-diffusing technology of the Internet to spread their hate-filled messages far beyond their previously circumscribed capabilities, and Pelley's name frequently appears on the web sites of the New Order, the Black Order, and Stormfront. So-called twenty-first century fascist movements such as Nucleus 21 also promote Pelley works in cyberspace.[11]

In his 1996 science-fiction novel *Expiration Date,* Tim Powers created the one-armed, "ghost-eating" character Sherman Oaks, who was a follower of William Dudley Pelley. The character and the book are fitting analogies for Pelley's career. The novel's surreal depictions of a world beyond rationality reflect Pelley's life in the twilight zone junction of anti-

Semitism, genteel fiction, spiritualism, and ufology. Like Oaks, Pelley was a marginal yet significant character in the history of American extremism and metaphysics. His legitimate heirs seem content to let his life and work fade into obscurity, but his legacy, buried under waves of cyberspace rancor and "Star Guest" pronouncements, can still be felt more than seventy years after the "seven minutes in eternity" that forever altered William Dudley Pelley's life.[12]

NOTES

BIBLIOGRAPHY

INDEX

Notes

PELLEY'S VOLUMINOUS ARTICLES are cited by title. In the rare case where another author wrote for Pelley's publications, the author's name is cited as well. The periodicals in which they appeared are abbreviated as follows:

AM	American Magazine	PW	Pelley's Weekly
CO	Current Opinion	RC	Roll Call
EM	Everybody's Magazine	SC	Scourge of Cords
Gal	Galilean	SLR	Silver Legion Ranger
Lib	Liberation	SJC	St. Johnsbury Caledonian
LVGA	Little Visits with Great Americans	SJEC	St. Johnsbury Evening Caledonian
NL	New Liberator	SM	Sunset Magazine
NLW	New Liberator Weekly	Val	Valor
OH	Over Here	WL	Weekly Liberation
PFM	People's Favorite Magazine	WO	World Outlook
Phil	The Philosopher		

Introduction

1. Leo Ribuffo, "Why Is There So Much Conservatism in the United States and Why Do So Few Historians Know Anything about It?" *American Historical Review* 99 (Apr. 1994): 438–39; Glen Jeansonne, *Gerald L. K. Smith: Minister of Hate* (New Haven, Conn.: Yale Univ. Press, 1988); Glen Jeansonne, *Women of the Far Right: The Mothers' Movement and World War II* (Chicago: Univ. of Chicago Press, 1996); Michael Barkun, *Religion and the Racist Right: The Origins of the Christian Identity Movement* (Chapel Hill: Univ. of North Carolina Press, 1994); Jeffrey Kaplan, ed., *The Encyclopedia of White Power: A Sourcebook on the Radical Racist Right* (Walnut Creek, Calif.: Altamira Press, 2000).

2. Previous scholarship on Pelley includes Leo Ribuffo, *The Old Christian Right: The Protestant Far Right from the Great Depression to the Cold War* (Philadelphia: Temple Univ.

Press, 1983), 25–79; Karen E. Hoppes, "William Dudley Pelley and the Silvershirt Legion: A Case Study of the Legion in Washington State, 1933–1942" (Ph.D. diss., City Univ. of New York, 1992); Donnell Portzline, "William Dudley Pelley and the Silver Shirt Legion of America" (Ph.D. diss., Ball State Univ., 1965); John Werly, "The Millenarian Right: William Dudley Pelley and the Silver Legion of America" (Ph.D. diss., Syracuse Univ., 1972). The prior Pelley studies, beyond failing to address his entire career, all show their age. Ribuffo's work, which is the best examination available of Pelley's Depression-era career, is twenty years old. Although Hoppes's dissertation was written only a decade ago, her study relies heavily on Portzline's work for background information and therefore does not incorporate much of the recent historiography.

1. Early Years: 1890–1915

1. Eckard V. Toy, Jr., "Silver Shirts in the Northwest: Politics, Prophecies, and Personalties in the 1930s," *Pacific Northwest Quarterly* 80, (Winter 1989): 143; Stanley High, "Star-Spangled Fascists," *Saturday Evening Post*, May 27, 1939, 70.

2. William Dudley Pelley, *The Door to Revelation* (Asheville N.C.: Pelley Publishers, 1939), 3; Albert N. Marquis, ed. *Who's Who in America, 1930–1931.* (New York: A. N. Marquis, 1932), 1746. Information on Pelley's early life is almost nonexistent. What information is available primarily derives from his autobiography. Although this work is very helpful in reconstructing the early years of his (nonpublic) life, Pelley's failure to provide dates for significant events and tendency to color the past with his then-current (1939) prejudices limit his memoir's usefulness. However, I have found no instances in which the autobiography contradicts verifiable facts. The opaque lens through which the adult Pelley viewed (and related) his early years is in some ways beneficial to the researcher, as it allows for insights into how Pelley perceived the degeneration of American society during the first third of the twentieth century.

3. Pelley, *Door to Revelation*, 3.

4. Ibid., 4.

5. Ibid., 10; Paul G. Faler, *Mechanics and Manufacturers in the Early Industrial Revolution: Lynn, Massachusetts 1780–1860* (Albany: State Univ. of New York Press, 1981), 8–27; Alan Dawley, *Class and Community: The Industrial Revolution in Lynn* (Cambridge, Mass.: Harvard Univ. Press, 1976), 97–128.

6. Pelley, *Door to Revelation*, 10.

7. William Dudley suggested that William G. A.'s decision to leave the ministry was based not only on financial problems, but also the realization that his sermons were not particularly good. In his autobiography Pelley related that his parents once discovered him at the rostrum of his father's church performing his own sermon, one which his father later admitted was "on a par with his own at the time." Pelley, *Door to Revelation*, 14. While Pelley's father never returned to active ministering, he (and his wife) maintained a devout

and strictly orthodox Methodist home. William Dudley later acknowledged his deep-rooted religious devotion (discounting a typical teenage rebellion against formal religion) derived primarily from the values inculcated in him by his father. Outside of the autobiography, the significance of his father's religion on William Dudley is best detailed by the autobiographical character Nat Forge in Pelley's novel *The Fog*. In that work Forge declared that his entire life (outside of school) revolved around the Methodist church. William Dudley Pelley, *The Fog* (Boston: Little, Brown, 1922), 67.

Pelley's mother also took an active role in his religious upbringing, but her relationship with William Dudley did not seem to leave as lasting an effect on his religious beliefs. Regardless, he was clearly very fond of his mother and presents her in a positive light in both the autobiography and his first novel, *The Greater Glory*, which is dedicated to her. William Dudley Pelley, *The Greater Glory* (Boston: Little, Brown, 1919), v.

John Werly has posited that Pelley's admiration for his mother surpassed that for his father, but this seems to be an exaggeration. While Pelley was more critical of his father in *Door to Revelation* (and in a smattering of his teenage publications), the fact that he chose to become a publisher and (broadly speaking) a minister, the two professions of William G. A. that his son was most proud of, suggests that William G. A. made a far more significant impact on the eldest Pelley child. Werly, "Millenarian Right," 1.

8. Pelley, *Door to Revelation,* 18.

9. Ibid., 22.

10. Ibid., 19.

11. Ibid., 19–20.

12. Ibid., 22–24.

13. Ibid., 25–26.

14. Pelley erroneously referred to the new century as beginning in 1900. As an individual with an abiding interest in numerology and, in particular, the prophetic dating system of pyramidism, this is a curious mistake. Pelley, *Door to Revelation,* 26–27.

15. Werly, "Millenarian Right," 4; "Paste-Pot Pelley," *Phil*, June 1909, 12–13; James A. Gelin, *Starting Over: The Formation of the Jewish Community of Springfield, Massachusetts, 1840–1905* (Lanham, Md.: Univ. Press of America, 1984), 1, 5; Michael H. Frisch, *Town into City: Springfield, Massachusetts, and the Meaning of Community, 1840–1880* (Cambridge, Mass.: Harvard Univ. Press, 1972), 238–41; William G. McLoughlin, *Revivals, Awakenings, and Reform: An Essay on Religious and Social Change in America* (Chicago: Univ. of Chicago Press, 1978), 149.

16. Pelley, *Door to Revelation,* 27, 29–31.

17. Ibid., 31–32; "Ma's Hairbrush and a Little Bear Behind," *Phil*, June 1909, 7.

18. Freeman Champney, *Art and Glory: The Story of Elbert Hubbard* (New York: Crown, 1978), 3. Champney also neatly sums up both the man and the difficulty in describing him: "He was both worshiped and hated. He was a tangle of passionate contradictions, and a prophet of the simple life. He was a rebel, a heretic, and a front man for big

business. He was a prolific writer, full of brilliance, bombast, sentimentality, calculated sincerity, pretense, and self-revelation—and sometimes he was straightforward and vivid." *Art and Glory,* 2. For more on Hubbard, see Brom Weber, "Spurious Sage: A Study of the Conspiracy Between Elbert Hubbard and His Times" (Ph.D. diss., Univ. of Minnesota, 1957); Frederick Lewis Allen, "Elbert Hubbard," *Scribner's Magazine,* Sept. 1938, 12–14.

19. For the arts and crafts movement in England, see Nikolaus Pevsner, *Pioneers of Modern Design: From William Morris to Walter Gropius* (New York: Metropolitan Museum of Art, 1949). The best introduction to Morris remains E. P. Thompson, *William Morris: Romantic Rebel* (London: Lawrence and Wishart, 1955). For the movement in the United States, see Coy L. Ludwig, *The Arts & Crafts Movement in New York State, 1890s–1920s* (Hamilton, N.Y.: Gallery Association of New York State, 1983); Wendy Kaplan, *"The Art That Is Life": The Arts and Crafts Movement in America, 1875–1920* (Boston: Little, Brown, 1987).

20. Marie Via and Marjorie Searl, eds., *Head, Heart, and Hand: Elbert Hubbard and the Roycrofters* (Rochester, N.Y.: Univ. of Rochester Press, 1994), 16.

21. For a solid examination of *The Philistine,* see Bruce A. White, *Elbert Hubbard's The Philistine, a Periodical of Protest (1895–1915): A Major American "Little Magazine"* (Lanham, Md.: Univ. Press of America, 1989).

22. Pelley continued to champion Hubbard throughout his career. In his 1939 autobiography he noted that "Lillian," the San Francisco aviatrix and newspaper writer who introduced him to clairvoyance, liked to quote Hubbard and that Frank Riley, inventor of the motorgraph (the electric news ticker in Times Square) and a Broadway producer, kept an autographed picture of the *Philistine* editor up on his office wall. As Pelley tried to portray both of these individuals in a positive light throughout the work, one can only surmise that their support for Hubbard was intended to be an indication of their intellectual acumen. Pelley, *Door to Revelation,* 167, 256.

23. Ibid., 33–34.

24. Ibid., 36. Pelley's brief description of *The Black Crow* in his autobiography is the only information available on the magazine; it appears no copies are extant.

25. Pelley detailed his lack of formal education (and pride in being self-educated) during his first sedition trial. For this testimony, see *Transcript of Record, United States of America vs. William Dudley Pelley, Lawrence A. Brown, Agnes Marian Henderson, Fellowship Press, Inc.,* No. Criminal 7391, in the District Court of the United States for the Southern District of Indiana, Indianapolis Division, May Term, 1942, 514.

26. Fulton Toilet Paper Company advertisement in *Phil,* June 1909, Pelley, *Door to Revelation,* 37, 44; Marquis, *Who's Who,* 1746; William Dudley Pelley, *No More Hunger: The Compact Plan of the Christian Commonwealth,* 2d ed. (Asheville, N.C.: Pelley Publishers, 1935). Pelley's economic plan and *No More Hunger* will be detailed in a later chapter.

27. Pelley, *Door to Revelation,* 39–46.

28. Ribuffo, *Old Christian Right,* 27.

29. "Ma's Hairbrush," 3–4; "What Is the Matter with Our Churches?" *Phil,* Nov. 1909, 5–6.

30. "A Common-Sense Education," *Phil,* Aug. 1909, 7; Steven Diner, *A Very Different Age: Americans of the Progressive Era* (New York: Hill and Wang, 1998), 212–17; Anthony Platt, *The Child Savers: The Invention of Delinquency* (Chicago: Univ. of Chicago Press, 1977), 43–67. The literature on the Progressive Era is legion. For a solid examination of American Progressivism in a global context, see James T. Kloppenberg, *Uncertain Victory: Social Democracy and Progressivism in European and American Thought, 1870–1920* (New York: Oxford Univ. Press, 1986).

31. "The New Christianity," *Phil,* Aug. (1909): 7; "New Declaration of Independence," *Phil,* Sept. 1909, 3; "What Is the Matter with Our Churches?" 6; "The Model Church," *Phil,* Oct. 1909, 10.

32. "The New Declaration of Independence," *Phil,* Sept. 1909, 3; Adelaide E. Bear, "Yellow Journalism—De Luxe," *Phil,* Nov. 1909, 16. One reflection of this difficulty is the variety of names New Thought ideas have been given. The ideas of these religious thinkers have also been called "harmonial religion" by Sydney Ahlstrom and the "religion of healthy-mindedness" by William James. Sydney Ahlstrom, *A Religious History of the American People* (New Haven, Conn.: Yale Univ. Press, 1972), 1019–37; William James, *Varieties of Religious Experience* (1902; Repr., New York: Random House, 1929), 78–115. For the growth of New Thought, see Charles S. Braden, *Spirits in Rebellion: The Rise and Development of New Thought* (Dallas: Southern Methodist Univ. Press, 1963).

33. "Punk Pastors and Pious Priests," *Phil,* Sept. 1909, 6–9.

34. While Rauschenbusch could be verbose and obtuse, his book is still the best place to start for those seeking to understand the Social Gospel movement. See Walter Rauschenbusch, *Christianity and the Social Crisis* (New York: Macmillan, 1907).

On the Social Gospel, see Robert Cross, *The Church and the City, 1865–1910* (Indianapolis: Bobbs-Merrill, 1967); Charles H. Hopkins, *The Rise of the Social Gospel in American Protestantism, 1865–1915* (New Haven Conn.: Yale Univ. Press, 1940); Donald Gorrell, *The Age of Social Responsibility: The Social Gospel in the Progressive Era, 1900–1920* (Macon Ga.: Mercer Univ. Press, 1988); Paul Phillips, *A Kingdom on Earth: Anglo-American Social Christianity* (University Park: Pennsylvania State Univ. Press, 1996); Ahlstrom, *Religious History,* 785–805.

Although Josiah Strong's nativist views do not appear to have affected Pelley, it is interesting to note that, like Pelley, one of the leading Social Gospelers mixed social and economic reform with a healthy dose of Anglo-Saxon racism. Strong's classic work was *Our Country: Its Possible Future and Its Present Crisis* (New York: Baker and Taylor, 1891). On Strong, see Dorothea Muller, "The Social Philosophy of Josiah Strong: Social Christianity and American Progressivism," *Church History* 28 (Oct. 1959): 183–201; Dong-Bai Chai, "Josiah Strong: Apostle of Anglo-Saxonism and Social Christianity" (Ph.D. dissertation, Univ. of Texas, 1972).

35. Ahlstrom, *Religious History,* 792. Bellamy's famous novel is the best place to start for his ideas. It has been reprinted several times, but *Looking Backward, 2000–1887* (New York: Modern Library, 1951) is recommended because of the inclusion of a solid introduction by Robert Shorter. For more on Bellamy, see Daphne Patai, ed. *Looking Backward, 1988–1888: Essays on Edward Bellamy* (Amherst: Univ. of Massachusetts Press, 1988); John Thomas, *Alternative America: Henry George, Edward Bellamy, Henry Demarest Lloyd, and the Adversary Tradition* (Cambridge Mass.: Belknap Press, 1983).

36. "New Christianity," 5; "Remedy," 10; "Wanted: A Religion of Laughter," *Phil,* Nov. 1909, 10–11. Bellamy was similarly vague in outlining the steps needed to achieve societal perfection by 2000.

37. Faler, *Mechanics and Manufacturers,* 30–35; Dawley, *Class and Community,* 35; John T. Cumbler, *Working-Class Community in Industrial America: Work, Leisure, and Struggle in Two Industrial Cities, 1880–1930* (Westport, Conn.: Greenwood Press, 1979), 19.

38. "Fool Socialism and the Other Kind," *Phil,* July 1909, 1; "Common-Sense Government," *Phil,* July 1909, 8–11; "Paste-Pot Pelley," 12.

39. William Dudley Pelley, *Seven Minutes in Eternity, with the Aftermath* (n.p., n.d. [1933]), 46.

40. "August 1st, 1959," *Phil,* Aug. 1909, 4; "500 Years Hence," *Phil,* Oct. 1909, 5; "New Christianity," 5, 7; "New Declaration of Independence," 2; "Wanted: A Religion of Laughter," 13.

41. The Mayflower claim seems, at best, dubious. In the autobiography Pelley stated that Mary Ann's mother's maiden name was Waste. He claimed that Waste was a corruption of West, and it was the Wests who could demonstrate a direct link to a Mayflower family. Pelley, *Door to Revelation,* 48, 61.

42. Pelley, *Door to Revelation,* 55–56.

43. Chicopee was also the hometown of Edward Bellamy. While Bellamy was deceased by the time Pelley moved to the city, his widow, Edna, still resided in Chicopee. Edna was something of a local celebrity, and as the editor of the town newspaper Pelley would certainly have met her. Surprisingly, Pelley makes no mention of contact with Edna Bellamy in his writings.

44. Pelley, *Door to Revelation,* 56–57. Many of Chicopee's leading figures agreed to assist Rivers in funding the newspaper venture. The financial backers included South Bridge Savings Bank treasurer Charles A. Seaver, real estate developer Eugene O'Neil, and Irving H. Page, owner of the Stevens-Duryea Motor Company and wealthiest man in Chicopee. Steve Jendrysik, "History of the Pioneer Valley" (Chicopee, Mass.: unpublished paper, n.d.), 28–29; *Chicopee Union-News,* May 31, 2000.

45. Pelley, *Door to Revelation,* 56, 60.

46. Ibid., 60

47. Ibid., 64. William G. A. Pelley's interest in Charles Taze Russell's Watch Tower Society (or Jehovah's Witnesses) may offer a clue to the surprising desertion of his family.

The most successful of the chiliastic movements arising in the early twentieth century, the Witnesses decried orthodox Christianity, tyrannical human government, and big business. Russell prophesied that the Second Advent had occurred in 1874 and that the end of all things would be in 1914. Had he fully accepted these beliefs, William G. A.'s decision to escape the worldly trappings of business and the Methodist Church and to spend the last few years of his earthly existence in spiritual contemplation would not be surprising. For Russell's views in the context of his times, see Ahlstrom, *Religious History,* 805–12.

48. Pelley, *Door to Revelation,* 65.

49. Ibid., 66–68.

50. Ibid., 75.

51. Ibid., 74.

52. Ibid., 79–80.

53. Ibid., 79.

2. Paris and Asia: 1916–1919

1. *Door to Revelation,* 81.

2. Ibid.

3. E. Jay Jernigan, *William Allen White* (Boston: Twayne, 1983), 76; Edward Gale Agran, *"Too Good a Town": William Allen White, Community, and the Emerging Rhetoric of Middle America* (Fayetteville: Univ. of Arkansas Press, 1998), 57. For White's specific inspiration, see Edgar W. Howe, *The Story of a Country Town* (Atchison, Kans.: Howe, 1883).

4. Sally Foreman Griffith, *Home Town News: William Allen White and the Emporia Gazette* (New York: Oxford Univ. Press, 1989), 151; William Allan White, *In Our Town* (1906; repr., New York: Doubleday, Page, 1909).

5. Ribuffo, *Old Christian Right,* 34; "Wanted: A Younger and More Practical Man," *AM,* Mar. 1918, 10–15; "Through Thick and Thin," *AM,* May 1918, 41–44; "Why the Judge Felt Safe," *AM,* Oct. 1918, 40–43; Henry Seidel Canby, *The Age of Confidence* (New York: Farrar and Rinehart, 1934), 177.

6. "Four-Square Man," *AM,* Oct. 1917, 28–31; "Russet and Gold," *AM,* Dec. 1917, 32–35; "One White Sheep in a Family of Black Ones," *AM,* June 1918, 46–49; "Wanted: A Younger Man," 14–15.

7. *SJEC,* Mar. 13, 1918; Robert Wiebe, *The Search for Order, 1877–1920.* New York: Hill and Wang, 1963), 133–36. For the small town in turn-of-the-twentieth-century literature, see Ima Honaker Herron, *The Small Town in American Literature* (1939; repr., New York: Pageant Books, 1959); Jay Martin, *Harvests of Change: American Literature, 1865–1914* (Englewood Cliffs, N.J.: Prentice-Hall, 1967).

8. Agran, *"Too Good a Town,"* 54–56; "Wanted: A Younger Man"; "The Face in the Window," *CO,* Nov. 1920, 637–48; "Bud Jones—Small Advertiser: The Story of a Man Who Stood by His Friend," *AM,* Feb. 1918, 20–23.

9. Anthony Channell Hilfer, *The Revolt from the Village, 1915–1930* (Chapel Hill: Univ. of North Carolina Press, 1969), 4–30; "Phantom Aeroplane," *Good Housekeeping,* July 1923, 49–51; "Sunset Derby," *AM,* Jan. 1926, 21–23, 161–66; "Martin's Tree," *AM,* Apr. 1927, 20–23.

10. Pelley, *Door to Revelation,* 81–83; "Their Mother," *AM,* Sept. 1917, 15–18. Slidell's affection for Pelley was certainly reciprocated. Pelley wrote very fondly of the editor in his 1939 autobiography. Slidell had also been a newspaper writer, most notably with the *Cleveland Plain Dealer,* and their shared interests helped propel a friendship that lasted until the *American* editor died in 1923. Pelley gave Slidell credit for his good judgment in fiction and "proper" racial background. He noted that he did not recall "ever getting a rejection slip from the *American Magazine* while [Slidell] remained its editor[,] but then, that was while Gentiles were running that enterprise." Pelley, *Door to Revelation,* 83. While it does not appear to have led to any personal connections between the two men, it is interesting to note that William Allan White was part owner of the *American Magazine* when Pelley began publishing stories in it.

Pelley won the O. Henry Award for 1920's "The Face in the Window." He won a second O. Henry in 1930 for "The Continental Angle," *Chicago Tribune,* Aug. 4, 1929.

11. Pelley, *Door to Revelation,* 90; *SJEC,* Mar. 13, 1918.

12. Pelley, *Door to Revelation,* 90–91; *SJEC,* Mar. 13, 1918.

13. Pelley, *Door to Revelation,* 91; *SJEC,* Mar. 3, 13, Sept. 18, 1918.

14. *SJEC,* Mar. 13, 1918.

15. *SJEC,* Sept. 5, 7, 20, 1918.

16. *SJEC,* Sept. 21, 25, Nov. 11, 1918.

17. *SJEC,* Sept. 3, Nov. 19, 1918.

18. *SJEC,* Sept. 3, 4, Nov. 19, 1918.

19. Ibid., Sept. 3, 20, 21, 1918; Betty M. Unterberger, *America's Siberian Expedition, 1918–1920: A Study of National Policy* (Durham, N.C.: Duke Univ. Press, 1956), 10–11; Richard Pipes, *The Russian Revolution* (New York: Vintage Books, 1990), 379, 411–12; John Higham, *Strangers in the Land: Patterns of American Nativism, 1860–1925* (1955; repr., New York: Atheneum, 1963), 218–23; Robert K. Murray, *Red Scare: A Study in National Hysteria, 1919–1920* (Minneapolis: Univ. of Minnesota Press, 1955), 15; Stanley Coben, "The American Red Scare of 1919–1920," in *Conspiracy: The Fear of Subversion in American History,* ed. Richard O. Curry and Thomas M. Brown (New York: Holt, Rinehart, and Winston, 1972), 149; Jan Cohn, *Creating America: George Horace Lorimer and the Saturday Evening Post* (Pittsburgh: Univ. of Pittsburgh Press, 1989), 130–34.

20. Pelley, *Door to Revelation,* 91–92; *SJEC,* Mar. 12, 1918. Pelley would later claim that the *Caledonian* was not the only successful newspaper venture he undertook during this period. In a 1922 interview he referred to himself as a "restorer of old or sick newspapers." His self-aggrandizement has led later scholars to overstate his success as a New England newspaperman. For Pelley's claim, see *San Francisco Chronicle,* Dec. 28, 1922. For

overstated assessments of his newspaper career, see Arthur Graham, "Crazy Like a Fox: Pelley of the Silver Shirts," *New Republic,* Apr. 18, 1934, 264–66, and Hoppes, "William Dudley Pelley and the Silvershirt Legion," 30–31.

21. Pelley, *Door to Revelation,* 93–94. The Methodist Centenary involved a year-long celebration in 1919 for the Methodist Episcopal Church's one-hundredth anniversary. The Centenary movement's goal was to recognize the church's past achievements, expand awareness (and financial support) of its current missionary activities, and promote democratic movements around the globe. For an overview of Methodist missionary work during this period, see Ralph E. Diffendorfer, ed., *The World Service of the Methodist Episcopal Church* (Chicago: Methodist Book Concern, 1923). For Taylor's perspective on the Centenary movement, see S. Earl Taylor, *The Christian Crusade for World Democracy* (New York: Methodist Book Concern, 1919). For Fisher's views, see Fred B. Fisher, *India's Silent Revolution* (New York: Macmillan, 1919).

22. Pelley, *Door to Revelation,* 94–95. Pelley's work was part of the Centenary's global survey program. The goal was to determine the specific financial needs of each Methodist missionary region around the world. Necessary funds would then be allocated to the area, with financial assessments being undertaken every five years. Diffendorfer, *World Service,* v–vi. The Centenary's missionary work, and Pelley's trip, received partial funding from the Rockefeller Foundation. Pelley, *Door to Revelation,* 94–96. The Rockefeller Foundation assisted foreign missions, primarily those affiliated with the Young Men's Christian Association (YMCA), through its Institute for Social and Religious Research. Jon Thares Davidann, *A World of Crisis and Progress: The American YMCA in Japan, 1890–1930* (Bethlehem, Pa.: Lehigh Univ. Press, 1998), 152; *Rockefeller Foundation Annual Report, 1917* (New York: Rockefeller Foundation, 1918), 63. For a survey of the Foundation's work, see Raymond B. Fosdick, *The Story of the Rockefeller Foundation* (New York: Harper and Brothers, 1952).

23. Pelley, *Door to Revelation,* 101–2; "When Brown Is Red," *SM,* Feb. 1919, 28. Pelley's position on the inherent weakness of Japan was undoubtedly influenced by his observation of the rice riots in 1918–1919, which he recounted in "When Brown Is Red." The riots demonstrated Japan's need to increase its involvement in Asian trade and, in part, helped lead to Japanese intervention in Siberia. Jon Albert White, *The Siberian Intervention* (Princeton, N.J.: Princeton Univ. Press, 1950), 165–67.

24. Pelley, *Door to Revelation,* 102–4; "Siberia with the Lid Off," *SM,* Nov. 1918, 18; "Behind the Dreadful Mask: The Sword-Rattling Japanese Giant Turns Out to Be a Bragging Boy," *SM,* July 1920, 32, 62.

25. "Lo, the Poor Cynic (Part 1)," *WO,* Feb. 1919, 26; "Lo, the Poor Cynic (Part 2)," *WO,* Mar. 1919, 13; "When Brown Is Red," 29; "Hustling the Far East," *SM,* Mar. 1919, 15; "Korea and Japan's Boot," *WO,* Oct. 1919, 23. *World Outlook* was the official magazine of the Methodist Centenary's missionary arm and was edited by Dr. S. Earl Taylor.

Pelley's belief that adoption of Christianity in Japan reflected an interest in expanding the Japanese role in international business appears at least partially correct. Later scholars have argued that some Japanese also converted to Christianity to forestall the moral decay they discerned in the wake of the Meiji Restoration. To protect themselves from charges of being tools of Western imperialists, these Japanese Christians developed a heightened nationalism and militarism, which helped Japanese expansionism during the mid-twentieth century. George S. Phelps, "Japan," in *The Red Triangle in the Changing Nations,* ed. Robert Wilder (New York: Association Press, 1918), 2; Davidann, *World of Crisis and Progress,* 30–79; Irwin Scheiner, *Christian Converts and Social Protest in Meiji Japan* (Berkeley: Univ. of California Press, 1970), 8; Fred G. Notehelfer, *American Samarai: Captain L. L. Janes and Japan* (Princeton, N.J.: Princeton Univ. Press, 1985), 139.

26. "Korea and Japan's Boot," 22–23.

27. Pelley, *Door to Revelation,* 105–6; "Should Americans Go to War to Save the Jew Dope Trade?" *WL,* May 7 1938, 1–3; "What Confronts America if Japan Should Lose," *WL,* Sept. 7 1938, 5; "What You Should Know About the Cosmic Role of Race," *Gal,* Mar. 2, 1942, 15.

28. Pelley, *Door to Revelation,* 106–7. Pelley also claimed Phelps hired him to do espionage work for the YMCA as well, a claim that has not been substantiated. For Phelps's views on the Red Triangle in the Far East, see Phelps, "Japan," 2–12.

29. Pelley, *Door to Revelation,* 117–20, 137. Lenin's alleged Jewish heritage would prove a long-lived myth within the anti-Semitic circles in which Pelley moved during the 1930s. Pelley staunchly maintained that Judaism was synonymous with Communism. His later views on Judaism will be detailed in a subsequent chapter.

Anti-Semitic claims that the Bolshevik Revolution was part of a Jewish conspiracy were often based upon the number of alleged Jews in the government. Although Jews did make up a relatively high percentage of the early Bolshevik cadre, their numbers dropped over time, and Russian Jews continued to face discrimination in the early years of the Soviet Union. David Vital, *A People Apart: The Jews in Europe, 1789–1939* (Oxford: Oxford Univ. Press, 1999), 702–13; Pipes, *The Russian Revolution,* 364–65.

30. Pelley, *Door to Revelation,* 120–21. Gleason later established himself as an Asian expert, primarily with the YMCA-sponsored Institute of Pacific Relations. George Gleason, *What Shall I Think of Japan?* (New York: Macmillan, 1921); Paul Hooper, "A Brief History of the Institute of Pacific Relations," in *Rediscovering the IPR: Proceedings of the First International Research Conference on the Institute of Pacific Relations* (Manoa, Hawaii: Center for Arts and Humanities, 1993), 110–41. For the development of the IPR, see John N. Thomas, *The Institute of Pacific Relations: Asian Scholars and American Politics* (Seattle: Univ. of Washington Press, 1974).

For anti-Semitism in the American military, see Joseph W. Bendersky, *The "Jewish Threat:" Anti-Semitic Politics of the U.S. Army* (New York: Basic Books, 2000); Albert Isaac Slomovitz, *The Fighting Rabbis: Jewish Military Chaplains and American History* (New York: New York Univ. Press, 1999), 26–62. For Jewish sentiments among the Czechs, see Ezra

Mendelsohn, *The Jews of East Central Europe Between the World Wars* (Bloomington: Indiana Univ. Press, 1987), 131–71.

For a detailed description of Vladivostok after the Allied intervention, see Carl W. Ackerman, *Trailing the Bolsheviki: Twelve Thousand Miles with the Allies in Siberia* (New York: Charles Scribner's Sons, 1919) 38–43. A reporter for the *New York Times,* Ackerman underwent an adventure very similar to Pelley's. Ackerman's report of traveling throughout Siberia in a YMCA canteen car provides an interesting supplement to Pelley's account. Although Ackerman described similar dire circumstances in the region, he made no reference to the sort of anti-Jewish sentiment Pelley recounted. Ackerman believed, as did Pelley prior to his trip to Siberia, that the Germans were solely responsible for the Bolshevik Revolution. Ackerman and Pelley traveled together briefly in Siberia (along with *New York World* writer Herman Bernstein), and the *Times* reporter's wife hosted the Pelleys' farewell party when they left Japan to return to the United States. Pelley, *Door to Revelation,* 151; *SJC,* Dec. 12, 1918.

31. Pelley, *Door to Revelation,* 123–24. Although Pelley never personally engaged in combat, he later asserted that he was a "soldier and United States courier in World War I." Pelley, *Something Better: How to Bring in the Christian Commonwealth* (Noblesville, Ind.: Soulcraft Chapels, 1952), 10.

32. Ibid., 125–27. Second only to Vladivostok in local importance, Blagovyeshchenck was the largest city in the Amur region, just south of Siberia. Jon White, *Siberian Intervention,* 26–35; William S. Graves, *America's Siberian Adventure, 1918–1920* (New York: Jonathan Cape and Harrison Smith, 1930), 162.

33. Pelley, *Door to Revelation,* 142–46. For Kolkchak's appointment as Supreme Ruler of Russia, see Jon White, *Siberian Intervention,* 115–17; John Bradley, *Allied Intervention in Russia* (London: Weidenfeld and Nicolson, 1968), 112–15.

Prior to the revolution, International Harverster invested very heavily in Russia. Harvester had its own factories and retail stores (more than two hundred in Siberia alone) in the country, and Russia accounted for one-third of the company's self-raking reaper sales. Hoping that Harvester would continue to invest money in Russia, the Bolsheviks did not immediately nationalize the company's factories. In 1924, however, after Harvester's refusal to aid them, the Russian Communists took over all company assets in the Soviet Union. Harvester estimated their total losses at over thirty million dollars. Fred V. Carstensen, *American Enterprise in Foreign Markets: Studies of Singer and International Harvester in Imperial Russia* (Chapel Hill: Univ. of North Carolina Press, 1984) 107–225; Cyrus McCormick, *The Century of the Reaper: An Account of Cyrus Hall McCormick* (Boston: Houghton Mifflin, 1931), 174; Jon White, *Siberian Intervention,* 31–36, 155, 327–28.

34. Pelley, *Door to Revelation,* 127–33. For an account of social dislocation during the Revolution, see Peter Gatrell, *A Whole Empire Walking: Refugees in Russia During World War I* (Bloomington: Indiana Univ. Press, 1999). Gatrell's account is a welcome corrective to

Pelley's views on the Revolution, as he demonstrates the persecution faced by Jewish refugees (often at the hands of other Russian refugees).

35. Pelley, *Door to Revelation*, 128–29, 136–38; "The World Problem Is a Matter of Race," *Lib*, Mar. 24, 1934, 4–5; "What Communism Hasn't Done to Judah's Glory," *WL*, June 6 1937, 5.

Pelley derived the "276 Jews" figure from the work of his friend Ernest Elmhurst, who picked the number up from the testimony of conservative Methodist minister George A. Simmons before a 1919 Senate committee investigating Bolshevik propaganda. Although there is no evidence to support Simmons's original claim, the figure still circulates in extreme right-wing circles. Ernest F. Elmhurst, *The World Hoax* (Asheville, N.C.: Pelley Publishers, 1938), 8–13; Michael Selzer, ed. *"Kike!": A Documentary History of Anti-Semitism in America* (New York: World Publishing, 1972), 176; Cheri Seymour, *Committee of the States: Inside the Radical Right* (Mariposa, Calif.: Camden Place, 1991), 73.

36. Pelley, *Door to Revelation*, 150–51; *SJC*, Dec. 18, 1918.

37. Pelley, *Door to Revelation*, 143, 150–52. Pelley claimed to have traveled over 37,000 miles during the trip. He never again left the United States.

38. Ibid., 82; "Their Mother," *AM*, Aug. 1917, 15–18.

39. Pelley, *Greater Glory*, 20, 99. Although Pelley wrote the novel after his exposure to anti-Semitism in Siberia, he did place Jewish characters in the work. That they are not villains (or unsympathetic) gives credence to Pelley's claim that he did not fully understand the threat of the Jewish "conspiracy" until the late 1920s. Ibid., 13, 51.

40. Ibid., 340.

41. Ibid., 111.

42. Ribuffo, *Old Christian Right*, 36–37.

43. *SJC*, Feb. 13, 1919; "Why I Am Glad I Married a Suffragist," *AM*, Apr. 1920, 49, 122.

44. Ibid., 122; Pelley, *Door to Revelation*, 170, 173, 225, 237; William Dudley Pelley, *Adam Awakes: Design for Romance* (1941; repr., Noblesville, Ind.: Soulcraft Chapels, 1953), 241–43.

45. Pelley, *Greater Glory*, 111, 310–15; "Why I Am Glad," 48–50; Pelley, *Adam Awakes*, 44; Pelley, *Door to Revelation*, 166–67, 225; Pelley, *Road into Sunrise: A Narrative of the Eternal Verities* (Noblesville, Ind.: Soulcraft Press, 1950), 66, 310; *SJC*, Feb. 20, 1919.

Late in his life Pelley would develop a theory, as part of his Soulcraft religious system, to "explain" why women feel the need to be dominated by men. Pelley posited that these women had unnaturally controlled their husbands in a previous incarnation, recognized (after death) the need to rectify this situation, returned in this incarnation as a subservient wife, and rejoiced "that she's getting what she's hungered for." He also argued this explained why battered women often refused to leave their abusive spouses. "The Long Table," *Val*, Oct. 1956, 31.

46. Pelley, *Door to Revelation*, 153–56; *SJC*, Dec. 12, 1918. The issues of the *Caledonian* published during Pelley's absence were clearly substandard. They contain numerous

typos, grammatical errors, articles printed twice in the same issue, upside down type, and (in one instance) a misspelling of Pelley. *SJC,* Sept. 18, 20, Nov. 11, 1918.

47. Pelley, *Door to Revelation,* 154–61. For examples of Pelley's fiction during this period, see "Human Nature, as the Country Editor Knows It," *AM,* Nov. 1919, 60–61; "Third-Speed Tarring," *EM,* Dec. 1920, 59–61.

Healy later became chief council for the Federal Trade Commission and was eventually appointed to the Securities and Exchange Commission by Franklin Delano Roosevelt. Pelley's previous personal relationship with Healy undoubtedly saved the attorney from inclusion on Pelley's list of Jews in the government. That Healy was not Jewish had nothing to do with his name being left off the list, as Pelley claimed numerous Gentiles in government service were Jewish (including Roosevelt, Cordell Hull, and Frances Perkins). "Jews in Our Government," *WL,* 8, Oct. 21 1937, 2–8; Ralph F. De Bedts, *The New Deal's SEC: The Formative Years* (New York: Columbia Univ. Press, 1964), 93–94, 103–4; Joel Seligman, *The Transformation of Wall Street: A History of the Securities Exchange Commission and Modern Corporate Finance* (Boston: Northeastern Univ. Press, 1995), 106–31.

48. *SJC,* Jan. 24, 30, Mar. 5, 1919.

49. *SJC,* May 16, 26, June 16, 1919.

50. *SJC,* Apr. 21, June 6, 19, 1919. For accounts of the antiradical sentiment in the immediate post-World War I period, see Murray, *Red Scare,* 12, 88; Jan Cohn, *Creating America* 149, 155; John George and Laird Wilcox, *American Extremists: Militias, Supremacists, Klansmen, Communists, and Others* (Amherst, N.Y.: Prometheus, 1996), 26–28; Brett Gary, *The Nervous Liberals: Propaganda Anxieties from World War I to the Cold War* (New York: Columbia Univ. Press, 1999), 15–55.

51. Pelley, *Door to Revelation,* 161–63.

3. Hollywood: 1920–1927

1. Pelley, *The Door to Revelation,* 164; "Behind the Dreadful Mask," 32–34. Although *Sunset* refused Pelley's nonfiction pieces, it was one of the primary publishers of his short stories during the early 1920s. "Birds of Passage," *SM,* Apr. 1920, 20–23; "Gamble Terrible," *SM,* May 1920, 5–8.

2. Pelley, *Door to Revelation,* 164–65. The articles went unpublished.

3. Ibid., 165–66.

4. Ibid., 170–75.

5. Ibid., 176–77.

6. Mark Schorer, ed. *Sinclair Lewis: A Collection of Critical Essays* (Englewood Cliffs, N.J.: Prentice-Hall, 1962); Hilfer, *Revolt from the Village,* 158–76; Martin Light, "The Quixotic Motifs of *Main Street,*" in *Critical Essays on Sinclair Lewis,* ed. Martin Bucco (Boston: G. K. Hall, 1986), 174–75.

7. Pelley, *The Fog,* 68, 218–19, 271.

8. Ibid., 4, 14. As Leo Ribuffo notes, Madge, "like all of Pelley's idealized women . . . personifies genteel refinement, appreciates sex without practicing it before marriage, and tries above all to help others." Ribuffo, *Old Christian Right,* 41. While Pelley's earlier works demonstrated his discomfort with women, *The Fog* takes his female objectification to new heights. Throughout the novel he routinely refers to the female characters simply as "The Sex."

9. Pelley, *The Fog,* 239.

10. The novel's financial success was not mirrored by literary critics, who found the book mediocre. Pelley later claimed that this unfavorable reception was part of the Jewish conspiracy in film and literature intended to denigrate the small town, causing Gentiles to move to the cities, where they could be "controlled or polluted." He also claimed that Jewish book reviewers were "obviously ignoring" the book. Pelley, *Door to Revelation,* 177–78, 185.

11. Ibid., 179–80.

12. Patricia King Hanson, ed. *The American Film Institute Catalog of Motion Pictures Produced in the United States: Feature Films, 1911–1920* (Berkeley: Univ. of California Press, 1988) 127, 678; *Variety,* Nov. 16, 1917, 52–53; *New York Daily Mail,* Nov. 17, 1917; Paul C. Spehr, *The Movies Begin: Making Movies in New Jersey, 1887–1920* (Newark, N.J.: Newark Museum, 1977), 108, 110; John T. Weaver, *Twenty Years of Silents, 1908–1928* (Metuchen, N.J.: Scarecrow Press, 1971), 196, 225, 282; Ephraim Katz, *The Film Encyclopedia* (New York: Perigee Books, 1979), 645.

13. Pelley, *Door to Revelation,* 182.

14. Ibid., 182–83. Pelley's daughter, Adelaide, seven years old at the time, later wrote of her first meeting with Chaney: "He came to dinner, bringing my mother a box of chocolates. After dinner he called me over to his side and put one of the little brown crinkled cups into each eye socket to give me my own personal little horror show. I was enchanted, of course, and didn't know for years that he made his living that way." Vance Pollock, "From Silverscreen to Silvershirt: Bill Pelley and Hollywood Antisemitism" (unpublished paper, in the author's possession, n.d.), 3.

15. Released by First National, the film premiered at the opening of the Strand Theater in Niagara Falls, N.Y., on Aug. 28, 1922. Andrew E. Mathis, *The King Arthur Myth in Modern American Literature* (Jefferson, N.C.: McFarland, 2002), 71–73; Kenneth Munden, *The American Film Institute Catalog of Motion Pictures Produced in the United States: Feature Films, 1921–1930* (New York: R. R. Bowker, 1971), 433; *Variety Film Reviews, 1921–1925* (New York: Garland, 1983), reviews for Sept. 1, 1922; Graham, "Crazy Like a Fox," 264; Michael Blake, *Lon Chaney: The Man Behind the Thousand Faces* (Vestal, N.Y.: Vestal Press, 1993), 85; Michael Blake, *The Films of Lon Chaney* (Lanham, Md.: Vestal Press, 1998), 120; Michael Blake, *A Thousand Faces: Lon Chaney's Unique Artistry in Motion Pictures* (Vestal, N.Y.: Vestal Press, 1995), 72; *San Francisco Chronicle,* Dec. 28, 1922; Katz, *Film Encyclopedia,* 171, 720–21; Weaver, *Twenty Years,* 160, 212; Pelley, *Door to Revelation,* 188; Spehr, *Movies Begin,* 45, 48.

16. Kalton Lahue, *Winners of the West: The Sagebrush Heroes of the Silent Screen* (New York: A. S. Barnes, 1970), 175–85; *Motion Picture News Booking Guide* 4, Apr. 1923, 29; Munden, *American Film Institute Catalog,* 27, 33; Weaver, *Twenty Years,* 135–36, 178–79; Spehr, *Movies Begin,* 132; *Variety Film Reviews, 1921–1925,* reviews for Dec. 15, 1922.

17. Pelley, *Door to Revelation,* 187. Despite its reputation as a Bohemian enclave, Greenwich Village also maintained a traditional "village" element throughout the 1920s. The melding of literary types and professionals, the increasing percentage of native white residents (particularly in the area north of Washington Square in which Pelley dwelled), and, by Manhattan standards, low population density obviously made the Village an attractive living environment for an individual such as Pelley (traditional but fiercely proud of his status as an artist). For an examination of Pelley's neighborhood, see Caroline F. Ware's classic study *Greenwich Village, 1920–1930: A Comment on American Civilization in the Post-War Years* (New York: Houghton Mifflin, 1935).

18. Pelley, *Door to Revelation,* 186–87.

19. Ibid., 193, 195.

20. Ibid., 183. Escaping from the watchful eye of his mother-in-law, who always required him to refer to her as Mrs. Holbrook, proved especially pleasing to Pelley. She had lived with the Pelleys for the majority of their marriage. Pelley later savagely characterized her in his novel *Drag* (Boston: Little, Brown, 1925).

21. Pelley, *Door to Revelation,* 198. Even after he concluded that the "Jewish question" represented the greatest danger to American society, Pelley still clearly felt proud of his tenure in Hollywood. In his autobiography Pelley noted with obvious glee that he found "zest and enticement in being part of necromantic picture-making in that flamboyant wild-cat period when the original Old Guard held all fronts." Ibid., 196. Pelley's decision to leave New York may also have been influenced by the 1923 death of his closest literary friend John Slidell of the *American Magazine.*

22. Blake, *Films of Lon Chaney,* 132; Blake, *A Thousand Faces,* 86; *Variety Film Reviews, 1921–1925,* reviews for June 7, 1923; Thomas Schatz, *The Genius of the System: Hollywood Filmmaking in the Studio Era* (New York: Pantheon, 1988), 15–28. With the success of *The Shock,* Universal boss Carl Laemmle allowed Chaney to handpick his next feature. Chaney chose to play the title character in *The Hunchback of Notre Dame* (1923); the film made him a star.

23. Munden, *American Film Institute Catalog,* 257–58, 340; Katz, *Film Encyclopedia,* 301, 535, 683–84; Weaver, *Twenty Years,* 98–99, 148; *Variety Film Reviews, 1912–1925,* reviews for July 12, 1923; *Santa Cruz Evening News,* Apr. 5, 1923.

24. Pelley, *Door to Revelation,* 197. For examples of Pelley's "plot" magazine, see Pelley, *Thrown Away* (New York: Cameo Picture Stories, 1923); Pelley, *Mother's Madness* (New York: Cameo Picture Stories, 1923). These unsold plots generally follow the same genteel lines as his short stories and produced scripts. However, one script, *Entrance in Rear* (New York: Cameo Picture Stories, 1923) uncharacteristically includes depictions of

homosexuality, prostitution, and white slavery. Pelley's pulp stories, quickly cranked out, often rehashed plots from the stories he previously sold to more reputable magazines. For representative examples, see "The Cloven Hoof," *PFM,* May 1921, 50–64, and "Right Miss Wright," *Pictorial Review,* Aug. 1925, 26–27.

25. Weaver, *Twenty Years,* 275, 317; Katz, *Film Encyclopedia,* 876; Munden, *American Film Institute Catalog,* 413; *Variety Film Reviews, 1921–1925,* reviews for May 21 and July 30, 1924; Larry Langman, *A Guide to Silent Westerns* (Westport, Conn.: Greenwood Press, 1992), 244.

26. Although it is unclear whether Chaney brought Pelley and Tourneur together, the director did work with Chaney on *Treasure Island* (1920). Spehr, *Movies Begin,* 170; Katz, *Film Encyclopedia,* 558, 736, 825, 1143; Munden, *American Film Institute Catalog,* 822; Weaver, *Twenty Years,* 220–21, 255–56; Kevin Brownlow, *Hollywood: The Pioneers* (New York: Knopf, 1979), 218.

27. *Drag,* 10, 172.

28. Pelley, *Door to Revelation,* 209–15.

29. Pelley had been particularly angered over Maurice Tourneur's rewrite of the script for *Torment,* which, in Pelley's original version, revolved around a modernization of the biblical tale of the feeding of the five thousand. Pelley, *Door to Revelation,* 196–97; Ribuffo, *Old Christian Right,* 45–46. On the Jewish studio heads that Pelley dealt with, see Schatz, *Genius of the System,* 15–48; Robert Sklar, *Movie-Made America: A Cultural History of American Movies,* rev. ed. (New York: Vintage, 1994), 38–42; Patricia Erens, *The Jew in American Cinema* (Bloomington, Ind.: Indiana Univ. Press, 1984), 53–54; Lester D. Friedman, *Hollywood's Image of the Jew* (New York: Frederick Ungar, 1982), 3–53; Benjamin B. Hampton, *A History of the Movies* (New York: Covici, Friede, 1931), 83–100; Neil Gabler, *An Empire of Their Own: How the Jews Invented Hollywood* (New York: Anchor, 1989), 47–64, 72–78.

30. Pelley, *Door to Revelation,* 197; Selzer, *"Kike!,"* 128–56; Gustavus Myers, *History of Bigotry in the United States* (New York: Random House, 1943), 277–313; William H. Short, *A Generation of Motion Pictures: A Review of Social Values in Recreational Films* (New York: National Committee for Study of Social Values in Motion Pictures, 1928), 112–17, 252–87; Harold Brackman, "The Attack on 'Jewish Hollywood': A Chapter in the History of Modern American Anti-Semitism," *Modern Judaism* 20 (Feb. 2000): 1–19. Lary May argues that the attacks on Hollywood during the 1920s reflect part of a larger Progressive attempt to regulate the new urban amusements that were perceived as a threat to middle-class children. While May is, to a degree, correct in his assessment, he is remiss in not recognizing the explicitly anti-Jewish nature at the core of much criticism of Hollywood during the decade. Lary May, *Screening Out the Past: The Birth of Mass Culture and the Motion Picture Industry* (New York: Oxford Univ. Press, 1980), 43–60. Scandalous behavior by motion picture stars and explicit portrayal of adult subject matter in films led to the first of several attempts to censor Hollywood product in the early 1920s. The literature on

film regulation is voluminous; for the best accounts see Annette Kuhn, *Cinema, Censorship, and Sexuality, 1909–1925* (New York: Routledge, 1988); Gregory D. Black, *Hollywood Censored: Morality Codes, Catholics, and the Movies* (New York: Cambridge Univ. Press, 1994); and Frank Miller, *Censored Hollywood: Sex, Sin, and Violence on Screen* (Atlanta: Turner Publishing, 1994).

31. Pelley, *Door to Revelation*, 197; Stanley Coben, *Rebellion Against Victorianism: The Impetus for Cultural Change in 1920s America* (New York: Oxford Univ. Press, 1991), 52–57.

32. Pelley, *Door to Revelation*, 218, 220.

33. Ibid., 230–31.

34. In mid-1926, Pelley also found time to file a lawsuit against the producers of a film who had "borrowed" the title of his novel *The Greater Glory*. The court found in Pelley's favor and awarded him $2500 in damages. Pelley developed a minor professional relationship with one of the defendants, scenarist June Mathis, who wrote parts of numerous box-office hits such as *Blood and Sand* (1922) and *Ben-Hur* (1925). After Pelley's conversion to spiritualism he began holding séances in his New York apartment. One of the first spirits to contact him in 1929, through medium George Wehner, was Mathis, who confided in him that all of her scripts were written clairaudiently. William Dudley Pelley, *Why I Believe the Dead Are Alive* (Indianapolis: Fellowship Press, 1942), 147–51.

35. Pelley, *Door to Revelation*, 229, 231, 283. Illustrating Pelley's developing anti-Semitism is the fact that German national Franz K. Ferenz, who operated Hollywood's Continental Theatre, served as *Hi-Hat*'s art director. Ferenz, one of five German-American Bundists arraigned, eventually stood with Pelley as a codefendant in the Mass Sedition Trial of 1944. Maximilian St.-George and Lawrence Dennis, *A Trial on Trial: The Great Sedition Trial of 1944* (National Civil Rights Committee, 1946), 321.

36. Pelley, *Door to Revelation*, 231.

37. Ibid., 231–32, 241–46; *New York Times*, June 29, 1927; June 30, 1927; July 2, 1927, July 4, 1927; July 5, 1927; July 6, 1927; Richard V. Grace, *Squadron of Death: The True Adventures of a Movie Planecrasher* (Garden City, N.Y.: Doubleday, Doran, 1929), 268–73. For accounts of the flying hysteria that arose in the wake of Lindbergh's trip, see Frederick Lewis Allen, *Only Yesterday* (New York: Harper and Row, 1931), 180–86; A. Scott Berg, *Lindbergh* (New York: G. P. Putnam's Sons, 1998), 161–65.

38. Munden, *American Film Institute Catalog*, 417; Katz, *Film Encyclopedia*, 688–89; *Variety Film Reviews, 1926–1929* (New York: Garland Publishing 1983), reviews for March 9, 1927.

39. Pelley, *Door to Revelation*, 273.

40. Ibid., 275–77.

41. Ibid., 286.

42. William Dudley Pelley, *The Blue Lamp* (New York: Fiction League, 1931), 72.

4. Seven Minutes in Eternity: 1928–1929

1. Selzer, *Kike!,* 228–29; David A. Gerber, "Anti-Semitism and Jewish-Gentile Relations in American Historiography and the American Past," in *Anti-Semitism in American History,* ed. David A. Gerber (Urbana: Univ. of Illinois Press, 1986), 24. The classic work on nativist thought is John Higham, *Strangers in the Land.* For a more recent assessment of nativist thought, see Juan F. Perea, ed. *Immigrants Out!: The New Nativism and the Anti-Immigrant Impulse in the United States* (New York: New York Univ. Press, 1997), 1–60.

2. Robert Singerman, "The Jew as Racial Alien: The Genetic Component of American Anti-Semitism," in *Immigrants Out! The New Nativism and the Anti-Immigrant Impulse in the United States,* ed. Juan F. Perea, 103–28 (New York: New York Univ. Press, 1997); Leonard Dinnerstein, *Antisemitism in America* (New York: Oxford Univ. Press, 1994), 58–77; Ivan Haddaford, *Race: The History of an Idea in the West* (Washington, D.C.: Woodrow Wilson Center Press, 1996), 348–59; David J. Goldberg, *Discontented America: The United States in the 1920s* (Baltimore: Johns Hopkins Univ. Press, 1999), 140–66; McLoughlin, *Revivals, Awakenings, and Reform,* 149–50. In 1916's *The Passing of the Great Race* (New York: C. Scribner's Sons), still widely circulated in racist circles, Madison Grant argued that education and environment were incapable of altering the lesser races. Grant believed that, to protect Anglo-Saxons from a demographic disaster, the United States needed to adopt complete racial segregation, official eugenics policies, and social engineering. For the connections between Grant, Gobineau, and Chamberlain, see Charles C. Alexander, "Prophet of American Racism: Madison Grant and the Nordic Myth," *Phylon* 23 (Spring 1962): 73–90. For the racist aspects of the eugenics movement, see Mark H. Haller, *Eugenics: Hereditarian Attitudes in American Thought* (New Brunswick, N.J.: Rutgers Univ. Press, 1963), 144–59.

3. Myers, *History of Bigotry,* 314–69. James Webb, *The Occult Establishment* (La Salle, Ill.: Open Court Press, 1976), 130. Although Brasol's translation was the first to appear in the United States, Victor Marsden of the English racist group the Britons holds the dubious distinction of first translating the *Protocols* into English. For Ford's anti-Semitic campaign, see Neil Baldwin, *Henry Ford and the Jews: The Mass Production of Hate* (New York: Public Affairs, 2001).

4. Leo Ribuffo, *Right Center Left: Essays in American History* (New Brunswick, N.J.: Rutgers Univ. Press, 1992), 72–103; John S. Curtiss, *An Appraisal of the Protocols of Zion* (New York: Columbia Univ. Press, 1942), 2, 58; Myers, *History of Bigotry,* 277–313; Ralph Lord Roy, *Apostles of Discord: A Study of Organized Bigotry and Disruption on the Fringes of Protestantism* (Boston: Beacon Press, 1953), 42–47. Although much of the *Protocols* was lifted from Joly's *Dialogue aux Enfers entre Montesquieu et Machiavel,* a portion of the book can also be traced to a short-story by Sir John Retcliffe [Herman Goedsche]. Herman Bernstein, *The History of a Lie: The Protocols of the Wise Men of Zion* (New York: J. S. Ogilvie, 1921), 16–43. The best work on the *Protocols* is Norman Cohn, *Warrant for Geno-*

cide:The Myth of the Jewish World-Conspiracy and the Protocols of the Elders of Zion (New York: Harper and Row, 1967). The *Protocols* continue to circulate in extremist circles and have obtained such "classic" status that they are now being reinterpreted as evidence of non-Jewish conspiracies. For example, William Cooper's 1991 work *Behold a Pale Horse* (Sedona, Ariz.: Light Technology Publishing) includes the *Protocols* with the proviso that the reader substitute the word "Illuminati" for "Jew," and "cattle" for "Goyim." The *Protocols* also recently served as the basis for parts of the Arab Radio and Television miniseries "Horseman Without a Horse." The thirty-part religious series ran on Egyptian television in the fall of 2001.

5. Werly, "Millenarian Right," 22-23. Pelley's increasingly anti-Semitic views also cost him his friendship with Lon Chaney. By 1928 Chaney made it clear to Pelley that, as a result of his anti-Jewish beliefs, the scriptwriter was not welcome in Lon's home. Pelley, *The Door to Revelation,* 262-63, 284-85; Blake, *A Thousand Faces,* 72.

6. Pelley, *Seven Minutes in Eternity,* 8; Pelley, *Door to Revelation,* 288-89. Chapter 4 of Houston Stewart Chamberlain's *Foundations of the Nineteenth Century* (New York: J. Lane, 1911) is devoted to answering this same question.

7. In most of his writings Pelley, in an attempt to demonstrate how surprising his conversion was, downplays any prior experience with spiritualism. However, furtive references to pre-1928 encounters with psychic phenomena do appear in some of his works. Pelley admits to communicating to his deceased brother-in-law through a ouija board in 1925 and reading a work on reincarnation by Sir Oliver Lodge (probably in 1927). Also, he was good friends with *American Magazine* fiction editor Mary Derieux, an open advocate of psychical research. Pelley, *Why I Believe,* 18-28; Pelley, *Seven Minutes in Eternity,* 8; Pelley, *Door to Revelation,* 247-55. Lodge, an English scientist, was probably the most famous spiritualist in the world during the early twentieth century. He gained international notoriety after the publication of his communications with his dead son, Raymond. Lodge also developed the psychic screen theory, which holds that the body is a device that limits a person's action in the material world and is so constructed that it prevents the mind from perceiving surrounding psychic realities. Clairvoyants, according to Lodge, have defective psychic screens and are thereby able to view the nonmaterial cosmos. Lodge's most famous work is *Raymond, or Life and Death* (London: Methuen, 1916). For a brief introduction to his views, see Oliver Lodge, "Design and Purpose in the Universe," in *The Great Design: Order and Intelligence in Nature,* ed. Frances Mason (New York: Macmillan, 1936), 225-33. On Lodge's career, see W. P. Jolly, *Sir Oliver Lodge* (London: Constable, 1974).

8. Pelley, *Seven Minutes in Eternity,* 10-11.

9. Pelley's anxiety over sexuality continued even during his spiritual conversion. In one account of the "seven minutes" he noted that, although naked, he "felt strangely sexless." Pelley, *Door to Revelation,* 292.

10. Pelley, *Seven Minutes,* 15. That "William," in some of Pelley's accounts of the ex-

perience, died in 1917 is troublesome, as Pelley also asserted that he was the disincarnated soul of Bert Boyden, deceased managing editor of *American Magazine.*

11. Ibid., 18, 22; Pelley, *Door to Revelation,* 287–309.

12. Pelley, *Seven Minutes,* 44, 47–48; Pelley, *Door to Revelation,* 310, 316.

13. Ibid., 281, 310; James, *Varieties of Religious Experience,* 188–258. Pelley's conversion experience is not unique among figures on the extremist right. Others who have undergone similar life-changing spiritual events include Lyndon LaRouche, Gerald L. K. Smith, and, according to some accounts, Adolf Hitler. Pelley fully believed that Hitler underwent a similar experience. Referring later to the "seven minutes," Pelley noted that "Adolf would understand exactly what happened that night in my bungalow." Pelley, *Door to Revelation,* 310; Glen Jeansonne, "Combating Anti-Semitism: The Case of Gerald L. K. Smith," in Gerber, *Anti-Semitism in American History,* 152–67; Dennis King, *Lyndon LaRouche and the New American Fascism* (New York: Doubleday, 1989), 33; Rudolf Olden, *Hitler, the Pawn* (New York: Covici, Friede, 1936), 69; Robert G. L. Waite, *The Psychopathic God: Adolf Hitler* (New York: Basic Books, 1977), 31–32.

14. Pelley, *Seven Minutes in Eternity,* 27–28; Pelley, *Door to Revelation,* 314–15. Sir Oliver Lodge's critics often fastened upon the sheer frivolity of much that he reported occurring in the spirit realms (the manufacturing of cigars and whiskey, for example), and Pelley opened himself up to similar attacks. Pelley's claim that "William" told him to start smoking again as it opened up his subconscious mind and made him a "better receiving organism," and the description of a séance during which his grandfather materialized and explained that he cut off his whiskers because they were no longer in fashion on the "other side," are difficult to take seriously and certainly undercut his credibility. Pelley's position as an ascetic mystic was also hampered by statements such as "some of the best telekinetic work which I myself have accomplished was done by a sort of lucky accident in a Buick coupe . . . when the windows of the coupe were all closed." Pelley, *Why I Believe,* 36–37, 290; Pelley, *Did the Sun Stand Still for Joshua?* (Asheville, N.C.: Fellowship Foundation, n.d. [1935]), 9; Jolly, *Sir Oliver Lodge,* 206.

15. For Derieux's views, see Mary Derieux, "Starting a New Era," *Psychic Research* 22 (Jan. 1928): 1–5.

16. Pelley, *Why I Believe,* 42–45. Although the notion that evil does not exist and is merely ignorance is traditionally associated with the East (the Hindu notion of *avidya,* for example), it is also a common belief among Western metaphysical movements; Alice Bailey's Arcane School is one promoter of this concept. Typically it is rooted in the theory that good is the totality of reality, hence evil is unreal (or ignorance). With God being good, and present in all things, evil is simply the absence of good and is unreal. J. Stillson Judah, *The History and Philosophy of the Metaphysical Movements in America* (Philadelphia: Westminster Press, 1967), 44, 119–31; Robert Laurence Moore, "Spiritualism," in *The Rise of Adventism: Religion and Society in Mid-Nineteenth-Century America,* ed. Edwin S. Gaustad (New York: Harper and Row, 1974), 79–104. For an example of this privative

doctrine of evil that influenced Pelley's thought, see Ralph Waldo Emerson, *Centenary Edition: The Complete Works* (New York: Houghton Mifflin, 1903), IV: 87. In the Western esoteric tradition this view of evil is largely derived from Neoplatonism. Plotinus argued that God emanated into all levels of reality, but his presence weakened the closer one came to the lowest depth of reality—the level of matter. In this bottom level his being (and purity) was no longer present, leaving matter evil. As man's divine spark was encased in a material skin, he was a participant in the process of evil. Accentuating the material side of being rather than the spiritual one, therefore, increased the evil one did. Philippus Villiers Pistorious, *Plotinus and Neoplatonism: An Introductory Study* (London: Bowes and Bowes, 1952), 117–29.

17. Pelley, *Why I Believe,* 45. Never one to shy away from his own bloated sense of self-importance, Pelley bombastically summarized that his brevet was to "contribute to a vast tidal-wave of enlightenment on the question of occupancy of flesh, and provide a prologue as I was able by means of my prestige in literary craftsmanship to the vast Aquarian Revelation that was slated to visit upon current humanity, altering the concepts of orthodox religion and giving man his correct cue as to what he might be doing in the three-dimensional octave and what evolutions of spirit await him when he has mastered the lessons of Mortality." Ibid., 32.

18. Judah, *History and Philosophy of Metaphysical Movements,* 82–84.

19. R. Laurence Moore, *In Search of White Crows: Spiritualism, Para-Psychology, and American Culture* (New York: Oxford Univ. Press, 1977), 142–67.

20. Ibid., 170–75; Seymour H. Mauskopf and Michael R. McVaugh, *The Elusive Science: Origins of Experimental Psychical Research* (Baltimore: Johns Hopkins Univ. Press, 1980), 44–71; Matthew Josephson, *Edison: A Biography* (New York: McGraw-Hill, 1959), 439. Pelley was well aware of Edison's spiritualist experiments; see John J. O'Neill, "Did Edison on His Deathbed Behold the Next World?" *NLW,* Nov. 21 1931, 208–9. Lodge and Doyle's tours consisted of lectures exclusively on the topic of spiritualism. Doyle's accounts of these tours are the basis of Sir Arthur Conan Doyle, *Our American Adventure* (London: Hodder and Stoughton, 1924) and *Our Second American Adventure* (London: Hodder and Stoughton, 1925). Although spiritualism first gained national attention in the United States with the "spirit rappings" of the nineteenth-century Fox sisters, scientific study of paranormal phenomena peaked in the 1920s and 1930s. ASPR members belittled much of the pop-culture aspects of spiritualism and sought to establish the scientific basis of "true" paranormal events through the development of psychical research, defined by R. Laurence Moore as "the systematic inquiry into whether human minds receive information in ways that bypass the normal channels of sensory communication, or interact with matter in ways not yet comprehensible to physical science." R. Laurence Moore, *White Crows,* 134. For an overview on development of spiritualism in the United States, see Judah, *History and Philosophy of Metaphysical Movements,* 50–91.

21. Mauskopf and McVaugh, *Elusive Science,* 95–164; R. Laurence Moore, *White*

Crows, 185–203. The unique nature of the Duke program is probably best illustrated by the difficulty graduate student John Thomas had with his dissertation committee in May 1932. The committee initially refused to accept the work because Thomas, in their judgment, did not state strongly enough that his test subject possessed supernormal means of acquiring information. Rhine's best-selling work was *Extra-Sensory Perception* (Boston: Boston Society for Psychic Research, 1934). For Rhine's career, see Denis Brian, *The Enchanted Voyager: The Life of J. B. Rhine* (Englewood Cliffs, N.J.: Prentice-Hall, 1982); K. Ramakhrishna Rao, ed. *J. B. Rhine: On the Frontiers of Science* (Jefferson, N.C.: McFarland, 1982).

22. For a discussion of "Margery" and other disputes of the period, see Thomas R. Tietze, *Margery* (New York: Harper and Row, 1973). Pelley believed "Margery's" ectoplasm was, in fact, material evidence of other planes of reality. Pelley, *Why I Believe,* 172.

23. Ibid., 58.

24. "My Seven Minutes in Eternity—The Amazing Experience That Made Me Over," *AM,* Mar. 7–9, 1929, 139–43; Pelley, *Why I Believe,* 102. The magazine version of the story is an abbreviated account of the narrative I outlined above. Although essentially identical in most details, only the pamphlet version contains an account of the second visit to the portico with its discussion of racial issues and meeting with deceased friends. Pelley's description of his clairaudient experience as "super radio" is not surprising. Spiritualists of the period often utilized terms relating to developing technologies, particularly those based upon invisible "forces," as metaphors and defenses for their own, unseeable powers. The most famous example of this phenomenon is Upton Sinclair, *Mental Radio* (New York: Albert and Charles Boni, 1930). Pelley also made the connection between spiritualism and technology in the *American* article. "Seven Minutes," 144. Pelley's tale of trance clairvoyance was one of many popular accounts during the decade. Other successful works along the same vein include Caroline D. Larsen, *My Travels in the Spirit World* (Rutland, Vt.: Tuttle Company, 1927) and Hereward Carrington, *The Projection of the Astral Body* (London: Rider, 1929).

25. Ribuffo, *Old Christian Right,* 51; Pelley, *Door to Revelation,* 310, 332, 351; House, Special Committee on Un-American Activities, *Hearings on Investigation of Un-American Propaganda Activities in the United States,* 75th–78th Cong., 1938–1941 (hereafter cited as HUAC), 6:4186. Among those who wrote positive responses to Pelley regarding the "seven minutes" was Sir Arthur Conan Doyle. Pelley, *Door to Revelation,* 332–35.

26. Pelley, *Why I Believe,* 140–52; Brad Steiger and Sherry Hansen-Steiger, *Hollywood and the Supernatural* (New York: St. Martin's Press, 1990), 3–11. Wehner established a name for himself in Hollywood by channeling messages from the spirit of Rudolph Valentino, who, while living, followed the advice of a spirit guide named "Meselope." Wehner earned a small fortune providing these messages for Valentino's widow, Natacha Rambova. Pelley spent a great deal of time with Wehner in New York during this period. Wehner often held séances in Pelley's apartment, where, allegedly, Valentino frequently

materialized. The standard format for this meetings involved a group recital of the Lord's Prayer, followed by the playing of "dreamy music," and, finally, Wehner's entrance into a trance state. The reciting of Christian prayers (or hymns) was very common during séances held by traditional-minded mediums of the period. They derived this practice from nineteenth-century spiritualist Andrew Jackson Davis's Law of Attractions. Under this Law, like attracted like and, Davis posited, love and kindness were essential to attracting the perfected spirits of higher planes during sessions. To his death, Davis encouraged prayer at the beginning of séances as a means of purifying the area and attracting positive energies. Judah, *History and Philosophy of Metaphysical Movements,* 39–40; Pelley, *Why I Believe,* 140–41; William Dudley Pelley, *Soul Eternal* (Noblesville, Ind.: Soulcraft Chapels, 1955), 246–47.

27. Pelley, *Why I Believe,* 130–33, 152–55.

28. William Dudley Pelley, *Golden Rubbish* (New York: G. P. Putnam's Sons, 1929), 103, 199–200, 223.

29. Ibid., 303. George also notes of Louise, in an example of the pompous verbosity of which the last two hundred pages of the book consists, that she "has a tendency to protest self-evident truths in order to prove their inherent legality—using the term in its literal sense. You have a weakness for taking things given you and denying their existence even as you take them—professing to be one thing and being quite another. I hope I don't offend you." One wishes Pelley had shown the same level of concern for his readers. Ibid., 274.

30. Ibid., 287–89, 298, 318.

31. Ibid., 410–11, 422.

32. Pelley's 1929 short stories include: "The Woman Across the Street," *AM,* Apr., 40–43; "The Higher Summons," *AM,* May, 14–17, 144–50; "Life Is to Find Out," *AM,* June, 36–39, 73–77; "Dark Happiness—Part I," *AM,* July, 18–21, 112–21; "Dark Happiness—Part II," *AM,* Aug., 40–43, 118–31; "Dark Happiness—Part III," *AM,* Sept., 64–67, 139–44; and "Dark Happiness—Part IV," *AM,* Oct., 62–65, 182–85.

33. Pelley, *Why I Believe,* 72; Pelley, *Door to Revelation,* 334–35; "Why I Have No Quarrel with Any Existent Creed," *NL,* May 1930, 118; Ribuffo, *Old Christian Right,* 51.

34. Munden, *American Film Institute Catalog,* 149, 201; Katz, *Film Encyclopedia,* 86; Weaver, *Twenty Years,* 43; Frederic Thrasher, *Okay for Sound* (New York: Duell, Sloan, and Pearce, 1946), 33; A. M. Sherwood, Jr., "The Movie Drag," *Outlook and Independent* 24, July (1929): 516; *Variety Film Reviews, 1926–1929,* reviews for June 26, Dec. 25, 1929; Colin Shindler, *Hollywood in Crisis: Cinema and American Society, 1929–1939* (London: Routledge, 1996), 3; Hampton, *History of the Movies,* 374–87; Harry M. Geduld, *The Birth of the Talkies* (Bloomington: Indiana Univ. Press, 1975), 153–59. Broadway producer Frank Riley also took out an option to produce a stage version of *Drag* in 1929, but the play never opened. Pelley, *Door to Revelation,* 256–57, 283.

35. "Seven Minutes," 144; Pelley, *Why I Believe,* 122; Pelley, *Door to Revelation,* 335.

5. Liberation: 1930–1932

1. James posited that attainment of unity may involve "some new stimulus or fash-ion" outside the spiritual, but "in all these instances we have precisely the same psycho-logical form of event—a firmness, stability, and equilibrium succeeding a period of storm and stress and inconsistency." James, *Varieties of Religious Experience,* 175–76.

2. Fred B. Bond, "Subjective Evidence for Survival or Continuity," *Journal of the American Society for Psychical Research* 24 (Jan. 1930): 35–38.

3. *The Door to Revelation,* 333; Ribuffo, *Old Christian Right,* 49; Pelley, *Seven Minutes in Eternity,* 47–48; "Why Do Thousands of People All Get the Same Details about Those in the After-Life?" *NL,* (Aug.-Sept. 1931): 110–11. Emanuel Swedenborg's influence on the Western esoteric tradition of the last two hundred years cannot be underestimated. His ideas served as the underlying principles for a variety of movements, including Mes-merism, transcendentalism, spiritualism, Theosophy, current New Age groups, and, most directly, the Church of the New Jerusalem (the New Church). After undergoing a con-version experience in 1743, at age fifty-six, Swedenborg became the first modern "chan-neler," receiving messages from Jesus, God, Plato, and other historical luminaries. Swedenborg's most significant contributions to modern esotericism include the concept of pre- and post-existence in a spiritual state, a monistic idea of God, initiates cognizant of important events occurring in invisible spirit realms, and the belief in an eternal, spiritual record of every thought, action, and emotion accumulated during a lifetime (a concept usually referred to in spiritualist circles as the "Akashic Records"). Despite the breadth of his influence, Swedenborg has few direct followers today. While his writings are still in print, the Church of New Jerusalem remains a small, insignificant player in current meta-physics. This state of affairs probably would not trouble Swedenborg as he exhibited a thorough ambivalence toward the establishment of a church, preferring his teachings to be passed by word-of-mouth among devotees. In the United States, for example, the New Church converted far fewer people than did John "Johnny Appleseed" Chapman, who left Swedenborg pamphlets in the frontier cabins he visited. Rosemary Ellen Guiley, *Harper's Encyclopedia of Mystical and Paranormal Experience* (Edison, N.J.: Castle Books, 1991), 590–93; Robert S. Ellwood and Harry B. Partin, *Religious and Spiritual Groups in Modern America,* 2d ed. (Englewood Cliffs, N.J.: Prentice-Hall, 1988), 51–52; Ahlstrom, *Religious History,* 483–88. Charles W. Ferguson, *The Confusion of Tongues: A Review of Modern Isms* (Garden City, N.Y.: Doubleday, Doran, and Company, 1929), 340–63. The literature of Swedenborg is extensive and rife with partisan bickerings; the best sources are Marguerite Block, *The New Church in the New World: A Study of Swedenborgianism in the New World* (New York: Henry Holt, 1932) and Signe Toksvig, *Emanuel Swedenborg, Scientist and Mys-tic* (New Haven, Conn.: Yale Univ. Press, 1948). A modern study addressing Sweden-borg's influence on Aquarian New Age movements is in order.

4. Pelley, *Door to Revelation,* 345–46, 350, 353; "Behold the Man," *NL,* May 1930, 1.

Pelley issued periodicals with a variety of similar titles for over a decade. The exact titles and dates of publication are as follows: *New Liberator* (1930–1931); *New Liberator Weekly* (1931–1932); *Liberation* (1932–1934); *New Liberation* (1937–1938); *Weekly Liberation* (1938); *Liberation* (1938–1941). The only article in the May 1930 issue not written by Pelley was Charlotte Chopin Koster. "Why the Present Wave of Spiritual Experiment." *NL,* 35–37. Employed by Pelley as New York secretary since early 1929, Koster accepted another position in mid-1930 and drifted out of Pelley's orbit. She was replaced by Mary Joyce Benner, an out-of-work theater director. She not only organized Pelley's correspondence, but also obtained one of the very few advertisers in the 1930 version of *New Liberation,* Sun Publishing Company. The Akron, Ohio, based Sun published numerous esoteric works (and was owned by Benner's father).

5. "Strange Mutterings and Rumblings Are Heard in the East," *NL,* May 1930, 6; "The True Significance of Present Russian Atheism," *NL,* May 1930, 38–39.

6. Pelley, *Door to Revelation,* 350–52.

7. Included in the early *New Liberation* advertisements were pitches for Robbins's own book, *How to Demonstrate Prosperity* (New York: Galahad Press, 1930). Robbins wrote extensively on a variety of spiritualist and harmonial topics during the 1920s, most extensively on the work of Emile Coue.

8. Walter Kafton-Minkel, *Subterranean Worlds: 100,000 Years of Dragons, Dwarfs, the Dead, Lost Races, and UFOs from Inside the Earth* (Port Townsend, Wash.: Loompanics Unlimited, 1989), 122–24; Wishar S. Cerve [H. Spencer Lewis], *Lemuria: The Lost Continent of the Pacific* (San Jose, Calif: AMORC, 1931); Judah, *History and Philosophy of Metaphysical Movements,* 96–97; Henry Steel Olcott, *Old Diary Leaves: The True Story of the Theosophical Movement* (New York: G. P. Putnam's Sons, 1895), 207; Ellwood and Partin, *Religious and Spiritual Groups,* 90–93. For discussions of Rosicrucian history and beliefs, see Arthur E. Waite, *The Brotherhood of the Rosy Cross* (London: William Rider and Son, 1924); Frances A. Yates, *The Rosicrucian Enlightenment* (London: Routledge and Keegan Paul, 1972); and H. Spencer Lewis, *Rosicrucian Questions and Answers* (San Jose, Calif.: AMORC, 1929). Although Pelley borrowed liberally from the AMORC in developing his own religious system, he later broke with Lewis and claimed the AMORC leader used Pelley's name without permission to further his own organization. Pelley, *Door to Revelation,* 349.

9. Charles S. Braden, *These Also Believe: A Study of Modern American Cults and Minority Religious Movements* (New York: Macmillan, 1949), 78–128; J. Gordon Melton, *Biographical Dictionary of American Cult and Sect Leaders* (New York: Garland, 1986), 239–40; Marcus Bach, *Strange Sects and Curious Cults* (New York: Dodd, Mead, 1961), 154–75. For a firsthand account, see Frank B. Robinson, *The Strange Autobiography of Frank B. Robinson* (Moscow, Idaho: Psychiana, 1941). Collier's *Secret of the Ages* sold over half a million copies, making it one of New Thought's best sellers. Braden, *Spirits in Rebellion,* 272–75.

10. *NL,* Apr. 1931, vi-viii; Harold Lavine, *Fifth Column in America* (New York: Dou-

bleday, 1940), 181–82; HUAC, 6:4186–88; Pelley, *Door to Revelation,* 353–54. Pelley legally changed the press's name to Galahad Press on Mar. 23, 1931.

11. Pelley, *Door to Revelation,* 343, 354–57. Pelley met Vinton while speaking before a group associated with Robert Collier's *Mind Magazine.*

12. Pelley, *Door to Revelation,* 374–75; "The League of Liberation," *NL,* July 1931, iii; *Program of Services for the Twenty-Second Assembly* (New York, [1931]), 11; Ribuffo, *Old Christian Right,* 56.

13. Pelley, *Door to Revelation,* 355–57, 390–91; *Program of Services for the Twenty-Second Assembly,* 11; Hoppes, "William Dudley Pelley and the Silvershirt Legion," 54, 108. Typical "Pink Script" topics included: "What Is the Holy Spirit and How Does It Cure?", "That Great Migration of Souls to This Planet," "Which Souls Make Up the Dark Forces," "Identify Your Soul in Eternity" and "How to Understand the Workings of Karma." Some of these weekly discussion groups devolved into truly absurd arguments. In the *Program of Services for the Thirty-Second Assembly* (New York, [1931]), Pelley claimed that a man he knew put dollar bills in his pockets, spent them, then found the same dollars (with the same serial numbers) returned to his pocket. Several local group leaders contacted the league for clarification of this matter as it led to heated debates over "if this were a general practice, a charge of counterfeiting [would be] brought against that person." Letter from Henry Montgomery Hardwicke to William Dudley Pelley, May 2, 1932, North Carolina State Archives, Buncombe County Criminal Action Papers, State vs. Pelley, 1931–1944, Folder 8 (hereafter cited as N.C. Archives).

14. *Program of Services for the Twenty-Eighth Assembly* (New York, [1931]), 4–5; "The League of Liberation," iii, vi–vii; Werly, "Millenarian Right," 32.

15. "For Sale!," *NL,* Aug.-Sept. 1931, v; "Liberator Master Assemblies," *NL,* vi; Pelley, *Door to Revelation,* 355–71; HUAC, 12:7308. Edgerton served as the INTA's first president from 1915 to 1924. For his views see, James A. Edgerton, *The Philosophy of Jesus: The Basis of a New Philosophy* (Boston: Christopher Publishing House, 1928) and *Invading the Invisible* (Washington, D.C.: New Age Press, 1931). For his career, see Tom Beebe, *Who's Who in New Thought: Biographical Dictionary of New Thought—Personnel, Centers, and Authors' Publications* (Lakemont, Ga.: CSA Press, 1977), 65; Braden, *Spirits in Rebellion,* 211–17.

16. Pelley, *Door to Revelation,* 334.

17. Ibid., 370–71. For Terry's views, see Lillian E. Terry, *The Beloved Order, Received by the Sword and the Cup* (Black Mountain, N.C.: The Printery, 1928).

18. Certified copy of chattel mortgage: Galahad Press, Inc. to Foundation for Christian Economics, N.C. Archives, Folder 6; Letter from Henry Montgomery Hardwicke to William Dudley Pelley, May 11, 1932, ibid., Folder 8; Notice of Annual Meeting of Common Stockholders of Galahad Press, Incorporated, ibid., Folder 14. Pelley kept sixty shares of the common stock for himself, dividing the other forty between Mina and Summerville. Pelley continued to hawk worthless Galahad stock in the spring of 1932. His questionable business practices bore the ruinous fruit of legal entanglements in 1934. "Put

Your Money under the Auspices of a Militant Christian Organization," *Lib,* Apr. 1932, vi-vii.

19. HUAC, 6:4201, 12:7204–5; Pelley, *Door to Revelation,* 386–88; "Put Your Money under the Auspices of a Militant Christian Institution," ii.

20. Pelley, *Door to Revelation,* 378–81; Hoppes, "William Dudley Pelley and the Silvershirt Legion," 54. That the Williamses were followers proved a fortuitous development, as they willingly agreed to continue printing Pelley's materials even during the long periods in which he could not pay them for these services.

21. Pelley, *Door to Revelation,* 388; Pelley, *Why I Believe,* 171–76.

22. Pelley, *Door to Revelation,* 397–98; Werly, "Millenarian Right," 35. John Werly studied the extant records of Galahad College's graduates and found that two-thirds were women and virtually all of them were 40–60 years of age. Ibid., 27. The gender and age of Pelley's students corresponds with general trends of spiritualism during the period. George Lawton, *The Drama of Life After Death: A Study of the Spiritualist Religion* (New York: Henry Holt, 1932), 175. Pelley based his lectures on the school's motto: "Make Public Stewardship Your Profession." His talks included the following topics: ethical history, public stewardship, spiritual eugenics, social metaphysics, Christian philosophy, educational therapy, college music, public expression, and cosmic mathematics.

23. HUAC, 6:4191; Werly, "Millenarian Right," 34–35; "What You Can Get!" circular letter, n.d. [1932], Parker Papers, Folder 10. Responsible for housekeeping at the college, Mina was undoubtedly happy no more students were coming.

24. Robert Summerville to George Parker, Dec. 20, 1932, Parker Papers, Folder 4.

25. Hoppes, "William Dudley Pelley and the Silvershirt Legion," 56–57; "M.B.C" to Sophia Parker, Nov. 5, 1932, Parker Papers, Folder 5.

26. "Why Do Thousands of People All Get the Same Details?" 110–12; Ribuffo, *Old Christian Right,* 53; William Dudley Pelley, *Stairs To Greatness* (Noblesville, Ind.: Soulcraft Fellowship, 1956), 115. Pelley's claim that he received his brevet from higher, otherwordly powers is a foreshadowing of his future career. As Jacques Vallee has noted these types of claims are a central precept of authoritarian regimes since the times of divine-right monarchs. Jacques Vallee, *Messengers of Deception: UFO Contacts and Cults* (Berkeley, Calif.: And/Or Press, 1979), 114–15.

27. William Dudley Pelley, *Star Guests: Design for Mortality* (Noblesville, Ind.: Fellowship Press, 1950). Although published much later, *Star Guests* consists of material originally written in 1928–30. Pelley also argued that the human mind "is divided into two parts, with the conscious retaining most of the memories of the present life-experience and the subconscious composed of the sum-total of all the lives we have ever experienced blended to make us the spiritual persons we are." "If We Have Lived Other Earthly Lives Why Do We Not Consciously Remember Them?" *NL,* Dec. 1931, 190.

28. Pelley, *Star Guests,* 39, 193–94.

29. Ibid, 40–41; Pelley., *Why I Believe,* 299–300; "You Can Remember Before You

Were Born," *NL,* May 1930, 10; Pelley, *How Divine Thought Shapes Events* (Asheville, N.C.: Pelley Publishers, n.d. [1933]), 12; Pelley, *Did the Sun Stand Still for Joshua?* 3; Steven E. Ozment, *Mysticism and Dissent: Religious Ideology and Social Protest in the Sixteenth Century* (New Haven, Conn.: Yale Univ. Press, 1973), 85. Pelley's attacks on orthodox Christian ministers also frequently included self-serving messages from the spiritual realms that the people most qualified to lead mass movements were artists and psychics. Because it did not correspond with his notions on karma and reincarnation, Pelley also decried the notion of Christ's vicarious atonement. Pelley's claim that the Bible had been purposefully misinterpreted is not unique. J. Stillson Judah noted that "nearly all the metaphysical sects interpret the Bible in this assertedly intuitive way so that the Bible may not be inconsistent with their particular 'scientific' beliefs. . . . [I]n this manner the Bible is made to reveal the laws of a spiritual science that the particular group believes it has found." This technique has been utilized by, among others, Swedenborg, Mary Baker Eddy, Helena Blavatsky, Guy and Edna Ballard, and the Universal Spiritualist Association. Judah, *History and Philosophy of Metaphysical Movements in America,* 37. Just as Pelley frequently received messages from the "Great Avatar," many other American spiritualists claimed to obtain information directly from Christ. Lawton, *Drama of Life After Death,* 569.

30. William Dudley Pelley, *Why the Holy Spirit Displays as Life* (Asheville, N.C.: Pelley Publishers, n.d. [1933]), 11–14.

31. Pelley, *Star Guests,* 44, 116.

32. Ibid., 45–46, 62, 75–76.

33. Ibid., 46; "A Stupendous Army of Celestial Instructors Has Come into Flesh in This Generation," *NL,* June-Oct. 1930, 56.

34. Pelley, *Star Guests,* 166–67. The theory that advanced souls assisted those in dark, lower spheres was previously worked out in G. Vale Owen, *The Life Beyond the Veil,* 4 vols. (London: Hutchinson, 1924), 1:91–92. Pelley undoubtedly derived this Catharite ternary system of humanity (initiates, adepts, masses) from Theosophy. Bruce F. Campbell, *Ancient Wisdom Revived: A History of the Theosophical Movement* (Berkeley: Univ. of California Press, 1980), 39.

35. Pelley, *Star Guests,* 30–31; "You Can Remember Before You Were Born," 10; "You May Go into the Next Life Unaware That You Have Experienced the Change Called Death," *NL,* May 1931, 252. The returning souls often exhibited the same personality as previous incarnations and sought out the souls they had known on earth before. In his spiritualist novel *Golden Rubbish,* Pelley also declared that last names are temporary and only affected "our most recent descent into the Vale of Experience," but first names were "utilized with permanence by the forces of Spirit." This peculiar belief may have derived from the religious significance that some spiritualists placed upon Pelley's first name, which can be interpreted as "Will of the I AM." Pelley, *Golden Rubbish,* 278.

36. Pelley, *Star Guests,* 49; Pelley, *Why I Believe,* 83. The issue of evil raised real problems for Pelley. At times he attacked the "crazy souls" for their actions, but in other writ-

ings he posited that hatred and evil were merely the absence of Love. As the decade progressed and his millenarian anti-Semitic views came to the fore, he dispensed with even this equivocal level of tolerance.

37. "And They Were Astonished at His Doctrine," *NL,* May 1930, 48. Pelley's inconsistencies were not surprising or unusual. In his classic study of spiritualism, George Lawton noted that "mediums are not systematic readers or students, neither are they systematic thinkers." Lawton, *Drama of Life After Death,* 184. For the closest Pelley ever came to concisely outlining his views on reincarnation, see "Do You Understand Reincarnation?" *NL,* Nov. 1930, 119–24.

38. Pelley, *Why I Believe,* 65, 94–96; "Are You Terrified at the Prospect of the Theological Day of Judgment?" *NL,* Dec. 1930, 171; George Parker to "E. G.," Jan. 7, 1933, Parker Papers, Folder 5.

39. "Why Do Thousands of People All Get the Same Details?" 110–12. For other examples of "Summerland," see Owen, *Life Beyond the Veil,* I, 50–52; Lawton, *Drama of Life After Death,* 92–132; W. T. Stead, *After Death, or Letters from Julia* (Chicago: Progressive Thinker Publishing House, 1909), 5–6.

40. Pelley, *Why I Believe,* 98. G. Vale Owen first detailed the existence of exactly ten spheres in *Life Beyond the Veil,* 1:223–24. Later, like Pelley, he ruminated on the possibility of fourteen spheres. Ibid., 4:139. Pelley also occasionally adopted the standard spiritualist view that only seven spheres existed. Lawton, *Drama of Life After Death,* 69–86; R. Laurence Moore, "Spiritualism," 90–91. According to Pelley, the soul that incarnated as Jesus Christ did so after leaving the Sixth Sphere. Pelley, *As Thou Lovest: The Biography of a Benefaction* (Noblesville, Ind.: Soulcraft Chapels, 1955), 189.

41. "Do You Know How to Put a Protective Armor about Your Mental Self?" *NL,* June 1931, 47; "Strange Mutterings and Rumblings Are Heard in the East," 6–8.

42. The literature of Theosophy is vast and unreliable. For the best accounts, see Campbell, *Ancient Wisdom Revived;* Braden, *These Also Believe,* 221–56; Gaius Glenn Adkins, *Modern Religious Cults and Movements* (London: George Allen and Unwin, 1924), 245–83; and Peter Washington, *Madame Blavatsky's Baboon: A History of the Mystics, Mediums, and Misfits Who Brought Spiritualism to America* (New York: Schocken Books, 1991). Blavatsky's primary works, *Isis Unveiled: A Master Key to the Mysteries of Ancient and Modern Science and Theology* (1877; repr., Pasadena, Calif.: Theosophical Univ. Press, 1972) and *The Secret Doctrine: The Synthesis of Science, Religion, and Philosophy* (1888; repr., Pasadena, Calif.: Theosophical Univ. Press), are recommended only for zealots and insomniacs. The curious are advised to start with the primer, Helena P. Blavatsky, *An Invitation to the Secret Doctrine* (1895; repr., Pasadena, Calif.: Theosophical Univ. Press, 1988). Something of a anti-Semite herself, HPB's theories of cosmic evolution and root-races were wide open for interpretations based upon racial superiority, particularly as she noted that stragglers from previous root races still survived on earth. Webb, *Occult Establishment,* 125–36, 213–67. Pelley's theories on human creation also belied a debt to Theosophy. Blavatsky

also argued that extraterrestrial life bred with earth creatures, in this case sixteen-foot-tall Lemurians (or the fourth subrace of the third root-race) to create humanity as we know it. In Blavatsky's version, however, the aliens brought sexual reproduction to earth, not, as in Pelley's system, the other way around. While Pelley's views most heavily reflected a Theo-sophical influence, his ideas on nonterrestrial life may also have developed from his read-ing of the esoterically minded French astronomer Camille Flammarion. For a summation of Flammarion's views, see Michael J. Crowe, *The Extraterrestrial Life Debate, 1750–1900: The Idea of a Plurality of Worlds from Kant to Lowell* (Cambridge: Cambridge Univ. Press, 1986), 367–86.

43. Emmett A. Greenwalt, *The Point Loma Community in California, 1897–1942: A Theosophical Experiment* (Berkeley: Univ. of California Press, 1955), 202. Blavatsky listed the most important Ascended Masters as Morya, Serapis, Koot Hoomi, the Venetian Mas-ter, Buddha, Moses, Confucius, and Jesus Christ. She most likely borrowed the notion of Masters from the Rosicrucians. For a summary of Western esoteric teachings on "hidden masters," see Kafton-Minkel, *Subterranean Worlds,* 108–19. The most famous of all Theo-sophical dissenters, Steiner established the Anthroposophical Society in 1913 after break-ing with the Theosophical establishment over potential "world-teacher" Khrishnamurti. Best remembered for creating eurythmy and the Waldorf Schools, Steiner developed a re-ligious system that replaced the Eastern orientation of orthodox Theosophy with a West-ern focus. He pushed Christ to the top of the Ascended Master pantheon and emphasized the significance of Christian scriptures. Steiner also developed his own peculiar version of the end times. He taught that Christ would return and reignite man's consciousness of his divine origins. Once Christ returns, those who accept him would undergo "etherization of the blood" and thus commingle with the etherized blood of Christ present throughout the universe. Webb, *Occult Establishment,* 61–72; see also A. P. Shepherd, *Rudolf Steiner: Sci-entist of the Invisible* (Rochester, Vt.: Inner Traditions International, 1983). Alice Bailey es-tablished the Arcane School in 1923 to offer correspondence courses in her own heterodox version of Theosophy. She accepted standard Theosophical views on karma, reincarnation, Ascended Masters, a divine plan, and humanity's slow return to divine sta-tus. Like Steiner, however, she propelled Christ to the top of the Master hierarchy. Bailey also believed in a literal second coming of Christ that will usher in peace on earth. Ac-cording to her teachings, the Arcane School's New Group of World Servers would func-tion as intermediaries between Christ and the masses, thereby facilitating a more rapid dispersal of his message. Bailey's group must have seemed to Pelley a serious threat; Arcane School doctrine is in many respects interchangeable with Liberation. Judah, *History and Philosophy of Metaphysical Movements,* 119–31; Campbell, *Ancient Wisdom Revived,* 150–55.

44. "Why the Human Race Is Allowed to Suffer Great Natural or Social Catastro-phes," *NL,* June 1931, 6–11; "Suppose That Portions of Ancient Atlantis Should Rise Again Off the American Coast," *NL,* July 1931, 58–61; Pelley, *Why I Believe,* 152–53; Isaac Newton Vail, *The Waters Above the Firmament, or the Earth's Annular System* (Philadelphia:

Ferris and Leach, 1902), 131–50 and *The Heavens and the Earth of Prehistoric Man* (Pasadena: Annular World Company, 1913), 5; L. Sprague de Camp, *Lost Continents: The Atlantis Theme in History, Science, and Literature* (New York: Gnome Press, 1954), 47–73; John Thomas Sladek, *The New Apocrypha: A Guide to Strange Science and Occult Beliefs* (New York: Stein and Day, 1974), 65–67; Werly, "Millenarian Right," 187. The Atlantis myth is popular with racist groups because it established a material and spiritual dominance of a white race over others since the beginning of time. Esoteric myths of superior ancient civilizations are generally tied to doctrines of the fall of man. These theories usually argue that some twelve thousand years ago the flood wiped out civilization, with survivors taking refuge in Iran, the Himalayas, Ethiopia, Peru, and the Rocky Mountains. The four great races (white, red, black, and yellow) then began repopulating the world. The white race (from Iran and Central Asia) migrated and split into three branches: in Europe, where they forgot their ancient wisdom and regressed into crude cults; some moved east and established India; and a third group, who settled in the Mediterranean basin, assimilated with other races, and established Assyria and Egypt. For groups like the Theosophists the goal was to reintroduce the "Secret Doctrine" preserved in the East to Western whites. Jean-Michel Angebert, *The Occult and the Third Reich: The Mystical Origins of Nazism and the Search for the Holy Grail* (New York: Macmillan, 1974), 57–68. Several groups tied the Lemurian myth to California's Mount Shasta, including AMORC. This tradition reached its pinnacle with the I AM cult of the 1930s. As I AM plays a role in Pelley's later career, the group will be detailed in a subsequent chapter.

45. Rolfe Boswell, *Prophets and Portents: Seven Seers Foretell Hitler's Doom* (New York: Thomas Y. Crowell, 1942), 97–121; Sladek, *New Apocrypha,* 70–81; Martin Gardner, *Fads and Fallacies in the Name of Science,* 2d ed. (New York: Dover, 1957), 173–85. Davidson's magnum opus was *The Great Pyramid, Its Divine Message,* rev. 8th ed. (London: Williams and Norgate, 1940). His "scientific" proof of the pyramid's prophetic message is a remarkable work, chock full of tables, graphs, formulae, and maps, that must be seen to be believed. The book's total unreadability does nothing to lessen its staggering achievement. Pelley relied heavily on this work during the 1930s.

46. Pelley, *Door to Revelation,* 288, 338, 392; "What Do You Know about the Pyramid," *NL,* Aug.-Sept. 1931, 97–99; "You Are Not in Life by Chance; You Are Working Out a Definite Program of Personal Experiences," *NL,* 100–101; Pelley, "Confidential Bulletin," Feb. 6, 1933, Parker Papers, Folder 13; Clyde J. Wright, "The Great Pyramid Proves Bible Prophecy," *NLW,* Dec. 19, 1931, 302–5 and "The Great Pyramid Foretells Events to Come in This Decade," *Lib,* Jan. 1932, 317–21, 344; David Davidson, *The Path to Peace in Our Time, Outlined from the Great Pyramid's Prophecy* (London: Covenant Publishing, 1942), 48–49. While it is not clear exactly when Pelley first became aware of pyramidism, his employee Robert Summerville carried on a correspondence with Davidson as early as March 1933. One of the most curious aspects of pyramidism is that it led to the development of British-Israelism in the nineteenth century, which developed into the

racist Christian Identity movement of the twentieth. Pelley, never a fan of the British people, refused to acknowledge that the lost tribes of Israel ended up in the British Isles, even though he supported Davidson's conclusion that the Adamic race was undoubtedly white. A few of Pelley's former followers helped to develop Identity Doctrine, which substitutes the "Two Seed Doctrine" for the pre-Adamite theory of the British-Israelites. Rather than claiming that God created nonwhite races before Adam and Eve, Identity followers argue that Satan, posing as the serpent, seduced Eve, producing Cain (while Abel was the son of Adam). Cain then married a "pre-Adamite," thereby starting the satanic seedline (of which, Identity theories posit, Jews belong), while Abel began the godly, white, "Adamic" line. Pelley, who frequently attacked both the "chosen people myth" and the Old Testament, had little use for such theories, particularly as they ran counter to his "three caste" system of humanity. Despite Pelley's objections to Anglo-Israelism, the Los Angeles Silver Shirt branches had numerous members, Reverend Joseph Jeffers being the most prominent, who promoted the creed. "E. G." to George Parker, May 22, 1933, Parker Papers, Folder 5; Barkun, *Religion and the Racist Right,* 91–96; Boswell, *Prophets and Portents,* 116–21; Braden, *These Also Believe,* 385–402; Donna Kossy, *Strange Creations: Aberrant Ideas of Human Origins from Ancient Astronauts to Aquatic Apes* (Los Angeles: Feral House, 2001), 69–116. The linkage between pyramidism and Anglo-Israelism was developed in C. Piazzi Smyth, *Our Inheritance in the Great Pyramid* (London: W. Isbister, 1880).

47. Werly, "Millenarian Right," 179; Paul Boyer, *When Time Shall Be No More: Prophecy Belief in Modern American Culture* (Cambridge, Mass.: Belknap Press, 1992), 1–80; Norman Cohn, *The Pursuit of the Millennium: Revolutionary Millenarians and Mystical Anarchists of the Middle Ages,* rev. ed. (New York: Oxford Univ. Press, 1970), 19–36.

48. William Dudley Pelley, *Did David Really Slay Goliath?* (Asheville, N.C.: Fellowship Foundation, n.d. [1935]), 1. Pelley also argued that many Masters incarnated in this generation because of its special spiritual significance. Presumably this also explained the presence of a great teacher such as himself. "Do You Know What Impends," *NL,* Nov. 1930, 99–102; "Strange Mutterings and Rumbles Are Heard in the East," 6; "Stupendous Army of Celestial Instructors," 55–56.

49. *Program of Services for the Tenth Assembly* (New York, [1931]), 2–3; *Program of Services for the Sixteenth Assembly* (New York, [1931]), 1, 7; *Program of Services for the Twelfth Assembly* (New York, [1931]), 8; *Program of Services for the Twenty-Second Assembly,* 11.

50. "The True Significance of Present Russian Atheism," 38–41.

6. Silver Shirts: 1933

1. William H. Schmaltz, *Hate: George Lincoln Rockwell and the American Nazi Party* (Washington: Brassey's, 1999), 31. Pelley's business manager, George Anderson, clearly recognized the marginalization associated with open anti-Semitism and warned Pelley to proceed with caution. Pelley, *Door to Revelation,* 396–97.

2. "The Strange Conduct of President Hoover," *NLW,* Nov. 21, 1931, 194; "Does This Mean Riot in Washington Soon?" *NLW,* Nov. 28, 1931, 217–18; "You Are Threatened by World Plotting for Revolution," *NLW,* Nov. 28, 1931, 226–29.

3. "You Are Not in Life by Chance; You Are Working Out a Definite Program of Personal Experiences," *NL,* Aug.-Sept. 1931, 101; "Are Europe's Great Money Barons Planning to Make the World a Debasing Proposal?" *NL,* Aug.-Sept. 1931, 104–6; "What Great Souls on the Other Side Have to Say about the Trend in Russia and Italy," *NLW,* Nov. 14, 1931, 176–77; "You Are Threatened by World Plotting," 226.

4. "Is Mr. Hearst Dumb or Has He Acquired a Bullet-Proof Vest?" *NLW,* Dec. 5, 1931, 249–50; "What Can Be Done by the Individual to Save Civilization?" *NLW,* Dec. 5, 1931, 253. English racist Nesta Webster remains a revered conspiracy exposer in extreme right circles. Her two most significant works were *World Revolution:The Plot Against Civilization* (London: Constable, 1921) and *Secret Societies and Subversive Movements* (London: Boswell, 1924). She believed the five powers behind the world conspiracy were Grand Orient Masonry, Theosophy, Pan-Germanism, international finance, and social revolution. Webster, *Secret Societies,* 382. While Pelley obviously did not find common ground with all of her pronouncements, he agreed with Webster's theory that Jews pulled the strings behind these oppressive movements. In her later years Webster became so convinced that the "conspiracy" was after her that she would only open her front door while holding a loaded revolver. Webb, *Occult Establishment,* 129; John Michell, *Eccentric Lives and Peculiar Notions* (Secaucus, N.J.: Citadel Press, 1984), 62–74. For Webster's career, see Richard Gilman, *Behind World Revolution: The Strange Career of Nesta H. Webster* (Ann Arbor, Mich.: Insights, 1982).

5. Pelley, *Door to Revelation,* 337–39, 392; Pelley, "Confidential Bulletin," February 6, 1933, Parker Papers, Folder 13. Pelley also promoted the idea that Hitler, like himself, received instructions from transcendental sources. Robert Summerville to George Parker, June 6, 1933, Parker Papers, Folder 6. Pelley's belief in the importance of January 31, 1933, was reinforced by the significance given to it in David Davidson's pyramid prophecy. Geoffrey S. Smith, *To Save a Nation:American "Extremism," the New Deal, and the Coming of World War II,* rev. ed. (Chicago: Elephant Paperbacks, 1992), 57; Curt Riess, *Total Espionage* (New York: G. P. Putnam's Sons, 1941), 47–48.

6. Pelley, *Door to Revelation,* 398–99; Johnpeter Horst Grill and Robert L. Jenkins, "The Nazis and the American South in the 1930s: A Mirror Image?" *Journal of Southern History* 58 (Nov. 1992): 679.

7. William Dudley Pelley, *Silver Shirts: A Personal Explanation* (Asheville, N.C.: n.p., n.d.), 1, 7.

8. *The Silvershirt Legion of America, Inc. Certificate of Incorporation and The Silvershirt Legion of America, Inc. By-Laws,* William Dudley Pelley Collection, Pack Memorial Library, Asheville, North Carolina (hereafter cited as Pack Collection). Harry F. Sieber served as the first treasurer, and Lee Collie initially acted as legion secretary. The nine divisions (and

most of the executive offices) existed only on paper. The Legion, despite Pelley's claims, never boasted enough members to develop such an elaborate national hierarchy. Pelley relied primarily on state liaison officers (not even mentioned in the initial organizational plan) for his contact with local members. Even Pelley seemed to forget what the structure was supposed to be. He routinely altered and co-opted titles. Generally he referred to himself as president, national commander, or chief.

9. William Dudley Pelley, *We Offer You the Scourge of Cords* (Asheville, N.C.: n.p, n.d. [1933]), 20–22.

10. William Dudley Pelley, *The Key To Crisis* (Asheville, N.C.: Pelley Publishers, 1939), 40–41; Robert Summerville, "Just What Is the Silver Legion?" *Lib,* Oct. 14, 1933, 10–11. In an attempt to attract more members the annual dues were quickly replaced with a one-time enrollment fee of $1.

11. John J. Smertenko, "Hitlerism Comes to America." *Harper's,* Nov. 1933, 663; Pelley, *Scourge of Cords,* 16; Graham, "Crazy Like a Fox," 264–65.

12. Samuel Levenson, "Pelley's Kampf." *Christian Century,* Apr. 10, 1940, 477.

13. Pelley, *Something Better,* 10. Pelley claimed that *No More Hunger,* like most of the articles that appeared in *Liberation,* was written with clairaudient assistance.

14. Pelley, *No More Hunger,* 27. Although Pelley claimed no violence need occur in the adoption of the Commonwealth program, he recognized the potential reticence of some Americans to accept it. Therefore, participants in the current "Jewish" government faced long prison sentences, and he posited that "the State has a solemn duty in declaring outlaws those among its citizenry who will not recognize the true tenets of peace and voluntary submission on which the State is projected." Ibid., 52–53. Not surprisingly, Pelley also contradicted this assertion by claiming the Commonwealth "cannot, by the very essence of its origin, be a government by any sort of physical or moral duress." Ibid., 51.

15. Ibid., 43–44.

16. Ibid., 57–58. Pelley frequently attacked the notion of democracy, but called for regular plebiscites to determine Christian Commonwealth policies. He reconciled these apparently contradictory ideas by limiting the franchise to Gentiles (after the United States had been purged of Jews and their henchmen). Pelley, then, found democracy palatable once the country underwent the proper political cleansing.

17. Ibid., 73–73, 113–24; Don Kirschner, *City and Country: Rural Responses to Urbanization in the 1920s* (Westport, Conn.: Greenwood Press, 1970), 23–53; John C. Burnham, *Bad Habits: Drinking, Smoking, Taking Drugs, Gambling, Sexual Misbehavior, and Swearing in American History* (New York: New York Univ. Press, 1993), 175–76; Richard T. Ely, *Hard Times—The Way In and the Way Out* (New York: Macmillan, 1931), 20, 25–16. Pelley was but one of many domestic right-wing extremists who decried the growth of urban areas in America. Morris Janowitz, "Black Legions on the March," in *America in Crisis: Fourteen Crucial Episodes in American History,* ed. Daniel Aaron (New York: Knopf, 1952), 318.

18. Pelley, *No More Hunger,* 201–2.

19. Interview with Melford Pearson, via e-mail, Aug. 18, 2003; Frederick Soddy, *Wealth, Virtual Wealth, and Debt: The Solution of the Economic Paradox* (New York: E. P. Dutton, 1933), xiii, 2–3, 289–93.

20. Ibid., 10, 12, 30. Unlike Father Charles Coughlin, Pelley did not meet with Douglas during the Social Credit leader's 1933 U.S. tour, but the Silver Shirt chief found much to agree with in Douglas's economic theories. Further, Douglas was something of an anti-Semite himself, although he claimed Jewishness was a philosophical description, not a racial term. Interview with Melford Pearson, Aug. 18, 2003; John L. Finlay, *Social Credit: The English Origins* (Montreal: McGill-Queen's Univ. Press, 1972), 102–4, 135.

21. Pelley, *No More Hunger,* 32–35; John Rutherford Everett, *Religion in Economics: A Study of John Bates Clark, Richard T. Ely, and Simon N. Patten* (Morningside Heights, N.Y.: King's Crown Press, 1946), 75–98.

22. Pelley, *No More Hunger,* 83–86, 110. The idiosyncratic nature of Pelley's thought led to some rather peculiar income classifications. For example, he noted that "in the non-essential professions—meaning those that are trimmings on our civilization and that we could get along without if we were living the kind of lives essayed by, say, Daniel Boone—we put attorneys and litigation, engineers, and to a degree dentists and clergy." The assignment of higher than 10-Q ratings also exhibits an unusual interpretation of importance. Pelley believed Thomas Edison and Henry Ford deserved 11-Q status, while writing the novel *Ben-Hur* garnered a 12-Q for Lew Wallace. Ibid., 101; Pelley, *Something Better,* 111.

23. Pelley, *No More Hunger,* 49, 64–70; "Liberate Wives Financially," *PW,* Feb. 26, 1936, 1.

24. Pelley, *No More Hunger,* 229; Pelley, *Door to Revelation,* 197–98; "Americans Face Menace of Negro Revolution," *PW,* Feb. 12, 1936, 3. Pelley's distrust of American Blacks echoed similar sentiments within Nazi Germany. Grill and Jenkins, "The Nazis and the American South," 667–68. Pelley's concern over miscegenation, however, proved minor compared to his disgust over potential unions between Jews and Gentiles. The mere thought of these couplings brought Pelley to a frothing. For a representative example, see William Dudley Pelley, *Nations-in-Law: An Unconventional Analysis of Civics,* 2 vols. (Asheville, N.C.: Pelley Publishers, 1938), 2:442.

25. Pelley, *Door to Revelation,* 197–98; Pelley, *No More Hunger,* 24–25, 184–88; "How I Would Treat the Jews," *PW,* May 6, 1936, 1; "Hanging Jews to Apple Trees Won't Pay the National Debt," *WL,* Feb. 14, 1938, 4–5; "How Many Jews Will Be Sent to State Ghettos," *WL,* June 7, 1938, 10; "Seriously What Is to Become of the Jews?" *WL,* Oct. 14, 1938, 12. Pelley also toyed with the idea of forced sterilization of all Jews, noting that it was "a compassionate thing to do for the Jew's own sake as well as that of outraged Aryans." Ibid., 11.

26. Pelley, *No More Hunger,* 47–49; Pelley, *Something Better,* 18; Pelley, *Scourge of Cords,*

22–23. Pelley's religiously backed Commonwealth plan is a classic, albeit failed, example of what Anthony F. C. Wallace termed "revitalization movements." Wallace posited that these movements attempted to utilize new prophetic teachings and methods to reawaken the desire for traditional lifestyles in societies racked with individual stress and cultural distortions. Although Wallace focused on preliterate and homogenous cultures, William G. McLoughlin has argued his system can be utilized to examine the United States (and to explain the recurring "great awakenings"). Anthony F. C. Wallace, *Religion: An Anthropological View* (New York: Random House, 1966), 157–66; McLoughlin, *Revivals, Awakenings, and Reform,* 12–23.

27. Hoppes, "William Dudley Pelley and the Silvershirt Legion," 112.

28. Smith, *To Save a Nation,* 53. A good example of the seething hatred of Jews that Pelley espoused during the 1930s is a Christmas card he proposed in 1937. Claiming Silver Shirts should "remember our enemies" during the holidays, Pelley suggested that all members send a card to Jews that read: "Dearest Shylock, in this season / When we're bereft of reason / As upon my rent you gloat / I would like to cut your throat." "Cogitations," *NL,* Feb. 1937, 11.

29. William Dudley Pelley, *Behold Life: Design for Liberation* (Asheville, N.C.: Pelley Publishers, 1937), 174; Portzline, "Pelley and the Silver Shirt Legion," 91–92; Oscar Handlin, *The American People in the Twentieth Century* (Cambridge, Mass.: Harvard Univ. Press, 1954), 152–53.

30. Pelley, *Star Guests,* 49, 166–67; "We've Got to Love the Jews or They'll Raise Cain," *WL,* Apr. 21, 1938, 5; "What You Should Know about the Cosmic Role of Race," 3.

31. "Will the Silver Shirts Decide American Affairs in 1934?" *Lib,* Dec. 30, 1933, 3; "The World Problem Is a Matter of Race," *Lib,* Mar. 24, 1934, 4.

32. William Dudley Pelley, *Thinking Alive: Design for Creation* (Noblesville, Ind.: Soulcraft Fellowship, 1938), 91; "Can Sincere Followers of Christ Endorse Anti-Semitism?" *WL,* Mar. 21, 1938, 7.

33. Pelley, *Behold Life,* 193–94; Pelley, *No More Hunger,* 137–42; Pelley, *Forty-Five Questions Most Frequently Asked about the Jews and the Answers* (Asheville, N.C.: Pelley Publishers, 1939), 33–40; "Onward Christian Soldiers Marching as to War," *Lib,* Feb. 18, 1933, 6; "We Should Stop the Slander That Jesus of Nazareth Was a Jew," *WL,* Dec. 21, 1938, 6–8; "How the Policy of Non-Resistance Has Been Wrongly Interpreted," *Gal,* Oct. 1941, 8; "Repeating the Cycle of Galilee in This Twentieth Century," *Gal,* Feb. 1942, 28. Reflective of earlier work by Houston Stewart Chamberlain, Alfred Rosenberg, and William J. Cameron, Pelley's Aryanization of Christ was not particularly unique as similar views were espoused by the Nazis and most domestic fascist groups. Peter Viereck, *Metapolitics: The Roots of the Nazi Mind,* rev. ed. (New York: Capricorn Books, 1965) 282–87. On the fate of mainstream Christianity under the Nazis, see Peter Matheson, ed. *The Third Reich and the Churches* (Grand Rapids, Mich.: Erdmans, 1981); Ernst

Christian Helmreich, *The German Churches under Hitler* (Detroit, Mich.: Wayne State Univ. Press, 1979).

34. Pelley, *No More Hunger,* 137–42; Pelley, *45 Questions,* 36–41; "What You Should Know about Jewish Holy Scripture," *NL,* Mar. 1937, 4.

35. Richard Hofstadter, *The Paranoid Style in American Politics* (New York: Vintage Books, 1967), 25–26; Ribuffo, *Old Christian Right,* 59. Pelley's historical views reflect a strong influence from *The Protocols of the Learned Elders of Zion* and W. J. Cameron's *The International Jew.*

36. William Dudley Pelley, *Dupes of Judah: A Challenge to the American Legion* (Asheville, N.C.: n.p., n.d.), 80.

37. Pelley, *Door to Revelation,* 467; "The Dead Bodies of Colonials Began International Banking," *Lib,* May 13, 1933, 5; "Will We Be Made to Fight Japan to Conserve Red Russia's Army?" *Lib,* Mar. 10, 1934, 1.

38. Pelley, *No More Hunger,* 198; Pelley, *45 Questions,* 44; "Silver Shirts Decide American Affairs in 1934?" 1; "The Coming Class War," *Lib,* Mar. 31, 1934, 12; "Does Trotsky Expect to Seize Power When Roosevelt Falls?" *WL,* Mar. 14, 1938, 6. Although connecting the contradictory beliefs of "international" bankers and Communists requires quite a leap of faith, it was a staple on the radical right during the 1930s. Morris Schonbach, *Native American Fascism During the 1930s and 1940s: A Study of Its Roots, Its Growth, and Its Decline* (New York: Garland, 1985), 269. Pelley's combustible combination of millennialism and hatred for "Jewish" Communism was not completely unique either. Timothy P. Weber, *Living in the Shadow of the Second Coming: American Premillennialism, 1875–1982,* expanded ed. (Chicago: Univ. of Chicago Press, 1987), 185–92.

39. William Dudley Pelley, *What Is a Jew-Baiter?* (Asheville, N.C.: n.p., n.d.), 15; "Desperate Condition in Labor Centers," *SLR,* June 6, 1934, 4. Like all conspiracy-minded anti-Semites, Pelley found it impossible to explain how Jews could control world finance at the same time they were being dominated by Gentiles, or why, if they were already in control, they chose to continue to remain in the shadows of "Jew-stooges."

40. "Should America Go to War to Save the Jew Dope Trade?" 3; "Don't Be Bamboozled by This Syphilis Tommyrot," ibid. 9, June 14 (1938): 11; "Yiddish Rabbi Heads Drug Ring," ibid. 9, August 14 (1938): 4.

41. "Did Benjamin Franklin Say This about the Hebrew?" *Lib,* Feb. 3, 1934, 5; Arnold Forster and Benjamin R. Epstein, *The Trouble-Makers* (Garden City, N.Y.: Doubleday, 1952), 148; Charles A. Beard, "Exposing the Anti-Semitic Forgery about Benjamin Franklin," *Jewish Frontier* 3 (Mar. 1935): 10–13. Not surprisingly, Pelley discounted Beard's work by noting that he conducted his work "in the large libraries from which most material referring to the Jews adversely has been removed." "How Benjamin Franklin Considered the Jews," *Lib,* Oct. 14, 1938, 4–5.

42. "What Silver Shirts Must Know about Our Federal Reserve," *Lib,* May 27, 1933, 1–2; "The Real Inside Story of the Rise of Rothschild," *Lib,* Jan. 27, 1934, 4–6; "Was the

House of Rothschild Responsible for Causing the Revolutionary War?" *Lib,* Dec. 14, 1939, 5; Portzline, "Pelley and the Silver Shirt Legion," 99; Pelley, *45 Questions,* 45–46; Pelley, *Door to Revelation,* 136–39; "The Mystery of the Civil War and Lincoln's Death," *Lib,* Feb. 10, 1934, 1–4; "Abraham Lincoln's Slayer," *Lib,* Oct. 28, 1940, 3.

43. Leon Surette, *Pound in Purgatory: From Economic Radicalism to Anti-Semitism* (Urbana: Univ. of Illinois Press, 1999), 239–60; William Chace, "Ezra Pound and the Marxist Temptation," *American Quarterly* 12 (Autumn 1970): 719–23; Ezra Pound and Robert C. Summerville, "Ezra Pound, Silvershirt," *New Masses,* Mar. 17, 1936, 15–16.

44. "The Good Old Days," *Lib,* July 21, 1940, 4; Pelley, *Dupes of Judah,* 56; Pelley, *Nations-in-Law,* 2:484; Lawrence Brown, "Weekly Research and Comment," *WL,* Apr. 7 1938, 9.

45. "Do You Clearly Discern the Spirit of Evil?" *Lib,* Apr. 1932, 54; "Do the Jews of America Wish Us to Reply with a Boycott," *Lib,* Aug. 5, 1933, 1; "Information You Can Get from No Other Source," *Lib,* Sept. 9, 1933, 7; "Compare the Protocols with Roosevelt's Policies," *Lib,* Jan. 20, 1934, 3; Pelley, *New Dealers in Office* (Indianapolis: n.p., n.d.), 3; Pelley, *Silver Shirts,* 1; "E.G" to George Parker, March 1, 1933, Parker Papers, Folder 5.

7. Extremists: 1934

1. Donald S. Strong, *Organized Anti-Semitism in America: The Rise of Group Prejudice During the Decade 1930–1940* (Washington, D.C.: American Council on Public Affairs, 1941), 2–4; David H. Bennett, *The Party of Fear,* 2d ed. (New Brunswick, N.J.: Rutgers Univ. Press, 1969), 244; Smith, *To Save a Nation,* 66–76; Ribuffo, *Old Christian Right,* 3–24.

2. Although Pelley's support for Lincoln (his "patron saint") seems odd, it actually is a logical development of his worldview. He believed Lincoln should be celebrated not only for smashing the "Jewish" bankers, but also for freeing the slaves who could then move to segregated communities or repatriate to Africa, thereby eliminating the spiritual damage done to Whites forced to live among them. To Pelley, then, Lincoln's actions were laudable; it was the policies of Reconstruction that were appalling. *WL,* July 14, 1938, 1; Pelley, *Nations-in-Law,* 166, 324; Princess Atalie , "What All Non-Nazis Should Know about the Swastika and Its Hidden Meaning," *WL,* July 28, 1938, 6; Harold E. Quinley and Charles Glock, *Anti-Semitism in America* (New York: Free Press, 197p), 168; Portzline, "Pelley and the Silver Shirt Legion," 73; Werly, "Millenarian Right," 112–55.

3. Raymond Gram Swing, *Forerunners of American Fascism* (New York: Julian Messner, 1935), 13–33; "E. G." to George Parker, March 1, 1933, Parker Papers, Folder 5. Morris Schonbach noted that the emotionally well-adjusted rarely joined domestic protofascist groups. Rather, typical followers were "nihilistic, cynical, and harsh, with many visceral, bizarre, unanalytical, race- and religious-prejudiced overtones." Schonbach, *Native American Fascism,* 22. For discussions of the older anti-Semitic and nativist el-

ements that contributed to domestic fascism in the depression decade, see John Higham, *Send These to Me: Jews and Other Immigrants in Urban America,* rev. ed. (Baltimore: Johns Hopkins, 1984); Michael N. Dobkowski, *The Tarnished Dream: The Basis of American Anti-Semitism* (Westport, Conn.: Greenwood Press, 1979); Smith, *To Save a Nation,* 75–76; Victor Ferkiss, "Populist Influences on American Fascism," *Western Political Quarterly* 10 (Summer 1957): 350–73; Naomi Cohen, "Anti-Semitism in the Gilded Age: The Jewish View," *Jewish Social Studies* 41 (Summer 1979): 187–201; Robert Singerman, "The American Career of the *Protocols of the Elders of Zion,*" *Journal of American History* 71 (Sept. 1981): 48–78; Leo Ribuffo, "Henry Ford and *The International Jew,*" *Journal of American History* 69 (June 1980): 437–77. For an excellent survey of the debate over the origins of American anti-Semitism, see Gerber, "Anti-Semitism and Jewish-Gentile Relations," 3–54.

4. Janowitz, "Black Legions on the March," 309–12.

5. Dinnerstein, *Antisemitism in America,* 112–13; Ribuffo, *Old Christian Right,* 5–13; Arthur M. Schlesinger, Jr., *The Age of Roosevelt: The Coming of the New Deal* (Boston: Houghton Mifflin, 1960), 44–48. For a statistical analysis of how right-wing extremists exaggerated the Communist threat in America, see Donald Strong, *Organized Anti-Semitism,* 17–20.

6. O. John Rogge, *The Official German Report: Nazi Penetration, 1924–1942: Pan-Arabism, 1939-Today* (New York: Thomas Yoseloff, 1961), 13–25, 113–29; Donald M. McKale, *The Swastika Outside Germany* (Kent, Ohio: Kent State Univ. Press, 1977), 13–17, 68–72; Sander A. Diamond, *The Nazi Movement in the United States, 1924–1941* (Ithaca, N.Y.: Cornell Univ. Press, 1974), 21–176; Philip Jenkins, *Hoods and Shirts: The Extreme Right in Pennsylvania, 1925–1950* (Chapel Hill: Univ. of North Carolina Press, 1997), 89–112; Alton Frye, *Nazi Germany and the American Hemisphere, 1933–1941* (New Haven, Conn.: Yale Univ. Press, 1967) 32–44; Schonbach, *Native American Fascism,* 70–158; Ludwig Lore, "Nazi Politics in America," *Nation,* Nov. 29, 1933, 615–16; J. B. Mathews, "Must America Go Fascist?" *Harper's,* June 1934, 8; Leland V. Bell, *In Hitler's Shadow: The Anatomy of American Nazism* (Port Washington, N.Y.: Kennikat Press, 1973), 14–15. For the most recent scholarship on the Bund, see Susan Canedy, *America's Nazis: A Democratic Dilemma* (Menlo Park, Calif.: Markgraf, 1990).

7. Schonbach, *Native American Fascism,* 224–29; Ribuffo, *Old Christian Right,* 80–105; Donald Strong, *Organized Anti-Semitism,* 104–5; Neil McMillen, "Pro-Nazi Sentiment in the United States, March 1933-March 1934," *Southern Quarterly* 2 (Oct. 1963): 62–64; Grill and Jenkins, "The Nazis and the American South," 677; Roy Tozier, *America's Little Hitlers: Who's Who and What's Up in U.S. Fascism* (Girard, Kans.: Haldeman-Julius, 1940) 25–29, 30–41. One of the more interesting domestic extremist groups, the Paul Reveres were incorporated in 1932 by Edwin Marshall Hadley and the infamous "Mrs." Elizabeth Dilling. Although their politics were no less extreme or paranoid than organizations like the Silver Shirts, the Reveres focused their energies on attracting the wealthy and well-bred. The group's members were highly educated, highly visible professionals.

Donald Strong, *Organized Anti-Semitism*, 118–23; John Roy Carlson, *The Plotters* (New York: E. P. Dutton, 1946), 77–79, 142–44. Dilling was the most active woman on the fascist circuit during the 1930s. She is best remembered for her book *The Red Network: A Who's Who and Handbook of Radicalism for Patriots* (Kenilworth, Ill.: Elizabeth Dilling, 1934). For one of the first attempts to analyze the beliefs that led many Americans to become extremist leaders during the Depression, see Leo Lowenthal and Norbert Guterman, *Prophets of Deceit: A Study of the Techniques of the American Agitator* (New York: Harper and Brothers, 1949). Lowenthal and Guterman preferred the term "agitator" for individuals such as Pelley. They defined an agitator as someone who "openly expressed admiration for Hitler and Mussolini, were rabidly anti-Semitic, indulged in intensive vituperation of our national leaders, . . .headed small 'movements,' published periodicals, . . .made frequent political speeches, and some gave comfort and aid to our enemies." ibid., xv. For a similar early account, see Alfred McClung Lee and Elizabeth Briant Lee, eds., *The Fine Art of Propaganda* (New York: Institute for Propaganda Analysis, 1939).

8. McMillen, "Pro-Nazi Sentiment," 48; Tozier, *America's Little Hitlers,* 8; Harold Loeb and Selden Rodman, "American Fascism in Embryo," *New Republic,* Dec. 27, 1933, 185; Alvin Johnson, "The Rising Tide of Anti-Semitism," *Survey Graphic,* Feb. 1939, 113–16. The Anglo-Saxon Federation (currently based in Haverhill, Mass.), although not associated with Pelley, promoted a worldview very similar to that of the Silver Shirt chief. The Federation was organized by W. J. Cameron, former editor of Henry Ford's *Dearborn Independent,* and Howard Rand, a pyramidist and Anglo-Israelite. Michael Barkun, *Religion and the Racist Right,* 29–36; Roy, *Apostles of Discord,* 92–117.

9. Henry Schwartz, "The Silver Shirts: Anti-Semitism in San Diego," *Western States Jewish History* 24 (Spring 1992): 56–57; Suzanne G. Ledeboer, "The Man Who Would Be Hitler: William Dudley Pelley and the Silver Legion," *California History* 6 (Summer 1986): 133; World Committee for the Victims of German Fascism, *The Brown Network: The Activities of the Nazis in Foreign Countries* (New York: Knight Publications, 1936), 254–55; Harold Lavine, *War Propaganda and the United States* (New York: Doubleday, 1940), 192–96; Smith, *To Save a Nation,* 59; Donald Strong, *Organized Anti-Semitism,* 104–5; Frye, *Nazi Germany,* 55; Lavine, *Fifth Column in America,* 191–210; Rogge, *Official German Report,* 207–12, 329; "Many a Man Has Lost His Job by Taking a Vacation," *Lib,* July 15, 1933, 2; Ribuffo, *Old Christian Right,* 80–127; Roy, *Apostles of Discord,* 26–58. High, "Star-Spangled Fascists," 72; "Get Ready to Save Your Country," *PW,* Sept. 26, 1936, 1; "Cogitations," *NL,* May 1937, 11.

10. Although Pelley and Long were occasionally lumped together by contemporary commentators (and Smith provided a direct conduit of Long's ideas to the Silver Shirt chief), Long's "share our wealth" distribution schemes and affirmations of the sanctity of private property bear little resemblance to Pelley's Christian Commonwealth system, which promoted governmental ownership of industry and hard work. Jeansonne, *Gerald L. K. Smith,* 28–30; Roy, *Apostles of Discord,* 59–84; Pelley, *Door to Revelation,* 413–15; "Compare the Protocols With Roosevelt's Policies," *Lib,* Jan. 1, 1934, 3.

11. Francis MacDonnell, *Insidious Foes: The Axis Fifth Column and the American Home Front* (New York: Oxford Univ. Press, 1995), 29–32; Henry Steele Commanger, *The American Mind* (New Haven, Conn.: Yale Univ. Press, 1950), 413; Carey McWilliams, *A Mask for Privilege: Anti-Semitism in America* (Boston: Little, Brown, 1948), 184–206.

12. Schonbach, *Native American Fascism,* 265–66; Donald Strong, *Organized Ant-Semitism,* 48; Graham, "Crazy Like a Fox," 265; Harold Lavine, "Fifth Column Literature," *Saturday Review of Literature,* Sept. 14, 1940, 179. Claims of Pelley's insanity were reinforced by the eccentricity of some of his supporters. Early in their existence the Silver Shirts received substantial financial backing from, among others, Marie Ogden and "Doctor" John R. Brinkley. Ogden ran the "Home of Truth" cult in Dry Valley, Utah. She gained national attention for claiming to be the reincarnation of the Virgin Mary. Ogden later faced legal difficulties when authorities discovered she had kept the corpse of a deceased follower in her home for a year while trying to revive him. Brinkley made a fortune and made an abortive attempt to create a political machine in Kansas, selling "goat-gland" treatments and surgeries to impotent men. Pelley, *Door to Revelation,* 360–63; Pelley, "Christmas at Silver Lodge," *SC,* Oct. 1937, 12; Smith, *To Save a Nation,* 57; Ledeboer, "The Man Who Would Be Hitler," 130; Ribuffo, *Old Christian Right,* 119–21; HUAC, 6:4191–93, 4226–27. For Brinkley's career, see Gerald Carson, *The Roguish World of Doctor Brinkley* (New York: Holt, Rinehart, and Winston, 1960); R. Alton Lee, *The Bizarre Careers of John R. Brinkley* (Lexington: Univ. Press of Kentucky, 2002).

13. Travis Hoke, *Shirts* (New York: American Civil Liberties Union, 1934), 20; John Spivak, *America Faces the Barricades* (New York: Covici Friede, 1935), 225–29; McMillen, "Pro-Nazi Sentiment," 63; Loeb and Redman, "American Fascism in Embryo," 185; House, Special Committee on Un-American Activities. *Investigation of Nazi Propaganda and Investigation of Certain Other Propaganda Activities.* 73d Cong. (hereafter cited as McCormack-Dickstein), 1st sess. Report No. 153, 11; A. B. Magil and Henry Stevens, *The Peril of Fascism: The Crisis of American Democracy* (New York: International Publishers, 1938), 215; Myers, *History of Bigotry,* 346–47, 399–401. Smith organized his group solely for the purpose of making money from the sale of Khaki Shirt uniforms. The group fell apart after an abortive march on Washington in October 1933.

14. Lore, "Nazi Politics," 617; "German Americans Should Support the Commonwealth," *PW,* Mar. 4, 1936, 4; Smertenko, "Hitlerism Comes to America," 660–70; Samuel D. McCoy, "Hitlerism Invades America," *Today,* Apr. 7, 1934, 3–4; Charles Angoff, "Nazi Jew-Baiting in America," *Nation,* May 1, 1935, 501–3; Frederick L. Schuman, "The Nazi International," *New Republic,* July 8, 1936, 275; Levenson, "Pelley's Kampf," 4; Hoke, *Shirts,* 8; High, "Star-Spangled Fascists," 5; George Britt, *The Fifth Column Is Here* (New York: Wilfred Funk, 1940), 117; Werly, "Millenarian Right," 94–96.

15. High, "Star-Spangled Fascists," 5; L. M. Birkhead, "Fascism in America," *Literary Digest,* Aug. 14, 1937, 16; Albert Kahn, *High Treason* (New York: Hour, 1950), 190; Donald Strong, *Organized Anti-Semitism,* 14.

16. Alfred M. Bingham, *Insurgent America: The Revolt of the Middle Classes* (New York: Harper and Brothers, 1935), 186–88; Donald Strong, *Organized Anti-Semitism*, 172–75; Schlesinger, *Age of Roosevelt*, 80–81; Janowitz, "Black Legions on the March," 307; Werly, "Millenarian Right," 221; Schonbach, *Native American Fascism*, 248–49.

17. Donald Strong, *Organized Anti-Semitism*, 50–52; Werly, "Millenarian Right," 219–20; Portzline, "Pelley and the Silver Shirt Legion," 215; Britt, *Fifth Column*, 113; McMillen, "Pro-Nazi Sentiment," 56–57; Hoke, *Shirts*, 19; Lowenthal and Guterman, *Prophets of Deceit*, 99–100.

18. Werly, "The Millenarian Right," 221–22; William Dudley Pelley, *We Offer You the Scourge of Cords* (Asheville, N.C.: n.p., 1933), 17.

19. McMillen, "Pro-Nazi Sentiment," 60; Smertenko, "Hitlerism Comes to America," 663; Werly, "Millenarian Right," 220; "Will the Silver Shirts Decide American Affairs in 1934?" *Lib*, Dec. 30, 1933, 3. The Silver Shirts were one of the few extremist groups operating in the Southeast. The majority of like-minded groups based their operations out of the Northeast and Mid-Atlantic regions. Donald Strong, *Organized Anti-Semitism*, 144–45.

20. Philip Jenkins, *Hoods and Shirts*, 13; Werly, "Millenarian Right," 229–52. The Silver Shirts were helped immeasurably in Pennsylvania by the presence of Paul Lillienfield-Toal and Louis T. McFadden in that state. Pelley's "foreign adjunct," Lillienfield-Toal, an exiled Estonian aristocrat, worked for the North German Lloyd shipping line in Philadelphia. He helped the nascent Silver Shirt movement gain entré into German-American circles. Hoke, *Shirts*, 17; Smith, *To Save a Nation*, 59; Philip Jenkins, *Hoods and Shirts*, 120–25,141. First elected to Congress in 1914, the conservative McFadden attacked internationalism, global finance, and socialism throughout his career. However, he shifted his focus toward anti-Semitism in the early 1930s and began making openly anti-Jewish speeches in the House of Representatives in 1933. Pelley found much common ground with McFadden and the two developed a deep friendship. He also reprinted the congressman's vitriolic speeches in *Liberation*. Interview with Melford Pearson, August 16, 2003; Smith, *To Save a Nation*, 15; Charles Higham, *American Swastika* (New York: Doubleday, 1985), 70; John Roy Carlson, *Under Cover* (New York: E. P. Dutton, 1943), 148; Hoke, *Shirts*, 25. For McFadden's ravings first hand, see Louis T. McFadden, *Collective Speeches of Congressman Louis T. McFadden* (Hawthorne, Calif.: Omni, 1970). To this day McFadden remains in the pantheon of congressional heroes for the anti-Semitic right.

21. Hoppes, "William Dudley Pelley and the Silvershirt Legion," 174–330. Although Hoppes found few former Ku Klux Klansmen active in the Washington Silver Shirts, Pelley's first Washington state lieutenant was former Klan leader Luther I. Powell. Pelley, *Door to Revelation*, 412. Pelley found it difficult to recruit former Klansmen or to coordinate activities with that organization because he did not share the Klan's anti-Catholic stance. Although anti-Catholic local leaders (including Lillienfield-Toal) might have balked at enrolling them, there were no official barriers to Roman Catholics joining the Silver Shirts.

22. George E. Rennar, "The Silvershirts" (unpublished paper, 1965) in George E. Rennar Papers, Univ. of Washington Library, Seattle Washington, 41–65; Eckard V. Toy, Jr., "Silver Shirts in the Northwest," 139–46; Roy Zachary, "What Silvershirts Should Know About Chief Pelley" *New Liberation* 7, July 7 (1937): 8.

23. Portzline, "Pelley and the Silver Shirt Legion," 214; HUAC, 6:4228–29; "Silver Ranger," *Lib,* Dec. 3, 1934, 9. Kenneth Alexander and Henry Allen were also important figures in the Los Angeles branches. With typical overstatement Pelley posited that "California has more Silver Shirts than either policemen or National Guardsmen." Pelley, *Door to Revelation,* 420.

24. Werly, "Millenarian Right," 253–59; Pelley, *Door to Revelation,* 424–27, 440, 444–46. Pelley responded to Case's attacks in kind and suggested that it was the L.A. Silver Shirt who was working for the Communists. Ibid., 445.

25. Pelley, *Door to Revelation,* 418, 434, 445; Hoppes, "William Dudley Pelley and Silvershirt Legion," 230–32; Max Vorspan and Lloyd P. Gartner, *History of the Jews of Los Angeles* (San Marino, Calif.: Huntington Library, 1970), 221. Craig's group should not be confused with the similarly named (and anti-Semitic) but much larger Constitutional Education League of Joseph P. Kamp. The reconstituted Silver Shirts frequently held joint meetings with the Bund at German House on West Fifteenth Street.

26. Werly, "Millenarian Right," 259–63; HUAC, 6:4260. San Diego's most famous extremist of the period, C. Leon de Aryan, maintained contact with the Silver Shirts in that city (and with Pelley), but Kemp, fearful of losing control of the group, kept de Aryan from developing a close relationship with the Legion. Arnold Forster, *A Measure of Freedom* (Garden City, N.Y.: Doubleday, 1950), 230. Although Pelley used a great deal of military and millennial rhetoric, he avoided openly advocating violence. While his "actionist" followers spoiled for confrontation, Pelley steadfastly clung to his prophetic faith that the Christian Commonwealth would inevitably redeem America without resorting to widespread bloodshed. "The United States Seal—A Christmas Prophecy," *Lib,* Dec. 23, 1933, 6; "You Asked for It, LaFollette, Our Answer Is Silvershirts," *WL,* Mar. 28, 1938, 2–3.

27. Ledeboer, "The Man Who Would Be Hitler," 132–34; Schwartz, "Silver Shirts in San Diego," 54–57.

8. Tribulation: 1934–1936

1. "The New Year Will Be Filled with Vital Occurrences," *Lib,* Dec. 30, 1933, 9.

2. Schwartz, "Silver Shirts in San Diego," 55; *New York Times,* Oct. 10, 1933.

3. McCormack-Dickstein, 2d sess., 1934, 1:1.

4. Werly, "Millenarian Right," 41–42; Pelley, *Door to Revelation,* 452.

5. Schwartz, "Silver Shirts in San Diego," 55–56; *Los Angeles Times,* Aug. 6, 1934; *New York Times,* Aug. 5, 1934, and Aug. 8, 1934; *New York Times,* Aug. 9, 1934; Ledeboer, "The Man Who Would Be Hitler," 132–33; Werly, "Millenarian Right," 42–43; Michael R.

Belknap, *Cold War Political Justice:The Smith Act, the Communist Party, and American Civil Liberties* (Westport, Conn.: Greenwood Press, 1977), 16–17; Schlesinger, *Age of Roosevelt*, 85,92; Walter Goodman, *The Committee:The Extraordinary Career of the House Committee on Un-American Activities* (New York: Farrar, Straus, and Giroux, 1968), 9–11. The McCormack-Dickstein Committee focused its attentions primarily on the perceived propaganda work of the Nazi government in the United States (and, to a surprising extent, the Soviet Union), while virtually ignoring followers of Italian fascism. Later commentators have suggested this was a by-product of Dickstein's heightened concerns over Nazi anti-Semitism (he was a Russian-born Jew). Pelley was also quick to point this out. However, it should be noted that a number of groups sprang up in the wake of Hitler's appointment as German chancellor, which gave credence to Dickstein's allegations that the Nazis were establishing a network in the United States, as did the flood of pro-Nazi propaganda entering the country onboard German ships. Schonbach, *Native American Fascism,* 85–89; McMillen, "Pro-Nazi Sentiment," 65–69; Diamond, *Nazi Movement in the United States,* 157–58. The United States military was concerned about the popularity of right-wing groups among servicemen by January 1934. These fears arose from the belief that groups such as the Silver Shirts were agents of Nazi Germany. *U.S. Military Intelligence Reports: Surveillance of Radicals in the United States, 1917–1941.* microfilm, Frederick, Md.: University Publications of America, 1984, reel 24, series 2662, file 0990; ibid., reel 26, series 2662, file 0671; ibid., reel 29, series 2666, file 0965.

6. Donald Strong, *Organized Anti-Semitism,* 40.

7. HUAC, 6:4190–99; Pelley, *Door to Revelation,* 443–47; Werly, "Millenarian Right," 43; Ribuffo, *Old Christian Right,* 71; *New York Times,* Apr. 25, 1934; Portzline, "Pelley and the Silver Shirt Legion," 187; Certificate of Incorporation, The Silvershirt Legion of America, Inc., N.C. State Archives, Folder 3. When it was declared bankrupt the press had only a paltry $8,176.33 in assets. Martin Dies, *The Trojan Horse in America* (New York: Dodd, Mead, 1940), 325–26.

8. William Dudley Pelley, "All Loyal Silver Shirts," June 27, 1934, mimeographed mailing; Smith, *To Save a Nation,* 65; *New York Times,* May 24, 1934. Summerville, who had been with Pelley since 1931, was one of the Silver Shirt chief's closest advisors and often ran the Asheville headquarters while Pelley was away. He was also a clairaudient adept, and even some within the Silver Shirt organization thought he was mentally unbalanced. Donald Strong, *Organized Anti-Semitism,* 47; Ledeboer, "The Man Who Would Be Hitler," 132. News of the indictments brought Kramer and U.S. District Attorney Marcus Erwin back to Asheville for another round of hearings, which only further compounded Pelley's difficulties. *New York Times,* May 27, 1934. Former Pelley confidant "Mont" Hardwicke was also involved in the initial investigation, but the grand jury declined to indict him.

9. Hoppes, "William Dudley Pelley and the Silvershirt Legion," 75–77.

10. Pelley, *Door to Revelation,* 454–55; Tozier, *America's Little Hitlers,* 45. Unable to

publish in North Carolina, Pelley began issuing *Pelley's Weekly* from Oklahoma City on August 29. The new magazine's subscription list was a fraction of *Liberation's*. Donald Strong, *Organized Anti-Semitism*, 49. Pelley hinted about possible divorce proceedings as early as 1930. In a *New Liberator* article that year he noted that "any human relationship that sets the soul back spiritually is immoral, and should not be tolerated." "Does Christ Sanction Divorce?" *NL*, June 1930, 90.

11. Floyd Hatfield, "The Case of William Dudley Pelley." *Lib*, Mar. 14, 1940, 1–2; Ribuffo, *Old Christian Right*, 71; Werly, "Millenarian Right," 45; State of North Carolina vs. W. D. Pelley, et al, N.C. State Archives, Folder 1.

12. Pelley, *Door to Revelation*, 460.

13. Hoppes, "William Dudley Pelley and the Silvershirt Legion," 76–78; Pelley, *Door to Revelation, 470; New York Times*, Jan. 23, 1935; Pelley, *Have I Been Foolish?* (n.p., n.d. [1935]), 3.

14. Lavine, *Fifth Column in America*, 191–210; Ribuffo, *Old Christian Right*, 72; HUAC, 6:3872–3973. It has also been suggested that Pelley's legal troubles were the actual cause of Gerald L. K. Smith's decision to switch his allegiance from Pelley to Huey Long. While this may have been a factor, Long's successes seem a much larger factor. To an ambitious young man like Smith, the "Kingfish" must have seemed a far brighter star to attach himself to than the marginalized Pelley. Roy, *Apostles of Discord*, 59–84; Jeansonne, *Gerald L. K. Smith*, 28–30. Those who remained loyal to Pelley faced difficulties owing to the adverse publicity from the trial. Many of the most vocal Silver Shirt members faced public ostracism and professional difficulties. For example, George L. Pafort was forced to resign his position as employment secretary of the Prison Association of New York after his ties to the organization (and his refusal to disavow them) were publicized. *New York Times*, Apr. 26, 1934; Samuel Walker, *Hate Speech: The History of an American Controversy* (Lincoln: Univ. of Nebraska Press, 1994), 40.

15. The extremist groups who gained the most Silver Shirt deserters as new members were the American White Guards, Constitutional League of America, and the Anti-Communist League of the World. Donald Strong, *Organized Anti-Semitism*, 40.

16. De Camp, *Lost Continents*, 72–73; Braden, *These Also Believe*, 257–307; Melton, *Biographical Dictionary of American Cult and Sect Leaders*, 24–26; David Stupple, "The I AM Sect Today: An Unobituary," *Journal of Popular Culture* 8 (Spring 1975): 897–905. Orthodox Theosophists were horrified and embarrassed by the I AM group. Greenwalt, *The Point Loma Community*, 211–12. At the end of the nineteenth century, for those describing outer space travel (or contact), Venus replaced Mars as the most popular contact planet. Reflecting this trend Blavatsky had, among her Masters, the "Lords of the Flame," who lived on Venus. Ballard swiped the "Lords" from her and raised them to the utmost spiritual significance in his cosmology, making Ballard the "first to actually build a religion on contact with extraterrestrials." Countless later contactee religions, including the Church Universal and Triumphant, Aetherius Society, and Astara Foundation borrowed

this idea directly from Ballard. J. Gordon Melton, "The Contactees: A Survey," in *The Gods Have Landed: New Religions From Other Worlds,* ed. James R. Lewis (Albany: State Univ. of New York Press, 1995), 1–15; Judah, *History and Philosophy of the Metaphysical Movements,* 133–45. For an account of the I AM lineage in modern esoteric groups, see Kenneth and Talita Paolini, *400 Years of Imaginary Friends: A Journey into the World of Adepts, Masters, Ascended Masters and Their Messengers* (Livingston, Mont.: Paolini International, 2000).

17. Ellwood and Partin, *Religious and Spiritual Groups* 98–102; Kafton-Minkel, *Subterranean Worlds,* 126–32; Gerald B. Bryan, *Psychic Dictatorship in America* (1940; repr. Livingston, Mont.: Paolini International, 2000), 20–29. Bryan was a disgruntled former I AM member and made no attempt to be impartial in his book. His work is a valuable source of information on the group but should be approached with caution. For the connections between the Ballards, Pelley, and Frank B. Robinson, see Philip Jenkins, "The Great Anti-Cult Scare, 1935–1945" (paper presented at CESNUR 1999 Conference, Bryn Athyn, Pa.).

18. Braden, *These Also Believe,* 269–71; Pelley, *Door to Revelation,* 457; Godfre Ray King [Guy Ballard], *The Magic Presence* (Chicago: St. Germain Press, 1935), 79.

19. David H. Bennett, *Demagogues in the Depression: American Radicals and the Union Party, 1932–1936* (New Brunswick, N.J.: Rutgers Univ. Press, 1969), 37–41; Alan Brinkley, *Voices of Protest: Huey Long, Father Coughlin, and the Great Depression* (New York: Knopf, 1982), 143–68; Donald Warren, *Radio Priest: Charles Coughlin, the Father of Hate Radio* (New York: Free Press, 1996), 60–61; Irving Howe and Lewis Coser, *The American Communist Party: A Critical History (1919–1957)* (Boston: Beacon Press, 1957), 328, 331–32; Frank A. Warren, *Liberals and Communism: The "Red Decade" Revisited* (Bloomington: Indiana Univ. Press, 1966), 50–62; Charles C. Alexander, *Nationalism in American Thought, 1930–1945* (Chicago: Rand McNally, 1969), 11–13; Judy Kutulas, *The Long War: The Intellectual People's Front and Anti-Stalinism, 1930–1940* (Durham, N.C.: Duke Univ. Press, 1995), 84, 88; Harvey Klehr, *The Heyday of American Communism* (New York: Basic Books, 1984), 186–206; Patrick D. Reagan, *Designing a New America: The Origins of New Deal Planning, 1890–1943* (Amherst: Univ. of Massachusetts Press, 1999), 168–95. Left-wingers leveled similar criticisms at Roosevelt's scattershot approach. For a representative example, see Bingham, *Insurgent America,* 179–85.

20. William Dudley Pelley, *Applying Horse-Sense to the Federal Mess* (Asheville, N.C.: Pelley Publishers, n.d.), 6–8; Elmhurst, *World Hoax,* 3; William Dudley Pelley, *What You Should Know about the Pelley Publications* (Asheville, N.C.: Pelley Publishers, n.d.), 3.

21. "Compare the Protocols with Roosevelt's Policies," *Lib,* Jan. 1, 1934, 3; Pelley, *New Dealers in Office,* 3; William Dudley Pelley, *No More Hunger,* 222; Pelley, *Door to Revelation,* 429–30; Werly, "Millenarian Right," 130. Owing to irregularities with her birth and marriage records, Perkins was a frequent target of paranoid extremists. Rumors of her alleged Jewish-Communist background eventually forced her to issue public statements

(and personal letters to a variety of American right-wingers) detailing her private affairs and genealogy. George W. Martin, *Madam Secretary: Frances Perkins* (Boston: Houghlin Mifflin, 1976), 398–99; Dov Fisch, "The Libel Trial of Robert Edward Edmondson: 1936–1938," *American Jewish History* 71 (Sept. 1981): 83–87.

22. "Where We Stand on N-I-R-A," *Lib,* Sept. 9, 1933, 12; "Heard above the Din of the Wailing Wall," *Lib,* Nov. 25, 1933, 7; "The New Year Will Be Filled with Vital Occurrences," *Lib,* Dec. 12, 1933, 9; "Compare the Protocols and Roosevelt," *Lib,* Dec. 12, 1933, 3; Pelley, *Our Secret Political Police* (Asheville, N.C.: Pelley Publishers, n.d.), 4–5; Portzline, "Pelley and the Silver Shirt Legion," 171.

23. Werly, "Millenarian Right," 130–40; "Silver Shirts Are Marching," *Lib,* 5, Aug. 26, 1933, 12; "Know America after Collapse," *PW,* Apr. 1, 1935, 1; "Nations Await Jewish Coup," *PW,* June 10, 1936, 1; Ribuffo, *Old Christian Right,* 67; "The Coming Class War," *Lib,* Mar. 31, 1934, 12.

24. Pelley, *Nations-in-Law,* 310–28; "Christian Party Is Autumn Dark Horse," *PW,* Jan. 15, 1936, 1; "Sacrifices Mean Utmost Economy," *PW,* Mar. 11, 1936, 2; Gaines M. Foster, *Moral Reconstruction: Christian Lobbyists and the Federal Legislation of Morality, 1865–1920* (Chapel Hill: Univ. of North Carolina Press, 2002), 27–30, 107–10; Christian Campaign Committee. "Christian Patriotism Stands at Bay," (circular letter, August 20, 1935), Parker Papers, Folder 2.

25. Toy, "Silver Shirts in the Northwest," 141. Pelley's incessant travel during this period resulted in the formation of Christian party units in sixteen states. These state organizations, however, proved tiny and ineffectual. Most Silver Shirt members paid lip service to the party but did little to actively support the organization. Looking to buoy confidence in his floundering campaign, Pelley claimed on at least one occasion to have Christian party groups active in forty states. Transcription of Pelley speech at Seattle Moose Hall, October 11, 1936, in Silver Shirt Legion of America, Inc., Washington State Division, Correspondence and related material of Orville W. Roundtree, liaison officer for the state division, 1933–1940, Univ. of Washington Libraries, Seattle, Washington (hereafter cited as Roundtree Collection).

26. Werly, "Millenarian Right," 266; Toy, "Silver Shirts in the Northwest," 142; Richard Rollins, *I Find Treason* (New York: William Morrow and Company, 1941), 77; Donald Strong, *Organized Anti-Semitism,* 53–54; Ledeboer, "The Man Who Would Be Hitler," 133–34; William Dudley Pelley, *The Councils of Safety* (Asheville, N.C.: n.p., 1936), 2. For the CPA's full slate of candidates, see State of Washington, Department of State. *Abstract of Votes Polled at General Election,* Nov. 3, 1936, 42.

27. Bennett, *Demagogues in the Depression,* 4; Toy, "Silver Shirts in the Northwest," 139–43; Hoppes, "William Dudley Pelley and the Silvershirt Legion," 137–40; Hofstadter, *Paranoid Style in American Politics,* 238–314. After his own organization began to falter, Frank Clark attempted a rapprochement with the Silver Shirts, only to be rebuked by Roy Zachary, who branded the National Liberty Party leader a cowardly "four-flusher and nat-

ural born liar." Clark responded by publicly criticizing Pelley and the Silver Shirts. To keep Clark quiet Zachary suggested sending "a committee of husky boys to call on him some dark and foggy night." Zachary to Orville Roundtree, April 18, 1938, Roundtree Collection; Zachary to Roundtree, December 6, 1938, ibid.

28. Toy, "Silver Shirts in the Northwest," 143; "Dictator for America Looms," *PW,* Apr. 15, 1936, 1; "Enter King's Chamber Today," *PW,* Sept. 16, 1936, 1; Pelley, *The Pillar of Cloud* (Asheville, N.C.: Christian Party Press, 1935), 11–15; Hoppes, "William Dudley Pelley and the Silvershirt Legion," 176–78.

29. "Get Ready to Save Your Country," *PW,* Jan. 22, 1936, 1–4; "Chief Answers Townsendite Who Bemoans Party Stand," *PW,* Feb. 12, 1936, 5; Portzline, "Pelley and the Silver Shirt Legion," 267.

30. Tozier, *America's Little Hitlers,* 12–13; Donald Strong, *Organized Anti-Semitism,* 133–34; Schonbach, *Native American Fascism,* 339–41; George Mintzer and Newman Levy, *The International Anti-Semitic Conspiracy* (New York: American Jewish Committee, 1946), 56–57; Roy, *Apostles of Discord,* 30–31; Hamilton Basso, "The Little Hitlers at Asheville," *New Republic,* Sept. 2, 1936, 100–101; Magil and Stevens, *Peril of Fascism,* 244–45. Most of the conference's extremist delegates were invited by two assistant organizers, Liberty Leaguer John Henry Kirby and Vance Muse of the Southern Committee to Uphold the Constitution. A second meeting, the American Christian Conference, was eventually held in Kansas City in August 1937. This gathering met with the same in-fighting as the Asheville conference and proved just as ineffectual. Morris Janowitz has persuasively argued that the native fascist movement failed to organize effectively because of a combination of factors including weak internal structure, a lack of organizational unity, poor administrative skill among leaders, and the inability to develop a comprehensive positive ideology. Janowitz, "Black Legions on the March," 313.

31. Charles J. Tull, *Father Coughlin and the New Deal* (Syracuse: Syracuse Univ. Press, 1965), 127–72; Lyman Tower Sargent, ed., *Extremism in America: A Reader* (New York: New York Univ. Press, 1995), 26–29; Bennett, *Demagogues in the Depression,* 187–292; James McGregor Burns, *Roosevelt: The Lion and the Fox* (New York: Harcourt, Brace, and Company, 1956), 209; Schlesinger, *Politics of Upheaval,* 555–59, 626–30; Hoppes, "William Dudley Pelley and the Silvershirt Legion," 181. Lemke's campaign, despite its relative success, did not receive blanket support from the radical right. German-American Bund leader Fritz Kuhn, for example, supported Republican candidate Alf Landon. Schonbach, *Native American Fascism,* 192–93.

32. The defeat proved too much for Willard Kemp to bear. In March 1937 he returned to San Diego, cleaned out all the supplies at the Silver Shirt ranch near that city, and vanished. Hoppes, "William Dudley Pelley and the Silvershirt Legion," 180, 204–5; Roy Zachary to Orville Roundtree, June 19, 1937, Roundtree Collection.

33. "Heavy Meetings in Washington State," *PW,* Oct. 4, 1936, 4; Hoppes, "William Dudley Pelley and the Silvershirt Legion," 80; "Why You Should Keep Your Faith in Pyra-

mid Prophecy," *NL,* Jan. 1937, 7; "How God's Plan Was Served by Roosevelt's Re-Election," *NL,* Jan. 1937, 9; "Chief's Viewpoint," *SC,* Jan. 1938, 3. Pelley also suggested that his defeat reflected that he was "thinking approximately six years in advance of the rest of the nation." Those intelligent folks who understood his thinking and wanted to vote for him, however, "discovered that handles on the voting machines had been plugged, so that votes could not be registered." Pelley, *Door to Revelation,* 433, 474. The classic study of a modern group dealing with an erroneous prophetic message is Leon Festinger, Henry W. Riecken, and Stanley Schachter, *When Prophecy Fails: A Social and Psychological Study of a Modern Group That Predicted the Destruction of the World* (Minneapolis: Univ. of Minnesota Press, 1956). The pseudonymous group studied by Festinger consisted of former Mighty I AM members.

9. Silver Shirts Redux: 1937–1939

1. Dies, *The Trojan Horse in America,* 327; Portzline, "Pelley and the Silver Shirt Legion," 193–94.

2. Pelley's metaphysical works from this period include *Behold Life: Design for Liberation; Thinking Alive: Design for Creation;* and *Earth Comes: Design for Materialization* (Asheville, N.C.: Pelley Publishers, 1939). This last volume represented Pelley's attempt to reconcile science and his religious system, making it an unusual work even for his oeuvre. In it Pelley rams through a survey of astronomical findings, then melds his "star guests" cosmology to recent scientific findings. Eventually even the trappings of scientism fall away as the author explains that Earth "came originally—we are led to believe—because spirits had to know of educational reactions from materials and their eccentricities, that in higher and grander octaves of the future, they might attain to those aspects of Consciousness that could of themselves attain to supernal subjectivity." Pelley, *Earth Comes,* 147. During this period he also began frequenting séances held by trance medium Bertie Lily Candler. Pelley, *Why I Believe,* 255–94; Pelley, *Soulcraft Scripts,* 12 vols. (Noblesville, Ind.: Soulcraft Chapels, 1954–56), vol. 3, Discourse 37, 15–18.

3. "Giovanni Verrazano," *LVGA,* Oct. 15, 1937, 11, 34; "Jacques Cartier," *LVGA,* Nov. 1, 1937, 23; "John Carver," *LVGA,* Feb. 1, 1938, 17; "John Cotton," *LVGA,* Mar. 5, 1939, 32–33.

4. "Cogitations," *NL,* Feb. 1937, 11; "Jews in Our Government." *NL,* Oct. 21, 1937, 2–6; "Jews in CIO," *NL,* Oct. 21, 1937, 8–9; "Hanging Jews to Apple Trees Won't Pay the National Debt," *WL,* Feb. 14, 1938, 5; "Roosevelt Rallies Riffraff to Form the Popular Front," *WL,* Sept. 7, 1938, 3; "Jewish Atrocity Fables," *Lib,* Feb. 14, 1939, 4.

5. Pelley, *Door to Revelation,* 196–98; "The Mask Is Now Stripped from the Movie Monopoly," *Lib,* Jan. 13, 1934, 1; "Poor Old George Arliss Becomes a Jewish Propagandist," *Lib,* Jan. 27, 1934, 3; Kenneth Alexander, "Who's Who in Hollywood—Find the Gentile," *WL,* Aug. 14, 1938, 4; "You Can't Print That," *WL,* Sept. 14, 1938, 9; "Movie

Hero President Muffs Everything," *WL,* Sept. 21, 1938, 1–2; "Are They Crazy in Holly-wood?" *WL,* Sept. 21, 1938, 4; "Sick Movies," *Lib,* July 14, 1940, 5; Ribuffo, *Old Christian Right,* 61–62. Despite Pelley's protests that it represented propaganda of the basest kind, 1934's *House of Rothschild* was anything but a pro-Jewish motion picture. As Lester Friedman has noted, the film "overtly intends to glorify the Rothschilds but its covert innuendos replace positive images with troubling doubts, as if a totally positive portrait is impossible." Friedman, *Hollywood's Image of the Jew,* 172. The film was remade in Germany as *The Rothschilds* (1940), an openly anti-Semitic (and anti-British) motion picture.

6. Sklar, *Movie-Made America,* 76; Erens, *The Jew in American Cinema,* 52–53, 125–65; Friedman, *Hollywood's Image of the Jew,* 3–85; Philip French, *The Movie Moguls: An Informal History of Hollywood Tycoons* (Chicago: Henry Regnery, 1971), 105–17; Gabler, *An Empire of Their Own,* 339–43; Colin Shindler, *Hollywood Goes to War* (London: Routledge and Keegan Paul, 1978), 2.

7. Erens, *The Jew in American Cinema,* 137–38; Friedman, *Hollywood's Image of the Jew,* 78–85; Gary Carey, *All the Stars in Heaven: Louis B. Mayer's MGM* (New York: E. P. Dutton, 1981), 241–50; Shindler, *Hollywood in Crisis,* 195–213; Clayton R. Koppes and Gregory D. Black, *Hollywood Goes to War: How Politics, Profits, and Propaganda Shaped World War II Movies* (Berkeley: Univ. of California Press, 1990), 31–39; David Stewart Hull, *Films in the Third Reich: A Study of the German Cinema, 1933–1945* (Berkeley: Univ. of California Press, 1969), 130–32, 155–77; Erwin Leiser, *Nazi Cinema* (New York: Macmillan, 1974), 73–95; Richard W. Steele, "The Great Debate: Roosevelt, the Media, and the Coming of War, 1940–1941," *Journal of American History* 71 (June 1984): 79–80; K. R. M. Short, "The White Cliffs of Dover: Promoting the Anglo-American Alliance in World War II," *Historical Journal of Film, Radio, and Television* 2 (March 1982): 3–25. For the congressional findings, see U.S. Senate, Hearings Before a Subcommittee of the Committee on Interstate Commerce on S. Res. 152, *Propaganda in Motion Pictures,* 77th Cong., 1st sess., Sept. 9–26, 1941.

8. MacDonnell, *Insidious Foes,* 30–31; Hilfer, *Revolt from the Village,* 228; Richard P. Blackmur, "Utopia, or Uncle Tom's Cabin," in *Sinclair Lewis: A Collection of Critical Essays,* ed. Mark Schorer , 108–10 (Englewood Cliffs, N.J.: Prentice-Hall, 1962); Robert L. McLaughlin, "Mark Schorer, Dialgic Discourse, and *It Can't Happen Here,*" in *Sinclair Lewis: New Essays in Criticism,* ed. James M. Hutchisson , 21–38 (Troy, N.Y.: Whitston, 1997); "John Cotton," 6. Although Metro-Goldwyn-Mayer (MGM) purchased the screen rights to Lewis's book, they decided against producing the film version for fear of creating a controversy. Lewis responded by adapting the novel to the stage and going on tour, with himself as the star, under the auspices of the WPA Federal Theatre Project. Jane DeHart Mathews, *The Federal Theatre, 1935–1939: Plays, Relief, and Politics* (Princeton, N.J.: Princeton Univ. Press, 1967), 95–101. While *A Cool Million* was not among his best works, West exhibited a keen understanding of the forces leading Americans to search out radical answers to domestic crises. At a time when many commentators sought to explain

the success of domestic extremists as resulting from their appeals to the ignorant and in-sane, he accurately noted that their followers were "of the middle class [who] are being crushed between two gigantic millstones [capital and labor]." Nathaniel West, *A Cool Million* (1934; repr., New York: Berkley, 1961), 173–74.

9. "The Great Spirit Still Speaking," *NL,* Feb. 15, 1937, 4; "Silver Shirts Propose Justice for the American Indian," *NL,* Mar. 1937, 1–2; Unkalunt, "What All Non-Nazis Should Know," 6; "John Eliot," *LVGA,* Aug. 1, 1938, 24–25; "Jacques Marquette," *LVGA,* Oct. 1, 1938, 17–20; Pelley, *Why I Believe,* 142–51; Pelley, *Indians Aren't Red: The Inside Story of the Administration's Attempt to Make Communists of the North Carolina Cherokees* (Asheville, N.C.: Pelley Publishers, n.d. [1940]), 83; Roy Zachary, "Zachary's Viewpoint," *SC,* 1, Jan. 1938, 6–7.

10. "Chief Pelley's Silver Program," *WL,* Mar. 28, 1938, 4–5. Pelley to Orville Roundtree, July 7, 1937, Roundtree Collection. The level of condescension in Pelley's Native American articles is stupefying. In one article he sought to simplify his program "in a language they understand," which concluded with: "in the tongue of the white children, the word Legion means tribe-that-has-neither-hunting-or-fishing-ground." "What Chief Pelley Would Do for America's Indians," *NL,* Feb. 1937, 9.

11. Toy, "Silver Shirts in the Northwest," 144–45; Elwood Towner speech to Silver Shirts, Redmen's Hall, Spokane, Washington, August 4, 1937, Roundtree Collection; Hoppes, "William Dudley Pelley and the Silvershirt Legion," 214–20. Towner's limited success with the Silver Shirts was also due to a significant amount of latent racism within the group; he eventually shifted his energies to exclusively cultivating contacts within the Bund, whose racial theories contended that Native Americans were pure Aryans. "Red Indians in Brown Shirts," *New Republic,* May 17, 1939, 31; Bell, *In Hitler's Shadow,* 90.

12. "Behind the Dreadful Mask," 32–34, 62–64; Toy, "Silver Shirts in the Northwest," 143: Pelley, *Door to Revelation,* 93–94.

13. William Dudley Pelley to Orville Roundtree, December 2, 1937, Roundtree Collection, Pelley to Dwight D. Clarke, December 11, 1937, ibid.

14. "Should Americans Go to War to Save the Jew Dope Trade?" 1–2; "What Confronts America If Japan Should Lose," *WL,* Sept. 7, 1938, 5; Werly, "Millenarian Right," 104–5.

15. Pelley to Roundtree, Dec. 11, 1937, Roundtree Collection; Schonbach, *Native American Fascism,* 200–222; Hoppes, "William Dudley Pelley and the Silvershirt Legion," 202–4; "Nigger Get Yo' White Gal," *PW,* Oct. 7, 1936, 8; David G. Goodman and Masanori Miyazawa, *Jews in the Japanese Mind: The History and Uses of a Cultural Stereotype* (New York: Free Press, 1995) 76–134.

16. Schonbach, *Native American Fascism,* 310; Rollins, *I Find Treason,* 103; Nathan Schachner, *The Price of Liberty: A History of the American Jewish Committee* (New York: American Jewish Committee, 1948), 121: Hoppes, "William Dudley Pelley and the Silvershirt Legion," 146–48.

17. Bell, *In Hitler's Shadow,* 74–83; Diamond, *Nazi Movement in the United States,* 305–23; McKale, *Swastika Outside Germany,* 141–44; Niel M. Johnson, *George Sylvester Viereck: German-American Propagandist* (Urbana: Univ. of Illinois Press, 1972), 208–9; Canedy, *America's Nazis,* 175–205; Werly, "Millenarian Right," 297–304.

18. "Twixt Bigger and Better Probes," *WL,* June 21, 1938, 12; Rogge, *Official German Report,* 57–59, 75–82; Alfred Goldschmidt to Pelley, March 21, 1938 in N.C. State Archives, Folder 7; A. H. Talpey to H. Adam, ibid.; Oscar Pfaus to Pelley, February 4, 1939, ibid., Folder #9; Talpey to Pfaus, February 6, 1939; Pfaus to Pelley Publishers, March 18, 1939, ibid.; Theodor Kessemeier to Lawrence A. Brown, August 9, 1939, ibid; McKale, *Swastika Outside Germany,* 83–119; Schonbach, *Native American Fascism,* 309. Pelley did not attend the conference. The phlegmatic Alfred Talpey, who earned a degree in electrical engineering from Harvard, became a Silver Shirt in 1934 and served as Skyland Press treasurer. Theodor Kessemeier worked with Paul Lillenfeld-Toal at North German Lloyd. As will be documented later in this study, federal investigators sought to prosecute Pelley by demonstrating how closely his writings followed the Nazi line, but his status as an independent operator is illustrated by the frequency with which his politics diverged from Third Reich policies. For example, Pelley believed several individuals favored by the Germans were actually tools of the Jewish conspiracy, including Charles Lindbergh, General Nicholas Rodriguez of the Mexican Gold Shirts, and Benito Mussolini (a "half-Jew" leading an entourage that "reeks of Jewry like a celebration of a feast of Purim"). "Will Mussolini Become the Wooden Horse Inside the Walls of a Nazi Troy?" *NL,* Sept. 21, 1937, 6; "Germans, Answer Dickstein by Ripping Open the Lindbergh Kidnapping," *WL,* May 7, 1938, 5; "The Pivot of Red Plotting Is Shifting to Mexico." *WL,* May 21, 1938, 5–6. Although Pelley later changed his views on Lindbergh and Mussolini, his original negative perspectives on these figures clearly demonstrates his freedom from the Berlin line. John Werly has painstakingly documented every distinction between Pelley and the Third Reich in an attempt to demonstrate that the Silver Shirt leader was not a Nazi. Werly did so to prove his thesis that Pelley represented a "paranoid-style" millenarian with a purely home-grown philosophy. However, Werly confuses independence and influence, and his argument is suspect. While his work is a welcome corrective to the assertions that Pelley worked for the Third Reich, claiming that the leader of a "shirt" movement owes no debt to European antecedents is untenable. Werly, "Millenarian Right," 112–55. However, Werly has correctly noted that Pelley, like most domestic fascists, was clearly not cognizant of Hitler's plans for the United States. In fact, Pelley assumed Germany and America would eventually unite as an "Aryan Confederation." Ibid., 131–33; Pelley, *Nations-in-Law,* 1:355, 2:457; Morris Janowitz, *Political Conflict: Essays in Political Sociology* (Chicago: Quadrangle Books, 1970), 155–56. For Hitler's plans for the United States, see Gerhard L. Weinberg, *World in the Balance: Behind the Scenes of World War II* (Hanover, N.H.: Univ. Press of New England, 1981), 53–95; Norman J. W. Goda, *Tomorrow the World: Hitler, Northwest Africa, and the Path Toward America* (College Station: Texas A&M Univ. Press, 1998).

19. HUAC, 3:2359; William Dudley Pelley to Orville Roundtree, June 19, 1937, Roundtree Collection; Roy Zachary to Roundtree, June 19, 1937, ibid.; Pelley to Roundtree, Dec. 2, 1937, ibid.; Pelley to Roundtree, Dec. 11, 1937, ibid.; Pelley to Roundtree, Mar. 18, 1938, ibid.; Toy, "Silver Shirts in the Northwest," 142–44; Donald Strong, *Organized Anti-Semitism,* 48–49.

20. Portzline, "Pelley and the Silver Shirt Legion," 195–96; Dies, *Trojan Horse in America,* 328; *Asheville Times,* Feb. 21, 1939.

21. *Chicago Daily-Times,* Nov. 18, 1938; *Chicago Tribune,* Nov. 24, 29, and 30, 1938; *New York Times,* Dec. 1, 1938; Portzline, "Pelley and the Silver Shirt Legion," 141–48; Bell, *In Hitler's Shadow,* 69; Philip Jenkins, *Hoods and Shirts,* 171–72.

22. Bell, *In Hitler's Shadow,* 69–74; Diamond, *Nazi Movement in the United States,* 273–304; Abraham Chapman, *Nazi Penetration in America* (New York: American League for Peace and Democracy, 1939), 9–11; Naomi W. Cohen, *Not Free to Desist: The American Jewish Committee, 1906–1966* (Philadelphia: Jewish Publication Society of America, 1972), 175–92; Magda Lauwers-Rech, *Nazi Germany and the American Germanists: A Study of Periodicals, 1930–1946* (New York: Peter Lang, 1995), 40–44. The German government's bumbling actions, particularly with regard to espionage, only added validity to claims of Nazi subversion in the United States. For example, in December 1938 four German citizens were convicted of espionage after being captured trying to steal American military documents, and two months later two more Germans were arrested for attempting to photograph military fortifications in the Panama Canal Zone. Such activities created a wellspring of anti-Hitler sentiment among the populace and government. Frye, *Nazi Germany,* 80–100; Ladislas Farago, *The Game of the Foxes: The Untold Story of German Espionage in the United States and Great Britain During World War II* (New York: David McKay, 1971), 51–67.

23. Ribuffo, *Old Christian Right,* 178–79; Magil and Stevens, *Peril of Fascism,* 11–12; Kutulas, *The Long War,* 96–97, 155–57; Gary, *Nervous Liberals,* 131 54; Justus D. Doenecke, "Non-interventionism of the Left: The Keep America Out of War Congress, 1938–1941," *Journal of Contemporary History* 12 (Apr. 1977): 221–36. For examples of material published by these anti-Nazi groups, see Tozier *America's Little Hitlers.*

24. "Fascism in America: Like Communism It Masquerades as Americanism," *Life,* Mar. 6, 1939, 57–63; Ribuffo, *Old Christian Right,* 181–82; Herman Klurfeld, *Winchell: His Life and Times* (New York: Praeger, 1976), 90–91; Douglas B. Craig, *Fireside Politics: Radio and Political Culture in the United States, 1920–1940* (Baltimore: Johns Hopkins Univ. Press, 2000), 182–83; Herbert J. Seligman, "The New Barbarian Invasion," *New Republic,* June 22, 1938, 175–77; "Uncle Sam's Nazis," *Newsweek,* July 18, 1938, 11; Stanley High, "Star-Spangled Fascists," 70–73; *New York Times,* Dec. 30, 1939.

25. "Jews in Our Government," *NL,* Oct. 21, 1937, 2–6; "Roosevelt Rallies Riffraff to Form the Popular Front," *WL,* Sept. 7, 1938, 3.

26. Ribuffo, *Old Christian Right,* 74; "Does Roosevelt Get All Proceeds of Birthday Paralysis Balls?" *WL,* May 28, 1939, 3; Pelley, *Cripple's Money: Who Gets the Proceeds of the*

Presidential Birthday Balls? (Asheville, N.C.: n.p., n.d. [1939]), 4, 15, 17; Werly, "Millenar-
ian Right," 52–54; A. H. Talpey to Orville Roundtree, May 31, 1939, Roundtree Col-
lection; Pelley, *Your Sacred Rights* (Indianapolis: Fellowship Press, n.d.), 7; Pelley, *Our Secret
Political Police* 4–5; Harold L. Ickes, *The Secret Diary of Harold L. Ickes,* 3 vols. (New York:
Simon and Shuster, 1954), 2:549; "The United Front Technique of Communists in the
United States," *WL,* Sept. 14, 1938, 6; "They Want J. Edgar Hoover Turned Out of FBI,"
WL, Oct. 7, 1938, 3; Harrison Fargo, "How to Become Dictator," *WL,* Oct. 7, 1938,
6–8. Beginning in 1934, Roosevelt sporadically requested that the FBI investigate Amer-
ican fascists. Schonbach, *Native American Fascism,* 386–95.

27. Schonbach, *Native American Fascism,* 396–400.

28. Frank J. Donner, *The Un-Americans* (New York: Ballantine Books, 1961), 25–31;
Schonbach, *Native American Fascism,* 193–99; Goodman, *The Committee,* 24–58; Dies, *Trojan Horse in America,* 324–31.

29. Dinnerstein, *Antisemitism in America,* 116–20; Schonbach, *Native American Fascism,* 366–73; "The Nazis Are Here," *Nation,* Mar. 4, 1939, 253; Walker, *Hate Speech,*
52–76; Mulford Sibley, *Conscientious Objectors in Prison, 1940–1945* (Philadelphia: Pacifist
Research Bureau, 1945), 20–28. The U.S. Congress discussed potential group-libel laws
throughout the World War II era, but failed to pass any meaningful legislation. This partly
derived from the blatant prejudices exhibited by congressmen themselves during the period. In one notorious example, Rep. John Rankin called fellow congressman L.
Emanuel Celler "the Jewish gentleman from New York" on the floor of the House of
Representatives. When Celler protested, Rankin responded by asking if he objected to
being called a Jew or a New Yorker. Goodman, *The Committee,* 182. More examples of
bigoted New Deal politicians are cited in Richard D. Breitman and Alan M. Kraut, "Anti-
Semitism in the State Department, 1933–44" in *Anti-Semitism in American History,* ed.
David A. Gerber (Urbana: Univ. of Illinois Press, 1986), 167–200.

30. Schonbach, *Native American Fascism,* 378–82; Frank A. Warren, *Noble Abstractions:
American Liberal Intellectuals and World War II* (Columbus: Ohio State Univ. Press, 1999),
40–41.

31. Werly, "Millenarian Right," 56–57; Portzline, "Pelley and the Silver Shirt Legion," 201–2; "Three Million Dollars!" *Lib,* Aug. 28, 1939, 2; "The Dies-Pelley Lawsuit
May Shape History," *Lib,* Aug. 28, 1939, 9; Pelley. *Newsletter No. 42,* Sept. 21, 1939, 5;
Asheville Times, Oct. 3, 1939. Pelley's decision to file against Dies probably derived from
his belief that a previous effort had been successful. In November 1937 the Senate Committee on Education and Labor, chaired by Robert La Follette, Jr., subpoenaed Ohio Silver Shirt leader Spencer Warwick as part of its investigation of strike breaking. Pelley filed
a lawsuit on Warwick's behalf, claiming the La Follette committee served as a Jewish tool
in the plot to silence Silver Shirt patriots. Warwick's own attorney successfully postponed
his appearance, and the committee, no longer needing the Silver Shirt's testimony, re-
scinded the subpoena. Pelley, however, claimed this as a victory over Communist agents

and declared his intent to expose governmental "Red stooges" in court. "Catching Bears by Their Tails," *WL,* Jan. 6, 1938, 5; "Legion Suddenly Wins," *WL,* Apr. 18, 1938, 3; Hoppes, "William Dudley Pelley and the Silvershirt Legion," 82–83; Pelley to liaison officers, May 8, 1938, Roundtree Collection. Despite their acrimonious relationship, Pelley and Dies had very similar worldviews. Both men yearned for a genteel America of small towns and traditional values that no longer existed, and their mutual attacks on radicalism reflected their anxieties over the changes being wrought in America. It is not too much of a stretch to suggest that Dies represented a "respectable Pelley." Goodman, *The Committee,* 163–64.

32. Portzline, "Pelley and the Silver Shirt Legion," 202–4; Schonbach, *Native American Fascism,* 310–11; Dies, *Trojan Horse in America,* 331.

33. William Dudley Pelley, *One Million Silver Shirts by 1939* (Asheville, N.C.: Pelley Publishers, 1938), 1; "More Congressional Red Help," *Lib,* June 7, 1939, 9; "Are You Playing the New Game?" *RC,* Feb. 24, 1941, 6; "Editorial," *RC,* Nov. 17, 1941, 16; William Dudley Pelley, *They Make Up Your Mind* (Indianapolis: Fellowship Press, n.d.), 41; John E. Moser, *Twisting the Lion's Tail: American Anglophobia Between the World Wars* (New York: New York Univ. Press, 1999), 97–119.

34. "Behind the Neutrality Hoax with Jewish Conspirators," *Lib,* July 21, 1939, 3; "Two Arguments for Neutrality That Have Business Sense Behind Them," *Lib,* Sept. 28, 1939, 6; "The Good Old Days," *Lib,* July 21, 1940, 4; William Dudley Pelley, *After Dictators, What?* (Asheville, N.C.: Pelley Publishers, n.d.), 43; "New World Order Pledged to Jews," *RC,* Mar. 24, 1941, 5; "Editorial," *RC,* Sept. 8, 1941, 16; "Every Cent of Next Year's Taxes Goes to a Foreign Nation," *RC,* Sept. 22, 1941, 1.

35. "What If a Second World War Is Won by Germany?" *Lib,* Apr. 28, 1939, 3; "What America Faces with Britain Invaded," *RC,* Feb. 17, 1941, 1; "Editorial," *RC,* Mar. 24, 1941, 16; "If Hitler Had Every Ship on Earth, He Could Not Invade United States," *RC,* Apr. 28, 1941, 7; Pelley, *The Hidden Empire* (Asheville, N.C.. Pelley Publishers, n.d.), 39; Wayne S. Cole, *America First: The Battle Against Intervention* (Madison: Wisconsin Univ. Press, 1953), 144; Justus D. Doenecke, *Not to the Swift: The Old Isolationists in the Cold War Era* (London: Associated Univ. Press, 1979), 29–31.

36. Schonbach, *Native American Fascism,* 253; Charles A. Beard, *Giddy Minds and Foreign Quarrels: An Estimate of American Foreign Policy* (New York: Macmillan, 1939), 63–65, 85–86; Stuart Chase, *The New American Front* (New York: Harcourt, Brace, and Company, 1939); Jeansonne, *Gerald L. K. Smith,* 83–86; Cole, *America First,* 35–68, 89–103; Manfred Jonas, *Isolationism in America, 1935–1941* (Ithaca, N.Y.: Cornell Univ. Press, 1966), 27–31, 100–135, 270–72; Craig, *Fireside Politics,* 159–60; David A. Horowitz, *Beyond Left and Right: Insurgency and the Establishment* (Urbana: Univ. of Illinois Press, 1997), 162–87. For the Nye Committee, see John E. Wiltz, *In Search of Peace: The Senate Munitions Inquiry, 1934–1936* (Baton Rouge: Louisiana State Univ. Press, 1963).

37. Kutulas, *The Long War,* 164–85; Frank Warren, *Liberals and Communism,*

193–215; Maurice Isserman, *Which Side Were You On?: The American Communist Party During the Second World War* (Middletown, Conn.: Wesleyan Univ. Press, 1982), 32–43; Howe and Coser, *The American Communist Party,* 387–95. The noninterventionist impulse also placed Pelley in the uncomfortable position of finding common cause with his nemesis Sinclair Lewis, who was one of the founders of the America First Committee.

38. Portzline, "Pelley and the Silver Shirt Legion," 178–86; "Berlin-Moscow Pact Gives Reds First Inkling of Their Duping," *Lib,* Aug. 21, 1939, 8–9; "Millions Are Sensing What Is Wrong about This War," *Lib,* Sept. 14, 1939, 3–4; Schonbach, *Native American Fascism,* 319–20.

39. Jonas, *Isolationism in America,* 206–43; Moser, *Twisting the Lion's Tail,* 135–48; Frank Warren, *Noble Abstractions,* 147–50; Robert Dallek, *Franklin D. Roosevelt and American Foreign Policy, 1932–1945* (New York: Oxford Univ. Press, 1979), 171–316.

40. Geoffrey Perret, *Days of Sadness, Years of Triumph: The American People, 1939–1945* (New York: Coward, McCann and Geoghegan, 1973), 158–61; Nathaniel Weyl, *The Jew in American Politics* (New Rochelle, N.Y.: Arlington House, 1968), 134–37; Cole, *America First,* 131–54; Jonas, *Isolationism in America,* 169–205; Justus D. Doenecke, ed., *In Danger Undaunted: The Anti-Interventionist Movement of 1940–1941 as Revealed in the Papers of the America First Committee* (Stanford, Calif.: Stanford Univ. Press, 1990), 25–26, 50–51. For the difficulties faced by congressional noninterventionists, see David L. Porter, *The Seventy-Sixth Congress and World War II, 1939–1940* (Columbia: Univ. of Missouri Press, 1979).

10. Sedition: 1940–1949

1. David M. Kennedy, *Freedom from Fear: The American People in Depression and War, 1929–1945* (New York: Oxford Univ. Press, 1999), 385–425; Wayne S. Cole, *Roosevelt and the Isolationists, 1932–1945* (Lincoln: Univ. of Nebraska Press, 1983), 223–383; Richard W. Steele, "American Popular Opinion and the War Against Germany: The Issue of Negotiated Peace, 1942," *Journal of American History* 65 (Dec. 1978): 710–14; John Morton Blum, *V Was for Victory: Politics and American Culture During World War II* (New York: Harcourt Brace Jovanovich, 1976), 45–52; Louis De Jong, *The German Fifth Column in the Second World War* (Chicago: Univ. of Chicago Press, 1956), 105–20. Espionage fears were reflected in an August 1940 Gallup poll in which 48 percent of Americans indicated that they believed their communities had been infiltrated by Nazi fifth columnists. MacDonnell, *Insidious Foes,* 7–8. During the war heightened fears of domestic fascists propelled a spate of highly successful exposés. The most famous of these works was Carlson's *Under Cover.* Carlson, in reality Washington attorney Avedis Derounian, spent four years infiltrating a number of extremist organizations. His sensationalized account of this work was the best-selling nonfiction book in America in 1943 and fourth in sales in 1944. Other successful lurid accounts included Allan Chase, *Falange: The Axis Secret Army in the Ameri-*

cas (New York: G. P. Putnam's Sons, 1943); Alan Hynd, *Passport to Treason: The Inside Story of Spies in America* (New York: R. M. McBride and Company, 1943), and Michael Sayers and Albert E. Kahn, *Sabotage! The Secret War Against America* (New York: Harper and Brothers, 1942). Fears of Nazi fifth columnists even permeated the esoteric societies of the period. The Ballards' I AM group, for example, claimed "Inner Secret Service" operated by Ascended Master K-17 destroyed over 300 Nazi spies and three submarines in late 1939. Paolini and Paolini, *400 Years of Imaginary Friends,* 214–15.

2. Mark Lincoln Chadwin, *The Warhawks: American Interventionists Before Pearl Harbor* (New York: Norton, 1970), 157, 168; Leonard Mosley, *Lindbergh: A Biography* (Garden City, N.Y.: Doubleday, 1976), 286–89; Walter Johnson, *The Battle Against Isolation* (Chicago: Univ. of Chicago Press, 1944), 63–71; Cole, *America First,* 104–20; Jonas, *Isolationism in America,* 253–57; MacDonnell, *Insidious Foes,* 139; Michele Flynn Stenehjem, *An American First: John T. Flynn and the America First Committee* (New Rochelle, N.Y.: Arlington House, 1976), 121–42.

3. Ribuffo, *Old Christian Right,* 186–87; Robert Justin Goldstein, *Political Repression in Modern America: From 1870 to the Present* (Cambridge, Mass.: Schenkman, 1978), 239–84.

4. Schonbach, *Native American Fascism,* 400–410; Francis B. Biddle, *The Fear of Freedom* (Garden City, N.Y.: Doubleday, 1951), 109; Stanley I. Kutler, *The American Inquisition: Justice and Injustice in the Cold War* (New York: Hill and Wang, 1982), 152–53; Goldstein, *Political Repression,* 256; Belknap, *Cold War Political Justice,* 22–27; Nicholas N. Kittrie and Eldon D. Wedlock, Jr., eds., *The Tree of Liberty: A Documentary History of Rebellion and Political Crime in America,* rev. ed. (Baltimore: Johns Hopkins Univ. Press, 1998), 355–69. The Smith Act, the precursor to a series of anti-immigrant measures during the war years, created a storm of protest. However, the Brown Scare fear of aliens, heightened by a series of munitions plants explosions in 1940, overrode all attempts at repeal. MacDonnell, *Insidious Foes,* 123–36. For an example of anti—Smith Act rhetoric, see Vito Marcantonio, *The Registration of Aliens* (New York: American Committee for Protection of Foreign Born, 1940).

5. Schonbach, *Native American Fascism,* 369–73.

6. Ibid., 328–33; Robert L. Taylor, "The Kampf of Joe McWilliams," *New Yorker,* Aug. 24, 1940, 32–39; Dinnerstein, *Antisemitism in America,* 121–22. Viereck and Zapp spearheaded the German government's somewhat less than secret campaign to defeat Roosevelt in the 1940 election. Alton Frye, *Nazi Germany,* 131–52.

7. Schonbach, *Native American Fascism,* 346–58; McMillen, "Pro-Nazi Sentiment," 67–70; Cole, *America First,* 122–23; Rogge, *Official German Report,* 130–72. Fish's indiscretions did incalculable harm to the noninterventionist movement. As well as getting himself mixed up in the franking scandal, Fish also made ill-conceived speeches at German-American Bund rallies. He was truly, in Rex Stout's phrase, one of the "illustrious dunderheads." Rex Stout, *The Illustrious Dunderheads* (New York: Knopf, 1942), 52–58.

8. Werly, "Millenarian Right," 58–60.

9. "The Probers," *Lib,* Sept. 28, 1939, 8–9; "American Jurisprudence, 1939," *Lib,* Oct. 14, 1939, 5; "Judges Nettles Denunciation Backfires Nationally." *Lib,* Nov. 21, 1939, 12; *Asheville Citizen,* Sept. 24, Oct. 20, 26, 1939; *New York Times,* Oct. 20, 1939. The claim that Pelley operated the Silver Shirts solely as a moneymaking racket was frequently reiterated in the immediate prewar years. Portzline, "Pelley and the Silver Shirt Legion of America," 220–23.

10. August Raymond Ogden, *The Dies Committee: A Study of the Special House Committee for the Investigation of Un-American Activities, 1938–1943* (Washington, D.C.: Catholic Univ. Press, 1943), 189; "Don't Spoil It, Mr. Dies," *WL,* Aug. 21, 1938, 3; "Some Inside Impressions of the Dies Committee in Session," *WL,* Aug. 28, 1938, 6–9; HUAC, 12:7533–7663. Pelley's appearance before the committee would have undoubtedly been more contentious if Dies had presided. The chairman exhibited no sympathy for his fellow anti-New Dealer and frequently charged Pelley with being a racketeer mulcting fanatics. *New York Times,* Nov. 14, 1938; *Asheville Times,* Feb. 7, 1940; William Gellerman, *Martin Dies* (New York: John Day, 1944), 112–13.

11. Goodman, *The Committee,* 90–95; Ledeboer, "The Man Who Would Be Hitler," 134–35; *New York Times,* Feb. 8, 1940; *Federal Reporter, Second Series* 122, Sept. 29, 1941, 12–14; Portzline, "Pelley and the Silver Shirt Legion," 204–7. Pelley appears to have played no active part in Mayne's plan. The entire incident was politically motivated, but who actually instigated it probably will never be determined. Mayne implicated Labor's Non-Partisan League in the scheme, while representatives of that left-wing organization claimed they merely purchased the letters from Mayne. Regardless, although the letters did eventually wind up in the *Congressional Record,* Mayne's scheme came to nothing and he was convicted of forgery. *New York Times,* Jan. 28, 1941.

12. Ribuffo, *Old Christian Right,* 76–77; "We Are Pro-Christian and Pro-American," *Lib,* Apr. 7, 1940, 1; "And Now, a Higher Octave," *Lib,* Nov. 28, 1940, 1–4; *Asheville Times,* Dec. 17, 1940; *Indianapolis News,* Oct. 25, 1941.

13. Werly, "Millenarian Right," 62–63.

14. Portzline, "Pelley and the Silver Shirt Legion," 234–37; Interview with Melford Pearson, July 31, 2002. Although Pelley had previously maintained that the Klan would never succeed because of its anti-Catholic stance and had maintained few connections with the various Klan groups around the country, he was certainly aware that Indiana had the nation's largest Klan organization in the 1920s and that residual elements of the group might assist him in his new environs. Despite newspaper broadsides against his move, Pelley did find a number of supporters in Noblesville. Located in Hamilton County, Noblesville had boasted a 1920s Klan branch that included 35 percent of all white males in the county as members. Given the area's history, it is not surprising that one Noblesville resident characterized Pelley as merely a "radical Republican." Leonard J. Moore, *Citizen Klansmen: The Ku Klux Klan in Indiana, 1921–1928* (Chapel Hill: Univ. of North Carolina Press, 1991), 48–50.

15. *Noblesville Ledger,* Dec. 7, 10, 1940; *Noblesville Times,* Dec. 20, 1940; *Indianapolis Star,* Dec. 21, 22, 24, 25, 1940; *Indianapolis Times,* Dec. 27, 1940. Pelley also created a stir by appearing in the area under an assumed name, despite being disguiseless and easily recognizable. Losey also facilitated Pelley's burgeoning relationships with several other former Indiana Klansmen still active in right-wing politics. Among the most significant of Pelley's new associates were Muncie's Court Asher, the colorful editor of *The X-Ray,* and Carl Mote, best remembered for his 1939 work *The New Deal Goose Step* (New York: Daniel Ryersom). E. A. Piller, *Time Bomb* (New York: Arco, 1945), 81. Stephenson was not released from prison until 1956. For his career, see M. William Lutholtz, *Grand Dragon: D. C. Stephenson and the Ku Klux Klan in Indiana* (West Lafayette, Ind.: Purdue Univ. Press, 1991). Although Lutholtz's work offers more details on Stephenson, Leonard J. Moore's *Citizen Klansmen* is a far more scholarly treatment of the Indiana Klan.

16. Werly, "Millenarian Right," 63; *Noblesville News,* Dec. 27, 1940; *Noblesville Ledger,* Dec. 30, 1940; *Indianapolis Times,* Jan. 1, 1941.

17. *Asheville Citizen,* Oct. 21, 1941; *Indianapolis News,* Oct. 31, 1941, Jan. 21, 1942; *Asheville Times,* Apr. 4, Sept. 23, 1942; *Asheville Citizen,* Sept. 24, 1942; Portzline, "Pelley and the Silver Shirt Legion," 225–27.

18. "Why International Bankers Have Financed Bolshevism," *RC,* Apr. 7, 1941, 3–4 ; "What Nation Is the Real Aggressor?" *RC,* May 5, 1941, 5–6; "Shoot 'em on Sight," *RC,* Sept. 22, 1941, 16; "America First, Last," *RC,* Dec. 1, 1941, 5–6. Perhaps realizing the inherent dangers of associating too closely with Pelley, Carl Losey discontinued his connection with the Fellowship Press in February 1941 and left Noblesville. *Noblesville Ledger,* Mar. 4, 1941.

19. "Big Time Significance Behind Apparent World Upset," *Gal,* Oct. 1941, 25–30; "From New Deal to Commonwealth," *Gal,* Dec. 22, 1941, 13–14; "The Resplendent Order on Its Way," *Gal,* Dec. 29, 1941, 2; "America Concurs in No Scheme to Regulate Earth," *Gal,* Jan. 19, 1942 4; *Noblesville Ledger,* Dec. 15, 1941.

20. *Indianapolis Star,* Apr. 1, 1942; Ribuffo, *Old Christian Right,* 77–78; "Tarnished Silver Shirt," *Newsweek,* Apr. 13, 1942, 29–30.

21. *Indianapolis Star,* June 4, 10, 1942. The issue of *Galilean* in question was found among the belongings of Private Paul D. Hoffman while he was undergoing basic training at Camp Wheeler in Georgia. Hoffman was a subscriber to the magazine and claimed he brought it with him to read on the train ride to the camp. Ibid., July 30, 1942.

22. Werly, "Millenarian Right," 68–69.

23. *Indianapolis Times,* July 28, 1942; *Indianapolis Star,* Aug. 6, 1942; *Chicago Sun,* Aug. 1, 1942; Gary, *Nervous Liberals,* 216–20. For Lasswell's explanation of the content analysis techniques he utilized in wartime sedition cases, see Harold D. Lasswell, ed., *Language of Politics: Studies in Quantitative Semantics* (New York: Stewart, 1949), 173–232; Harold F. Gosnell, "Instruction and Research: Public Opinion Research in Government," *American Political Science Review* 43 (June 1949): 565–66. On Lasswell and content analysis, see Janowitz, *Political Conflict,* 207–22.

24. Although they were not personal friends, Pelley held a deep respect for Van Horn Moseley and occasionally reprinted the retired officer's speeches. Christian also served as one of D. C. Stephenson's defense attorneys in the Klansman's 1925 murder trial.

25. *Indianapolis Times,* July 30, 1942; *Chicago Sun,* July 30, 1942; *Indianapolis Star,* Aug. 3, 1942; *Indianapolis News,* Aug. 4, 1942; Charles Lindbergh, *The Wartime Journals of Charles A. Lindbergh* (New York: Harcourt Brace, 1970), 539–41; Werly, "Millenarian Right," 73–74; "Are You as Panicky over Hitler as Marc Anthony Hull and His Caesar?" *RC,* Feb. 3, 1941, 7; Berg, *Lindbergh,* 444–45; Portzline, "Pelley and the Silver Shirt Legion," 201. Lindbergh's appearance at Pelley's trial severely damaged his public reputation. Despite his having never met Pelley, his appearance helped link Lindbergh with shady political elements and undercut his public support. Wayne S. Cole, *Charles A. Lindbergh and the Battle Against American Intervention in World War II* (New York: Harcourt Brace Jovanovich, 1974), 230.

26. *Indianapolis Star,* Aug. 6, 13, 1942.

27. MacDonnell, *Insidious Foes,* 137–84; Michael Linfield, *Freedom under Fire: U.S. Civil Liberties in Times of War* (Boston: South End Press, 1990), 69–111; James MacGregor Burns, *Roosevelt: The Soldier of Freedom, 1940–1945* (New York: Harcourt Brace Jovanovich, 1970), 453–54; Portzline, "Pelley and the Silver Shirt Legion," 258–59. Pelley's decision to continue assailing Roosevelt and the war effort during a politically volatile period resulted from his beliefs that the war was illegal, that alignment with the Soviet Union was suicidal, and that civil liberties would continue to be respected. The mistreatment of hyphenate Americans during World War II has recently received a great deal of scholarly attention. For representative studies, see Roger Daniels, *Concentration Camps USA: Japanese Americans and World War II* (New York: Holt, Rinehart, and Winston, 1972); John Christgau, *"Enemies:" World War II Alien Internment* (Ames: Iowa State Univ. Press, 1985); Stephen Fox, *America's Invisible Gulag: A Biography of German American Internment and Exclusion in World War II* (New York: Peter Lang, 2000); Arthur D. Jacobs, ed., *German-Americans in the World Wars,* 4 vols. (Munchen: K.G. Saur, 1995). For conscientious objectors, Cynthia Eller, *Conscientious Objectors and the Second World War: Moral and Religious Arguments in Support of Pacifism* (New York: Praeger, 1991). The violation of political extremists' civil liberties, however, remains largely unexamined.

28. Werly, "Millenarian Right," 78–80; Rogge, *Official German Report,* 173–232. The thirty individuals listed on the final indictment were: Joseph McWilliams, Pelley, Howard Victor Broenstrupp, Gerald Winrod, George Deatherage, Edward James Smythe, Ellis O. Jones, Robert Noble, Franz Ferenz (who worked for Pelley in Hollywood), Lois de Lafayette Washburn, Frank W. Clark, E. J. Parker Sage, William Lyman, Garland Alderman, Ernest Elmhurst, Robert Edmondson, James True, Charles Hudson, Elmer Garner, David Baxter, Eugene Sanctuary, Peter Stahrenberg, Elizabeth Dilling, Lawrence Dennis, George Sylvester Viereck, Prescott Dennett, Gerhard Kunze, August Klapprott, Herman Schwinn, and Max Diebel. When the trial finally began Pelley, Jones, Noble,

Ferenz, Viereck, and Kunze were already incarcerated for prior sedition convictions. Father Charles Coughlin and Gerald L. K. Smith were conspicuously absent from the indictments. The full indictment is reprinted in Kittrie and Wedlock, *Tree of Liberty,* 369–71.

29. Leo P. Ribuffo, *"United States v. McWilliams:* The Roosevelt Administration and the Far Right," in *American Political Trials,* rev. ed., ed. Michael R. Belknap (Westport, Conn.: Praeger, 1994), 180–86; Schonbach, *Native American Fascism,* 415–17.

30. Ribuffo, *Old Christian Right,* 197–99; Gary, *Nervous Liberals,* 220–42; Portzline, "Pelley and the Silver Shirt Legion," 259–67. Much of the evidence utilized by Rogge was already used in the Indiana trial. Given that they were included in a second indictment against Pelley for sedition, the rules against "double jeopardy" were clearly violated in this case.

31. Werly, "Millenarian Right," 82–83; Charles Higham, *American Swastika,* 57–68. Despite the failure of the wartime mass sedition trial, the Justice Department attempted a similar venture in 1949 against American Communists. The lengthy trial of nineteen CPUSA leaders also led to no convictions. Kutler, *American Inquisition,* 152–82.

32. Schonbach, *Native American Fascism,* 418–19; Maximilian St.-George and Lawrence Dennis, *Trial on Trial,* 70; Portzline, "Pelley and the Silver Shirt Legion," 270–79; William Preston, Jr., "The 1940s: The Way We Really Were," *Civil Liberties Review* 2 (Winter 1975): 9–10; Ronald Radosh, *Prophets on the Right: Profiles of Conservative Critics of American Globalism* (New York: Simon and Schuster, 1975), 290–95; Neil Johnson, *George Sylvester Viereck,* 243–50. The government made sporadic attempts to revive the prosecution after the war ended, and as a result the proceedings did not officially end until June 30, 1947.

33. Werly, "Millenarian Right," 84; *Washington Times-Herald,* Nov. 23, 1946. The end of the mass sedition trial and his quiet return to prison did help fulfill one of Pelley's prophecies. In 1940, based upon his Great Pyramid readings, Pelley predicted that his public career would end in 1945. This assertion was probably based upon the standard pyramidist belief that March 20, 1945, would witness the change from man-rule on earth to God-rule. *Indianapolis Star,* Dec. 28, 1940; Boswell, *Prophets and Portents,* 110–11. Baltzell's letter asserted that he intended for Pelley to remain incarcerated only for the duration of the war.

34. Interview with Melford Pearson, July 31, 2002; Pelley, *Soulcraft Scripts,* vol. 4, Discourse 46, 150.

35. Werly, "Millenarian Right," 85–86; Portzline, "Pelley and the Silver Shirt Legion," 282–91; *Chicago Tribune,* Oct. 19, 1947, May 19, 1949, Nov. 9, 1949; *Washington Times-Herald,* Oct. 2, 1947; *Congressional Record* 95, Sept. 19, 1949, 13260, 13281. Langer even visited Pelley in prison to offer his assistance.

36. *Chicago Tribune,* Feb. 7, 1950; Melford Pearson, *The Price of Truth* (Noblesville, Ind.: Aquila, 1947), 4, 8; Pearson, *Life Imprisonment for Exposing Communists* (Noblesville, Ind.: Fellowship Press, 1947), 5, 29–30. The difficulties faced by Communists in the

1950s have been frequently recounted. For a short, useful summation, see Athan Theoharis, "The Threat to Civil Liberties" in *Cold War Critics: Alternatives to American Foreign
Policy in the Truman Years,* ed. Thomas G. Paterson (Chicago: Quadrangle Books, 1971),
266–98.

11. Soulcraft: 1950–1965

1. Werly, "Millenarian Right," 87; *Indianapolis News,* Feb. 7, 15, 1950, Jan. 13, 1951;
Noblesville Ledger, Feb. 12, 1950; *Indianapolis Times,* July 1, 1952; *Asheville Citizen,* Jan. 18,
1952.

2. Portzline, "Pelley and the Silver Shirt Legion," 294–95; *Indianapolis Times,* Sept. 1,
1953; *Indianapolis News,* June 24, 1954, Jan. 10, 1955; Pearson, *Price of Truth,* 28; Roy, *Apostles of Discord,* 40–42; Jeffrey Kaplan, *Encyclopedia of White Power,* 96–98; June Melby
Benowitz, *Days of Discontent: American Women and Right-Wing Politics, 1933–1945* (Dekalb:
Northern Illinois Univ. Press, 2002), 161–63.

3. Werly, "Millenarian Right," 87–88; *Indianapolis Star,* Apr. 13, 1950.

4. Pelley, *Road into Sunrise,* 266, 314.

5. Ibid., 66.

6. "Cogitations," *Val,* Oct. 17, 1953, 14.

7. *Indianapolis Times,* July 1, 1952.

8. Pelley, *No More Hunger,* 47–57.

9. Ibid., 84, 158; Pelley, *Nations-in-Law,* 17.

10. Pelley, *Nations-in-Law,* 28, 104, 186–89, 199; "Are We Truly Without a Chart as
a Nation?" *Val,* Aug. 30, 1952, 4; "That Thing," *Val,* Sept. 6, 1952, 8; "Adams Is Aroused
by What Is Being Allowed to Happen to U.S," *OH,* Apr. 1959, 25–26. Until his death Pelley continued to maintain that the USSR was Jew-controlled and refused to comment on
the anti-Semitic purges that occurred in several eastern bloc countries during the 1950s.
These purges led many neo- and residual Nazi groups to adopt the position that the Soviet Union was a lesser threat to their continued existence than the United States. Pelley,
however, continued to assail the USSR and promote the United States as holding a special
position in millennial prophecy. Martin A. Lee, *The Beast Reawakens* (Boston: Little,
Brown, 1996), 106–7.

11. Pelley, *Nations-in-Law,* 249, 333; "When the Wheel Turns Over," *Val,* Sept. 12,
1952, 2; "Kremlin Headache," *Val,* Oct. 3, 1953, 8; "Collapse, Not War," *Val,* Oct. 10,
1953, 8; "China Afresh," *Val,* July 1956, 25; "We Can Take It," *Val,* Oct. 1956, 24–25; "Are
We to Fight Russia?" *Val,* June 1959, 1–2. The Pan-Aryan Federation consisted of the residents of the United States, Canada, Australia, England, Scotland, Ireland, and Germany.
Although Pelley was persona non grata among respectable spiritualists, his views on international affairs were not necessarily unique. Duke University's J. B. Rhine, the father of
professional psychical research, for one, shared Pelley's concern over Communism. Dur-

ing the 1950s Rhine stressed the importance of promoting parapsychological phenomena in the west as a refutation of Communist materialism. J. B. Rhine, "Why National Defense Overlooks Parapsychology," *Journal of Parapsychology* 21 (Dec. 1957): 245–58.

12. Pelley, *Stairs to Greatness*, 131, 153–55, 160–63, 242–43.

13. Pelley, *Star Guests*, 205; Pelley, *Stairs to Greatness*, 165, 210–11, 273–76; "Cataclysm," *Val*, Sept. 20, 1952, 8; "Stairs to Happiness," *Val*, July 1956, 2; Pelley, *Soulcraft Scripts*, vol. 1, Script 2, 18–19; ibid., vol. 8, Script 96, 11; ibid., vol. 10, Script 123, 3–7; ibid., vol. 12, Script 149, p. 20.

14. "No Argument," *Val*, Oct. 3, 1953, 8; "Soulcraft Conventions Everywhere," *Val*, Oct. 31, 1953, 3. Despite the organization's small size, Pelley was able to support himself solely from the sale of Soulcraft literature. In 1958 the Indiana Employment Security Board, seeking to collect payroll taxes from Pelley, unsuccessfully challenged Soulcraft Fellowship Incorporated's nonprofit status. Testimony during the hearing disclosed that Soulcraft received approximately $92,000 from literature sales and contributions during the years 1956–1957. *Indianapolis Times*, Nov. 25, 1958. Pelley failed, however, in his attempt to obtain federal tax-exempt status for Soulcraft. *Indianapolis Times*, Oct. 26, 1961.

15. "Soulcraft Is Organized Fact," *Val*, Mar. 1959, 5–6, 23–24; Portzline, "Pelley and the Silver Shirt Legion," 298. Portzline's point is well-taken, and even veteran Soulcrafters must have been off-put by statements such as: "the Soul-Consciousness, or the sentient intellect, by residing primarily in the etheric self, which in turn resides by day in the body, feels a speeding up of its atomic energies with detachment from the flesh." Pelley, *Soul Eternal*, 112.

16. Pelley *Star Guests*, 42–45. Pelley also explained the "constitution of the created universe" with the following formula: "self-awareness = Soul, soul in manifestation = Spirit, spirit's etheric maneuvers = Materials, spirit's purposeful conceivings = Thought, thought's technical instrumentality = Light." Pelley, *Soulcraft Scripts*, vol. 4, Script 42, 70.

17. Pelley, *Stairs to Greatness*, 139–43; Pelley, *Soul Eternal*, 106–8; "Misinterpreting Plane One," *Val*, July 1959, 3–4.

18. Pelley, *Star Guests*, 30; Pelley, *Stairs to Greatness*, 143; Pelley, *Soul Eternal*, 189–205; Pelley, *Thinking Alive: Design for Creation*, 217–31.

19. Pelley, *Star Guests*, 46–51.

20. Pelley, *Stairs to Greatness*, 22, 131; Pelley, *Star Guests*, 88; Pelley, *Soulcraft Scripts*, vol. 7, Script 80, 9, Script 81, 9–10; Pelley, *Why I Believe*, 94–96. Although published before his incarceration, Pelley trumpeted *Why I Believe* as one of the foundations of Soulcraft.

21. Pelley, *Stairs to Greatness*, 110, 242–43, 276; Pelley, *Star Guests*, 65; Pelley, *Soulcraft Scripts*, vol. 5, Script 63, 18.

22. Among Pelley's favorite metaphysical authorities were medium Bertie Lily Candler (with whom he had prewar ties), English psychic Geraldine Cummins, and the work of Meade Layne's Borderlands Sciences Research Associates (BSRA). Pelley was particularly enamored with BSRA medium Mark Probert, who received clairaudient messages

from a spirit-guide named Yada Di Shi'ite. Probert claimed Yada was the discarnate soul of a teacher from the ancient Himalayan civilization called Yuga. Yada spoke to him in the Yugan language, Kethra E Da, and he then translated the messages. Probert's eschatology stressed reincarnation on multiple planes, advanced ancient civilizations, soul seeds made of light, and life on other planets. His views corresponded considerably with Pelley's, and the Soulcraft Recorder frequently reprinted Probert's work in the pages of *Valor*. For Probert's beliefs, see Mark Probert, *The Magic Bag*, 2 vols. (San Diego, Borderlands Sciences Research Associates, 1950). Although Pelley no longer maintained formal ties with spiritualist organizations as he did during the Liberation era, his focus on life on other planes after death unwittingly placed him in middle of the most contentious debate among psychical researchers of the period. Having given up on establishing Rhinian-style scientifically provable psi phenomena, the American Society for Psychical Research returned to its 1920s position and promoted exploration of communication with the dead. R. Laurence Moore, *White Crows*, 207–9. Along with *Bright Horizons*, Pelley also tried to assist bewildered Soulcrafters by publishing a Soulcraft "dictionary" in 1952, *The Soulcraft Elucidata* (Noblesville, Ind.: Soulcraft Chapel).

23. "Are We Truly Without a Chart?" 1–2; "This Autumn Is Prelude to Eventful 1953," *Val*, Sept. 26, 1952, 2; "The World Is in the Process of Becoming Different," *Val*, Oct. 17, 1953, 4; Davidson, *The Great Pyramid*, 390.

24. "Don't Declare War Upon the Saucers," *Val*, Aug. 30, 1952, 3; "A Statement about Soulcraft," *Val*, Oct. 24, 1953, 3; "Afterthought," *Val*, Oct. 3, 1953, 16; "Headline Stuff," *Val*, Nov. 21, 1953, 8; Pelley, *Soulcraft Scripts*, vol. 10, Script 123, 16–17. While Pelley decried the level of violence in movie westerns, he frequently wrote approvingly of Hollywood product. Pelley made film recommendations in the pages of *Valor* and was particularly supportive of biblical epics (with *The Robe* and *Salome* being notable favorites). He also frequently recounted his own career in Hollywood. Typically Pelley over-inflated his own role in the growth of the motion picture industry during the 1920s. His bloated self-importance led Pelley to lash out at James Cagney's plans to make a Lon Chaney biopicture without a "Bill Pelley character in it." Pelley noted that it was impossible to make the Chaney story without him, but Cagney's actions were not surprising from an "Israelite." "Cogitations," *Val*, Oct. 1956, 26–27.

25. "Saucer Discretion," *Val*, Aug. 30, 1952, 8; "The Businessman's Thinking Must Alter," *Val*, Nov. 14, 1953, 2–3; "Should Moon-Shots Arrive," *Val*, Mar. 1959, 11; Robert E. Bartholomew and George S. Howard, *UFOs and Alien Contact: Two Centuries of Mystery* (Amherst, N.Y.: Prometheus Books, 1998), 189–206; Paul Devereux and Peter Brookesmith, *UFOs and Ufology: The First Fifty Years* (New York: Facts on File, 1997), 21–26; Curtis Peebles, *Watch the Skies: A Chronicle of the UFO Myth* (Washington: Smithsonian Institution Press, 1994), 67–71; Jerome Clark, *The UFO Book: Encyclopedia of the Extraterrestrial* (Detroit: Visible Ink, 1998), 119–41; Sladek, *New Apocrypha*, 30–35. The early years of ufology are ably surveyed in John A. Keel, "The Flying Saucer Subculture," *Journal of Popular Culture* 8 (Spring 1975): 871–96.

26. Peebles, *Watch the Skies,* 102; Vallee, *Messengers of Deception,* 192–93.

27. Clark, *UFO Book,* 18–19; Peebles, *Watch the Skies,* 93–99. There is some evidence to suggest that Adamski's Laguna Beach, California, Royal Order of Tibet monastery was simply a front for making "sacramental" wine during Prohibition. Lynne Picknett, *The Mammoth Book of UFOs* (New York: Carroll and Graf, 2001), 282. For a sympathetic portrait of Adamski, see Lou Zinsstag and Timothy Good, *George Adamski— The Untold Story* (London: Ceti Publications, 1983).

28. Devereux and Brookesmith, *UFOs and Ufology,* 27–29; Clark, *UFO Book,* 20–23; David W. Stupple, "Mahatmas and Space Brothers," *Journal of American Culture* 7 (Summer 1984): 131–39. Adamski's primary saucer works of the period were *Flying Saucers Have Landed* (New York: The British Book Centre, 1953) and *Inside the Spaceships* (New York: Abelard-Schuman, 1955). Adamski, like Pelley, made increasingly outlandish claims as he got older. By the early 1960s Adamski contended he had made a trip to Saturn and discussed the saucers in private sessions with John F. Kennedy and Pope John XXIII. Peebles, *Watch the Skies,* 148; James Lewis, ed., *The Gods Have Landed,* 259–66. For a summation of Adamski's religious system, see George Adamski, *Cosmic Philosophy* (1961; repr., Freeman, S.Dak.: Pine Hill Press, 1972). The "Aryan" appearance of spacemen spotted by Adamski and others helped give rise to a theory that UFOs represented a secret weapon of remnants of the Third Reich (who were usually said to be hiding out in the Arctic). To his credit, Pelley ignored such nonsense. For the development of this theory, see David Hatcher Childress, ed., *Lost Continents and the Hollow Earth* (Kempton, Ill.: Adventures Unlimited Press, 1999), 257–74; Nicholas Goodrick-Clarke, *Black Sun: Aryan Cults, Esoteric Nazism, and the Politics of Identity* (New York: New York Univ. Press, 2002), 151–72; Picknett, *Mammoth Book of UFOs,* 406–11; Joscelyn Godwin, *Arktos: The Polar Myth in Science, Symbolism, and Nazi Survival* (Kempton, Ill.: Adventures Unlimited Press, 1996).

29. "He Talked With a Saucer-man From Venus," *Val,* Aug. 29, 1953, 1–6; "Sorrowful Planet," *Val,* Oct. 10, 1953, 10; "Space-Ship Guests Not Permitted to Alter Earth Destiny," *Val,* 4–5; "Afterthought," *Val,* Oct. 17, 1953, 16; "More about Saucers," *Val,* Oct. 31, 1953, 10–11; "Let's Call Them Ventlas Instead of Saucers," *Val,i* Nov. 7, 1953, 4, 10; Jim Keith, *Saucers of the Illuminati* (Lilburn, Ga.: IllumiNet Press, 1999), 49–52. Adamski's adoption of a Theosophy-based belief system is not unique among UFO cults. Ufologist David Stupple has noted that most current contactee groups have neo-I AM connections. Curtis G. Guller, ed., *Proceedings of the First International UFO Congress* (New York: Warner Books, 1980), 307.

30. Pelley, *Soulcraft Scripts,* vol. 11, Script 135, 6; "Would You Raise the Dead If You Knew How?" *Val,* Aug. 30, 1952, 5–6; "Just What Is Psychological Research?" *Val,* Mar. 1959, 13; "Famous Voices," *Val,* May 1959, 17.

31. Pelley, *As Thou Lovest,* 21–22, 44–45, 90–91, 114, 147, 190–91.

32. Pelley, *Stairs to Greatness,* 121, 153–55, 210–11; "Stairs to Happiness," 2; "Birthday," *Val,* Mar. 1959, 16; "Nostradamus," *Val,* May 1959, 28; Pelley, *New Quatrains of the Modern Michel Nostradamus* (Noblesville, Ind.: Soulcraft Fellowship, 1956), 9–14. Pelley

enclosed a mimeographed sheet with *New Quatrains* that translated the terms found in the new stanzas. These definitions showed that Nostradamus and Pelley displayed remarkably similar interests. For example, in the quatrains the "weevils" were "the Marxist Zionists," the "grinning fool" was Nikita Khrushchev, the "man with the umbrella" was Bernard Baruch, and, most curious, the "vortexes" were hurricanes named after women. Anyone who continues to harbor notions of Nostradamus as a metaphrast is advised to read James Randi's devastating monograph *The Mask of Nostradamus* (New York: Charles Scribner's Sons, 1990).

33. "Cogitations," *Val,* Mar. 1959, 25.

34. "How the Deceased Employ Themselves," *Val,* Mar. 1959, 20; "Revere Proclaims Cosmic Fact," *OH,* Apr. 1959, 6. According to Melford Pearson, Pelley himself came to believe these "Great Voices" were probably bogus and quietly removed these materials from the Soulcraft library. While I have no reason to doubt the validity of Pearson's statements, the "Great Voices" series did represent a significant aspect of Pelley's teachings in the late 1950s and, therefore, is detailed here. Interview with Melford Pearson, July 31, 2002.

35. "How the Deceased Employ Themselves," 20; "Mark Twain Sees Life on Mississippi Humorously," *OH,* Jan. 1959, 17; "Henry Ward Beecher Is Strong for Soulcraft," *OH,* 22; "Samuel Adams Is Aroused by What Is Being Allowed to Happen to U.S.," *OH,* Apr. 1959, 25–26; *Indianapolis Times,* Aug. 10, 1955.

36. "Birthday," 16; *Noblesville Ledger,* July 3, 1965.

Epilogue

1. Interview with Melford Pearson, July 31, 2002. Pearson's three primary works are *Challenge to Crisis* (Noblesville, Ind.: Aquila Press, 1969), *There Is a Way to Peace and Social Justice* (Noblesville, Ind.: Aquila Press, 1995), and *A Blueprint for Survival: Peace and Economic Justice Await the Adoption of a National Cooperative Commonwealth* (Victoria, B.C.: Trafford and Aquila, 2002). Unlike his father-in-law, however, Pearson's works display what seems to be a genuine interest in promoting the Civil Rights movement.

2. Jack Kerlin, "William D. Pelley's Legacy" (unpublished paper, Provo, Utah, 2003).

3. Benn E. Lewis, *I, John: The Reincarnated Apostle* (New York: Exposition Press, 1970), 27, 89, 119, 246, 279–87; John Godwin, *Occult America* (Garden City, N.Y.: Doubleday, 1972), 135–37. Lewis also seemed to swipe material from George Adamski. For example, Lewis depicted secret interviews with John F. Kennedy and Pope John XIII that are almost verbatim recountings of Adamski's tales. Benn Lewis, *I, John,* 224–26.

4. George Hunt Williamson, undated document #0124N, in George Hunt Williamson Papers, maintained by Michael D. Swords, 1025 Berkshire Drive, Kalamazoo, Michigan (hereafter cited as Williamson Papers). Williamson's spiritual system is outlined in *Other Tongues—Other Flesh* (Amherst, Wisc.: Amherst Press, 1953) and *Other Voices,* rev. ed. (Scottsdale, Ariz.: Abelard, 1995).

5. Kossy, *Strange Creations,* 9–43; David Hatcher Childress, "Tunnel Systems Beneath South America," in *Lost Continents and the Hollow Earth,* ed. David Childress (Kempton, Ill.: Adventures Unlimited Press, 1999), 295–301; Clark, *UFO Book,* 429–44. Pelley's ideas have also found a home in the peculiar metaphysical no-man's-land where spiritualism, ufology, and Christianity converge. For example, the *Star Beacon,* a well-known magazine that mixes extraterrestrials, New Age channeling, Christianity, and Native American mythology, frequently cites Pelley's work, particularly *The Golden Scripts,* seemingly oblivious to his racist and anti-Semitic past. For a representative example, see Julian Joyce, "Cosmic Thoughts," *Star Beacon* 11, Mar. 1997, 8. The "ancient astronauts" theory of human creation proved to be a highly lucrative subject for paperback publishers in the early 1970s. Among the best-known works on the topic are Erich von Daniken, *Chariots of the Gods? Unsolved Mysteries of the Past* (London: Souvenir, 1969); Raymond Drake, *Spacemen in the Ancient East* (London: Neville Spearman, 1968); Robert Charroux, *The Mysterious Unknown* (London: Neville Spearman, 1972); Max Flindt and Otto Binder, *Mankind—Child of the Stars* (Greenwich, Conn.: Fawcett Gold Medal, 1974); and Alan and Sally Landsburg, *The Outer Space Connection* (New York: Bantam Books, 1975).

6. Kossy, *Strange Creations,* 15; Devereux and Brookesmith, *UFOs and Ufology,* 83–84; Vicki Cooper, "Fascist Trends Spotted in UFO Past," *UFO,* Apr. 1992, 28; Peebles, *Watch the Skies,* 104; Vallee, *Messengers of Deception,* 114–15; Martin Cannon, *The Controllers: A New Hypothesis of Alien Abductions* (Aptos, Calif.: Tom Davis Books, n.d.), 58–59; Picknett, *Mammoth Book of UFOs,* 411. Much of Williamson's work was openly anti-Semitic and, in classic Pelley fashion, linked global oppression with Jews, international bankers, and Communism. For a representative example, see George Hunt Williamson and John McCoy, *UFOs Confidential* (Corpus Christi: Essene Press, 1958).

7. Paolini and Paolini, *400 Years of Imaginary Friends,* 207–354; Stupple, "The "I AM Sect Today," 897–905; Campbell, *Ancient Wisdom Revived,* 163; Judah, *History and Philosophy of Metaphysical Movements,* 133 45; Ellwood and Partin, *Religious and Spiritual Groups,* 102–6; J. Gordon Melton, "The Church Universal and Triumphant: Its Heritage and Thoughtworld," in *Church Universal and Triumphant in Scholarly Perspective,* eds. James R. Lewis and J. Gordon Melton, 1–20 (Stanford: Center for Academic Publications, 1994).

8. Raymond E. Wolfinger, et al., "America's Radical Right: Politics and Ideology," in *Ideology and Discontent,* ed. David E. Apter (Glencoe, Ill.: Free Press, 1964), 262–93.

9. Hoppes, "William Dudley Pelley and the Silvershirt Legion," 318.

10. Bennett, *Party of Fear,* 352–56; James Coates, *Armed and Dangerous: The Rise of the Survivalist Right* (New York: Hill and Wang, 1987), 104–22; James Corcoran, *Bitter Harvest: Gordon Kahl and the Posse Comitatus, Murder in the Heartland* (New York: Viking, 1990), 91–251; Vincent Coppola, *Dragons of God: A Journey Through Far-Right America* (Marietta, Ga.: Longstreet, 1996), 87–104; Philip Finch, *God, Guts, and Guns: A Close Look at the Radical Right* (New York: Seaview, 1983), 66–81; Sargent, *Extremism In America,* 343–50; Ted Daniels, ed., *A Doomsday Reader: Prophets, Predictors, and Hucksters of Salvation* (New York: New York Univ. Press, 1999), 171–98. In the mid-1970s Beach founded an

"above-ground" organization, the Citizens Law Enforcement and Research Committee (CLERC). This group published pro-Posse and Christian Identity materials. Barkun, *Religion and the Racist Right,* 96. Given their decentralized nature (and shunning of publicity), it is difficult to establish either an exact lineage or specific connections with other groups for the Posse. It appears that Beach established the Posse independently, but at roughly the same time that William Potter Gale created a similar organization, initially known as the California Rangers, in California. These groups often share an overlapping membership, as well as a commonality of beliefs. Gale credits Beach with developing the Posse idea but is himself probably a more significant figure on the extreme right. While working at Hughes Aircraft Company during the 1950s, Gale was introduced to proto-Identity Doctrine through Gerald L. K. Smith and Wesley Swift. Gale later established his Identity and Posse-related Committee of the States, which served as an ideological training ground for Richard Butler of the Aryan Nations and Ty Hardin (who played Bronco Lane on the 1950s television show *Cheyenne*) of the Arizona Patriots. See also Jeansonne, *Gerald L. K. Smith,* 101–14; Ann Burlein, *Lift High the Cross: Where White Supremacy and the Christian Right Converge* (Durham, N.C.: Duke Univ. Press, 2002), 39–41; Goodrick-Clarke, *Black Sun,* 232–56.

11. George and Wilcox, *American Extremists,* 323–53; Martin Lee, *The Beast Reawakens,* 337–44; Philip Lamy, *Millennium Rage: Survivalists, White Supremacists, and the Doomsday Prophecy* (New York: Plenum Press, 1996), 127–29.

12. Tim Powers, *Expiration Date* (New York: TOR Fantasy, 1996), 225.

Bibliography

Archival Materials

Buncombe County Criminal Action Papers. 1933–1944. *State vs. Pelley.* North Carolina State Archives, Raleigh, N.C.

George and Sophia Parker Papers. Pikes Peak Library District, Colorado Springs, Colo.

George E. Rennar Papers. Univ. of Washington Library, Seattle, Wash.

George Hunt Williamson Papers. Maintained by Michael D. Swords, Kalamazoo, Mich.

Silver Shirt Legion of America, Inc., Washington State Division, correspondence and related material of Orville W. Roundtree, liaison officer for the state division, 1933–1940. Univ. of Washington Library, Seattle, Wash.

William Dudley Pelley Collection. Pack Memorial Library, Asheville, N.C.

William Dudley Pelley Collection. Southeast Public Library, Noblesville, Ind.

Published Works and Dissertations

Aaron, Daniel, ed. *America in Crisis: Fourteen Crucial Episodes in American History.* New York: Knopf, 1952.

Abrahams, Edward. *The Lyrical Left: Randolph Bourne, Alfred Stieglitz, and the Origins of Cultural Radicalism in America.* Charlottesville: Univ. of Virginia Press, 1986.

Ackerman, Carl W. *Trailing the Bolsheviki: Twelve Thousand Miles with the Allies in Siberia.* New York: Charles Scribner's Sons, 1919.

Adamski, George. *Cosmic Philosophy.* 1961. Reprint, Freeman, S.Dak.: Pine Hill Press, 1972.

———. *Flying Saucers Have Landed.* New York: British Book Centre, 1953.

————. *Inside the Spaceships.* New York: Abelard-Schuman, 1955.

Adkins, Gaius Glenn. *Modern Religious Cults and Movements.* London: George Allen and Unwin, 1924.

Agran, Edward Gale. *"Too Good a Town:" William Allen White. Community, and the Emerging Rhetoric of Middle America.* Fayetteville: Univ. of Arkansas Press, 1998.

Ahlstrom, Sydney. *A Religious History of the American People.* New Haven, Conn.: Yale Univ. Press, 1972.

Alexander, Charles C. *Nationalism in American Thought, 1930–1945.* Chicago: Rand McNally, 1969.

————. "Prophet of American Racism: Madison Grant and the Nordic Myth." *Phylon,* 23 (Spring 1962): 73–90.

Allen, Frederick Lewis. "Elbert Hubbard." *Scribner's Magazine* 104 (Sept. 1938): 12–14.

Amann, Peter H. "Vigilante Fascism: The Black Legion as an American Hybrid." *Comparative Studies in Society and History* 25 (July 1983): 490–524.

Angebert, Jean-Michel. *The Occult and the Third Reich: The Mystical Origins of Nazism and the Search for the Holy Grail.* New York: Macmillan, 1974.

Angoff, Charles. "Nazi Jew-Baiting in America." *Nation,* May 1, 1935.

Anti-Defamation League of B'nai B'rith. *Extremism on the Right: A Handbook.* New York: Anti-Defamation League of B'nai B'rith, 1983.

Apter, David E., ed. *Ideology and Discontent.* Glencoe, Ill.: Free Press, 1964.

Arendt, Hannah. *The Origins of Totalitarianism.* New York: Meridian, 1958.

Armbruster, Howard. *Treason's Peace: German Dyes and American Dupes.* New York: Beechurste, 1947.

Bach, Marcus. *Strange Sects and Curious Cults.* New York: Dodd, Mead, 1961.

Baldwin, Neil. *Henry Ford and the Jews: The Mass Production of Hate.* New York: Public Affairs, 2001.

Barkun, Michael. *Religion and the Racist Right: The Origins of the Christian Identity Movement.* Chapel Hill: Univ. of North Carolina Press, 1994.

Barrett, Jr., Edward, *The Tenney Committee: Legislative Investigation of Subversive Activities in California.* Ithaca, N.Y.: Cornell Univ. Press, 1951.

Bartholomew, Robert E., and George S. Howard. *UFOs and Alien Contact: Two Centuries of Mystery.* Amherst, N.Y.: Prometheus Books, 1998.

Basinger, Jeanine. *Silent Stars.* New York: Knopf, 1999.

Basso, Hamilton. "The Little Hitlers at Asheville." *New Republic,* Sept. 2, 1936.

Bayor, Ronald. "Klans, Coughlinites and Aryan Nations: Patterns of American Anti-Semitism in the Twentieth Century." *American Jewish History* 76 (Dec. 1986): 181–96.

Beard, Charles A. "Exposing the Anti-Semitic Forgery about Benjamin Franklin." *Jewish Frontier,* Mar. 1935, 10–13.

———. *Giddy Minds and Foreign Quarrels: An Estimate of American Foreign Policy.* New York: Macmillan, 1939.

Beebe, Tom. *Who's Who in New Thought: Biographical Dictionary of New Thought— Personnel, Centers, and Authors' Publications.* Lakemont, Ga.: CSA Press, 1977.

Belknap, Michael. *American Political Trials.* Rev. ed. Westport, Conn.: Praeger, 1994.

———. *Cold War Political Justice: The Smith Act, the Communist Party, and American Civil Liberties.* Westport, Conn.: Greenwood Press, 1977.

Bell, Daniel, ed. *The Radical Right.* Garden City, N.Y.: Doubleday, 1963.

Bell, Leland V. *In Hitler's Shadow: The Anatomy of American Nazism.* Port Washington, N.Y.: Kennikat Press, 1973.

Bendersky, Joseph W. *The "Jewish Threat:" Anti-Semitic Politics of the U.S. Army.* New York: Basic Books, 2000.

Bennett, David H. *Demagogues in the Depression: American Radicals and the Union Party, 1932–1936.* New Brunswick, N.J.: Rutgers Univ. Press, 1969.

———. *The Party of Fear: From Nativist Movements to the New Right in American History.* Chapel Hill: Univ. of North Carolina Press, 1988.

Benowitz, June Melby. *Days of Discontent: American Women and Right-Wing Politics, 1933–1945.* Dekalb: Northern Illinois Univ. Press, 2002.

Berg, A. Scott. *Lindbergh.* New York: G. P. Putnam's Sons, 1998.

Bergier, Jacques. *Extraterrestrial Visitations from Prehistoric Times to the Present.* Chicago: Regnery, 1973.

Bergon, Doris. *The Twisted Cross: The German Christian Movement in the Third Reich.* Chapel Hill: Univ. of North Carolina Press, 1996.

Bernstein, Herman. *The History of a Lie: The Protocols of the Wise Men of Zion.* New York: J. S. Ogilvie, 1921.

Biddle, Francis. *In Brief Authority.* Garden City, N.Y.: Doubleday, 1962.

———. *The Fear of Freedom.* Garden City, N.Y.: Doubleday, 1951.

Bingham, Alfred M. *Insurgent America: The Revolt of the Middle Classes.* New York: Harper and Brothers, 1935.

Birkhead, L. M. "Fascism in America." *Literary Digest,* Aug. 14, 1937.

Black, Gregory D. *Hollywood Censored: Morality Codes, Catholics, and the Movies.* New York: Cambridge Univ. Press, 1994.

Blackmur, Richard P. "Utopia, or Uncle Tom's Cabin." In *Sinclair Lewis: A Collection of Critical Essays,* edited by Mark Schorer, 108–10. Englewood Cliffs, N.J.: Prentice-Hall, 1962.

Blake, Michael. *The Films of Lon Chaney.* Lanham, Md.: Vestal Press, 1998.

———. *Lon Chaney: The Man Behind the Thousand Faces.* Vestal, N.Y.: Vestal Press, 1993.

———. *A Thousand Faces: Lon Chaney's Unique Artistry in Motion Pictures.* Vestal, N.Y.: Vestal Press, 1995.

Block, Marguerite. *The New Church in the New World: A Study of Swedenborgianism in the New World.* New York: Henry Holt, 1932.

Blum, John Morton. *V Was for Victory: Politics and American Culture During World War II.* New York: Harcourt Brace Jovanovich, 1976.

Bond, Fred B. "Subjective Evidence for Survival or Continuity." *Journal of the American Society for Psychical Research* 24 (Jan. 1930): 35–38.

Boswell, Rolfe. *Prophets and Portents: Seven Seers Foretell Hitler's Doom.* New York: Thomas Y. Crowell, 1942.

Bosworth, Allan R. *America's Concentration Camps.* New York: W. W. Norton, 1967.

Boyer, Paul. *When Time Shall Be No More: Prophecy Belief in Modern American Culture.* Cambridge, Mass.: Belknap Press, 1992.

Brackman, Harold. "The Attack on 'Jewish Hollywood': A Chapter in the History of Modern American Anti-Semitism." *Modern Judaism* 20 (Feb. 2000): 1–19.

Braden, Charles S. *Spirits in Rebellion: The Rise and Development of New Thought.* Dallas, Tex.: Southern Methodist Univ. Press, 1963.

———. *These Also Believe: A Study of Modern American Cults and Minority Religious Movements.* New York: Macmillan, 1949.

Bradley, John. *Allied Intervention in Russia.* London: Weidenfeld and Nicolson, 1968.

Breitman, Richard D., and Alan M. Kraut, "Anti-Semitism in the State Department, 1933–44." In *Anti-Semitism in American History,* ed. David A. Gerber, 167–200. Urbana: Univ. of Illinois Press, 1986.

Brian, Denis. *The Enchanted Voyager: The Life of J. B. Rhine.* Englewood Cliffs, N.J.: Prentice-Hall, 1982.

Brinkley, Alan. *Voices of Protest: Huey Long, Father Coughlin, and the Great Depression.* New York: Knopf, 1982.

Britt, George. *The Fifth Column Is Here.* New York: Wilfred Funk, 1940.

Brown, Croswell. *They Went Wrong.* New York: McGraw-Hill, 1954.

Brownlow, Kevin. *Hollywood: The Pioneers.* New York: Knopf, 1979.

Bryan, Gerald B. *Psychic Dictatorship in America.* 1940. Reprint, Livingston, Mont.: Paolini International, 2000.

Bucco, Martin, ed. *Critical Essays on Sinclair Lewis.* Boston: G. K. Hall, 1986.

Burlein, Ann. *Lift High the Cross: Where White Supremacy and the Christian Right Converge*. Durham, N.C.: Duke Univ. Press, 2002.

Burlingham, Charles C., et al. *The German Reich and Americans of German Origin*. New York: Oxford Univ. Press, 1938.

Burns, James McGregor. *Roosevelt: The Lion and the Fox*. New York: Harcourt, Brace, and Company, 1956.

———. *Roosevelt: The Soldier of Freedom, 1940–1945*. New York: Harcourt Brace Jovanovich, 1970.

Cameron, Evan William, ed. *Sound and the Cinema: The Coming of Sound to American Film*. Pleasantville, N.Y.: Redgrave, 1980.

Campbell, Bruce F. *Ancient Wisdom Revived: A History of the Theosophical Movement*. Berkeley: Univ. of California Press, 1980.

Canby, Henry Seidel. *The Age of Confidence*. New York: Farrar and Rinehart, 1934.

Canedy, Susan. *America's Nazis: A Democratic Dilemma*. Menlo Park, Calif.: Markgraf, 1990.

Cannon, Martin. *The Controllers: A New Hypothesis of Alien Abductions*. Aptos, Calif.: Tom Davis Books, n.d.

Carey, Gary. *All the Stars in Heaven: Louis B. Mayer's MGM*. New York: E. P. Dutton, 1981.

Carlson, John Roy. *The Plotters*. New York: E. P. Dutton, 1946.

———. *Under Cover: My Four Years in the Nazi Underworld of America*. New York: E. P. Dutton, 1943.

Carmichael, Joel. *The Satanizing of the Jews: Origin and Development of Mystical Anti-Semitism*. New York: Fromm, 1992.

Carr, Joseph J. *The Twisted Cross*. Shreveport, La.: Huntington House, 1985.

Carrington, Hereward. *The Projection of the Astral Body*. London: Rider, 1929.

Carson, Gerald. *The Roguish World of Doctor Brinkley*. New York: Holt, Rinehart, and Winston, 1960.

Carstensen, Fred V. *American Enterprise in Foreign Markets: Studies of Singer and International Harvester in Imperial Russia*. Chapel Hill: Univ. of North Carolina Press, 1984.

Cerve, Wishar S. [H. Spencer Lewis]. *Lemuria: The Lost Continent of the Pacific*. San Jose, Calif.: AMORC, 1931.

Chace, William. "Ezra Pound and the Marxist Temptation." *American Quarterly* 12 (Autumn 1970): 719–23.

Chadwin, Mark Lincoln. *The Warhawks: American Interventionists Before Pearl Harbor*. New York: Norton, 1970.

Chai, Dong-Bai. "Josiah Strong: Apostle of Anglo-Saxonism and Social Christianity." Ph.D. diss., Univ. of Texas, 1972.

Chamberlain, Houston Stewart. *The Foundations of the Nineteenth Century*. New York: J. Lane, 1911.

Champney, Freeman. *Art and Glory: The Story of Elbert Hubbard*. New York: Crown, 1968.

Chapman, Abraham. *Nazi Penetration in America*. New York: American League for Peace and Democracy, 1939.

Chase, Allan. *Falange: The Axis Secret Army in the Americas*. New York: G. P. Putnam's Sons, 1943.

Chase, Stuart. *The New American Front* New York: Harcourt, Brace, 1939.

Childress, David Hatcher, ed. *Lost Continents and the Hollow Earth*. Kempton, Ill.: Adventures Unlimited Press, 1999.

Christgau, John. *"Enemies": World War II Alien Internment*. Ames: Iowa Univ. Press, 1985.

Clark, Jerome. *The UFO Book: Encyclopedia of the Extraterrestrial*. Detroit: Visible Ink, 1998.

Coates, James. *Armed and Dangerous: The Rise of the Survivalist Right*. New York: Hill and Wang, 1987.

Coben, Stanley. "The American Red Scare of 1919–1920." In *Conspiracy: The Fear of Subversion in American History,* ed. Richard O. Curry and Thomas M. Brown. New York: Holt, Rinehart, and Winston, 1972.

———. *Rebellion Against Victorianism: The Impetus for Cultural Change in 1920s America*. New York: Oxford Univ. Press, 1991.

Cohen, Naomi W. "Anti-Semitism in the Gilded Age: The Jewish View." *Jewish Social Studies* 41 (Summer 1979): 187–201.

———. *Not Free to Desist: The American Jewish Committee, 1906–1966*. Philadelphia: Jewish Publication Society of America, 1972.

Cohen, Sarah Blacher, ed. *From Hester Street to Hollywood: The Jewish-American Stage and Screen*. Bloomington: Indiana Univ. Press, 1983.

Cohn, Jan. *Creating America: George Horace Lorimer and the* Saturday Evening Post. Pittsburgh, Pa.: Univ. of Pittsburgh Press, 1989.

Cohn, Norman. *Warrant For Genocide: The Myth of the Jewish World-Conspiracy and the Protocols of the Elders of Zion*. New York: Harper and Row, 1967.

Cole, Wayne S. *America First*. Madison: Univ. of Wisconsin Press, 1953.

———. *Charles A. Lindbergh and the Battle Against American Intervention in World War II*. New York: Harcourt Brace Jovanovich, 1974.

———. *Roosevelt and the Isolationists, 1932–1945*. Lincoln: Univ. of Nebraska Press, 1983.

Commager, Henry Steele. *The American Mind*. New Haven, Conn.: Yale Univ. Press, 1950.

————, ed. *Civil Liberties Under Attack*. Philadelphia: Univ. of Pennsylvania Press, 1951.

Cooper, Vicki. "Fascist Trends Spotted in UFO Past." *UFO,* Apr. 1992.

Cooper, William. *Behold a Pale Horse*. Sedona, Ariz.: Light Technology Publishing, 1991.

Coppola, Vincent. *Dragons of God: A Journey Through Far-Right America*. Marietta, Ga.: Longstreet, 1996.

Corcoran, James. *Bitter Harvest: Gordon Kahl and the Posse Comitatus, Murder in the Heartland*. New York: Viking, 1990.

Craig, Douglas B. *Fireside Politics: Radio and Political Culture in the United States, 1920–1940*. Baltimore: Johns Hopkins Univ. Press, 2000).

Cross, Robert. *The Church and the City, 1865–1910*. Indianapolis, Ind.: Bobbs-Merrill, 1967.

Crowe, Michael J. *The Extraterrestrial Life Debate, 1750–1900: The Idea of a Plurality of Worlds from Kant to Lowell*. Cambridge: Cambridge Univ. Press, 1986.

Cumbler, John T. *Working-Class Community in Industrial America: Work, Leisure, and Struggle in Two Industrial Cities, 1880–1930*. Westport, Conn.: Greenwood Press, 1979.

Curry, Richard O., and Thomas M. Brown, eds. *Conspiracy: The Fear of Subversion in American History*. New York: Holt, Rinehart, and Winston, 1972.

Curtiss, John S. *An Appraisal of the Protocols of Zion*. New York: Columbia Univ. Press, 1942.

Dallek, Robert, *Franklin D. Roosevelt and American Foreign Policy, 1932–1945*. New York: Oxford Univ. Press, 1979.

Daniels, Roger. *Concentration Camps USA: Japanese Americans and World War II*. New York: Holt, Rinehart, and Winston, 1972.

Daniels, Ted, ed. *A Doomsday Reader: Prophets, Predictors, and Hucksters of Salvation*. New York: New York Univ. Press, 1999.

Davidann, Jon Thares. *A World of Crisis and Progress: The American YMCA in Japan, 1890–1930*. Bethlehem, Pa.: Lehigh Univ. Press, 1998.

Davidson, David. *The Great Pyramid, Its Divine Message*. Rev. 8th ed. London: Williams and Norgate, 1940.

————. *The Path to Peace in Our Time, Outlined from the Great Pyramid's Prophecy*. London: Covenant Publishing, 1942.

Davis, David Brion, ed. *The Fear of Conspiracy: Images of Un-American Subversion From the Revolution to the Present*. Ithaca, N.Y.: Cornell Univ. Press, 1971.

Dawley, Alan. *Class and Community: The Industrial Revolution in Lynn.* Cambridge, Mass.: Harvard Univ. Press, 1976.

De Bedts, Ralph E. *The New Deal's SEC: The Formative Years.* New York: Columbia Univ. Press, 1964.

de Camp, L. Sprague. *Lost Continents: The Atlantis Theme in History, Science, and Literature.* New York: Gnome Press, 1954.

De Jong, Louis. *The German Fifth Column in the Second World War.* Chicago: Univ. of Chicago Press, 1956.

Derieux, Mary. "Starting a New Era." *Psychic Research* 22 (Jan. 1928): 1–5.

Devereux, Paul, and Peter Brookesmith. *UFOs and Ufology: The First Fifty Years.* New York: Facts on File, 1997.

Diamond, Sander A. *The Nazi Movement in the United States, 1924–1941.* Ithaca, N.Y.: Cornell Univ. Press, 1974.

Dies, Martin. *The Trojan Horse in America.* New York: Dodd, Mead, 1940.

Diffendorfer, Ralph E., ed. *The World Service of the Methodist Episcopal Church.* Chicago, Ill.: Methodist Book Concern, 1923.

Diner, Steven. *A Very Different Age: Americans of the Progressive Era.* New York: Hill and Wang, 1998.

Dinnerstein, Leonard. *Antisemitism in America.* New York: Oxford Univ. Press, 1994.

District Court of the United States for the Southern District of Indiana, Indianapolis Division. *Transcript of Record, United States of America vs. William Dudley Pelley, Lawrence A. Brown, Agnes Marian Henderson, Fellowship Press, Inc.* May Term, 1942.

Dobkowski, Michael N. *The Tarnished Dream: The Basis of American Anti-Semitism.* Westport, Conn.: Greenwood Press, 1979.

Doenecke, Justus D. *In Danger Undaunted: The Anti-Interventionist Movement of 1940–1941 as Revealed in the Papers of the America First Committee.* Stanford, Calif.: Stanford Univ. Press, 1990.

———, ed. "Non-interventionism of the Left: The Keep America Out of War Congress, 1938–1941." *Journal of Contemporary History* 12 (Apr. 1977): 221–36.

———. *Not to the Swift: The Old Isolationists in the Cold War Era.* London: Associated Univ. Press, 1979.

Donner, Frank J. *The Age of Surveillance: The Aims and Methods of America's Political Intelligence System.* New York: Vintage, 1981.

———. *The Un-Americans.* New York: Ballantine, 1961.

Dudman, Richard. *Men of the Far Right.* New York: Pyramid, 1979.

Dumond, Dwight. *America in Our Time, 1896–1946*. New York: Holt, 1947.

Edgerton, James A. *The Philosophy of Jesus: The Basis of a New Philosophy*. Boston: Christopher Publishing House, 1928.

———. *Invading the Invisible*. Washington, D.C.: New Age Press, 1931.

Eller, Cynthia. *Conscientious Objectors and the Second World War: Moral and Religious Arguments in Support of Pacifism*. New York: Praeger, 1991.

Ellwood, Robert S., and Harry B. Partin. *Religious and Spiritual Groups in Modern America*. 2d ed.: Englewood Cliffs, N.J.: Prentice-Hall, 1988.

Elmhurst, Ernest F. *The World Hoax*. Asheville, N.C.: Pelley Publishers, 1938.

Ely, Richard T. *Hard Times—The Way In and the Way Out*. New York: Macmillan, 1931.

Erens, Patricia. *The Jew in American Cinema*. Bloomington: Indiana Univ. Press, 1984.

Everett, John Rutherford. *Religion in Economics: A Study of John Bates Clark, Richard T. Ely, and Simon N. Patten*. Morningside Heights, N.Y.: King's Crown Press, 1946.

Faler, Paul G. *Mechanics and Manufacturers in the Early Industrial Revolution: Lynn, Massachusetts 1780–1860*. Albany: State Univ. of New York Press, 1981.

Farago, Ladislas. *The Game of the Foxes: The Untold Story of German Espionage in the United States and Great Britain During World War II*. New York: David McKay, 1971.

Ferkiss, Victor. "Populist Influences on American Fascism." *Western Political Quarterly* 10 (Summer 1957): 350–73.

Ferguson, Charles W. *The Confusion of Tongues: A Review of Modern Isms*. Garden City, N.Y.: Doubleday, Doran, 1929.

Festinger, Leon, Henry W. Riecken, and Stanley Schachter. *When Prophecy Fails: A Social and Psychological Study of a Modern Group that Predicted the Destruction of the World*. Minneapolis: Univ. of Minnesota Press, 1956.

Finch, Philip. *God, Guts, and Guns: A Close Look at the Radical Right*. New York: Seaview, 1983.

Finlay, John L. *Social Credit: The English Origins*. Montreal: McGill-Queen's Univ. Press, 1972.

Fisch, Dov. "The Libel Trial of Robert Edward Edmondson: 1936–1938." *American Jewish History* 71 (Sept. 1981).

Fisher, Fred B. *India's Silent Revolution*. New York: Macmillan, 1919.

Flynn, John T. *As We Go Marching*. Garden City, N.Y.: Doubleday, Doran, 1944.

Forster, Arnold. *A Measure of Freedom*. Garden City, N.Y.: Doubleday, 1950.

Forster, Arnold, and Benjamin R. Epstein. *The Trouble-Makers*. Garden City, N.Y.: Doubleday, 1952.

Fosdick, Raymond B. *The Story of the Rockefeller Foundation*. New York: Harper and Brothers, 1952.

Foster, Gaines M. *Moral Reconstruction: Christian Lobbyists and the Federal Legislation of Morality, 1865–1920*. Chapel Hill: Univ. of North Carolina Press, 2002.

Fox, Stephen. *America's Invisible Gulag: A Biography of German American Internment and Exclusion in World War II*. New York: Peter Lang, 2000.

French, Philip. *The Movie Moguls: An Informal History of the Hollywood Tycoons*. Chicago: Regnery, 1971.

Friedman, Lester D. *Hollywood's Image of the Jews*. New York: Frederick Ungar, 1982.

Frisch, Michael H. *Town into City: Springfield, Massachusetts, and the Meaning of Community, 1840–1880*. Cambridge, Mass.: Harvard Univ. Press, 1972.

Frye, Alton. *Nazi Germany and the American Hemisphere, 1933–1941*. New Haven, Conn.: Yale Univ. Press, 1967.

Gabler, Neil. *An Empire of Their Own: How the Jews Invented Hollywood*. New York: Anchor, 1989.

Gardner, Martin. *Fads and Fallacies in the Name of Science*. 2d ed. New York: Dover, 1957.

Gary, Brett. *The Nervous Liberals: Propaganda Anxieties from World War I to the Cold War*. New York: Columbia Univ. Press, 1999.

Gatrell, Peter. *A Whole Empire Walking: Refugees in Russia During World War I*. Bloomington: Indiana Univ. Press, 1999.

Gaustad, Edwin S., ed. *The Rise of Adventism: Religion and Society in Mid-Nineteenth-Century America*. New York: Harper and Row, 1974.

Geduld, Harry M. *The Birth of the Talkies*. Bloomington: Indiana Univ. Press, 1975.

Gelin, James A. *Starting Over: The Formation of the Jewish Community of Springfield, Massachusetts, 1840–1905*. Lanham, Md.: Univ. Press of America, 1984.

Gellerman, William. *Martin Dies*. New York: John Day, 1944.

George, John, and Laird Wilcox. *American Extremists: Militias, Supremacists, Klansmen, Communists, and Others*. Amherst, N.Y.: Prometheus, 1996.

Gerber, David A., ed. *Anti-Semitism in American History*. Urbana: Univ. of Illinois Press, 1986.

Gertz, Elmer. *Odyssey of a Barbarian: The Biography of George Sylvester Viereck*. Buffalo: Prometheus, 1978.

Gilman, Richard. *Behind World Revolution: The Strange Career of Nesta H. Webster.* Ann Arbor, Mich.: Insights, 1982.

Gleason, George. *What Shall I Think of Japan?* New York: Macmillan, 1921.

Goda, Norman J. W. *Tomorrow the World: Hitler, Northwest Africa, and the Path Toward America.* College Station: Texas A&M Univ. Press, 1998.

Godwin, John. *Occult America.* Garden City, N.Y.: Doubleday, 1972.

Godwin, Joscelyn. *Arktos: The Polar Myth in Science, Symbolism, and Nazi Survival.* Kempton, Ill.: Adventures Press, 1996.

Goldberg, David J. *Discontented America: The United States in the 1920s.* Baltimore: Johns Hopkins Univ. Press, 1999.

Goldstein, Robert Justin. *Political Repression in Modern America: From 1870 to the Present.* Cambridge, Mass.: Schenkman, 1978.

Goodman, David G., and Masanori Miyazawa. *Jews in the Japanese Mind: The History and Uses of a Cultural Stereotype.* New York: Free Press, 1995.

Goodman, Walter. *The Committee: The Extraordinary Career of the House Committee on Un-American Activities.* New York: Farrar, Straus, and Giroux, 1968.

Goodrick-Clarke, Nicholas. *Black Sun: Aryan Cults, Esoteric Nazism and the Politics of Identity.* New York: New York Univ. Press, 2002.

———. *The Occult Roots of Nazism: The Ariosophists of Austria and Germany, 1890–1935.* Wellingsborough, U.K.: Aquarian, 1985.

Gorrell, Donald. *The Age of Social Responsibility: The Social Gospel in the Progressive Era, 1900–1920.* Macon, Ga.: Mercer Univ. Press, 1988.

Grace, Richard V. *I Am Still Alive.* New York: Rand McNally, 1931.

———. *Squadron of Death: The True Adventures of a Movie Planecrasher.* Garden City, N.Y.: Doubleday, Doran, 1929.

Graham, Arthur. "Crazy Like a Fox: Pelley of the Silver Shirts." *New Republic,* Apr. 18, 1934, 264–66.

Grant, Madison. *The Passing of the Great Race.* New York: C. Scribner's Sons.

Graves, William S. *America's Siberian Adventure, 1918–1920.* New York: Jonathan Cape and Harrison Smith, 1931.

Greenwalt, Emmett A. *The Point Loma Community in California, 1897–1942: A Theosophical Experiment.* Berkeley: Univ. of California Press, 1955.

Griffith, Sally Foreman. *Home Town News: William Allen White and the Emporia Gazette.* New York: Oxford Univ. Press, 1989.

Grill, Johnpeter Horst, and Robert L. Jenkins. "The Nazis and the American South in the 1930s: A Mirror Image?" *Journal of Southern History* 58 (Nov. 1992): 667–94.

Grzesinski, Albert. "Hitler's Branch Offices, U.S.A." *Current History and Forum,* Nov. 26, 1940, 11–13.

Guller, Curtis G., ed. *Proceedings of the First International UFO Congress*. New York: Warner Books, 1980.

Gwaltney, John Langston. *The Dissenters: Voices from Contemporary America*. New York: Random House, 1986.

Haddaford, Ivan. *Race: The History of an Idea in the West*. Washington, D.C.: Woodrow Wilson Center Press, 1996.

Haller, Mark H. *Eugenics: Hereditarian Attitudes in American Thought*. New Bunswick, N.J.: Rutgers Univ. Press, 1963.

Hampton, Benjamin. *A History of the Movies*. New York: Covici, Friede, 1931.

Handlin, Oscar. *The American People in the Twentieth Century*. Cambridge, Mass.: Harvard Univ. Press, 1954.

Hanson, Patricia King, ed. *The American Film Institute Catalog of Motion Pictures Produced in the United States: Feature Films, 1911–1920*. Berkeley: Univ. of California Press, 1988.

Hapgood, Norman, ed. *Professional Patriots*. New York: A. C. Boni, 1927.

Helmreich, Ernst Christian. *The German Churches under Hitler*. Detroit: Wayne State Univ. Press, 1979.

Herron, Ima Honaker. *The Small Town in American Literature*. 1939. Reprint, New York: Pageant Books, 1959.

Hewitt, Andrew. *Fascist Modernism*. Stanford, Calif.: Stanford Univ. Press, 1993.

High, Stanley. "Star-Spangled Fascists." *Saturday Evening Post,* May 27, 1939, 5–7, 70–73.

Higham, Charles. *American Swastika*. Garden City, N.Y.: Doubleday, 1985.

Higham, John. *Send These to Me: Jews and Other Immigrants in Urban America*. Rev. ed. Baltimore: Johns Hopkins, 1984.

———. *Strangers in the Land: Patterns of American Nativism, 1860–1925*. 1955. Reprint, New York: Atheneum, 1963.

Hilfer, Anthony Channell. *The Revolt from the Village, 1915–1930*. Chapel Hill: Univ. of North Carolina Press, 1969.

Hofstadter, Richard. *The Paranoid Style in American Politics*. New York: Vintage Books, 1967.

Hoke, Henry. *Black Mail*. New York: Reader's Book Service, 1944.

———. *It's a Secret*. New York: Reynal and Hitchcock, 1946.

Hoke, Travis. *Shirts*. New York: American Civil Liberties Union, 1934.

Hooper, Paul, ed. *Rediscovering the IPR: Proceedings of the First International Research Conference on the Institute of Pacific Relations*. Manoa, Hawaii: Center for Arts and Humanities, 1993.

Hopkins, Charles H. *The Rise of the Social Gospel in American Protestantism, 1865–1915*. New Haven, Conn.: Yale Univ. Press, 1940.

Hoppes, Karen E. "William Dudley Pelley and the Silvershirt Legion: A Case Study of the Legion in Washington State, 1933–1942." Ph.D. diss., City Univ. of New York, 1992.

Horowitz, David A. *Beyond Left and Right: Insurgency and the Establishment.* Urbana: Univ. of Illinois Press, 1997.

Howe, Edgar W. *The Story of a Country Town.* Atchison, Kans.: Howe, 1983.

Hull, David Stewart. *Film in the Third Reich: A Study of the German Cinema, 1933–1945.* Berkeley: Univ. of California Press, 1969.

Hutchisson, James M., ed. *Sinclair Lewis: New Essays in Criticism.* Troy, N.Y.: Whitston, 1997.

Hyman, Harold. *To Try Men's Souls: Loyalty Tests in American History.* Berkeley: Univ. of California Press, 1960.

Hynd, Alan. *Passport to Treason: The Inside Story of Spies in America.* New York: R. M. McBride, 1943.

Ickes, Harold L. *The Secret Diary of Harold L. Ickes.* 3 vols. New York: Simon and Schuster, 1954.

Isserman, Maurice. *Which Side Were You On?: The American Communist Party During the Second World War.* Middletown, Conn.: Wesleyan Univ. Press, 1982.

Jacobs, Arthur D., ed. *German-Americans in the World Wars.* 4 vols. Munich: K. G. Saur, 1995.

James, William. *Varieties of Religious Experience.* 1902. Reprint, New York: Random House, 1929.

Janowitz, Morris. "Black Legions on the March." In *America in Crisis: Fourteen Crucial Episodes in American History,* edited by Daniel Aaron. New York: Knopf, 1952.

———. *Political Conflict: Essays in Political Sociology.* Chicago: Quadrangle, 1970.

Janson, Donald, and Bernard Eismann. *The Far Right.* New York: McGraw-Hill, 1963.

Jeansonne, Glen. "Combating Anti-Semitism: The Case of Gerald L. K. Smith." In *Anti-Semitism in American History,* ed. David A. Gerber, 152–67. Urbana: Univ. of Illinois Press, 1986.

———. *Gerald L. K. Smith: Minister of Hate.* New Haven, Conn.: Yale Univ. Press, 1988.

———. *Women of the Far Right: The Mothers' Movement and World War II.* Chicago: Univ. of Chicago Press, 1996.

Jenkins, Philip. *Hoods and Shirts: The Extreme Right in Pennsylvania, 1925–1950.* Chapel Hill: Univ. of North Carolina Press, 1997.

Jernigan, E. Jay. *William Allen White.* Boston: Twayne Publishers, 1983.

Johnson, Alvin. "The Rising Tide of Anti-Semitism." *Survey Graphic,* Feb. 1939, 113–16.

Johnson, George. *Architects of Fear: Conspiracy Theories and Paranoia in American Politics.* Los Angeles: Jeremy P. Tarcher, 1983.

Johnson, Neil. *George Sylvester Viereck: German-American Propagandist.* Urbana: Univ. of Illinois Press, 1972.

Johnson, Walter. *The Battle Against Isolation.* Chicago: Univ. of Chicago Press, 1944.

Jolly, W. P. *Sir Oliver Lodge.* London: Constable, 1974.

Jonas, Harold. *Anti-Semitica Americana.* New York: American Jewish Committee, 1941.

Jonas, Manfred. *Isolationism in America, 1935–1941.* Ithaca, N.Y.: Cornell Univ. Press, 1966.

Joyce, Julian. "Cosmic Thoughts." *Star Beacon,* Mar. 1997.

Judah, J. Stillson. *The History and Philosophy of the Metaphysical Movements in America.* Philadelphia: Westminster Press, 1967.

Kafton-Minkel, Walter. *Subterranean Worlds: 100,000 Years of Dragons, Dwarfs, the Dead, Lost Races, and UFOs from Inside the Earth.* Port Townsend, Wash.: Loompanics Unlimited, 1989.

Kahn, Albert. *High Treason.* New York: Hour, 1950.

Kamp, Joseph. *The Fifth Column in the South.* New Haven, Conn.: Constitutional Education League, 1940.

Kaplan, Jeffrey, ed. *The Encyclopedia of White Power: A Sourcebook on the Radical Racist Right.* Walnut Creek, Calif.: Altamira Press, 2000.

Kaplan, Wendy. *"The Art That Is Life:" The Arts and Crafts Movement in America, 1875–1920.* Boston: Little, Brown, 1987.

Katz, Ephraim. *The Film Encyclopedia.* New York: Perigree Books, 1979.

Keel, John A. *The Flying Saucer Subculture.* New York: New York Fortean Society, 1994.

———. "The Flying Saucer Subculture." *Journal of Popular Culture* 8 (Spring 1975): 871–96.

Kennedy, David M. *Freedom from Fear: The American People in Depression and War, 1929–1945.* New York: Oxford Univ. Press, 1999.

King, Dennis. *Lyndon LaRouche and the New American Fascism.* New York: Doubleday, 1989.

King, Godfre Ray [Guy Ballard]. *The Magic Presence.* Chicago: St. Germain Press, 1935.

Kirschner, Don. *City and Country: Rural Responses to Urbanization in the 1920s.* Westport, Conn.: Greenwood Press, 1970.

Kittrie, Nicholas N., and Eldon D. Wedlock, Jr., eds. *The Tree of Liberty: A Documentary History of Rebellion and Political Crime in America.* Rev. ed. Baltimore: Johns Hopkins Univ. Press, 1998.

Kloppenberg, James T. *Uncertain Victory: Social Democracy and Progressivism in European and American Thought, 1870–1920.* New York: Oxford Univ. Press, 1986.

Koppes, Clayton, and Gregory D. Black. *Hollywood Goes to War: How Politics, Profits, and Propaganda Shaped World War II Movies.* Berkeley: Univ. of California Press, 1990.

Kossy, Donna. *Strange Creations: Aberrant Ideas of Human Origins from Ancient Astronauts to Aquatic Apes.* Los Angeles: Feral House, 2001.

Kramer, Dale. "The American Fascists." *Harper's,* Sept. 1940, 380–93.

Kris, Ernst. "German Propaganda Instructions of 1933." *Social Research* 9 (Feb. 1942): 46–81.

Kuhn, Annette. *Cinema, Censorship, and Sexuality, 1909–1925.* New York: Routledge, 1988.

Kutler, Stanley, I. *The American Inquisition: Justice and Injustice in the Cold War.* New York: Hill and Wang, 1982.

Kutulas, Judy. *The Long War: The Intellectual People's Front and Anti-Stalinism, 1930–1940.* Durham, N.C.: Duke Univ. Press, 1995.

Lahue, Kalton. *Winners of the West: The Sagebrush Heroes of the Silent Screen.* New York: A. S. Barnes, 1970.

Lamont, Corliss. *Freedom Is as Freedom Does: Civil Liberties Today.* New York: Horizon Press, 1956.

Lamy, Philip. *Millennium Rage: Survivalists, White Supremacists, and the Doomsday Prophecy.* New York: Plenum Press, 1996.

Langman, Larry. *A Guide to Silent Westerns.* Westport, Conn.: Greenwood Press, 1992.

Larsen, Caroline D. *My Travels in the Spirit World.* Rutland, Vt.: Tuttle Company, 1927.

Lasswell, Harold D., ed. *Language of Politics: Studies in Quantitative Semantics.* New York: Stewart, 1949.

Lauwers-Rech, Magda. *Nazi Germany and the American Germanists: A Study of Periodicals, 1930–1946.* New York: Peter Lang, 1995.

Lavine, Harold. *Fifth Column in America.* New York: Doubleday, 1940.

———. "Fifth Column Literature." *Saturday Review of Literature,* Sept. 14, 1940.

———. *War Propaganda and the United States.* New York: Doubleday, 1940.

Lawton, George. *The Drama of Life After Death: A Study of the Spiritualist Religion.* New York: Henry Holt, 1932.

Ledeboer, Suzanne. "The Man Who Would Be Hitler: William Dudley Pelley and the Silver Legion." *California History* 65 (Summer 1986): 126–36.

Lee, Alfred McClung, and Elizabeth Briant Lee, eds. *The Fine Art of Propaganda.* New York: Institute for Propaganda Analysis, 1939.

Lee, Martin A. *The Beast Reawakens.* Boston: Little, Brown, 1996.

Lee, R. Alton. *The Bizarre Careers of John R. Brinkley.* Lexington: Univ. Press of Kentucky, 2002.

Leiser, Erwin. *Nazi Cinema.* Translated by Gertrud Mander and David Wilson. New York: Macmillan, 1974.

Levenson, Samuel. "Pelley's Kampf." *Christian Century,* Apr. 10, 1940, 477–78.

Lewis, Benn E. *I, John: The Reincarnated Apostle.* New York: Exposition Press, 1970.

Lewis, H. Spencer. *Rosicrucian Questions and Answers.* San Jose, Calif.: AMORC, 1929.

Lewis, James R., ed. *The Gods Have Landed: New Religions from Other Worlds.* Albany: State Univ. of New York Press, 1995.

Libstadt, Deborah E. *Beyond Belief: The American Press and the Coming of the Holocaust, 1933–1945.* New York: Free Press, 1986.

Light, Martin. "The Quixotic Motifs of *Main Street.*" In *Critical Essays on Sinclair Lewis,* edited by Martin Bucco, 174–75. Boston: G. K. Hall, 1986.

Lindbergh, Charles. *The Wartime Journals of Charles A. Lindbergh.* New York: Harcourt Brace, 1970.

Linfield, Michael. *Freedom under Fire: U.S. Civil Liberties in Times of War.* Boston, Mass.: South End Press, 1990.

Lipset, Seymour M. *Political Man: The Social Basis of Politics.* Garden City, N.Y.: Doubleday, 1963.

Lodge, Oliver. "Design and Purpose in the Universe." In *The Great Design: Order and Intelligence in Nature,* edited by Frances Mason, 225–33. New York: Macmillan, 1936.

———. *Raymond, or Life and Death.* London: Methuen, 1916.

Loeb, Harold, and Selden Rodman. "American Fascism in Embryo." *New Republic,* Dec. 27, 1933, 185–87.

Lopez, Claude-Anne. "Prophet and Loss." *New Republic,* Jan. 27, 1997, 28–31.

Lore, Ludwig. "Nazi Politics in America." *Nation,* Nov. 29, 1934, 3–6, 26–31.

Lowenthal, Leo, and Norbert Guterman. *Prophets of Deceit: A Study of the Techniques of the American Agitator.* New York: Harper and Brothers, 1949.

Ludvig, Coy. *The Arts & Crafts Movement in New York State, 1890s–1920s.* Hamilton, N.Y.: Gallery Association of New York State, 1983.

Lutholtz, M. William. *Grand Dragon: D.C. Stephenson and the Ku Klux Klan in Indiana.* West Lafayette, Ind.: Purdue Univ. Press, 1991.

MacDonnell, Francis. *Insidious Foes: The Axis Fifth Column and the American Home Front.* New York: Oxford Univ. Press, 1995.

Magil, A. B., and Henry Stevens. *The Peril of Fascism: The Crisis of American Democracy.* New York: International Publishers, 1938.

Maguire, Daniel. *The New Subversives: Anti-Americanism of the Religious Right.* New York: Continuum, 1982.

Marks, Kathy. *Faces of Right Wing Extremism.* Boston: Branden, 1996.

Marquis, Albert N., ed. *Who's Who in America, 1930–1931.* New York: A. N. Marquis, 1932.

Martin, George W. *Madam Secretary: Frances Perkins.* Boston: Houghton Mifflin, 1976.

Martin, Jay. *Harvests of Change: American Literature, 1865–1914.* Englewood Cliffs, N.J.: Prentice-Hall, 1967.

Mason, Frances, ed. *The Great Design: Order and Intelligence in Nature.* New York: Macmillan, 1936.

Matheson, Peter, ed. *The Third Reich and the Churches.* Grand Rapids, Mich.: Eerdmans, 1981.

Mathews, J. B. "Must America Go Fascist?" *Harper's,* June 1934, 8.

Mathis, Andrew E. *The King Arthur Myth in Modern American Literature.* Jefferson, N.C.: McFarland, 2002.

Mauskopf, Seymour H., and Michael R. McVaugh. *The Elusive Science: Origins of Experimental Psychical Research.* Baltimore: Johns Hopkins Univ. Press, 1980.

May, Lary. *Screening Out the Past: The Birth of Mass Culture and the Motion Picture Industry.* New York: Oxford Univ. Press, 1980.

McCormick, Cyrus. *The Century of the Reaper: An Account of Cyrus Hall McCormick.* Boston: Houghton Mifflin, 1931.

McCoy, Samuel D. "Hitlerism Invades America." *Today,* Apr. 7, 1934.

McFadden, Louis T. *Collective Speeches of Congressman Louis T. McFadden.* Hawthorne, Calif.: Omni, 1970.

McKale, Donald M. *The Swastika Outside Germany.* Kent, Ohio: Kent State Univ. Press, 1977.

McLoughlin, William G. *Revivals, Awakenings, and Reform: An Essay on Religious and Social Change in America.* Chicago: Univ. of Chicago Press, 1978.

McMillen, Neil. "Pro-Nazi Sentiment in the United States: March 1933–March 1934." *Southern Quarterly* 2 (June 1963): 48–70.

McWilliams, Carey. *A Mask for Privilege: Anti-Semitism in America.* Boston: Little, Brown, 1948.

———. *Witch Hunt: The Revival of Heresy.* Boston: Little, Brown, 1950.

Melton, J. Gordon. *Biographical Dictionary of American Cult and Sect Leaders.* New York: Garland, 1986.

———. "The Contactees: A Survey." In *The Gods Have Landed: New Religions from Other Worlds,* edited by James R. Lewis, 1–15. Albany: State Univ. of New York Press, 1995.

———. "The Church Universal and Triumphant: Its Heritage and Thought-world." In *Church Universal and Triumphant in Scholarly Perspective,* edited by James R. Lewis and J. Gordon Melton, 1–20. Stanford, Calif.: Center for Academic Publications, 1994.

Michell, John. *Eccentric Lives and Peculiar Notions.* Secaucus, N.J.: Citadel Press, 1984.

Miller, Frank. *Censored Hollywood: Sex, Sin, and Violence on Screen.* Atlanta: Turner Publishing, 1994.

Mintz, Frank. *The Liberty Lobby and the American Right: Race, Conspiracy, and Culture.* Westport, Conn.: Greenwood Press, 1985.

Mintzer, George, and Newman Levy. *The International Anti-Semitic Conspiracy.* New York: American Jewish Committee, 1946.

Mitchie, Allan A., and Frank Ryhlick. *Dixie Demagogues.* New York: Vanguard Press, 1939.

Moore, Leonard J. *Citizen Klansmen: The Ku Klux Klan in Indiana, 1921–1928.* Chapel Hill: Univ. of North Carolina Press, 1991.

Moore, Robert Laurence. *In Search of White Crows: Spiritualism, Parapsychology, and American Culture.* New York: Oxford Univ. Press, 1977.

———. "Spiritualism." In *The Rise of Adventism: Religion and Society in Mid-Nineteenth-Century America,* edited by Edwin S. Gaustad, 79–104. New York: Harper and Row, 1974.

Moser, John E. *Twisting the Lion's Tail: American Anglophobia Between the World Wars.* New York: New York Univ. Press, 1999.

Mosley, Leonard. *Lindbergh: A Biography.* Garden City, N.Y.: Doubleday, 1976.

Mote, Carl. *The New Deal Goose Step.* New York: Ryerson, 1939.

Munden, Kenneth, ed. *The American Film Institute Catalog of Motion Pictures Produced in the United States: Feature Films, 1921–1930.* New York: R. R. Bowker, 1971.

Muller, Dorothea. "The Social Philosophy of Josiah Strong: Social Christianity and American Progressivism." *Church History* 28 (Oct. 1959): 183–201.

Murray, Robert K. *Red Scare: A Study in National Hysteria, 1919–1920.* Minneapolis: Univ. of Minnesota Press, 1955.

Myers, Gustavus. *History of Bigotry in the United States.* New York: Random House, 1943.

Neiwert, David A. *In God's Country: The Patriot Movement and the Pacific Northwest.* Pullman: Washington State Univ. Press, 1999.

Ogden, August R. *The Dies Committee: A Study of the Special House Committee for the Investigation of Un-American Activities, 1938–1943.* Washington, D.C.: Catholic Univ. Press, 1943.

———. *The Dies Committee: A Study of the Special House Committee for the Investigation of Un-American Activities, 1938–1944.* Westport, Conn.: Greenwood Press, 1984.

Olcott, Henry Steel. *Old Diary Leaves: The True Story of the Theosophical Movement.* New York: G. P. Putnam's Sons, 1895.

Olden, Rudolf. *Hitler, the Pawn.* New York: Covici, Friede, 1936.

O'Neill, John J. "Did Edison on His Deathbed Behold the Next World?" *New Liberation Weekly,* Nov. 21, 1931, 208–9.

O'Reilly, Kenneth. *Hoover and the Un-Americans: The FBI, HUAC, and the Red Menace.* Philadelphia, Pa.: Temple Univ. Press, 1983.

Owen, G. Vale. *The Life Beyond the Veil.* 4 vols. London: Hutchinson, 1924.

Ozment, Steven E. *Mysticism and Dissent: Religious Ideology and Social Protest in the Sixteenth Century.* New Haven: Yale Univ. Press, 1973.

Paolini, Kenneth, and Talita Paolini. *400 Years of Imaginary Friends: A Journey into the World of Adepts, Masters, Ascended Masters, and Their Messengers.* Livingston: Mont.: Paolini International, 2000.

Patai, Daphne, ed. *Looking Backward, 1988–1888: Essays on Edward Bellamy.* Amherst: Univ. of Massachusetts Press, 1988.

Pearson, Melford. *A Blueprint for Survival: Peace and Economic Justice Await the Adoption of a National Cooperative Commonwealth.* Victoria, B.C.: Trafford and Aquila, 2002.

———. *Challenge to Crisis.* Noblesville, Ind.: Aquila Press, 1969.

———. *Life Imprisonment for Exposing Communists.* Noblesville, Ind.: Fellowship Press, 1947.

———. *The Price of Truth.* Noblesville, Ind.: Aquila, 1947.

———. *There Is a Way to Peace and Social Justice.* Noblesville, Ind.: Aquila Press, 1995.

Peebles, Curtis. *Watch the Skies: A Chronicle of the UFO Myth.* Washington: Smithsonian Institution Press, 1994.

Pelley, William Dudley. *Adam Awakes: Design for Romance.* 1941. Reprint, Noblesville, Ind.: Soulcraft Chapels, 1953.

———. *After Dictators, What?* Asheville, N.C.: Pelley Publishers, n.d.

———. *Applying Horse-Sense to the Federal Mess.* Asheville, N.C.: Pelley Publishers, n.d.

———. *As Thou Lovest: The Biography of a Benefaction.* Noblesville, Ind.: Soulcraft Chapels, 1955.

———. *Behold Life: Design for Liberation.* Asheville, N.C.: Pelley Publishers, 1937.

———. *The Blue Lamp.* New York: Fiction League, 1931.]

———. *The Councils of Safety.* Asheville, N.C.: n.p., 1936.

———. *Cripple's Money: Who Gets the Proceeds of the Presidential Birthday Balls?* Asheville, N.C.: n.p., n.d. [1939].

———. *Did David Really Slay Goliath?* Asheville, N.C.: Fellowship Foundation, n.d. [1935].

———. *Did the Sun Stand Still for Joshua?* Asheville, N.C.: Fellowship Foundation, n.d. [1935].

———. *The Door to Revelation.* Asheville, N.C.: Pelley Publishers, 1939.

———. *Drag.* Boston: Little, Brown, 1925.

———. *Dupes of Judah: A Challenge to the American Legion.* Asheville, N.C.: n.p., n.d.

———. *Earth Comes: Design for Materialization.* Asheville, N.C.: Pelley Publishers, 1939.

———. *Entrance in Rear.* New York: Cameo Picture Stories, 1923.

———. *The Fog.* Boston: Little, Brown, 1922.

———. *Forty-Five Questions Most Frequently Asked About the Jews and the Answers.* Asheville, N.C.: Pelley Publishers, 1939.

———. *Golden Rubbish.* New York: G. P. Putnam's Sons, 1929.

———. *The Golden Scripts.* Noblesville, Ind.: Soulcraft Chapels, 1951.

———. *The Greater Glory.* Boston: Little, Brown, 1919.

———. *Have I Been Foolish?* Asheville, N.C.: n.p., n.d. [1935].

———. *The Hidden Empire.* Asheville, N.C.: Pelley Publishers, n.d.

———. *How Divine Thought Shapes Events.* Asheville, N.C.: Pelley Publishers, n.d. [1933].

———. *Indians Aren't Red: The Inside Story of the Administration's Attempt to Make Communists of the North Carolina Cherokee.* Asheville, N.C.: Pelley Publishers, n.d. [1940].

———. *The Key To Crisis* Asheville, N.C.: Pelley Publishers, 1939.

———. *Know Your Karma: Design for Destiny.* Noblesville, Ind.: Soulcraft Chapels, 1954.

———. *Mother's Madness.* New York: Cameo Picture Stories, 1923.

———. *Nations-in-Law: An Unconventional Analysis of Civics.* 2 vols. Asheville, N.C.: Pelley Publishers, 1938.

———. *New Dealers in Office.* Indianapolis: n.p., n.d.

———. *New Quatrains of the Modern Michel Nostradamus.* Noblesville, Ind.: Soulcraft Fellowship, 1956.

———. *No More Hunger: The Compact Plan of the Christian Commonwealth.* 2d ed. Asheville, N.C.: Pelley Publishers, 1935.

———. *One Million Silver Shirts By 1939.* Asheville, N.C.: Pelley Publishers, 1938.

———. *Our Secret Political Police.* Asheville, N.C.: Pelley Publishers, n.d.

———. *The Pillar of Cloud.* Asheville, N.C.: Christian Party Press, 1935.

———. *Road into Sunrise: A Narrative of the Eternal Verities.* Noblesville, Ind.: Soulcraft Press, 1950.

———. *Seven Minutes in Eternity: With the Aftermath.* New York: n.p., n.d. [1933].

———. *Silver Shirts: A Personal Explanation.* Asheville, N.C.: n.p., n.d.

———. *Something Better: How to Bring in the Christian Commonwealth.* Noblesville, Ind.: Soulcraft Chapels, 1952.

———. *The Soulcraft Elucidata.* Noblesville, Ind.: Soulcraft Chapels, 1952.

———. *Soulcraft Scripts.* 12 vols. Noblesville, Ind.: Soulcraft Chapels, 1952–54.

———. *Soul Eternal.* Noblesville, Ind.: Soulcraft Chapels, 1955.

———. *Stairs to Greatness.* Noblesville, Ind.: Soulcraft Fellowship, 1956.

———. *Star Guests: Design for Mortality.* Noblesville, Ind.: Fellowship Press, 1950.

———. *They Make Up Your Mind.* Indianapolis: Fellowship Press, n.d.

. *Thinking Alive: Design for Creation.* Noblesville, Ind.: Soulcraft Fellowship, 1938.

———. *Thrown Away.* New York: Cameo Picture Stories, 1923.

———. *We Offer You the Scourge of Cords* Asheville, N.C.: n.p, n.d. [1933].

———. *What Is a Jew-Baiter?* Asheville, N.C.: n.p., n.d.

———. *What You Should Know about the Pelley Publications.* Asheville, N.C.: Pelley Publishers, n.d.

———. *Why I Believe the Dead Are Alive.* Indianapolis: Fellowship Press, 1942.

———. *Why the Holy Spirit Displays as Life.* Asheville, N.C.: Pelley Publishers, n.d. [1933].

———. *Your Sacred Rights.* Indianapolis: Fellowship Press, n.d.

Perea, Juan, ed. *Immigrants Out!: The New Nativism and the Anti-Immigrant Impulse in the United States.* New York: New York Univ. Press, 1997.

Perret, Geoffrey. *Days of Sadness, Years of Triumph: The American People, 1939–1945.* New York: Coward, McCann and Geoghegan, 1973.

Pevsner, Nikolaus. *Pioneers of Modern Design: From William Morris to Walter Gropius.* New York: Metropolitan Museum of Art, 1949.

Phelps, George S. "Japan." In *The Red Triangle in the Changing Nations,* edited by Robert Wilder. New York: Association Press, 1918.

Phillips, Paul. *A Kingdom on Earth: Anglo-American Social Christianity.* University Park: Pennsylvania State Univ. Press, 1996.

Picknett, Lynne. *The Mammoth Book of UFOs.* New York: Carroll and Graf, 2001.

Piller, E. A. *Time Bomb.* New York: Arco, 1945.

Pipes, Richard. *The Russian Revolution.* New York: Vintage Books, 1990.

Pistorious, Philippus Villiers. *Plotinus and Neoplatonism: An Introductory Study.* London: Bowes and Bowes, 1952.

Platt, Anthony. *The Child Savers: The Invention of Delinquency.* Chicago: Univ. of Chicago Press, 1977.

Polenberg, Richard. *War and Society: The United States, 1941–1945.* Philadelphia: Lippincott, 1972.

Porter, David L. *The Seventy-Sixth Congress and World War II, 1939–1940.* Columbia: Univ. of Missouri Press, 1979.

Portzline, Donnell. "William Dudley Pelley and the Silver Shirt Legion of America." Ph.D. diss., Ball State Univ., 1965.

Pound, Ezra, and Robert C. Summerville, "Ezra Pound, Silvershirt," *New Masses,* Mar. 17, 1936, 15–16.

Preston, Jr., William. *Aliens and Dissenters: Federal Suppression of Radicals, 1903–1933.* Urbana: Univ. of Illinois Press, 1994.

———. "The 1940s: The Way We Really Were," *Civil Liberties Review* 2 (Winter 1975): 9–10.

Probert, Mark. *The Magic Bag.* 2 vols. San Diego: Borderlands Sciences Research Associates, 1950.

Quinley, Harold E., and Charles Gloat. *Anti-Semitism in America.* New York: Free Press, 1979.

Radosh, Ronald. *Prophets on the Right: Profiles of Conservative Critics of American Globalism.* New York: Simon and Schuster, 1975.

Randi, James. *The Mask of Nostradamus.* New York: Charles Scribner's Sons, 1990.

Rao, K. Ramakhrishna, ed. *J. B. Rhine: On the Frontiers of Science.* Jefferson, N.C.: McFarland, 1982.

Rauschenbusch, Walter. *Christianity and the Social Crisis.* New York: Macmillan, 1907.

Reagan, Patrick D. *Designing a New America: The Origins of New Deal Planning, 1890–1943*. Amherst: Univ. of Massachusetts Press, 1999.

Remak, Joachim. "Friends of the New Germany: The Bund and German American Relations." *Journal of Modern History* 29 (Mar. 1957): 38–41.

Rhine, J. B. *Extra-Sensory Perception*. Boston: Boston Society for Psychic Research, 1934.

———. "Why National Defense Overlooks Parapsychology." *Journal of Parapsychology* 21 (Dec. 1957): 245–57.

Ribuffo, Leo. "Henry Ford and *The International Jew.*" *American Jewish History* 69 (June 1980): 437–77.

———. *The Old Christian Right: The Protestant Far Right from the Great Depression to the Cold War*. Philadelphia: Temple Univ. Press, 1983.

———. *Right Center Left: Essays in American History*. New Brunswick, N.J.: Rutgers Univ. Press, 1992.

———. "*United States v. McWilliams*: The Roosevelt Administration and the Far Right." In *American Political Trials*, rev. ed., edited by Michael R. Belknap, 180–86. Westport, Conn.: Praeger, 1994.

———. "Why Is There So Much Conservatism in the United States and Why Do So Few Historians Know Anything about It?" *American Historical Review* 99 (Apr. 1994): 438–39.

Riess, Curt. *Total Espionage*. New York: G. P. Putnam's Sons, 1941.

Robbins, Olive. *How to Demonstrate Prosperity*. New York: Galahad Press, 1930.

Robinson, David. *Hollywood in the Twenties*. New York: A. S. Barnes, 1968.

Robinson, Frank B. *The Strange Autobiography of Frank B. Robinson*. Moscow, Idaho: Psychiana, 1941.

Rockefeller Foundation Annual Report, 1917. New York: Rockefeller Foundation, 1918.

Rogge, O. John. *The Official German Report: Nazi Penetration, 1924–1942: Pan-Arabism, 1939-Today*. New York: Thomas Yoseloff, 1961.

Rogin, Michael. *Black Face, White Noise: Jewish Immigrants in the Hollywood Melting Pot*. Berkeley: Univ. of California Press, 1996.

Rollins, Richard. *I Find Treason: The Story of an American Anti-Nazi Agent*. New York: William Morrow, 1941.

Rothschild, Richard. *Are American Jews Falling into the Nazi Trap?* New York: American Jewish Committee, 1940.

Roy, Ralph Lord. *Apostles of Discord: A Study of Organized Bigotry and Disruption on the Fringes of Protestantism*. Boston: Beacon Press, 1953.

Sargent, Lyman Tower, ed. *Extremism in America: A Reader.* New York: New York Univ. Press, 1995.

Sayers, Michael, and Albert E. Kahn. *Sabotage! The Secret War Against America.* New York: Harper and Brothers, 1942.

Schaefer, Eric. *Bold! Daring! Shocking! True!: A History of Exploitation Films, 1919–1959.* Durham, N.C.: Duke Univ. Press, 1999.

Schatz, Thomas. *The Genius of the System: Hollywood Filmmaking in the Studio Era.* New York: Pantheon, 1988.

Schlesinger, Arthur M., Jr. *The Age of Roosevelt: The Coming of the New Deal.* Boston: Houghton Mifflin, 1960.

Schmaltz, William H. *Hate: George Lincoln Rockwell and the American Nazi Party.* Washington: Brassey's, 1999.

Scholnick, Myron. *The New Deal and Anti-Semitism in America.* New York: Garland, 1990.

Schonbach, Morris. *Native American Fascism During the 1930s and 1940s: A Study of Its Roots, Its Growth, and Its Decline.* New York: Garland, 1985.

Schorer, Mark, ed. *Sinclair Lewis: A Collection of Critical Essays.* Englewood Cliffs, N.J.: Prentice-Hall, 1962.

Schultz, Bud, and Ruth Schultz. *It Did Happen Here: Recollections of Political Repression in America.* Berkeley: Univ. of California Press, 1989.

Schuman, Frederick L. "The Nazi International." *New Republic,* July 8, 1936.

Schwartz, Henry. "The Silver Shirts: Anti-Semitism in San Diego." *Western States Jewish History* 25 (Spring 1992): 52–60.

Seldes, George. *Facts and Fascism.* New York: New Union Press, 1943.

Seligman, Joel. *The Transformation of Wall Street: A History of the Securities Exchange Commission and Modern Corporate Finance.* Boston: Northeastern Univ. Press, 1995.

Selzer, Michael, ed. *Kike!: A Documentary History of Anti-Semitism in America.* New York: World Publishing, 1972.

Seymour, Cheri. *Committee of the States: Inside the Radical Right.* Mariposa, Calif.: Camden Place, 1991.

Shay, Felix. *Elbert Hubbard of East Aurora.* New York: William Wise, 1926.

Sherwin, Mark. *The Extremists.* New York: St. Martin's Press, 1963.

Shindler, Colin. *Hollywood Goes to War.* London: Routledge and Keegan Paul, 1978.

———. *Hollywood in Crisis: Cinema and American Society, 1929–1939.* London: Routledge, 1996.

Short, K. R. M. "The White Cliffs of Dover: Promoting the Anglo-American

Alliance in World War II." *Historical Journal of Film, Radio, and Television* 2 (Mar. 1982): 3–25.

Short, William H. *A Generation of Motion Pictures: A Review of Social Values in Recreational Films.* New York: National Committee for Study of Social Values in Motion Pictures, 1928.

Sibley, Mulford. *Conscientious Objectors in Prison, 1940–1945.* Philadelphia: Pacifist Research Bureau, 1945.

Singerman, Robert. "The American Career of the *Protocols of the Elders of Zion.*" *Journal of American History* 71 (Sept. 1981): 48–78.

———. "The Jew as Racial Alien: The Genetic Component of American Anti-Semitism." In *Immigrants Out!: The New Nativism and the Anti-Immigrant Impulse in the United States,* edited by Juan F. Perea, 103–28. New York: New York Univ. Press, 1997.

Sitkoff, Harvard. *A New Deal for Blacks: The Emergence of Civil Rights as a National Issue.* Vol. 1. New York: Oxford Univ. Press, 1978.

Sklar, Robert. *Movie-Made America: A Cultural History of American Movies.* Rev. ed. New York: Vintage, 1994.

Sladek, John Thomas. *The New Apocrypha: A Guide to Strange Science and Occult Beliefs.* New York: Stein and Day, 1974.

Slomovitz, Albert Isaac. *The Fighting Rabbis: Jewish Military Chaplains and American History.* New York: New York Univ. Press, 1999.

Smallwood, Frank. *The Other Candidates: Third Parties in Presidential Elections.* Hanover, N.H.: Univ. Press of New England, 1980.

Smertenko, Johan. "Hitlerism Comes to America." *Harper's,* Nov. 1933, 600–607.

Smith, Geoffrey S. *To Save a Nation: American "Extremism," the New Deal, and the Coming of World War II.* Chicago: Elephant Paperbacks, 1992.

Smyth, C. Piazzi. *Our Inheritance in the Great Pyramid.* London: W. Isbister, 1880.

Soddy, Frederick. *Wealth, Virtual Wealth, and Debt: The Solution of the Economic Paradox.* New York: E. P. Dutton, 1933.

Sparrow, Bartholomew. *From the Outside In: World War II and the American State.* Princeton, N.J.: Princeton Univ. Press, 1996.

Spehr, Paul. *The Movies Begin: Making Movies in New Jersey, 1887–1920.* Newark, N.J.: Newark Museum, 1977.

Spivak, John. *America Faces the Barricades.* New York: Covici Friede, 1935.

———. *Pattern for American Fascism.* New York: New Century, 1947.

Staiger, Janet, ed. *The Studio System.* New Brunswick, N.J.: Rutgers Univ. Press, 1995.

Stead, W. T. *After Death, or Letters from Julia.* Chicago: Progressive Thinker Publishing House, 1909.

Steele, Richard W. "American Popular Opinion and the War Against Germany: The Issue of Negotiated Peace, 1942." *Journal of American History* 115 (Dec. 1978): 704–23.

———. "Franklin D. Roosevelt and His Foreign Policy Critics." *Political Science Quarterly* 94 (Spring 1979): 15–32.

———. "The Great Debate: Roosevelt, the Media, and the Coming of War, 1940–1941." *Journal of American History* 71 (June 1984).

Steiner, H. Arthur. "Fascism in America." *American Political Science Review* 29 (Oct. 1935, 821–30.

Stenehjem, Michele Flynn. *An American First: John T. Flynn and the America First Committee.* New Rochelle, N.Y.: Arlington House, 1976.

Stephan, Alexander. *Communazis: FBI Surveillance of German Emigre Writers.* New Haven, Conn.: Yale Univ. Press, 2000.

Sternhell, Zeev. *The Birth of Fascist Ideology.* Princeton, N.J.: Princeton Univ. Press, 1995.

St.-George, Maximilian, and Lawrence Dennis. *A Trial on Trial: The Great Sedition Trial of 1944.* Washington, D.C.: National Civil Rights Committee, 1946.

Strausz-Hupe, Robert. *Axis America: Hitler Plans Our Future.* New York: G. P. Putnam's Sons, 1941.

Strong, Donald S. *Organized Anti-Semitism in America: The Rise of Group Prejudice During the Decade 1930–1940.* Washington, D.C.: American Council on Public Affairs, 1941.

Strong, Josiah. *Our Country: Its Possible Future and Its Present Crisis.* New York: Baker and Taylor, 1891.

Stupple, David. "The I AM Sect Today: An Unobituary." *Journal of Popular Culture.* 8 (Spring 1975): 897–905.

———. "Mahatmas and Space Brothers." *Journal of American Culture* 7 (Summer 1984): 131–39.

Surette, Leon. *Pound in Purgatory: From Economic Radicalism to Anti-Semitism.* Urbana: Univ. of Illinois Press, 1999.

Swing, Raymond Gram. *Forerunners of American Fascism.* New York: Julian Messner, 1935.

Taylor, Robert L. "The Kampf of Joe McWilliams." *New Yorker,* Aug. 24, 1940, 32–39

Taylor, S. Earl. *The Christian Crusade for World Democracy.* New York: Methodist Book Concern, 1919.

Terry, Lillian *The Beloved Order, Received by the Sword and the Cup.* Black Mountain, N.C.: The Printery, 1928.

Theoharis, Athan. "The Threat to Civil Liberties." In *Cold War Critics: Alternatives to American Foreign Policy in the Truman Years,* edited by Thomas G. Paterson, 266–98. Chicago: Quadrangle Books, 1971.

Thomas, John L. *Alternative America: Henry George, Edward Bellamy, Henry Demarest Lloyd, and the Adversary Tradition.* Cambridge, Mass.: Belknap Press, 1983.

Thomas, John N. *The Institute of Pacific Relations: Asian Scholars and American Politics.* Seattle: Univ. of Washington Press, 1974.

Tietze, Thomas R. *Margery.* New York: Harper and Row, 1973.

Toksvig, Signe. *Emanuel Swedenborg, Scientist and Mystic.* New Haven, Conn.: Yale Univ. Press, 1948.

Toy, Eckard V., Jr. "Silver Shirts in the Northwest: Politics, Prophecies, and Personalities in the 1930s." *Pacific Northwest Quarterly* 80 (Winter 1989): 139–46.

Toye, Lori Adaile. *I AM AMERICA New World Atlas.* Socorro, N.Mex.: Seventh Ray Publishing, 1991.

Tozier, Roy. *America's Little Hitlers: Who's Who and What's Up in U.S. Fascism.* Girard, Kans.: Haldeman-Julius, 1940.

Tull, Charles J. *Father Coughlin and the New Deal.* Syracuse, N.Y.: Syracuse Univ. Press, 1965.

Unterberger, Betty M. *America's Siberian Expedition, 1918–1920: A Study of National Policy.* Durham, N.C.: Duke Univ. Press, 1956.

U.S. Congress. House. Special Committee on Un-American Activities. *Hearings on Investigation of Un-American Propaganda Activities in the United States.* 75th–78th Cong., 1938–1941, vols. 1–14.

U.S. Congress. House. Special Committee on Un-American Activities. *Investigation of Nazi Propaganda Activities and Investigations of Certain Other Propaganda Activities.* 73rd Cong., 2d sess., 1934.

U.S. Congress. Senate. Hearing Before a Subcommittee of the Committee on Interstate Commerce on S. Res. 152. *Propaganda in Motion Pictures, 77th Cong.* 1st sess., Sept. 9–26, 1941.

U.S. Military Intelligence Reports: Surveillance of Radicals in the United States, 1917–1941. microfilm, Frederick, Md.: University Publications of America, 1984.

Vail, Isaac Newton. *The Heavens and the Earth of Prehistoric Man.* Pasadena: Annular World Company, 1913.

———. *The Waters above the Firmament, or the Earth's Annular System.* Philadelphia: Ferris and Leach, 1902.

Vallee, Jacques. *Messengers of Deception: UFO Contacts and Cults.* Berkeley, Calif.: And/Or Press, 1979.

Variety Film Reviews, 1921–1925. New York: Garland, 1983.

Variety Film Reviews, 1926–1929. New York: Garland, 1983.

Via, Marie, and Marjorie Searl, eds. *Head, Heart, and Hand: Elbert Hubbard and the Roycrofters.* Rochester, N.Y.: Univ. of Rochester Press, 1994.

Viereck, Peter. *Metapolitics: The Roots of the Nazi Mind.* Rev. ed. New York: Capricorn Books, 1965.

Vital, David. *A People Apart: The Jews in Europe, 1789–1939.* Oxford: Oxford Univ. Press, 1999.

Volkman, Ernest. *A Legacy of Hate: Anti-Semitism in America.* New York: Franklin Watts, 1982.

Von Strempel, Herbert. "Confessions of a German Propagandist." *Public Opinion Quarterly* 10 (Summer 1946): 216–33.

Vortan, Max, and Lloyd P. Gartner *History of the Jews of Los Angeles.* San Marino, Calif.: Huntington Library, 1970.

Waite, Arthur E. *The Brotherhood of the Rosy Cross.* London: William Rider and Son, 1924.

Waite, Robert G. L. *The Psychopathic God: Adolf Hitler.* New York: Basic Books, 1977.

Walker, Samuel. *Hate Speech: The History of an American Controversy.* Lincoln: Univ. of Nebraska Press, 1994.

Wallace, Anthony F. C. *Religion: An Anthropological View.* New York: Random House, 1966.

Ware, Caroline F. *Greenwich Village, 1920–1930: A Comment on American Civilization in the Post-War Years.* New York: Houghton Mifflin, 1935.

Warren, Donald. *Radio Priest: Charles Coughlin, the Father of Hate Radio.* New York: Free Press, 1996.

Warren, Frank A. *Liberals and Communism: The "Red Decade" Revisited.* Bloomington: Indiana Univ. Press, 1966.

———. *Noble Abstractions: American Liberal Intellectuals and World War II.* Columbus: Ohio State Univ. Press, 1999.

Washington, Peter. *Madame Blavatsky's Baboon: A History of the Mystics, Mediums, and Misfits Who Brought Spiritualism to America.* New York: Schocken Books, 1991.

Weaver, John T. *Twenty Years of Silents, 1908–1928*. Metuchen, N.J.: Scarecrow Press, 1971.

Webb, James. *The Occult Establishment*. La Salle, Ill.: Open Court Press, 1976.

Weber, Brom. "Spurious Sage: A Study of the Conspiracy Between Elbert Hubbard and His Times." Ph.D. diss., Univ. of Minnesota, 1957.

Weber, Timothy P. *Living in the Shadow of the Second Coming: American Premillennialism, 1875–1982*. Expanded ed. Chicago, Ill.: Univ. of Chicago Press, 1987.

Webster, Nesta. *Secret Societies and Subversive Movements*. London: Boswell, 1924.

———. *World Revolution: The Plot Against Civilization*. London: Constable, 1921.

Weinberg, Gerhard L. "Hitler's Image of the United States." *American Historical Review* 69 (July 1964): 1006–21.

———. *World in the Balance: Behind the Scenes of World War II*. Hanover, N.H.: Univ. Press of New England, 1981.

Weintraub, Stanley. *Disraeli: A Biography*. New York: Truman Talley, 1993.

Werly, John. "The Millenarian Right: William Dudley Pelley and the Silver Legion of America." Ph.D. diss., Syracuse Univ., 1972.

West, Nathaniel. *A Cool Million*. 1934. Reprint, New York: Berkley, 1961.

Weyl, Nathaniel. *The Battle Against Disloyalty*. New York: Thomas Y. Crowell, 1951.

———. *The Jew in American Politics*. New Rochelle, N.Y.: Arlington House, 1968.

———. *Treason: The Story of Disloyalty and Betrayal in American Wars*. Washington: Public Affairs Press, 1950.

White, Bruce A. *Elbert Hubbard's The Philistine, A Periodical of Protest (1895–1915): A Major American "Little Magazine."* Lanham, Md.: Univ. Press of America, 1989.

White, Jon Albert. *The Siberian Intervention*. Princeton, N.J.: Princeton Univ. Press, 1950.

White, William Allen. *In Our Town*. 1909. Reprint, New York: Doubleday, Page, 1909.

Wiebe, Robert. *The Search for Order, 1877–1920*. New York: Hill and Wang, 1963.

Wilder, Robert, ed. *The Red Triangle in the Changing Nations*. New York: Association Press, 1918.

Williamson, George Hunt. *Other Tongues—Other Flesh*. Amherst, Wisc.: Amherst Press, 1953.

———. *Other Voices*. Rev. ed. Scottsale, Ariz.: Abelard, 1995.

Williamson, George Hunt, and John McCoy. *UFOs Confidential.* Corpus Christi: Essene Press, 1958.

Winter, Ella. "California's Little Hitlers." *New Republic,* Dec. 27, 1933, 188–90.

Wittner, Lawrence. *Rebels Against War: The American Peace Movement, 1941–1960.* New York: Columbia Univ. Press, 1969.

Wolfinger, Raymond E., et al. "America's Radical Right: Politics and Ideology" In *Ideology and Discontent,* edited by David E. Apter, 262–93. Glencoe, Ill.: Free Press, 1964.

Wood, Frederic H. *Through the Psychic Door: The Facts about Death and Human Survival.* London: Spiritualist Press, 1956.

World Committee for the Victims of German Fascism. *The Brown Network: The Activities of the Nazis in Foreign Countries.* New York: Knight Publications, 1936.

Yates, Frances A. *The Rosicrucian Enlightenment.* London: Routledge and Keegan Paul, 1972.

Zalampas, Michael. *Adolf Hitler and the Third Reich in American Magazines, 1923–1939.* Bowling Green, Ohio: Bowling Green State Univ. Popular Press, 1989.

Zeskind, Leonard. *The Christian Identity Movement.* Washington: Center for Democratic Renewal, 1986.

Zinsstag, Lou, and Timothy Good. *George Adamski-The Untold Story.* London: Ceti Publications, 1983.

Magazines and Newspapers

Adventure Magazine, 1917–20.

American Magazine, 1915–29.

Asheville Times, 1930–45.

Bright Horizons, 1953–54.

Chicopee Journal, 1913–14.

Chicopee Union-News, 2000.

Current Opinion, 1918–21.

Daily Worker, 1940–45.

Galilean, 1941–42.

Good Housekeeping, 1922–23.

Indianapolis News, 1940–50.

Indianapolis Times, 1940–50.

Liberation, 1933–40.

Little Visits with Great Americans, 1937–39.

New Liberator, 1930–32.

New Liberator Weekly, 1931–33.

New York Times, 1933–65.

Over Here, 1958–60.

Pelley's Weekly, 1934–36.

People's Favorite Magazine, 1920–25.

Philosopher, 1909–12.

Pictorial Review, 1922–27.

Popular Magazine, 1914–15.

Reality, 1937–39.

Roll Call, 1941.

Saturday Evening Post, 1916–39.

Silver Legion Ranger, 1933–35.

Star Beacon, 1995–2002.

St. Johnsbury Evening Caledonian, 1918–19.

Sunset Magazine, 1919–22.

Valor, 1950–61.

Variety, 1920–30.

World Outlook, 1919–22.

Unpublished Works and Others

Hall, Michelle. E-mail to author, Aug. 15, 2002.

Hamilton, Cendi. "The Asheville Times Meets William Dudley Pelley." Unpublished paper, Asheville, N.C., 2002.

Jendrysik, Steve. "History of the Pioneer Valley." Unpublished paper, Chicopee, Mass., n.d.

Jenkins, Philip. "The Great Anti-Cult Scare, 1935–1945." Unpublished paper presented at CESNUR 1999 Conference, Bryn Athyn, Pa.

Kerlin, Jack. "William D. Pelley's Legacy." Unpublished paper, Provo, Utah, 2003.

Pearson, Melford. E-mail interview by author, July 31, 2002, Aug. 18, 2003.

Pollock, Vance. "From Silverscreen to Silvershirt: Bill Pelley and Hollywood Antisemitism." Unpublished paper in the author's possession, n.d.

Index

www.ingramcontent.com/pod-product-compliance
Lightning Source LLC
Chambersburg PA
CBHW031551151125
35463CB00002B/127